Faulkner at 100
FAULKNER AND YOKNAPATAWPHA
1997

Faulkner at 100
Retrospect and Prospect

FAULKNER AND YOKNAPATAWPHA, 1997

EDITED BY
DONALD M. KARTIGANER
AND
ANN J. ABADIE

UNIVERSITY PRESS OF MISSISSIPPI
JACKSON

www.upress.state.ms.us

Copyright © 2000 by University Press of Mississippi
All rights reserved
Manufactured in the United States of America

⊗

Library of Congress Cataloging-in-Publication Data

Faulkner and Yoknapatawpha Conference (24th : 1997 : University of Mississippi)
  Faulkner at 100 : retrospect and prospect / edited by Donald M. Kartiganer and
Ann J. Abadie.
     p. cm.
  Includes bibliographical references and index.
  ISBN: 978-1-61703-845-7
     1. Faulkner, William, 1897–1962—Criticism and interpretation—Congresses.
2. Yoknapatawpha County (Imaginary place)—Congresses. 3. Mississippi—
In literature—Congresses. I. Kartiganer, Donald M., 1937– II. Abadie, Ann J.
III. Faulkner, William, 1897–1962. IV. Title.
PS3511.A86Z78321186 1997
813'.52—dc21
                                                          00-027753

British Library Cataloging-in-Publication Data available

For Evans Harrington
1925–1997

Contents

Evans Harrington

"Faulkner at 100: Retrospect and Prospect" was the last conference
Evans Harrington attended. Cofounder of the conference in 1974, with
Ann J. Abadie, and its director through 1993, he died of cancer December 1, 1997. At the 1998 Faulkner and Yoknapatawpha Conference, Donald Kartiganer, who succeeded Evans as director, made the following
remarks.

Before introducing the speaker for this evening, I want to say a few words
about the man who, with Ann Abadie, cofounded Faulkner and Yoknapatawpha twenty-five years ago. Evans died this past year of cancer at the
age of seventy-two. Although many of you here tonight may not have
known Evans, simply by virtue of your presence you are sharing in his
legacy, for certainly one of the most significant of his many contributions
to our lives and to literary study was Faulkner and Yoknapatawpha. Together, Evans and Ann created a literary event that reflected perfectly
Evans's conception of what literature is and what it is for: Faulkner's
work positioned in the context of its writing, the books considered not as
isolated, breathless wonders, like stars, but as living organisms, inti-
mately related to, reflecting the real world in which and of which they
were made. The conference came to represent the genuine liberalism of
Evans Harrington: a gathering not just of scholars and critics but of people from all walks of life bound together by a fascination with Faulkner's
fiction. I do not think there is a gathering quite like it in America. The
general reader—it was something Evans Harrington, for all his advanced
degrees, never ceased to be, and never ceased to respect—the general
reader is alive and well, assembling in one-hundred-degree heat in Oxford, Mississippi, to listen to academic lectures on one of the most difficult writers in American literature. Evans believed that, as someone said
about war and generals, Faulkner was too important to be left to the
scholars.

In Oxford Evans's achievement and value were so well known that, at
his passing, we have hardly had to deliberately, formally remember them,
since they have never been really very far from our minds. But there is a
time for public, communal acknowledgment. So let me say this.

He was a good novelist; he was a superb teacher; he was a passionately involved, deeply committed citizen; he loved this town and this Southern land and people and was fearless in his desire to make them worthy: as Faulkner has Chick Mallison think in *Intruder in the Dust*: "that *fierce desire* that they should be perfect because they were his and he was theirs." And so, along with everything else, this university professor, this writer and teacher, this creator of academic conferences, became, when the times demanded, a hero as well. When the crises came to Mississippi and Oxford: the registration of James Meredith at the University in 1962, the integration of the Southern Literary Festival in 1965, the attempt to censor a student literary magazine in 1972—in each case, Evans Harrington was there: standing up, being counted, the right man at the right time, one of those necessary people without whom nothing truly important ever gets done.

There are passages from Faulkner's Nobel Prize speech that are among the most quoted of all his writing. I must confess that I have never been quite as enamored of these passages as others are. For me they seem too abstract, too remote from the real ground of his power and his meaning. And yet, thinking now about Evans Harrington, I can finally put a concrete life behind some of those elegant, high-sounding words. Think of Evans, what he was and how he lived: "courage and honor and hope and pride and compassion and pity and sacrifice." And if you could just add a glorious sense of humor, you'd have something like the man.

In Place of an Introduction: Reading Faulkner

> In the very essence of poetry there is something indecent:
> a thing is brought forth which we didn't know we had in us,
> so we blink our eyes, as if a tiger had sprung out
> and stood in the light, lashing his tail.
> —CZESLAW MILOSZ, *"Ars Poetica?"*

Two images, Centennially inspired:

Faulkner in the fall of 1928. Lean, stiff-backed, dark-haired, dark-mustached, with a manner at once courteous and cocky, the arrogance of absolute confidence, crossing the cool October morning streets of Greenwich Village, carrying the typescript of a novel he has finished revising the day before—perhaps thinking, as he would later write, "I wont have to worry about publishers liking or not liking this at all," even as he is convinced that he has created "something to which the shabby term Art not only can, but must, be applied." He walks into the apartment of Ben Wasson—his friend and occasional agent and editor—and casually tosses The Sound and the Fury *on the bed: "Read this, Bud. It's a real son of a bitch."*

Faulkner in the summer of 1997. Represented in an oversized framed photograph suspended on a backdrop of the stage of an auditorium at the University of Mississippi: hair turned white, the mustache still striated with black yet fuller and curving upward to the illusion of a smile; the old arrogance replaced by benign aloofness, the quiet confidence of completion—perhaps thinking, as he had anticipated, "that it was all pretty good," but that now he has "put it all away forever that I anguished and sweated over, and it [will] never trouble me anymore." He seems to be listening intently, but to a voice only he can hear, as a speaker at the front of the stage holds forth before an audience of over four hundred people, gathered from around the world to celebrate, pay homage, continue the task of making plain.

Does he remember—does anyone?—what it was that made that novel of sixty-eight years ago a "real son of a bitch"?

Thirty-five years after his death he looms as large as ever: revered by writers throughout the world; analyzed by literary critics according to whatever theoretical approach is currently in vogue; assumed by nearly all writers and readers, including those who do not acknowledge his influence or feel especially compelled to reread him, as a fixture, perhaps *the* fixture, in our American literary constellation. Flannery O'Connor's famous remark—"Nobody wants his mule and wagon stalled on the same track the Dixie Limited is roaring down"—is rich with implication: wonder, resignation, the need for strategies of containment and creative survival.[1]

Faulkner has taken his place among the canonized high modernists, with all the usual effects of official authorization, one of which is our assumption of familiarity—that we know quite well which track the Dixie Limited is roaring down as well as its maximum speed. "One cannot too often symbolically underscore the moment," Fredric Jameson has written, "in which the modern 'classics' entered the school system and the college reading lists. . . . This was a kind of revolution in its own way, with unexpected consequences, forcing the recognition of the modern texts at the same time that it defused them, like former radicals finally appointed to the cabinet."[2]

The danger is clear enough. Like many of his modernist contemporaries, Faulkner may be in the process of losing precisely that power that distinguishes any major writer—the modernists in particular—namely, the power of his recalcitrance. The driving force of Faulkner's fiction is the offense, the turn within and yet against the very conditions of its existence: the elaborate network of conventions—linguistic, generic, social, economic, political, cultural, moral—that permit it to be. At its best the fiction tells us what we are never quite ready to know. However exacting the scholarship that clarifies a puzzling reference, however imaginative the appropriated theory that illuminates a concealed corner of Faulkner's imagination, the novels possess a resisting voice, sounding what André Bleikasten calls, in one of the essays in this volume, their "singularity," the power to "wrench . . . readers from their certitudes."

Ideally, even in the context of canonization, the familiarization that (especially these days) cannot help being accompanied by a degree of contempt, Faulkner's fiction remains a still unsettled world of words, "readable" yet strange, capable of evoking responses beyond what a reader is prepared to make. The scene of the dying, castrated Joe Christmas in *Light in August* is a scene of Faulknerian instruction on what the experience of reading can become. "[F]rom out the slashed garments about his hips and loins the pent black blood seemed to rush like a released breath. It seemed to rush out of his pale body like the rush of sparks from a rising rocket." Three men have witnessed Percy Grimm's assault on Christmas, brutally and eternally defining this enigmatic being: " 'Now you'll let white women alone, even in hell.' " Yet they recognize, in the very horror of knowledge, that it is they themselves who have been seized, have become the prisoners of their vision: "the man

seemed to rise soaring into their memories forever and ever. They are
not to lose it, in whatever peaceful valleys, beside whatever placid and
reassuring streams of old age, in the mirroring faces of whatever children
they will contemplate old disasters and newer hopes. It will be there,
musing, quiet, steadfast, not fading and not particularly threatful, but of
itself alone serene, of itself alone triumphant."[3]

Those readers of *Light in August* safely outside the novel rather than
within it may not be so susceptible to its singular power. Wittily comparing the reader to the obsessively alert young driver of an automobile,
Philip Weinstein calls for a deliberate act of surrender to the text: "You
must, at a certain point, submit to the vehicle if you want it to take you
anywhere. We must revalidate the experience of submitting to the literary vehicle, learning all we can about the tricky and far from obvious
moves it can make, yet granting it the power to take us somewhere."
His comment is echoed several times in the essays that follow. Susan
Donaldson refers to the Faulkner who "lead[s] us by the hand into those
regions where we would just as soon not venture," Minrose Gwin to the
journey of reading, the value of which is "this possibility of the *someone
else* who returns."

And yet, for all our desire to open ourselves to the strangeness of the
new, there is an irresistible urge to take our pleasures in the text not
from its abundance and plurality, its power to alarm, but from our own
power to read it into order, situating it within an aesthetic, political, and
moral scheme that gives us comfort because the scheme is our own. We
read and judge according to the consistency between the text and our
beliefs. Either it does what our reading strategies require it to do, albeit
in its own way, or it doesn't. In the latter case it is a flawed work: out of
date or incorrect or both. As for the particular mode of reading that has
governed the entire process from beginning to end, it remains unchanged
and usually unquestioned.

The strongest examples of reading as the act of discovering in a text
confirmation of the values implicit to the reading strategy itself have
come from the academy. Literary criticism is always an armed vision,
capable of converting any text into an opportunity rather than a problem,
a vehicle to validate a reading strategy rather than to test it. André Bleikasten cogently addresses what he regards as the particular tendencies
of recent cultural criticism, with its emphasis on social and historical
issues, to disregard the specificity of Faulkner's texts, reading them as
"prooftexts . . . for preconceived general views . . . illustrations of our
ideas about culture and society." The power of reading, however, to exploit any text into a banner for its critical cause—or to point up the failure

of the text to become that banner—is a power every reader, whatever the critical strategy, finds difficult to lay aside.

New Criticism, for example, largely responsible not only for establishing Faulkner as a popular subject for critical analysis but also for revealing the enormous, ultimately intelligible subtlety of his work, implemented a strict and delimiting agenda. In stressing the importance of a "close reading" of the text itself, it ignored the author's biography and historical and cultural context. Analyzing the text's every word and nuance, with at least the appearance of objectivity, it nevertheless gave the highest value—according to criteria determined prior to the actual reading—to the text's achievement of total coherence, its power to resolve thematic contradiction and formal fragmentation into wholeness. Moreover, the passion for order often translated into a preference for a fundamentally conservative, "traditional" politics and ethics.

Deconstruction, on the other hand—to single out the most extreme version of the suspicion that dominates much of poststructualism— borrowed New Criticism's excessive attention to textual detail, but was based on an opposing sense of disparity at the heart of all language: the fact, as Faulkner's Addie Bundren puts it, "that words dont ever fit even what they are trying to say at."[4] Rather than complexly achieved wholeness as the criterion for literary excellence, the deconstructionists privileged the sheer multiplicity of meaning, abandoning any need to resolve or harmonize the clashing possibilities. Yet deconstruction also had its agenda, chiefly the deferral of meaning itself—what its American adherents emphasized as "undecidability"—as a possibly impassable stage of reading. Ultimately such reading seemed less an acknowledgment of the full power of the subversive fiction than an elaborately played out demonstration that all language is doomed to imprecision. The text was freed not only of the constraint of single, straightforward meaning (even if New Critically resolved in "fruitful tension") but also of its significance. In the place of meaning predetermined, deconstruction substituted meaning perpetually postponed.

The mode of reading presently holding sway in the academy, historical and cultural criticism, objects to what it regards as the elitist, reactionary implications of New Criticism, and what, among American deconstructionists at least, seems to be political indifference, the celebration of multiplicity itself. The cultural critics have focused sharply on the representation in literature of race, class, and gender, as well as the entanglement of any text within its entire cultural context. Their purpose, borrowed from the deconstructionist attack on imposed hierarchies of every sort, has been to explore Faulkner's texts in hopes of bringing to the surface something of their hidden, marginalized life. The result has been a new awareness of the richness and power of Faulkner's female characters, the unexpected profusion of gender roles—far more varied and complex than the social conventions of compulsory heterosexuality and male dominance allow—and in general a more comprehensive understanding of and sympathy for the unprivileged groups within society. Behind these discoveries—enabling them—is a program, commonly on the political left, feminist, egalitarian, that is refreshing for the candid disclosure of its commitment, although no less prone than other forms of reading to find in Faulkner what it wishes to find.

Obviously, there can be no such thing as a "naked," purely submissive reading; we are determined at the outset by everything we are, everything our personal backgrounds and public culture have contrived that we should be. The question is whether a book can ever subvert the mode of its reading and all that has gone into the making of it. In other words, what is the possibility of a reading that does not confirm its origins but alters them? a reading that finds what it was not supposed to find—in fact finds the very truth it may have been designed to hold at bay?

The secret passion of reading—it is also the passion of writing—is that despite everything that militates against it (not least our passion to remain as we are), a book will at some point break through the bonds of strategy, changing our convictions into questions, our assumed identities into the masks of unexplored selves, our theories into abstractions that cannot contain the action on the ground. Somehow, the book *turns*, seemingly within the very grip of our valid and coherent reading, and begins to read *us*, telling us what we are and the worth of what we believe.

Bleikasten reminds us of one of the great expressions of the hope for a literature of genuine confrontation in his reference to a famous letter of Kafka's, which calls for "the kind of books that wound and stab us." "[B]ooks that make us happy," Kafka continues, "we could write ourselves if we had to. . . . A book must be the axe for the frozen sea inside us."[5] One of our contemporary descendants of Kafka, Philip Roth, has put it this way: "I read fiction to be freed from my own suffocatingly narrow perspective on life and to be lured into imaginative sympathy with a fully developed narrative point of view not my own. It's the same reason that I write."[6]

Roth's abrupt move from the act of reading to that of writing is crucial, for what makes them both valuable activities is the willingness to encounter what he calls "the crises." For the writer it is the moment when "you turn . . . against your material" (140); for the reader, it is the moment when the material turns against you.

But how does that happen? How does a book turn against its reading,

like a word turning against the massive weight of its accumulated meaning, and still be read, *still mean*? How does a book become an axe? In
Faulkner's words, what, quite apart from its sheer difficulty of access,
might make a book "a real son of a bitch"?

That literature should have that goal is a dream peculiar to the nineteenth-century modernists and their twentieth-century successors, although it is clear enough that the desire is an attribute of modernism
whenever it appears. The need, as Paul de Man writes, "to wipe out
whatever came earlier, in the hope of reaching at last a point that could
be called a true present, a point of origin that marks a new departure," is
the perennial quest of any literature to expand what might be regarded
as its given cultural boundaries.[7] The figures of Oedipus or Clytemnestra
in Classical drama have a catastrophic power—sufficient to arouse in an
audience pity and fear—that the communally invested chorus dares not
aspire to; Shakespeare's Shylock, unlike his Marlovian counterpart of
Malta, sporadically breaks through the anti-Semitic culture fundamental
to his creation; Swiftean and Popean rage employs the language of reason
in order to convey the threat of universal darkness.

But in the nineteenth century, the questioning of linguistic reference
itself becomes a paramount principle, an attempt to subvert the very
nature of representation and recover for the word a solidity, a corporeal-
ity that allows it to resist its role as a transparent vehicle of external
meaning and achieve some degree of autonomous presence. As Michel
Foucault writes, a poet such as Mallarmé tries to free language from
functional sign-making, the "art of naming," and achieve for it "a radical
intransitivity." The result is that literature "leads language back from
grammar to the naked power of speech, and there it encounters the
untamed, imperious being of words."[8] Focussing also on the Symbolist
revolution, Julia Kristeva identifies in language a semiotic force, which—
while serving within the existing cultural conventions of language—
nevertheless exerts a creative, revisionary power, one that simultaneously
adheres to the laws of signification and dislocates them.

The drive toward a language capable of freeing itself of reference, capable of *meaning* in a way that violates the very laws that constitute the
possibilities of meaning, is the drive toward the book that turns against
its reader. In his reading in the French Symbolists, in Dostoevsky, Conrad, and later Joyce, Faulkner found various forms of the modernist urge
to foster a language beyond representation: to achieve the status of what,
in *Crime and Punishment*, Roskolnikov calls a "new word," or what Joyce
would describe as the moment of epiphany, when the ordinary image

suddenly assumes, as if out of a hitherto unrevealed, inherent power, the resonance of icon.

Conrad exemplifies a different version of the possibilities of textual power in his use of the narrative strategy of the "divided protagonist," common throughout the modernist period, in which the novel becomes a dramatization of reading. In *Heart of Darkness* and *Lord Jim*, Conrad, following the technique of *Frankenstein*, *Moby Dick*, and *Wuthering Heights*, and anticipating a spate of twentieth-century English and American fiction, from *The Good Soldier*, *The Great Gatsby*, *The Sun Also Rises*, *My Antonia*, to *Absalom, Absalom!*—to name just a few novels leading toward Faulkner—explores the possibility of the radically compromised reading: what happens when a reader, fully determined by an elaborate cultural background, encounters a textual "other" who will not yield to the reading most consistent with that background. In *Heart of Darkness*, Conrad demonstrates the tremendous impact of Kurtz on Marlow, as the latter draws into the circle of Kurtz's powerful presence. Without simplifying the ensuing confrontation, we yet recognize the powerful pull of Kurtz on the liberal, humane, moderate, ethically bound Marlow, which compels him to grant the mad Kurtz a victory: " 'a moral victory paid for by innumerable defeats, by abominable terrors, by abominable satisfactions. But it was a victory!' "9

In the extreme experiments of Symbolist poetry, in fin de siècle celebrations of the superiority of art over life, in dramatizations of how reading can give way, at least partially, to meanings it has little vested interest in accepting, there is a common thread of the modernist dream of textual power: the *word* that undoes the very cultural conditions within which it is spoken and interpreted.

There is an obvious recalcitrance in Faulkner's fiction at both the stylistic and thematic levels, one which, like that of Joyce's or Eliot's, never quite loses its capacity to challenge even the most experienced readers. Whether because of the constant disruptions of sentence and structure, the incessant qualification and digression apparently designed to break up the falsely fluent line of narrative, or because of his often grotesque and violent subject matter, there remains in Faulkner an initial difficulty of access that even seasoned critics occasionally feel. And yet it is clear that readers have learned either to accommodate both challenges, reconciling them with their own stylistic and cultural criteria, or to dismiss the fiction as fundamentally flawed. For the most part the academy has chosen the first option, with each shift in critical criteria finding new possibilities for taking pleasure in Faulkner.

As I have suggested earlier, the several schools of criticism that have focussed on Faulkner's work since the 1950s have been able to contain its resistance: the New Critics, for example, by absorbing fictional fragmentation into wholes, and seemingly perverse subject matter into traditional moral and social values; the deconstructionists, through an opposing gesture, by demonstrating just how resistant to ultimate coherence—formal or thematic—Faulkner's fiction can be.

Of particular interest to current historicist and cultural critics is Faulkner's apparent willingness to revise the Southern stereotypes he works with: the debased poor white, the impotent aristocrat, the frustrated spinster, the black man as either obsequious or dangerous. At times the fiction seems to anticipate some of the most deeply held current attitudes: in *As I Lay Dying* (1930), for example, the depiction of a family of poor white farmers who display an unexpected psychic richness, not to mention—in their grotesque efforts to transport Addie Bundren's corpse to Jefferson—an early instance of Faulknerian indomitability; in *Light in August* (1932) the recognition of race as in many ways a cultural construct, a human perception rather than a biological fact—and at a time when blood was regarded in the South as the most telling fact of identity; or in *If I Forget Thee, Jerusalem* (1939) the exploration—and subversion—of fixed ideas of gender position, as Harry and Charlotte enact and reverse a series of presumably "male" and "female" roles.

Of course there are those readers, operating out of the same cultural mindsets as those who value Faulkner, who attack his portrayals of marginal groups as in fact confirming the stereotypes or, if challenging them, not challenging them enough. The Bundrens still retain some of the attributes of the subhuman—setting a broken leg with cement, viciously casting out the visionary, Darl; Joe Christmas, as the murderer of a white woman, still calls up images of the black beast incarnate; and Charlotte Rittenmeyer pays for her gender reversals with her life.

With both the sympathetic readers and the unsympathetic, however—and I say this as one who finds the arguments for Faulkner's capacity to rewrite his own cultural determinants extremely persuasive—the fact remains that we cannot help but understand these breakthrough "meanings," suggesting extraordinary novelistic foresight by Faulkner in the 1930s, as at least the half-creations of 1980s and 1990s readers. We have lived a cultural experience that has prepared us to focus on Faulkner's treatment of various marginalized groups, invariably from a perspective of sympathy with those groups and a readiness to evaluate Faulkner's fiction according to its ability to match that sympathy. Moreover, and most tellingly, ours has been an experience that has made us quite comfortable with the new focus and its accompanying values. Such "discoveries" would undoubtedly have shocked readers of the 1930s—and might well have shocked Faulkner-as-reader as well—but now there is little shock, which is probably a good indication that the recovered relevance of dead writers is inextricably bound up with current cultural need.

That this is the case should neither be surprising nor distressing; it is one of the ways in which some writers remain alive—and some decline—and there is no question but that it is to the credit of the writer that he or she can be "recovered," as well as to the reader that he or she can validly install a new basis for understanding and appreciation. Nevertheless, whether readers praise Faulkner for the moral insight he shares with them, or condemn him for the blindness he shares with his contemporaries, the fiction continues to reflect the reading process rather than alter it. The only change in the transaction that may have taken place is not with the reader, who operates out of a fixed prior perspective, but with Faulkner's text, which has revealed an understanding hitherto unnoticed.

The question is whether literature can be more than this. Can it deliver what we are not prepared to receive? Can it be what Kafka proposed: the axe for the frozen sea of ourselves?

What continues to strike me about Faulkner is a recalcitrance that yields nothing but the hard opaque surface of its mystery, and this may well be the key to our enduring interest, compelling us—beyond our culturally determined convictions—to discover *more*. Each of the major novels, as well as the great stories, stages a collapse, or at the very least refuses to dispel the dubiousness of, the most imaginative attempts within the text—and therefore without—to bring its materials to some kind of valid order. The pleasures of that order are such that we, all of us, find it both necessary and justifiable to cling to it, even as we know that some absolutely crucial event or situation in the text remains unclear, unexplained. Significantly, this gap in our knowing of the text—which seems a gap in the text's knowing of itself—has the effect of enhancing the power of its images, as if rendering them all the more brilliant for the revealed blankness of their background. The gap is a summons to attend to the particulars, inspired by the pervading sense that the particulars are ultimately beyond, or beneath, interpretation.

There is no escaping the enigma of Caddy Compson, who remains forever concealed, not so much behind as within the words of her psychically disturbed brothers. The journey of the Bundrens to Jefferson is mandated by Addie for a reason never actually divulged, so that both the alleged motives of the family in taking her there and the ulterior ones almost become interchangeable fictions. Joe Christmas is the complete cultural embodiment of all that race has come to mean in the South precisely because the novel preserves the mystery of his origin: we cannot

begin to guess at Christmas's racial genealogy, and are thus forever
thrown back on the particulars for what must remain tentative exploration. In all three novels, the interpreters within and without are themselves *read by* the mysteries they explore, which ultimately ascend to the
level of symbol: not *having* meaning but *creating* meaning, meaning that
overflows the fiction without ever fully explaining its power.

Perhaps the most remarkable example is *Absalom, Absalom!*, which
provides two major disruptions, one as another instance of Faulknerian
instruction in reading, the other as the novel's refusal to modify the abiding opacity of its particulars. The first involves the dramatic "turning" in
the narrative of Quentin and Shreve as they attempt to explain the central
event of the novel: Henry Sutpen's murder of his best friend, Charles
Bon, presumably to prevent Bon's marriage to Henry's sister, Judith.
Having decided that Charles is the half brother of Henry and Judith—a
half brother whom Thomas Sutpen, for some unknown reason, refuses to
acknowledge as his son—Quentin and Shreve invent a tragic love story
in which Bon is torn between a longing for recognition from his father
and an incestuous desire for his half sister. Henry shoots Bon, despite his
love for him, in order to prevent the incest. Like the narratives that pre-
cede theirs, Quentin and Shreve's is clearly marked by cultural precon-
ceptions and personal biases; two young Harvard freshmen, they invent
a romantic tragedy of star-crossed lovers divided between the demands
of love and honor, the blameless victims of a powerful, unfathomable
father.

The great shift in the established pattern of the novel occurs when
Quentin and Shreve change their reading. They decide that Henry would
not kill his half brother over the threat of incest with their sister Judith,
that there must be some other reason for the murder. That other reason,
which Quentin and Shreve arrive at in a burst of almost mystical intuition, collectively imagining the episode that reveals it to them, is that
Charles Bon was part black, and that the violation Henry is protecting
Judith from is not primarily incest but miscegenation.

The novel never reveals the source of this insight, nor, for that matter,
for the boys' belief that Bon was Sutpen's son by a former marriage. Did
Henry Sutpen tell Quentin when they met briefly in 1909? Is it the figure
of Clytie, Sutpen's mulatto slave daughter, telling or implying that blood
and blackness are always the key? Or is it Shreve, the foreigner profoundly caught up in the Sutpen story, who draws Quentin toward the
final interpretation? Blackness haunts the edges of the story, like Aeschy-
lean furies promising vengeance or a shadow family patiently waiting for
the whites to turn and see: the black servant who dismisses the young
Sutpen from the door of the great Tidewater plantation; Sutpen's Haitian

slaves; his daughter Clytie; Charles Bon's octoroon mistress and one-drop black son. But only Quentin and Shreve make blackness the story's absolute center. Do we resort to a theory of unconscious desire in Quentin (that somehow has penetrated Shreve as well) to confess the guilt of the South? Does the novel possess some communal unconscious, acknowledging the entire nation's great collective crime? Or are these speculations only a screen, readings that repress the novel's turn against readings?

Quentin's and Shreve's interpretation is remarkable for two reasons. The first is that theirs is the only reading in the novel that radically changes from its original theme, and just at the moment when it has apparently completed itself, with at least as much persuasiveness as the readings preceding it have had. The second reason, even more important, is that it is a reading which neither Quentin nor Shreve can take much comfort in: it is not the reading they desire. For Shreve, the Northerner who has been trying to enter the thick complexities of Southern history, largely through his identification with the "outsider" of the story, Charles Bon, the blackness of Bon renders Shreve far more foreign than he cares to be. No longer the gallant lover rejected by an inscrutable father, Bon is now the supreme Other who horrifies all:

—*You are my brother.*
—*No I'm not. I'm the nigger that's going to sleep with your sister. Unless you stop me, Henry.*[10]

Shreve's game of vicarious engagement with Southern memory and tragic glory is over; in the novel's concluding chapter Quentin dismisses him from the privilege of interpretation, even as Henry has violently dismissed Bon from the Sutpen family: "You cant understand it. You would have to be born there" (289).

For Quentin, the wages of this new reading are more dire. The eldest son of a distinguished Southern family, he has somehow found himself compelled into that reading of Southern history that he wishes most to resist: that the root of the Sutpen tragedy, of the tragedy of the South, the American tragedy, is that the white man kills the black man who is his brother.

The power of this reading is inescapable; it is the one that most of us, ourselves readers, come to believe in. Not because it is confirmed in the chronology Faulkner appended to the novel, but because it is the transgression—Kafka's axe—the reading that emerges not for its comfort but for what its two readers somehow cannot help but accept as its truth.

There remains, however, a still larger disruption, the one reserved not so much for Quentin and Shreve as for us. This is the disruption that exists throughout the novel—impossible to deny and yet almost impossible to accept, since it requires us to withhold assent from *all* the novel's internal readings. Is Sutpen the demon whose punishment requires the decimation of the South in war? Is Bon's marriage to an octoroon the social violation Henry cannot pass? Above all—since Quentin and Shreve's reading is the most persuasive (and even writes its way into the appended Chronology and Genealogy of the text)—*is* Charles Bon the part-black son of Sutpen and his part-black first wife?

The difference between fact and conjecture in *Absalom, Absalom!* is painfully clear; there is little unequivocal basis for any of these interpretations, including the last. Yet virtually everything written about *Absalom, Absalom!* for several decades depends on the largely unfounded assumption of the truth of at least some of those conjectures, especially the one that identifies Bon as Sutpen's part-black son. Finally, all we have are the particulars themselves, the imaginers and their imaginings, whose ultimate meaning is always dubious but whose brilliantly realized actions we cannot forget or leave uninterpreted.

We need not relax into undecidability, but rather attend to the continuous drive toward significance. The gift—in all of Faulkner's major fictions—if we are willing to receive it, is the surprising renewal of the text before us. As Faulkner memorably put it, "[we] are not to lose it. . . . It will be there, musing, quiet, steadfast, not fading and not particularly threatful, but of itself alone serene, of itself alone triumphant."

Faulkner's greatest novels invariably enact a rhetorically imposing, ultimately overwhelming flight from language: a subversion of all telling, his and ours. His unique modernism is his passionate pursuit and rejection of a dream of rhetorical adequacy—the supreme fiction—analagous to his relationship to a Southern culture he also appropriated and opposed. The novels turn on us because they are always about the insufficient attempts of language to control, to articulate an unfathomable Otherness, with the writer tortuously divided between the language he gorgeously assumes and the unwordable Other he desires to keep in motion, uncontained. The result is the rhetorical failure that triumphantly confirms that language has dared everything.

In interviews he talked of the "gallantry of the failure," "the splendidly magnificent bust" of the writing he most admired: the grand defeat of language which only the total resources of language could register. The pleasure of the Faulknerian text is the experience of its ultimate subversion of reading, perhaps most succinctly exemplified in the effort of the community in *Light in August* to identify Joe Christmas, and their fury at his resistance: " 'He never acted like either a nigger or a white man. That was it. That was what made the folks so mad' " (350). Like the writer seeking to contain his vision in a fiction, we seek to contain the fiction in a reading whose subversion is what the fiction is *about*, and which it calls us to reenact: the turning that assures us we have read well, that we have come to the heart of Faulkner's repudiation of the language he inhabits and from which he longs to break free.

Faulkner said, "The aim of every artist is to arrest motion, which is life, by artificial means and hold it fixed so that a hundred years later, when a stranger looks at it, it moves again since it is life."[11]

And so we come to the books, now or in a hundred years, readers and critics all, anxious to drape Faulkner in our myriad desires: our formalist designs, our insistence on unmeaning or meanings both moral and profound, our politically engaged determination to remake the dishonest world. For a while the books behave, accept the particular shape of our attention; but then, if we are lucky, they begin to move. The life arrested by art yields to flow, unmaking artifice, frees itself in a stranger's eye, unfolding as motion.

Read him again and see.

Donald M. Kartiganer
The University of Mississippi
Oxford, Mississippi

Acknowledgments

An earlier version of this essay appeared in the *Oxford American*. I am grateful to the editor, Marc Smirnoff, and the publisher, John Grisham, for their continued support.

NOTES

1. Flannery O'Connor, "Some Aspects of the Grotesque in Southern Fiction," in *Mystery and Manners: Occasional Prose*, ed. Sally Fitzgerald and Robert Fitzgerald (New York: Farrar, Straus, and Giroux, 1969), 45.

2. Fredric Jameson, *Postmodernism, or The Cultural Logic of Late Capitalism* (Durham: Duke University Press, 1991), 314–15.

3. William Faulkner, *Light in August*, The Corrected Text (1932; New York: Vintage International, 1990), 464–65.

4. William Faulkner, *As I Lay Dying*, The Corrected Text (1930; New York: Vintage International, 1990), 171.

5. Franz Kafka, *Letters to Friends, Family, and Editors*, trans. Richard and Clara Winston (New York: Schocken Books, 1977), 16.

6. Philip Roth, "Interview with *Le Nouvel Observateur*," *Reading Myself and Others* (New York: Penguin Books, 1985), 120.

7. Paul de Man, *Blindness and Insight: Essays in the Rhetoric of Contemporary Criticism* (New York: Oxford University Press, 1971), 148.

8. Michel Foucault, *The Order of Things: An Archaeology of the Human Sciences* (1966; New York: Vintage, 1973), 43, 300.

9. Joseph Conrad, *Heart of Darkness*, ed. Robert Kimbrough, rev. ed. (New York: Norton, 1971), 72. For a full discussion of this narrative technique see my "The Divided Protagonist: Reading as Repetition and Discovery," *Texas Studies in Language and Literature* 30 (Summer 1988): 151–78.

10. William Faulkner, *Absalom, Absalom!*, The Corrected Text (1936; New York: Vintage International, 1990), 286.

11. "Interview with Jean Stein Vanden Heuvel," *Lion in the Garden: Interviews with William Faulkner, 1926–1962*, ed. James B. Meriwether and Michael Millgate (New York: Random House, 1969), 253.

A Note on the Conference

"Faulkner at 100"—the 1997 Faulkner and Yoknapatawpha Conference celebrating the one hundredth anniversary of the author's birth—took place July 27–August 1, and was the largest since the conference began twenty-four years ago. Over four hundred people registered for the conference and twenty-five speakers made presentations. Because of the large number of scholars invited to speak, the conference program committee decided, in addition to a number of full-length presentations, to organize a series of panels in order to raise in a fairly direct way some of the key questions that seem appropriate on such occasions. In this volume we have grouped the papers comprising each of the panels together, interspersing them with the longer presentations. In addition to the Faulkner scholars, Albert Murray, closest among the speakers to being a contemporary of Faulkner's, gave an address discussing, among other things, his response to Faulkner in the 1930s while a student at the Tuskegee Institute in Alabama. Randall Kenan, about to begin a year at the University of Mississippi as the Southern Writer in Residence, sponsored by John and Renée Grisham, gave a reading.

The conference opened with a reception hosted by the University Museums and an exhibition entitled *Faulkner's World: The Photographs of Martin J. Dain*, curated by Tom Rankin. At the opening session Chancellor Robert C. Khayat welcomed participants, and William Ferris, director of the Center for the Study of Southern Culture, presented the 1997 Eudora Welty Awards in Creative Writing to Olivia Foshee of Oxford and Charles Johnson of West Point. The awards are selected annually through a competition held in high schools throughout Mississippi. This was followed by presentation of the winner of the eighth annual Faux Faulkner write-alike contest, sponsored by the Jack Daniel Distillery, the University of Mississippi, and Yoknapatawpha Press and its *Faulkner Newsletter*. The winner was Wendy Goldberg, who read her prize-winning entry, "Dyin' to Lie Down." The program concluded with *Voices from Yoknapatawpha*, readings of passages from Faulkner's fiction selected and arranged by former conference director Evans Harrington. Participants then gathered at the home of Dr. and Mrs. M. B. Howorth Jr. for a buffet supper, followed by the opening lecture of the conference by Michael Millgate.

In addition to the lectures and panel discussions, highlights of the conference included reminiscences of Faulkner during his visit to West Point by Joseph L. Fant, coeditor of *Faulkner at West Point*; the presentation "Knowing William Faulkner," by the writer's nephew, J. M. Faulkner, and Meg Faulkner DuChaine; a panel discussion, "Faulkner in Oxford," including local residents Charles M. Murry, Patricia Young, and M. C. Falkner, another of the writer's nephews; "Teaching Faulkner" sessions, conducted by visiting scholars James B. Carothers, Robert W. Hamblin, and Charles A. Peek; and bus tours of North Mississippi and the Delta. Social highlights were a party at Tyler Place hosted by Charles Noyes, Sarah and Allie Smith, and Colby Kullman; a walk through Bailey's Woods and a picnic at Faulkner's home, Rowan Oak; a party at Square Books, and a closing party at the Gary home.

The conference planners are grateful to all the individuals and organizations who support the Faulkner and Yoknapatawpha Conference annually. In addition to those mentioned above, we wish to thank the Appalachian Regional Council, the Mississippi Humanities Council, the University of Mississippi Sesquicentennial Committee, Mr. Richard Howorth of Square Books, Mr. James Rice of Downtown Inn, St. Peter's Episcopal Church, the City of Oxford, the Oxford Tourism Council, and Mississippi Madness.

A Note on the Faulkner Centennial

Throughout 1997, the centennial year of William Faulkner's birth, celebrations took place in universities and libraries in all parts of the world. In addition to papers marking the event presented during the annual Faulkner and Yoknapatawpha Conference, "Faulkner at 100: Retrospect and Prospect," this volume contains records of two other celebrations in Mississippi, plus a list of events that took place throughout the year in the United States and abroad.

In Oxford, the writers's home for most of his life and the imaginative site of much of his great fiction, the commemoration included exhibitions, lectures, panel discussions, commentaries, readings, birthday cake—decorated with maps of Yoknapatawpha County—served in the Student Union, and champagne toasts at Square Books. In New Albany, Faulkner's birthplace, residents organized a weekend of celebratory events that included scholarly address and performances of *"Oh, Mr. Faulkner, Do You Write?"* and a musical version of *As I Lay Dying.*

Testimonials presented on the University of Mississippi campus in Oxford and Robert Hamblin's keynote address in New Albany are printed here, demonstrating William Faulkner's extraordinary impact one hundred years after his birth.

Faulkner at 100
FAULKNER AND YOKNAPATAWPHA
1997

Some Brief Recollections of Then—for Now

JOSEPH BLOTNER

First I must thank Don Kartiganer and Ann Abadie for permitting me to insert myself into the proceedings belatedly, and for this I offer explanation. A year ago, when Don had very kindly reminded me of the opportunity to submit a paper I replied, too hastily, that I was so pressed with the completion of work on Robert Penn Warren and with other concerns that I thought I had better decline. Then, about a month ago, with those concerns long since met, I began to confront something that had begun to nag at the fringes of my consciousness. More than I had realized, I wanted to be here for this special celebration. It was no consolation to read the words of another who had made the same mistake I had: "I [had] declined, saying that I really couldn't concentrate enough to collect remarks on 'Faulkner and Women' because I was deeply involved in writing a book myself and I didn't want any distractions whatsoever." And it was no consolation to me that the person was someone as smart as Toni Morrison.

I kept thinking of a novel and a particular passage which begins with the image of a wheel and goes on, "In the lambent suspension of August into which night is about to fully come, it seems to engender and surround itself with a faint glow like a halo. The halo is full of faces." I thought of the faces I would not see by failing to come here: your own, but also faces which many of you never had the chance to see: the faces of Mac Reed and Bob Farley, Ben Wasson and Phil Mullen, Calvin Brown and Howard Duvall—and more: Cleanth Brooks and Elizabeth Kerr, even Carvel Collins, and others too. I began to feel as if it was up to me to name those names—friends of Faulkner and townspeople and scholars—though for all I knew someone else might do it, but I did not think there would be a great many here who had been here twenty-three summers ago when "Faulkner and Yoknapatawpha" began. Toni Morrison said that the conference directors (she must have meant Evans Harrington and Ann Abadie, and perhaps Doreen Fowler) had asked her to come anyway and read from her manuscript. Fortunately she accepted, and took part in a panel too. I decided to try to recoup my mistake and sent in the registration form and bought my air tickets. Then I asked Ann and Don Kartiganer if I could have a little time to allow memory to speak.

Of the beginnings, Evans wrote, "Even before William Faulkner's death, visitors often came to his home town of Oxford to see firsthand the area which he had transformed into Yoknapatawpha County and made world famous. In the years that followed his death, the stream of visitors grew increasingly larger. Members of the English Department . . . were beset by questioners about the man and his area. . . . So constant were the visits and persistent the inquiries . . . that a number of individuals at the University came to be spending a large part of their time just advising and escorting Faulkner enthusiasts. . . . Thus was conceived Faulkner and Yoknapatawpha. . . . The first such conference was held in August of 1974, and so great was the attendance that the whole program had to be repeated a second week." It was nothing like the smooth production you experience now, but again the response was encouraging.

In the ensuing years we came to date events by their intersection with the days of the conference. Of the many, one is paramount. During the second week of that command repeat performance, some of us were gathered for dinner at the Holiday Inn, then the Downtowner, on Friday night, August 9th. Among the tables of polite and quiet Oxford citizens, I sat with Malcolm Cowley, Elizabeth Kerr, and Betty and Evans Harrington as a network news bulletin was piped into the dining room. In the wreckage of Watergate Richard M. Nixon was resigning the Presidency of the United States of America. We five leaped cheering to our feet, as the other diners regarded us in silence.

In the closing ceremonies of another conference, a different mood was evoked. The same Elizabeth Kerr, a veteran scholar and professor emerita, had distinguished herself by her wide-ranging knowledge and passionate enthusiasm for all things Yoknapatawphan. In the farewell dinner some young wags had prepared a memento for her: a corsage fashioned of a bed of Kudzu on which reposed a corn cob. As game as she was knowledgeable, Elizabeth accepted the trophy with good humor. Another conference-closing occasion was different. That year we held the dinner in a restaurant established by Faulkner's boyhood friend, Aubrey Seay, and grandly called the Mansion. It was a jolly and boisterous occasion, so much so that most people couldn't hear, above the after-dinner chatter, the voice of an old man: Malcolm Cowley, reading from his 1929 volume of poems, *Blue Juniata*. It was, I think, his last "Faulkner and Yoknapatawpha."

Over the next decade and a half, the pilgrimage of native scholars was augmented by the stream from abroad: Michael Millgate, then the lone Englishman; François Pitavy, presaging the French contingent to be augmented soon by Michel Gresset and André Bleikasten. Before long came the Russians: Sergei Chakovsky, Alexandre Vaschenko, and Peter Palievsky. Lothar Hönnighausen was blazing his own trail, and Kenzaburo Ohashi, at first a solitary representative, but not for long. The parade of scholars continued, brightened by the women: Ilse Dusoir Lind, Panthea Reid, Judith Wittenberg, Thadious Davis, Judith Sensibar, and Susan Donaldson, and this brief mention does not include the 1990s. Who were their fellow participants? Cleanth Brooks, Hugh Kenner, John Pilkington, the two Louises (Rubin and Simpson), and the young stars hot on their trail: Noel Polk, Jim Carothers, Tom McHaney, Jim Watson, and Bob Hamblin. (But this is a losing game, which I must stop immediately; for there are more scholars and critics who deserve mention in this same breath as well as the creative writers, who paid tribute in more than one coin.)

Now I'll run the time machine backward even further, to Charlottesville, and another closing just under forty years ago. William Faulkner's term as writer in residence was finally coming to an end. (We did not know then that there would be another one.) Introducing him with an attempt at lightheartedness, I recalled the turn-of-the-century concert artists who would make several farewell appearances for "positively the last time." When he began he said that yes, this "interminable valedictory" was finally coming to an end. I know he didn't regret the public part of it, but my colleague and partner, Fred Gwynn, and I certainly did.

There were other such occasions in that spring of 1957. Fred and I took the question-and-answer format and "put the show on the road," as the star of our one-man production phrased it. We went to Mary Washington college for a fine, lively occasion, but the scene I remember best was a quiet one: the only ones there, we wandered through the cemetery in the sunny April silence, reading the fading names and ranks and dates and regimental numbers carved under the legend C.S.A. on the rows of the small dark weathered stones. What are his thoughts, I wondered, a private ode to the Confederate dead? On the way home we paused for a commemorative libation of Jack Daniel's. Three weeks later, with his stepson and son-in-law, we made a trip to places even more deeply steeped in memory: the bloody Seven Days' battlefields, finally to stand at the memorial marking the Crater and the carnage of the dying days of the war.

Four years later, his second term completed, and now a Charlottesville homeowner, he was ready for more battlefielding, as Howard Duvall used to call it. Fred Gwynn had left, and so our Balch Hangar-Flying Squadron was reduced to two, one lieutenant and one leader, the Chief, as Fred had dubbed him. He loved to make plans, even those I suspected he knew we might never carry out. We decided that next year we would go to Gettysburg. As we talked about Matthew Brady's photographs he uttered the only literary phrase I ever heard from him. Of the unbearable stench of the battlefields he said, "the Confederate corpses didn't have enough meat on them to produce it; it was the effluvium from the Yankee corpses that permeated the circumambience." But we did not linger on mortality and the lugubrious. My birthday was approaching, with his following a few months later. Thinking of his mother's longevity, I told him that one of my ambitions was to see the year 2000 in. "That's a good date," he said. "We'll have a party then." We could not know that it was his last birthday that was approaching.

And now, speeding up the machine, I am back in our time again. Looking ahead to the William Faulkner Centenary at the University of Rennes 2, some time ago I decided to give myself a course in contemporary literary criticism. After finishing the work I did with Noel Polk (a caboose to his engine) for the third Library of America volume of Faulkner novels three years ago, and then the Warren biography four months ago, I could no longer put it off. The course proved to be a difficult one. For years I had been a card-carrying Brooks and Warren New Critic. Years before that I had even written some Freudian and Jungian criticism only to learn subsequently that Freud was passé. (Imagine my feelings when I read this month in the *New York Times Magazine*, "Save Sigmund Freud: What we can still learn from a discredited, scientifically challenged misogynist.") So I have been trying to learn what I can about the worlds and works of Lévi-Strauss and Saussure and Jakobsen and Barthes and Derrida and Foucault and Lacan and Althusser, and even De Man and Miller and Hartman and Bloom. It hasn't been easy. But there have been a few smiles along the way.

I owe one to last year's Special William Faulkner issue of the *Mississippi Quarterly*, more particularly to M. Nell Sullivan's essay, "Persons in Pieces: Race and Aphanisis in *Light in August*." She writes that Byron Bunch "comments upon the radical disjunction between the word and the thing." Then she goes on to explain that

> Byron, Lena, and *all* the residents of Jefferson are caught in a web of signifiers, what Faulkner calls "the lack of words" in an uncanny anticipation of Lacanian rhetoric. According to Lacan, "the subject appears first in the Other, in so far as the first signifier . . . emerges in the field of the Other and represents the subject for another signifier, which other signifier has as its effect the *aphanisis* of the subject." . . . The subject is eclipsed in his dialogue with the Other by the signifier that represents him. For Byron Bunch, as for Lacan, the symbolic realm, the world of words, mediates the Real for the subject and mediates the

subject for the Other. But for Joe Christmas, the dilemma of being represented by a signifier for yet another signifier is more dire than for Byron. . . ."[1]

The rest of Professor Sullivan's paragraph is equally challenging. What seized my imagination was the link between Byron Bunch and Jacques Lacan, and there began to open out for me a world of possibility. Could there also, perhaps, be a link between Dr. Lacan treating words and signifiers in *Light in August* and Dr. Peabody treating the words and signifiers of Addie and Dewey Dell Bundren, for example, in *As I Lay Dying*? And more than that, in the vast saga of Yoknapatawpha were there not, perhaps, other doppelgangers—for Gail Hightower and Gavin Stevens, and even perhaps, for V. K. Ratliff? As one who has himself been the Other—one Yankee amid three Southerners on the field of Petersburg—I earnestly commend this possibility to your study as I pursue it in mine.

At last I return to the names I came here to say. But having already said them once, I shall not repeat them. Instead, I'll take the liberty of saying something for them, and perhaps for the rest of us as well, certainly for myself. "I'm sorry, Chief, that in the flesh you did not make it to the year 2000 or even to your 100th, but it is clear to see that in the worlds of the spirit and the word you did make it, and beyond."

NOTE

1. *Mississippi Quarterly* 49 (Summer 1996): 502.

WHO WAS WILLIAM FAULKNER?
Growing Up in Faulkner's Shadow

W. KENNETH HOLDITCH

Who was Faulkner? A challenging question indeed, and it is one with which the participants in this conference have been struggling one way or another for twenty-four years. My response to that query makes me feel—to paraphrase an old and humorous description of North Carolina—somewhat like a valley of humility among these towering examples of Faulknerian erudition that are gathered here this week.

My primary research has not been in Faulkner, but in other Southern authors—Tennessee Williams and John Kennedy Toole, for example—for I was early steered rather forcefully away from Faulkner scholarship, for reasons that will be clear later.

What scholarly attention I have directed to Faulkner has been in regard to his connection with New Orleans, and that, of course, is certainly one key to the identity of the man—his relationship to place. For Faulkner was, more than most, a part of all that he had met and seems never to have lost those early impressions from the 1920s in the French Quarter. Today, however, I am concerned with his relationship to the Yoknapatawpha country, or North Mississippi if you will, and I hope that this does not imply that I would label him a regionalist.

I was told by Donald Kartiganer that I might be the only person presenting a paper in this year's gathering who had met Faulkner, and if that is indeed the case, and I do not know that it is, I think it incumbent on me to report on the man himself as opposed to the novelist or to the mythic gentleman into which he has evolved since his death in 1962.[1] As a consequence, my answer to the question "Who was Faulkner?" will take the form of an impressionistic portrait of the man, and I trust you will pardon the very personal tone of the following remarks. I will leave to my cospeakers the larger questions of Faulkner and the world or Faulkner and the cosmos.

We are, all of us, products of all the family generations that preceded us, even if we are unconcerned with genealogical research and have no idea from whom we sprang, beyond our parents and the grandparents we remember. I know that I was a product, in part, and I speak not

6

merely of genes, of my paternal great-grandfather. Although he was long dead when I was born, his presence was very powerfully felt in the old Pontotoc County house—located six miles south of New Albany, Faulkner's birthplace—in which my grandfather, my father, and I all were born. The same connection with his past certainly existed for William Faulkner, for the mythic stature of W. C. Falkner, the Old Colonel, remained for his family a brooding force long after his assassination in 1889, and he and his memory constitute part of who William Faulkner became.

It is through the connection between Faulkner's ancestor and mine that my first association with and knowledge of the novelist came about. My great-grandfather, Sidney F. Holditch, enlisted in Colonel Falkner's second regiment in 1861, and later followed Falkner, who, when he was voted out of leadership, left General Joe Johnston's division to form the Fourth Mississippi Cavalry. Their association continued through the war and after. When the Old Colonel determined that New Albany would be the southernmost station on his railroad because of problems with the terrain to the South, my great-grandfather persuaded him to extend the line across the Holditch land in Pontotoc County.

Colonel Falkner, who named the new stations along the line, towns such as Falkner and Ingomar (from a character in his popular novel, *The White Rose of Memphis*), chose "Ecru" for the hamlet that grew up on my great-grandfather's land. He had planned to name the town Holditch, but my great-grandfather resisted, pointing out that he had already made numerous enemies because he had pulled strings with his old friend to get the railroad built across his land. Why Ecru? Because it was the color of the railroad station. I have always, I guiltily admit, regretted my great-grandfather's decision, for it has deprived me of the privilege of introducing myself as "Kenneth Holditch of Holditch, Mississippi."

Early in childhood I began to hear stories from members of my family and other Ecru residents about W. C. Falkner and his friendship with my ancestor. "Your great-grandfather bought the railroad with a turkey dinner and a bottle of wine" became something of a litany through the years. George Holditch, my grandfather, who lived to the age of ninety-three, remembered the Old Colonel, an imposing and imperious figure of whom he was frightened, in his childhood. One of the grievances often voiced by my older relatives was the fact that two autographed copies of Falkner's *The White Rose of Memphis* owned by the family had been borrowed and never returned. Later I even discovered the location of one of those volumes but was never able to reclaim it.

Limited as it may seem to some, this was the world in which I grew to maturity. I truly did not discover that the South had lost "*The* War" until

I was eight years old, and quite a shock it was! Obviously Quentin Compson was not the only one who grew up among ghosts.

In addition to hearing stories of the Old Colonel's valor and daring in the War Between the States and of his financial and political and literary activities during Reconstruction, I knew about other Faulkners. Louise Hale, who with her sister Clara Mae had grown up in Ecru across the street from my family home and attended high school with my father, married Dean Faulkner. I also heard of William and John, the two writers, who were accounted rather wild by older residents of north Mississippi and who had, of course, written those "awful" and "scandalous" books that "defamed" the South. I remember a classmate in junior high school who had acquired a copy of *Sanctuary*—literally encased in a "plain brown wrapper"—about which he snickered, though I suspect that he had no comprehension of its contents or what was shocking about it.

Although my family may not have held William Faulkner in high esteem as an author, they did not subscribe to some of the more bizarre rumors about him. For example, there were those who insisted that when drinking, he was inclined to take off all his clothes, climb into a tree in front of Rowan Oak, and spring down to surprise any unwary intruder who chanced to enter his private domain. Such cautionary stories served, of course, to create in a bookish and curious boy the opposite effect from what was intended, and I early determined to read those books!

In 1949 in Tupelo, Mississippi, Florence Bogan, one of those wonderful high school English teachers to whom many of us owe an inestimable debt, introduced me to the short stories of William Faulkner—"A Rose for Emily" and "Dry September" specifically—and encouraged me to read more. I acquired the *Collected Stories* when it was published and read it straight through, then moved on to the novels, first *Intruder in the Dust*, which my mother had checked out of the Lee County Library and professed not to have enjoyed. In all honesty, I was not especially impressed by that work either on my first encounter, but I soon found *Light in August*, became lost in those labyrinthine sentences and paragraphs, and was forever hooked. At the time, I was engaged in my first attempts at writing fiction, and I recall being stunned by the greatness of that novel and saddened at the same time because I realized that Faulkner had done what I wished passionately and hopelessly that I could have done myself. He had written of the people and places that I knew, and I felt somehow deprived of my native material even as I marveled at his talents. Years later I would read and identify completely with Flannery O'Connor's observation that for Southern writers, "The presence alone of Faulkner in our midst makes a great difference in what the writer can and cannot permit himself to do. Nobody wants his mule and wagon stalled on the same track the Dixie Limited is roaring down."

In May of 1951, William Faulkner delivered the commencement address to his daughter's high school graduating class, and I prevailed on my parents to drive me and a high school friend, Gwen Posey, to Oxford. That was before the days when such young people had their own cars. When Faulkner, dapper and elegant as a nineteenth-century gentleman, walked onto the stage at Fulton Chapel on the Ole Miss campus, Gwen and I were sitting on the front row to the side, my parents having discreetly chosen to take places in the back of the auditorium. It was my first sight of the great man, or any great person for that matter, or any celebrity, save a few ancient Confederate veterans. Of course, I had gone to junior high school with a boy named Elvis Presley, but in those days, nobody knew what a phenomenon he would become. At the risk of sounding maudlin, I must admit that on that night in Fulton Chapel, with Faulkner standing behind the podium, I was awe-struck. "So that is what genius looks like," I thought: a physically small man who casts a very large shadow.

Sitting in the first row turned out to have been a very good decision, for Faulkner spoke softly, hardly above a mutter, and those further back would later complain, as one Oxford resident expressed it, that they heard "nary a word" of his speech. It was brief, lasting little more than four minutes, but now, as an academician who has suffered through thirty-five years of interminably long university graduations, I can attest to the fact that it is the only commencement address I ever heard in which anything of substance was said.

In those few words, he urged the young people, his daughter Jill among them, to avoid fear and to accept the human obligation to "see that justice and truth and pity and compassion are done." By so doing, he assured them, their generation could "change the earth." Mixed with echoes of the Nobel Prize Acceptance Speech, there was another typical Faulkner touch, an oblique attack on government programs to provide food and money to those who had not earned it, thereby, he said, depriving the populace of its independence. The large audience, more than a thousand people I understand, many of them surely come out of curiosity to see that strange reclusive author and hear what he might say or do, seemed impressed, and the applause was loud and sustained. Certainly the brevity of the talk was a plus for many, but in addition, there was nothing in it to offend the more conservative Mississippians gathered there.

Exhibiting perhaps more nerve than brain, I rushed backstage immediately after the ceremony to find Faulkner being interviewed by Phil

Mullen, an editor of the *Oxford Eagle*. I approached the author with some trepidation, held out my hand, and told him how much I admired his work. He smiled, took my hand, bowed slightly, and said, "Why, thank you." Joseph Blotner records that significant moment in my life in his biography, writing that Faulkner was "in an almost expansive mood" and "talked to a young admirer." Well, as you can see from the wrinkles, the youth is long gone, but the admiration has only grown with the passage of time.

The next year, 1952, I saw Faulkner, accompanied by Shelby Foote, striding across the fields at Shiloh on the occasion of the ninetieth anniversary of that bloody engagement. Three years after that, November 10, 1955, I drove from Ole Miss, where I was a student, to Memphis to hear Faulkner address the very first integrated audience at the Peabody Hotel, the annual convention of the Southern Historical Association. Once again, Faulkner, when he stood at the podium, was strikingly elegant and commanding, despite his height or lack thereof, and again I was amazed just to be in the presence. The speech that night, though still brief and succinct, was more than twice as long as the commencement address, and, as many of you know, it was to be the source of considerable controversy, containing as it did Faulkner's views on integration, including the now famous assertion that "To live anywhere in the world of A.D. 1955 and be against equality because of race or color, is like living in Alaska and being against snow." The discussion that followed was both supportive and adverse, and the attacks by the author's enemies in the press within the next few days were often virulent. Among the severest critics was Fred Sullens, the editor of the Jackson *Clarion-Ledger*, whose animosity endured through several decades, manifested in such pronouncements as his description of Faulkner as "a propagandist of degradation," who "properly belongs to the privy school of literature."

In the eight more years Faulkner was to live, I saw him occasionally on the streets of Oxford, where I was a graduate student at Ole Miss. Several times, returning from late hours at the library, I spotted him walking through the dark streets and once even waved to him, a greeting he returned. Fortunately I had more sense than to approach him during his solitary rambles, remembering the experience of the chairman of the university honors program, a brusque and outspoken woman, who met him on the square one day, stopped in front of him and launched into a request that he speak to her students—while Faulkner, without a pause, stepped down off the raised sidewalk onto the street, walked around her, and proceeded on his way.

In 1962, I stood on a hill in Oxford Cemetery amid a small cluster of silent people, most grieving, some perhaps merely curious, and looked down on the gathering of family and friends laying to rest the man who had written much of the greatest fiction of the century. It seemed impossible that his physical presence in Oxford would no longer exist. For the first time, the town seemed almost as a unit to realize that something very important had gone out of its life.

Never did the sight of that small, neat, and dapper figure—on stage, on Shiloh battlefield, or striding through the town he had immortalized—fail to excite and inspire me. Seeing him in the flesh was, for me, tantamount to having one's dreams incarnated, akin perhaps to the experience of some eighteenth-century Londoner, having just been overwhelmed by the premier performance of *Messiah*, brushing against George Frederick Handel in the street. Or a sixteenth-century Italian, having craned his neck to view and marvel at the splendor of the Sistine Chapel, turning to see Michelangelo mixing paints on his palette.

Excuse a cliché, but I cannot resist pointing out that times have changed. We are gathered here on his "little postage stamp of native soil" to commemorate the centenary of the birth of a man who in his fiction created a mythic microcosm that will, I am sure, continue to astound readers in ages to come—and I do not share the reticence of some scholars to proclaim that. However, in the late 1950s, at the University of Mississippi, when I proposed writing my dissertation on William Faulkner, I was told that he had been "done" and I should choose another author. My protests and pleas were of no avail, and I abandoned that dream. Now, in retrospect, surely it is clear that so rich and layered is his fiction that there will always be issues to be raised and questions to be answered—for example, "Who was Faulkner, really?"

Well, now you at least know something of what he was and who he was for me and many of us who grew up in the Yoknapatawpha region at our particular time, the time in which he trod these hills and made them an unforgettable part of the landscape of literature and memory.

NOTE

1. As he recounts in his essay, "Some Brief Recollections of Then—for Now," Joseph Blotner became a part of the conference program belatedly, doubling the number of speakers who had met Faulkner. [Eds.]

Faulkner, the Role-Player

LOTHAR HÖNNIGHAUSEN

"What then is truth? A mobile army of metaphors, metonymics, and anthropomorphism."
—FRIEDRICH NIETZSCHE as quoted by Jacques Derrida

"Part of the fun of writing is putting on masks."
—TOM WHALEN[1]

The rediscovery of Friedrich Nietzsche by Jacques Derrida is one of the characteristic manifestations of the spirit of our times, as is Tom Whalen's enjoyment of writing as a putting on of masks. In fact, the pronouncement of the nineteenth-century philosopher Friedrich Nietzsche, as transmitted through the deconstructive spirit of Jacques Derrida, and the casual remark of the contemporary American poet Tom Whalen on a writer's pleasure in role-playing mark the wide range of our theme of Faulkner as role-player. It contains cognitive, ethical, and aesthetic aspects, centering on "masks and metaphors" and comprising the sociopsychic implications of Faulkner's personae and of his imagery for his readers. Nietzsche's replacement of truth by metaphor accords well with his conviction that the modern artist can best be understood as a wearer of masks. ("Every complex spirit needs a mask: even more, around every complex spirit a mask continually grows."[2]) Indeed, Nietzsche's interrelated views on masks and metaphor constitute the threshhold of my approach to Faulkner.[3]

In recent years, the approach to metaphor has developed well beyond the taxonomic registering of rhetorical figures and the sensitive but essentially formalist image studies of the previous generation. Discourse theory, women's studies, and reader response criticism as well as new historicism and communication theory have "modified our sensibility" and created a new awareness of the interrelationship between metaphoric forms and ideological contents. The idea inspiring my approach of an essential affinity between the transfer in role-playing and in metaphorizing opens up a new view of the processes of the artistic imagination as well as of the functioning of metaphor. From this perspective, metaphor appears not so much as a single rhetorical device than as a complex

12

shaping power, as "metaphoricity," inspiring whole contexts and respective reader responses. Connected with these new concepts is the replacement of "the work" as ruling aesthetic metaphor by that of "the illimitable text." Clearly, the new fascination with intertextuality and contextuality, with the logistics of role-playing, and the transgression of categorical boundaries in metaphor is concomitant with a more comprehensive sociopolitical deconstruction of which the traditional notions of race and gender are the most prominent examples. While the Romantics insisted on sincerity, we appreciate the aesthetics of role-play; while the New Critics focused on the "well-wrought" urn and the definiteness of structure, we cherish the Bakhtinian "openness" of Faulkner's novels.

In trying to answer the question of our panel, we find relevant quotations not only in Faulkner's own novel *Mosquitoes* but also in an essay by an American author he held in high esteem, Herman Melville. In his review essay, "Hawthorne and His Mosses," Melville assures us: "And if you rightly look for it, you will almost always find that the author himself has somewhere furnished you with his own picture." Authors "furnish us with pictures of themselves," but the following quotation from Faulkner's *Mosquitoes* indicates that these pictures are not nearly as clear as Melville's remark would lead us to believe: "But you, straying trustfully about this park of dark and rootless trees which Dr. Ellis and your Germans have recently thrown open to the public. . . . A book is the writer's secret life, the dark twin of a man: you can't reconcile them. And with you, when the inevitable clash comes, the author's actual self is the one that goes down, for you are one of those for whom fact and fallacy gain verisimilitude by being in cold print."[4]

The examples of both Melville and Faulkner—"Ishmael is the witness in *Moby Dick* as I am Quentin in *The Sound and the Fury*"—illustrate that what artists give us are not so much pictures as projections and distorted reflections of themselves. Noel Polk, in *Children of the Dark House*, illustrates a comic aspect of the problem by recounting how Faulkner in the 1952 *Omnibus* television program about himself grants the former editor of the *Oxford Eagle* permission to "Do your story," but then, putting on the mask of the "Writer as Recluse," insists, "But no pictures."[5] Another famous example of Faulkner's role-play is the startling pronouncement that he, the Nobel Prize-winning author, is not a writer at all but a grain and feed producing farmer.[6] The metaphors in the quotation from *Mosquitoes* and its eerie, psychoanalytic scenery uncover some of Faulkner's unconscious motifs in shaping his masks: an author's book is envisioned as his sinister *Doppelgänger* revealing the mysterious superiority of this other self.

As the study of Faulkner's masking practice shows, the elusive master did not only employ one but a "multitude of masks" to transform himself. This is not surprising if it is understood that a mask not only disguises but also constitutes an essential mode of living and writing, as Wallace Stevens puts it: "Authors are actors, books are theaters." Consequently, to describe the entire diversity of Faulkner's roles, to assess their related-ness, and to evaluate their psychological motifs and literary functions would involve a complete overview of his entire biography and work. On the present occasion, I cannot do more than ask some methodological questions and offer a few reflections. How does one reconcile the depres-sive side of Faulkner's personality and the respective role-playing (reck-less horseman and ruthless drinker) with his human sympathy and humor, with his self-confidence and clear awareness of being one of the world's greatest novelists?[7] Do these oppositions, if they really are oppo-sitions, resurface as particular masks which he assumed in his life or in his writing?

While it is tempting to dismiss Faulkner's dandyism as a means for him to compensate for his diminuitive size, there is little doubt that such a simplistic approach would prove unsatisfactory. The dandy mask should not be viewed in isolation; it must be seen in relation to the opposing mask of the vagabond or bum. Furthermore, the coexistence of the dandy with the persona of the country boy, farmer, and country gentleman—all three having different symbolic implications—is worthy of consideration and evaluation. Finally, the differing appearances of the dandy and his close relative, the aesthete, must be discussed in both psychological and artistic terms, as they appear to be related to the polar features of the self-effacing minuteness of Faulkner's handwriting and its calligraphic elevation in his handcrafted art nouveau manuscripts. Critics have rarely taken these stylizing details of Faulkner's masks and the circumstances of their use into account. But the dandy mask, while serving compensa-tory and supplementary functions in Faulkner's life, also proved to be inspirational in his writing. Its *élan* and irony embodied the artist's cre-ative buoyancy and his emerging sense of form.

If it is accepted that the reader's experience of Faulkner's fiction also involves considering the artist as "hero of a thousand faces" (Joseph Campbell), it is obviously necessary to consider the several media in which Faulkner cast images of himself because the impact of Faulkner's role-playing in his photos, letters, and interviews is quite different from that of his artist-personae in his fiction. Clearly, one must take into ac-count the different media of Faulkner's self-projections, whether they be a group of drawings, a poetry volume, or a short story about a living or a marble faun. It does matter whether a portrayal as a fighter pilot is to serve to impress some lady friend or whether two novelistic Quentins are to express different sides of himself. But whether Faulkner poses for a photo in his new riding gear or identifies with suicidal flyers, these artist-personae appear as historically and individually conditioned foci of the text and as aesthetically transforming its sociocultural contents. The awareness that fictionalizing plays as considerable a part in Faulkner's biography as in his literary works will lead to new approaches in biographical criticism as well as in the study of his works.

However, assessing the impact of the different personae of the artist on our reception of his art is complicated by several factors, particularly, how the various media through which these several personae—the drawn faun or the photographed war veteran—are established and affect us simultaneously yet differently. Further, little is yet known about how these personae or images interact and in which ways their interaction influences our reception of Faulkner's writing. The readers' encounters with Faulkner's literary self-portraits or masks constitute a very different kind of experience from their exposure to his images in sculpture, drawing, and photography. Above all, the personae of the author, whom readers help create by sensuously and intellectually realizing the metaphorics that constitute them, remain subordinate to the laws of the narrative cosmos of each story or novel. In contrast, the Faulkner masks conveyed through nonliterary media such as interviews and photographs seem to affect us more directly although they, too, do not give us "the real thing."

So far the few critics who have dealt with Faulkner's masks have tended to focus on the thematic aspects and on a small number of masks, often conceived of as complementary pairs, such as "rustic and aesthete" or "dandy and bum."[8] While one need not quarrel with these models per se, one obviously should avoid their exclusive use. A commendable alternative to both—the exclusive treatment of single masks or complementary pairs—seems to be a method of observing the variants of particular masks as they occur in shifting configurations and constellations in both his life and his works.

Thus Josh, in *Mosquitoes*, appears as a specialization and further development of one aspect of the title hero of *Elmer*, and the sterile immobility of Hightower in *Light in August* can be regarded as a fuller realization of character problems anticipated in the "paralysis" of the "marble faun." The most telling examples of recurring personae in changing constellations are, of course, the Quentins and Gavins who were to be "rewritten" in several novels and stories. The characters we can read as masks of the artist—Pierrot or Darl, "marble faun" or Horace Benbow—are neither representations of "right" or "wrong" attitudes nor mimetic, self-gratulatory autobiography, but exploratory impersonations of certain aesthetic and psychological problems, solutions, and failings, arising with the

changes in the author's outer and inner life story. They appear as
sketches of an intensely stylized, albeit unflattering self-portrait which
remained unfinished, ultimately, because in Faulkner's tragic life the an-
ticipations of death and love cancelled each other out.

To speak of the "development" of Faulkner's persona, in other words,
to employ evolutionary diction and metaphorics would suggest a clear-
ness of direction and singleness of purpose alien to his perspectivist philosophy and narration. However, there are noticeable currents in
Faulkner's role-playing, such as the fascination in his early work with the
radically different and frequently changing personae of the artist (the
late romantic marble faun, the symbolist Pierrot of Paris, the Sherwood
Anderson-type of a young man in "The Hill," and the glass blowing lawyer in the first Yoknapatawpha novel). This tendency, culminating in a
kind of "artists' convention" of different artist personae (*Mosquitoes*), not
surprisingly becomes less pronounced after Faulkner's emergence as
"major writer." There are also characteristic preoccupations—like the
contrast between the several painfully reflecting personae (Horace, Darl,
Quentin) and their active counterparts (Bayard, Jewel, Sutpen). Finally,
there are repetitions, like the use of the Cyrano de Bergerac and Don
Quixote metaphors in the fictionalizing of both the early Helen Baird
encounter and the late Joan Williams affair, or continuities like the interest in the fox hunting country gentleman and the motif of the war veteran. Given the many different and similar masks overlaying each other,
the metaphor of the palimpsest or of an endless "all-over painting"
should perhaps be employed to define Faulkner's biographical and literary self-fashionings.

The image of the "true" Faulkner as opposed to his "false" appearances presupposes an organicist model with a holistic identity that
evolves in orderly stages towards maturity. In view of Faulkner's role-
playing and his many "false" stories, particularly those about military
honors he had not earned and war wounds he never sustained, some
critics have had recourse to psychological imposture theories, or have
approached Faulkner's career in terms of "The Psychopathology of Vocation."[9] The drawback of this approach is that the very complex phenomenon of Faulkner's role-playing, comprising sociological, psychological,
historical, and aesthetic aspects, appears reduced to a scientific determinism and a moral perspective. Of equal importance, the wearing of masks
and role-playing are perceived not as a matter of discourse but as an
ontological issue.

The imposture theory presupposes "philosophical realism" and ontological or causal oppositions such as "being-seeming," "original-copy,"
"character-mask," "underlying causes-surface appearances." "Impos-

ture" implies a dichotomy of "true and false," "normal and pathological" with moralistic and clinical implications that are closer to the tradition of Cesare Lombroso's *Genio e follia* (1864) than to our present-day conviction that role-playing functions as a decisive factor in all human behavior and, particularly, in any artistic transformation of life. Indeed we can give a more satisfactory answer to the question who was Faulkner if we regard his many masks as so many shifting responses to contemporary social, psychological, and literary contexts and, above all, if we see him as participating in a discursive practice in which role-playing is understood as a communicative act and an artistic strategy.

NOTES

1. Jacques Derrida, "White Mythology," *Enclitic* 2.2 (1978): 14; Tom Whalen, poetry reading, 14 June 1994, Bonn, Germany.

2. Friedrich Nietzsche, "Number 40," *Beyond Good and Evil*, trans. R.J. Hollingdale (London: Penguin Classics, 1990), 69–70.

3. See Wesley Morris, with Barbara Alverson Morris, *Reading Faulkner* (Madison: University of Wisconsin Press, 1989); Joseph Blotner, "Metafiction and Metalife: William Faulkner's Masks as Man and Artist," *The Artist and His Masks: William Faulkner's Metafiction*, ed. Agostino Lombardo (Roma: Bulzoni Editore, 1991), 9–26, and other contributors to the Rome session of the International Faulkner Symposium; see also my articles, " 'Point of View' and Its Background in Intellectual History," *Comparative Criticism* 2 (1980): 151–61, and "Metaphor in the Twentieth-Century Novel," *Modes of Narrative: Approaches to American, Canadian, and British Fiction*, ed. Reingard M. Nischik and Barbara Korte (Würzburg: Könighausen und Neumann, 1990), 3–19.

4. William Faulkner, *Mosquitoes* (New York: Liveright, 1955), 251.

5. Noel Polk, *Children of the Dark House* (Jackson: University Press of Mississippi, 1996), 242–43.

6. James B. Meriwither and Michael Millgate, eds., *Lion in the Garden: Interviews with William Faulkner, 1926–1962* (New York: Random House, 1968), 169.

7. See Blotner, "Metafiction and Metalife," *The Artist and His Masks*, ed. Lombardo: "I am an artist, a sincere one and of the first class. . . . I am the best in America, by God . . . what an amazing gift" (11).

8. Michael Grimwood, *Heart in Conflict: Faulkner's Struggles with Vocation* (Athens: University of Georgia Press, 1987), 287; Blotner, "Metafiction and Metalife," *The Artist and His Masks*, ed. Lombardo.

9. Judith Sensibar, *The Origins of Faulkner's Art* (Austin: University of Texas Press, 1984); Grimwood, *Heart in Conflict*, 35–84.

Was Not Was Not Who Since Philoprogenitive

NOEL POLK

One approaches such occasions as these, especially such a topic as this one—*who indeed was Faulkner?*—with lots of misgivings and misprisions. It is a topic at once both too broad and too specific and, more problematically, it calls for comment at one end or the other of the scale: either broad sweeping statements so general as to be banal and meaningless, or comments so particular as to be clinical and soulless. The topic allows for little in between, certainly not in the twenty minutes I've been allotted.

Who was Faulkner? We've spent sixty collective years trying to figure that one out, and it's a hell of a question to begin a conference like this with, investing the occasion with an ontological solemnity that Don Kartiganer has already belied by putting this panel at nine o'clock on Monday morning and to a certain extent betraying the great sense of celebration, of community, in Faulkner studies that we all feel every year when we come here to Oxford to pray and meditate and pour oblations on his grave at midnight. Our annual visits to Oxford are pilgrimages, doubtless for many of us even spiritual quests, which we secularize by assembling in the spirit of Chaucer's pilgrims, in all our lusty variety, telling each other tales that we pretend are about Faulkner when they are mostly about ourselves—who *we* are, where we come from, what we believe, what we seek, and what we *do* with what we discover here. We tell whopping good tales, each of them creating a jolly good and worthy Faulkner for our collective delectation, and the litany of Faulkners we have created in our own evolving likenesses is an impressive one in which we hear regularly chanted our own cultural and literary histories.

But enough of this religious metaphor, which smacks too much of the sort of bardolatry that we are too sophisticated to admit to these days but which, of course, still blurbles along under the surface of everything we do here. We are acolytes all, to one degree or another, and most of us are heavily invested with a devotion that goes beyond simple intellectual

18

stimulation, with some sense of mystery at the complex of things William Faulkner means to each of us: we know that to define him is at the same time to try to define ourselves. Thus in trying to discuss who William Faulkner was, or is, I am more than ever conscious that "words are no good: that words dont ever fit even what they are trying to say at."

We still don't have a complete fix on William Faulkner. He remains elusive for us, even with umpteen volume-length biographies, several volumes of letters, and more than a zillion essays that explore various aspects of his life in his works and out of them. Like Caddy Compson, Thomas Sutpen, Flem Snopes, and Eula Varner, he is the absent center of all our narrations, the gap we keep trying to fill, and we keep trying to fill it even though we now understand that he is all the more interesting to us precisely because he is unfixable, no matter how many marble slabs we create in the cemetery, how many critical studies, conferences, or New Corrected Texts to which we all must perforce transfer our crinkly old notes from graduate school (and don't tell me that isn't your *primary* reaction to the new texts: I've heard too many of you complain!).

I have come to think that even to try to fix William Faulkner is somehow to cancel him, such a chameleon is he: and I feel him standing by, pretending to ignore but watching closely our proceedings, ready always to laugh demonically at such attempts, with perhaps something in him of the Cyrano de Bergerac he loved, waiting for me to pronounce the critical equivalent of Valvert's lame observation that Cyrano's nose was "rather large!," to be bemused by my banality, and then to insert himself with great good humor into the proceedings, in sardonic soliloquy howling with glee and contradiction: Is that the best you can do?

> Ah no, young sir!
> You are too simple. Why, you might have said—
> Oh, a great many things! Mon dieu, why waste
> Your opportunity? For example, thus:—[1]

WRITER: He was the best in America, by God!

PHILOSOPHER: He declined to accept the end of man.

HORSEMAN: *And he on a buckskin pony with eyes like blue electricity and a mane like tangled fire, galloping up the hill and right off into the high heaven of the world.*

PRIVATE CITIZEN: It was his ambition to be, as a private individual, abolished and voided from history, leaving it markless, no refuse save the printed books; he wished he had enough sense to see ahead thirty years ago and, like some of the Elizabethans, not signed them.

HUSBAND: Poor bloke, Hemingway, to have to marry three times to find out that marriage is a failure, and the only way to get any peace out of it is (if you are fool enough to marry at all) keep the first one and stay as far away from her as much as you can, with the hope of some day outliving her. At least you will be safe then from any other one marrying you—which is bound to happen if you ever divorce her. Apparently man can be cured of drugs, drink, gambling, biting his nails and picking his nose, but not of marrying.

FATHER: Nobody remembers Shakespeare's children.

MISSISSIPPIAN: He hoped it would never come to it, but if it did he would make the choice Robert E. Lee made and defend Mississippi against the United States even if it meant going out into the street and shooting Negroes.

MAN OF LETTERS AND PUBLIC ICON: He was a mild retiring little man over yonder at Oxford.

NUTRITIONIST: There's a whole lot of nourishment in an acre of corn.

GENTLEMAN: Mammie Callie taught him to tell the truth, to refrain from waste, to be considerate of the weak and respectful to age.

LOVER: He said: I just showed you once. You want me to show you again?

ROMANTIC: He said she said: I reckon *I* don't mind if *you* don't.

TRAGEDIAN: He said she said: I reckon *I* don't mind if you *don't*.

SAGE: He knows now that you don't love because, you love despite; not for the virtues, but despite the faults.

Well, there are at any rate far too many Faulkners for us ever to hope to contain him or define him, even in or by his own words. Nevertheless, conference rules require that we make a stab at it occasionally if only to justify the partying that we are really here for and so I want to turn, in the spirit of serious play, to a couple of places where I believe we spot him most readily.

Who was William Faulkner? First, foremost, and finally, he was the man who wrote the books, and *there* is where we are most likely to find him, if we find him at all. Michel Gresset[2] and others have discussed at illuminating length the number of self-portraits in Faulkner's work, none of them particularly flattering. We know him as the fey young poet Faulkner in *Mosquitoes*, as an adulterous fey young poet in "Artist at Home," as an alcoholic who wants to get drunk and wallow around in the gutter with humanity in the late and openly autobiographical "Mr. Acarius," and as the gray-haired sage coming to terms with a lifetime of conflict in "Mississippi." We know how physically similar he is to Flem Snopes and Popeye. Such self-portraiture, however deeply into the author's psyche it may lead us, is perhaps at one level perhaps more a series of private jokes for author and friends than anything else, part and parcel of the tall-tale narrator's necessary self-deprecation: indeed, we cannot forget, even if we wanted to, that he apparently told a dowager that he appeared in *Sanctuary* as the corncob.

We spot him first, I think, as the unnamed narrator and central character of the early autobiographical fragment called "And Now What's to Do?" which he wrote around 1926. The narrator describes the adolescenting hero as one descended from a great-grandfather like Faulkner's and who grows up very democratically among blacks and whites who populate his father's livery stable, learning about horses and dice and women from them. Adolescence makes him conscious of class and sex distinctions, both of which work powerfully on him: he begins

> to acquire a sort of inferiority complex regarding his father's business. He had gone through grammar school and one year in high school with girls and boys . . . whose fathers were lawyers and doctors and merchants—all genteel professions, with starched collars. He had been unselfconscious, then, accepting all means of earning bread as incidental to following whatever occupation a man preferred. But not now. All this was changed by his changing body. Before and during puberty he learned about women from their negro hostlers and the white night-man, by listening to their talk. Now, on the street, he looked after the same girls he had once taken to school in his father's hack, watching their forming legs, imagining their blossoming thighs, with a feeling of defiant inferiority. There was a giant in him, but the giant was muscle-bound.[3]

I do not accept Frederick Karl's grotesquely reductive notion that Faulkner was mostly a horny short guy who wrote to get laid.[4] Much more interesting is Faulkner's sense of "defiant inferiority," his consciousness of the specific tensions between his small body, which he so early recognized as a "defiant inferiority," and his large mind, a "muscle-bound giant" held captive in that small frame. We have long noted these tensions in our ongoing discussions of certain powerful images of dynamic stasis. I'm also interested in the class-consciousness, the class antagonisms, the loss of that democratic livery-stable innocence that his body created for him when he began to be aware of himself as an inferior product on the sexual market.

Who was William Faulkner? Only in that split, that bifurcation, which becomes a multiplication, can we hope to locate him. He was, I think, Wilfred Midgleston, the ersatz hero of "Black Music" and, no doubt, of "Carcassonne." In "Carcassonne," he dreams nightly of the contest between his body and his soaring spirit, of conquering his constraining body by riding that well-known buckskin pony *up the hill and right off into the high heaven of the world.*[5] In "Black Music," he is "fortune's favorite, chosen of the gods. For fifty-six years, a clotting of the old gutful compulsions and circumscriptions of clocks and bells, he met walking the walking image of a small, snuffy, nondescript man whom neither man nor woman had ever turned to look at twice. . . . Then," like his unnamed counterpart dreamer/poet in "Carcassonne," his "apotheosis soared glaring, and to him at least not brief, across the unfathomed sky above his lost earth like that of Elijah of old" (CS 799). Like the dreamer in "Carcassonne," Midgleston lives in Rincon as one alien to the people he lives among. Faulkner describes him in language not unlike that he would later use to describe his own life in Oxford: Midgleston "hasn't learned more than ten words of Spanish. . . . [H]e hadn't learned to speak hardly a word of the language of the people with whom he had lived twenty-five years and among whom it appeared that he intended to die and be buried. . . . [H]e had no job: a mild, hopelessly mild man who looked like a book-keeper in a George Ade fable dressed as a tramp for a Presbyterian social charade in 1890, and quite happy" (CS 799–800). He is a "small, snuffy man in a pair of dirty drill trousers which had not been made for him" and he lives among "men a little soiled and usually unshaven . . . loud, violent, maintaining the superiority of the white race and their own sense of injustice and of outrage" (CS 802).

Midgleston tells his interlocutor a fantastic story of his afternoon as a "farn" in the Virginia mountains, when he performed "something outside in the lot and plan for mortal human man to do" (CS 805). He became a mythical creature "used" by the gods to save the sacred grapes that a New York society woman planned to destroy, in order to build upon that sacred ground a "community house [that would] look like the [Roman] Coliseum and the community garage . . . [that would] look like it was a Acropolis" (CS 807) for the amusement of her New York Park Avenue society friends. In his story Midgleston is a mere New York architect's draftsman gone to Virginia to take the architect's plans to the builder. But he becomes the marble faun made flesh who preserves the ancient grove from destruction through the accident of his first drink of alcohol when he unlocks the gate that constrains a bull—for Faulkner the quintessence of natural power—which scares the bejesus out of the citified Mrs. Van Dyming so badly that she abandons the project. Midgleston is, then, the faun, the slight-bodied half-goat half-man artist, the musician who unleashes his defiance in the form of that muscle- and fence-bound bullish masculinity that does his work for him. Midgleston becomes a writer, too; escaped to Rincon after his escapade, he carries with him a written record of the event, the story as it appeared in the New York Times as well as his own correction, which he wrote and which was published also in the Times, of certain factual errors in the story.

In 1936, Faulkner writes these two Midglestons into a single work. In Absalom, Absalom! Faulkner/Midgleston becomes both Sutpen and Sutpen's French architect, but with a significant difference: in "Black Music" he is the artist who releases the muscle-bound giant; in Absalom he is the artist of iron discipline who constrains and controls that selfsame bullish giant, Thomas Sutpen, and in the constraining makes possible even a lesser form of the magnificence that the bullish giantish Sutpen conceives for himself:

And not only an architect . . . but an artist since only an artist could have borne those two years in order to build a house which he doubtless not only expected but firmly intended never to see again. . . . [O]nly an artist could have borne Sutpen's ruthlessness and hurry and still manage to curb the dream of grim and castlelike magnificence at which Sutpen obviously aimed, since the place as Sutpen planned it would have been almost as large as Jefferson itself at the time; that the little grim harried foreigner had singlehanded given battle to and vanquished Sutpen's fierce and overweening vanity or desire for magnificence or for vindication or whatever it was . . . and so created of Sutpen's very defeat the victory which, in conquering, Sutpen himself would have failed to gain.[6]

By 1936, then, Faulkner had both conquered and freed the muscle-bound giant, and by 1937 he had become comfortable enough, or at least analytical enough, to write about it with great good humor, in a little-read piece called "Afternoon of a Cow," putatively written by one Ernest V. Trueblood, who tells us that he has been "writing Mr. Faulkner's novels and short stories for years."[7] The story begins one evening when a landed gentrified julep-sipping *faux* gentleman William Faulkner, a man of "almost violently sedentary habits" (*US* 426) starts to tell Trueblood what to write the next day. News that the pasture is on fire interrupts him; in the ensuing action the "almost violently sedentary" Faulkner chases down the cow of the title in order to rescue her. He finds her in a ditch and like Isaac Snopes in a similar situation, he gets under her to push her out of it. I quote Mr. Trueblood:

Remember how the poor spent terrified creature had for an entire afternoon been the anguished and blind victim of a circumstance which it could not comprehend, had been sported with by an element [fire] which it instinctively feared, and had now been hurled recently and violently down a precipice whose crest it doubtless now believed it would never see again.——I have been told by soldiers (I served in France, in the Y.M.C.A) how, upon entering battle, there often sets up within them, prematurely as it were, a certain impulse or desire which brings on a result quite logical and quite natural, the fulfillment of which is incontestible and of course irrevocable.——In a word, Mr. Faulkner underneath received the full discharge of the poor creature's afternoon of anguish and despair. (*US* 430)

Ernest V. Trueblood is thus the architect of Faulkner's literary mansion, the artist who contains and tames the buckskin pony of his imagination. The narrative and its title evoke both the "Afternoon of a Faun" of his early poem, and of "Black Music." Faulkner had identified himself with fey adulterous poets, a psychopathic criminal, and an impotent Baptist banker; now he can lampoon both the giant and the inferiority by identifying himself with an idiot lover who gets defecated upon by his bovine amoureuse!

The Faulkner-Trueblood split is a particularly interesting one, partly because Faulkner had used the Trueblood pseudonym very early in his career. At its simplest level, the split suggests some of the distance that Faulkner the man by this time in his career had gained on Faulkner the writer. "Afternoon of a Cow" is the single best parody of Faulkner that I know; nobody knew better than Faulkner how Faulkner wrote or why he wrote as he did. The two Faulkners, the Faulkner Faulkner and the Trueblood Faulkner—the faun and the bull, the gentleman farmer presumptive from the backwoods and the sophisticated architect—lived side by side with each other, in the same household: Faulkner, like Sutpen, holding court and giving orders and living as grandly as possible, Trueblood taking the orders and getting the creation down on paper. The Trueblood Faulkner is constantly ragged at by Malcolm and James and Rover or Grover, though he has tried, he says "on more than one occasion (this was years ago; I have long since ceased) to explain to them that my position in the household is in no sense menial" (US 424).

The two Faulkners didn't always live in harmony with each other, and perhaps came at times to hold each other in a kind of disdain or even contempt. I suspect that they didn't always understand each other completely, and there's some evidence in his later life—witness the serious depression in the years immediately following the Nobel Prize—that they didn't always like each other very much and frequently lived in contention. Thus we have the Faulkner who could write powerful novels of racial injustice in Mississippi coexisting with the Faulkner who would shoot Negroes in the street to defend Mississippi against the United States; Faulkner the lover, the older man, who could write the most mawkish and clumsy love letters to his much younger beloved co-existing with the Faulkner who could create a Gavin Stevens to give him precisely that analytical distance on his aging Lothario self that his lover self could not manage; we have the depressed alcoholic coexisting with the analytical Faulkner who wrote "Mr. Acarius"; the Faulkner who could write such powerful portraits of family dysfunction *and* the Faulkner who could tell his own daughter that nobody remembers Shakespeare's children.

At some celestial level, Faulkner was Cyrano de Bergerac himself, rapier always ready, from an early age, to defend, even if by parodying and ridiculing, his nose or his small stature, sweeping aside those limitations of size, of class, and of regional background that he seems to have felt sometimes very acutely: the muscle-bound giant freed, flexing its own muscles to give him the strength to defy that perceived inferiority, that perceived deformity, like Cyrano dazzling his critics with his wit and his language, challenging them implicitly to fence, composing a sonnet as he did so, and then thrusting home on the sonnet's final line, with a swirl and a buckle of his swash.

Finally—*finally*—he wrote the books—he or, as someone said of Shakespeare, someone exactly like him living in his house and his shoes, whether Ernest V. Trueblood or the Earl of Oxford. Finally indeed he wrote the books. Like Wilfred Midgleston, he was a man that had "done and been something outside the lot and plan for mortal human man to do and be" (*CS* 821).

NOTES

1. Edmond Rostand, *Cyrano de Bergerac*, trans. Brian Hooker (New York: Bantam, 19950), 30.

2. Michel Gresset, "Faulkner's Self-Portraits," *Faulkner Journal* 2 (Fall 1986): 2–13.

3. Faulkner, "And Now What's to Do?," *A Faulkner Miscellany*, ed. James B. Meriwether (Jackson: University Press of Mississippi, 1974), 146.

4. *William Faulkner: American Writer* (New York: Weidenfeld & Nicolson, 1989).

5. William Faulkner, "Carcassonne," *Collected Stories* (New York: Random House, 1950), 805.

6. *Absalom, Absalom!*, The Corrected Text (New York: Random House, 1986), 29.

7. *Uncollected Stories*, ed. Joseph L. Blotner (New York: Random House, 1979), 424.

Defining Moment:
The Portable Faulkner Revisited

MICHAEL MILLGATE

It is a privilege to be giving the opening lecture on this auspicious occasion and before this impressive audience. I had almost said, with standard oratorical redundancy, a proud privilege, were it not for the dark suspicion that my position on the program reflects my having been cast in the Dickensian role of the Spirit of Criticism Past, speaking, as Faulkner once put it, in a language you do not even need to not understand. If the theme of the conference is Prospect and Retrospect, I represent Retrospect. After this evening you will have Prospect all before you. On previous visits to Oxford I have sometimes been confused with that other intrusive Canadian, Shreve McCannon, Quentin Compson's fresh-air fiend of a friend from Alberta, but although Shreve was still living and practicing in Edmonton at the end of *Absalom, Absalom!* he must surely by this time have gone to his reward—though getting out of *Absalom, Absalom!* in one piece was perhaps reward enough.

Some personal retrospection first. At the University of Michigan, in the early months of 1957, I was a member of a graduate class in the Modern American Novel taught by Malcolm Cowley. The class didn't, as I recall, spend as much time on Faulkner as on Hemingway, but we certainly worked fairly intensively through *Go Down, Moses* and I luckily impressed Cowley early on by resolving, in class and off-the-cuff, a crux in "Delta Autumn" that he had still been puzzling over—the identity of the character referred to as "that one that was its own mother too."[1] A friendship quickly developed. He was a visiting professor, I was a visiting student, a little older than most. And British, more unusual then than now. I stayed with Cowley that summer at his home in Connecticut; he gave me introductions that led to some early writing assignments; and when he found I had no solid plans for the future he told me to go back to England, get "one of those easy British Ph.Ds," and then return to the States to teach. It was excellent advice, even if I didn't follow it quite through to the end. Needless to say, I valued Cowley's friendship and

26

advice; I dedicated my second book to him; I honor his memory; and I want this evening to look back at his contribution to Faulkner studies in a spirit of affectionate interrogation. But interrogation none the less.

Malcolm Cowley was, of course, a poet, a writer, an editor, and a prominent marcher and countermarcher of the highly politicised twenties and thirties, probably best remembered for *Exile's Return*, a rich evocation— part critical commentary, part personal memoir—of the American writers of the so-called Lost Generation who gravitated to Paris in the years following the First World War. But when Cowley died in 1989, at the age of ninety, many of the obituaries stressed the role played by his editing of *The Portable Faulkner* in bringing the work and name of William Faulkner to national prominence at the end of the Second World War and thus to international fame in 1950 as the winner of the previous year's held-over Nobel Prize. One obituary spoke of Cowley's "outstanding service to literature" as being his "rescue" of Faulkner "from out-of-print oblivion," and actually used "The rescuing of Faulkner" as its headline.

Whether *The Portable Faulkner* was in fact an effectual lifeline for Faulkner, whether it was a lifeline flung with covert political intent— whether, indeed, Faulkner needed a lifeline—these and other questions I'll turn to later. I must first say something about the book itself and the context in which it was originally produced—now more than half a century ago.

The Portable Faulkner, then, was—and is—an anthology of Faulkner short stories and novel segments that Cowley prepared in the latter half of 1945 and published with a long and important introduction in April 1946. The "Portable" series of compact, well-produced, hardcover, mostly single-author anthologies did not of course originate with the Faulkner volume: Viking—the publishing house Cowley worked for as an editorial advisor—had previously brought out more than a dozen of them, ranging from a Portable Shakespeare to a Portable Dorothy Parker. Cowley himself had recently done *The Portable Hemingway*, and in 1990, after his death, there was even *The Portable Malcolm Cowley*—edited by Donald W. Faulkner. No relation, so far as I know, but certainly a nicely appropriate choice. I have to say that the "Portable" concept, although now so familiar, has always struck me as a little ungainly when applied, not to individual books, but to the authors themselves: as one might say *The Travel-size Tolstoy*, *The Carry-on Balzac*, *The Collapsible Conrad*, *The Vest-pocket Proust*, or *The Available Austen*. There is absurdity in the sound of it, as Faulkner doesn't quite say in *Sartoris*, like a dying fall of horns along the road to Random House. But the *Portable* format was proving commercially viable, and indeed *The Portable Faulkner* itself has remained in print, in formats of decreasing attractiveness, right down to the present day.

Work on *The Portable Faulkner* began just as the Second World War was ending, and Cowley, renewing his contacts with writers in Europe, became aware of Faulkner's already high reputation there: in an August 1945 letter to Faulkner he quoted Jean-Paul Sartre as saying that for young people in France Faulkner was a god.[2] Faulkner also knew something of his European reputation, but when approached by Cowley, first with a suggestion for a long essay about his work, subsequently with the proposal for *The Portable Faulkner* itself, he responded eagerly enough, declaring that he had worked too hard at his trade to be ready "to leave no better mark on this our pointless chronicle than I seem to be about to leave."[3] Faulkner, at forty-six, was young to be contemplating imminent departure and his remark seems both extreme and more than a little ambiguous—like so many other passages in the marvellous letters Faulkner wrote to Cowley at this time and that Cowley later collected (at my suggestion, I might add) in *The Faulkner-Cowley File* of 1966.[4] But Faulkner was writing from Hollywood, where he had been trapped by a bad contract into scriptwriting for derisory sums; he had published no novel since 1940 apart from *Go Down, Moses*, wrongly described on its title page as a collection of short stories; very little of his work was in print (probably only *Sanctuary* and *Mosquitoes*); and he may already have sensed the intractability of the manuscript that ten years later became *A Fable*. And he was, as always, desperately short of money. The voice of propertied poverty is heard so often in his letters to his agent and to Random House that it's a wonder they never suggested that he might sell Rowan Oak and move into one of those nice new bungalows on the edge of town.

Absolutely central to all aspects of *The Portable* was Cowley's pre-existing perception of Faulkner's work as integrated in terms of a single cohesive design—a "living pattern" that manifested itself narratively in the "story" of the "mythical kingdom" of Yoknapatawpha County, and conceptually in a reading of that story as "the Yoknapatawpha saga," "a parable or legend of all the Deep South."[5] That terminological salvo (myth, saga, parable, legend) is indicative of both the strength and the weakness of Cowley's scheme—the fact that it was, precisely, a scheme, a theory in search of a practice: not a personal or consensual selection of Faulkner's finest or most powerful or best-known writings but the projection of an abstractable pattern perceived as pervasive and potentially repeatable throughout an entire corpus—an attempt, as it were, to make Faulkner portable through essentialization.

It was an ambitious—perhaps impossibly ambitious—approach, pursued by Cowley with intelligence and panache and implicitly endorsed by Faulkner's readiness to supply comments, explanations, and answers to specific questions. He even contributed what may now seem the volume's outstanding feature, the specially written "Compson Appendix,"[6] begun as a contextualizing induction to Cowley's chosen excerpt from *The Sound and the Fury* but constituting in its final form a rich meditation on all the Compsons in his fiction and, as Susan Donaldson has pointed out,[7] a highly problematic supplement to *The Sound and the Fury* itself. When Faulkner first saw a draft of Cowley's Introduction, however, he objected both to its biographical portions and to its comprehensive emphasis on his Southernness: the South, he insisted, was not in fact "very important" to him, just what he happened to know, the material he had readily at hand.[8]

Cowley stuck to his central idea, however, and it was presumably to allow himself the space in which to work it out that he chose not to include any novel in its entirety, backing up the decision in his Introduction by arguing, rather too strenuously, that Faulkner was at his best in the long short story and not really a novelist at all.[9] Cowley's first preference, therefore, was for actual short stories—such as "A Justice" and "Red Leaves"[10]—but distinctions of genre or even of textual integrity otherwise became somewhat blurred. His position, after all, was that all Faulkner's books were part of the "living pattern" of the Yoknapatawpha saga, and that it was in the pattern, not the individual constituent volumes, that Faulkner's "real achievement" lay.[11] The admired "long stories" thus proved in practice to include "Spotted Horses," "Old Man," and "The Bear," all in versions possessing no valid claim to an independent existence outside of the novels in which Faulkner had published them. *The Portable*'s "Spotted Horses" is not the short story of that title but a chunk of *The Hamlet*; its "Old Man" is compiled from the successive chapters of the counterpointed subplot of *The Wild Palms*, hence cruelly separated from its nested, though not identical, twin; and the five-section version of "The Bear" belongs, and makes sense, only within the complex novelistic structure of *Go Down, Moses*.

Cowley's central notion of a Yoknapatawpha "saga" of course demanded validation in terms of specifically narrative material, and he had some difficulty in finding passages from Faulkner's novels that were sufficiently detachable and self-contained.[12] The extract he called "Dilsey," from the fourth section of *The Sound and the Fury*, actually breaks off in mid-paragraph, and in his editorial notes Cowley acknowledges that he chose the Percy Grimm episode from *Light in August* and the wedding of Thomas Sutpen and Ellen Coldfield from *Absalom, Absalom!* not because he especially admired them but because no other passages in those novels were so nearly capable of standing alone.[13]

Cowley constructed the volume by arranging the various stories and extracts into a single chronological sequence subdivided under seven general headings, beginning with "The Old People" and ending with "Modern Times." The dating of individual items, based for the most part on textual evidence, seems at times a little arbitrary, as if adjusted to schematic requirements. Thus the single year 1883 is assigned to the wide-ranging narrative of "The Bear," and Cowley himself worried over the inconvenient fact that the present time of "A Justice" was some seventy years later than the events being described.[14] The misdating of the Sutpen wedding by five years seems to have been simply an error. Cheryl Lester, in a forceful critique of *The Portable Faulkner*, has objected to Cowley's sectional or, as she calls them, "topic" headings not only as unnecessary, in that the contents of *The Portable* are in any case chronologically ordered, but also as excessively bland, in that none of them even hints at what she nicely calls the "less hygienic subjects"—violence, incest, etc.—for which Faulkner had become notorious.[15] Violence and racism, however, are certainly present in several of the items—in "Percy Grimm," for instance, "Wash," and "That Evening Sun"—and while it is certainly a serious weakness in Cowley's introduction that it nowhere engages with the darker side of Faulkner's imagination I'm not sure that his textual selections convict him of deliberate sanitization, of presenting a Faulkner not merely portable but potable.

Cowley's essentializing project achieved its purest realization, as Claude-Edmonde Magny long ago pointed out,[16] in the map of Yoknapatawpha that appeared inside *The Portable*'s front and back covers. Although it was Cowley who suggested the map, it was Faulkner who decided to draw a new one, omitting much of the detail he had supplied in the fold-out map for the first edition of *Absalom, Absalom!* and inserting instead the titles and locations of all the stories and excerpts in *The Portable* that could plausibly be assigned a Yoknapatawpha setting. "Ad Astra" and "Delta Autumn" don't appear, but "Death Drag"—whose omission Faulkner had at one point recommended on the grounds that it "could have happened anywhere"[17]—is duly located at the Jefferson airport and even "Old Man," textually devoid of any direct Yoknapatawphan relevance, is worked in by Faulkner's subtle retroactive location of the convict's birthplace in the extreme southeast corner of the map, south of the Yoknapatawpha River—on the map but not in the county itself. With the possible exception of the "Compson Appendix," nothing more clearly demonstrates Faulkner's commitment to *The Portable* than his investment, or reinvestment, in the map—though the version actually included in *The Portable*, like the map in the Modern Library *Absalom*, was professionally redrawn.

2

Given the strength and coherence of *The Portable*'s version of Faulkner's work and the virtual absence of competing versions, it is worth considering what impact it had, then and later, on the evolution of a Faulkner canon—on the texts that critics, publishers, teachers, and readers consensually (if sometimes mysteriously) identify as being of central importance. The 1950 Book Society issue of *The Portable* was called *The Indispensable Faulkner*, and while that title makes a claim that the original *Portable* did not, it nonetheless indicates how Cowley's selection was beginning to be regarded.

In 1954 Random House published *The Faulkner Reader*, with a new foreword written by Faulkner himself. It included the complete text of *The Sound and the Fury* and one item published since 1945,[18] but its remaining contents substantially replicated *The Portable*'s, only four of the thirteen items not having appeared there.[19] "The Bear," "Old Man," and "Spotted Horses" were all present, in *The Portable*'s dubious versions, and in 1958 they gained even wider circulation when Random House published them together in one volume under a breathtakingly disingenuous title, *Three Famous Short Novels*, in which only the first word is beyond dispute. Three of the four new stories in *The Faulkner Reader* had Yoknapatawpha settings,[20] it extolled Yoknapatawpha in its jacket copy,[21] and its slightly variant British counterpart, published in 1955, was actually called, with emphatic redundancy, *Faulkner's County: Tales of Yoknapatawpha County*.[22] Perhaps not surprisingly, Cowley made few revisions to the new edition of *The Portable* that appeared in 1967,[23] five years after Faulkner's death, though he did expand and slightly modify the introduction.[24]

In France the original 1946 *Portable Faulkner* obviously had some impact on the construction of *Jefferson, Mississippi*, an anthology of stories and novel extracts in French translation, that was edited by Michel Mohrt and published in Paris in 1956. Its contents overlapped with *The Portable*'s to some degree but it actually outdid its predecessor in playing the Yoknapatawpha game by using the principal Yoknapatawphan families as its organizing principle (a possibility Cowley had mentioned) and including elaborately drawn genealogical charts for those families, together with an expressive if somewhat disproportioned map of the county imaginatively derived from the map for *Absalom, Absalom!* And though it could scarcely be called a direct descendant of *The Portable*, the densely packed *Album Faulkner,* issued by Gallimard in 1995 and offered free to purchasers of three Pléiade editions, certainly contains a generous supply of Mississippi photographs.

Of course, even when direct descent from *The Portable* can be traced or hypothesized, that is not necessarily to say that *The Portable* was indeed the point of origin. It could be argued that Cowley represented in *The Portable* not only the majority of the Faulkner short stories that are at all frequently reprinted, taught, and critically discussed but also—with the single exception of *As I Lay Dying*—all of the novels currently accepted as canonical. But some of the stories included in *The Portable* had already been extensively reprinted: writing to Faulkner in August 1945 Cowley himself could speak of "That Evening Sun" as "anthologized till its bones are picked, like Nancy's in the ditch."[25] And so far as the novels were concerned, he was, after all, drawing upon what everyone agrees to have been Faulkner's "major phase." If Cowley can be said to have defined the canon for his particular moment, he can scarcely be said to have determined it for the future. In this respect, at least, he was not so much an originator as a shrewd assessor and transmitter, playing at a crucial time and on an almost empty stage a crystallizing role that no single critic or editor could dream of playing today.

One wonders what, if anything, Faulkner himself may have contributed to these faintly Darwinian processes of textual survival and success, how far he can be said to have consciously promoted this text rather than that other—as we know that he tried to persuade Random House that *The Sound and the Fury*'s partner in the Modern Library double-volume of 1947 should be, not *As I Lay Dying*, but the "Wild Palms" section of *The Wild Palms*, otherwise left stranded by Cowley's enthusiasm for "Old Man."[26] He certainly abetted Cowley in some of *The Portable*'s other textual manipulations. It was Faulkner, I regret to report, who first recommended that "Spotted Horses" be taken from *The Hamlet* rather than from its magazine publication—on the grounds, accurate in itself, that the story had been "conceived in that form."[27]

But what part, if any, he played in selecting the contents of *The Faulkner Reader* is unclear. Meriwether assigns editorship of the *Reader* to Saxe Commins,[28] but since Faulkner wrote the Foreword for the *Reader* and spoke of going to Princeton to see Commins and "edit" it,[29] it seems reasonable to assume that at least he didn't *dis*approve of its contents. The British *Faulkner's County* actually claims on its title page to have been "chosen by the author," but with what validity I do not pretend to know. I can't help remembering what Faulkner replied when asked by the editor of a volume entitled *This Is My Best* to "select the one unit which in his own, uninfluenced opinion represent[ed] him at his best creative moment." "Dear Mr Burnett," Faulkner wrote in July 1942. "Choose anything of mine you want to, and that is convenient."[30] It seems almost needless to add that Burnett chose "That Evening Sun."

The most impressive endorsement of *The Portable*'s organization and arguments—as Cowley quietly notes in a footnote to his expanded introduction of 1967[31]—was Faulkner's own deployment of specifically Yoknapatawphan settings, characters, and narrative strands in all but one of his post-*Portable* volumes—in *Knight's Gambit, Intruder in the Dust, Requiem for a Nun, Collected Stories,* and *Big Woods,* and finally in *The Town, The Mansion,* and *The Reivers.* It's also striking that the contents of *Collected Stories* are organized under headings—The Country, The Village, The Wilderness, and so on—closely reminiscent of the section headings of *The Portable Faulkner.* There's some evidence, indeed, that Cowley may actually have suggested them.[32] *A Fable,* the one non-Yoknapatawphan text of this period, has recently been read as a rebelliously antiauthoritarian work deliberately hostile to Cowley's interpretations and emphases, but the evidence of the surviving manuscripts and typescripts seems clearly to indicate that the novel published in 1954 remained essentially faithful to Faulkner's original conception of 1943, well before his correspondence with Cowley began.[33]

3

If the presence of the *Portable* can be traced in some of the publications that followed in its wake, were Cowley's obituarists correct in making the larger claim that he had effectively restored Faulkner's reputation and opened the way to the Nobel Prize? Because the Nobel Prize followed so hard on the heels of *The Portable,* Cowley is sometimes perceived—most notably by Lawrence H. Schwartz in his *Creating Faulkner's Reputation*[34]—as having played a specifically political role within a vague conspiracy, somehow involving Random House, the State Department, the Rockefeller Foundation, and the academic New Critics, to construct Faulkner as a major "nationalist writer,"[35] promote him to international fame, and deploy him as a powerful weapon in the ideological battles of the Cold War.

If you work back from the end result, the perception is plausible enough. Faulkner may sometimes have had personal reasons for going on overseas trips, but in the latter half of the 1950s he did indeed lend himself, for good or ill, to the policies and purposes of the U.S. State Department, serving as an active and effective if sometimes unpredictable ambassador for American values and interests. Meriwether and Millgate, indeed, as the editors of *Lion in the Garden,* were perhaps a little

ungenerous in not acknowledging the State Department as the only be-
getter of many important Faulkner interviews.[36] But while Cowley was
genuinely eager to enhance Faulkner's American readership and reputation, and said as much when seeking the cooperation of Random House
as Faulkner's publishers,[37] his personal stake in *The Portable* was also
high. Politically, he was anxious to put behind him his fellow-travelling
past, and it doubtless suited him to be associated instead with conservative Southerners such as Tate and Warren and indeed Faulkner himself.
Professionally, he had his living to make and was eager to enhance still
further the standing in the field of twentieth-century American writing
that he had recently gained by editing *The Portable Hemingway* and writing two and a half chapters for the prestigious new Spiller, Thorp, Johnson, and Canby *Literary History of the United States*.[38]

Nor were Faulkner's American audience and reputation in 1945 by
any means nonexistent. He had made the cover of *Time* in 1939 and been
elected, at the age of forty-one, to the National Institute of Arts and Letters. His work had been the subject of major articles by critics such as
Warren Beck, Conrad Aiken, and George Marion O'Donnell, and even
Maxwell Geismar, no admirer, would prove to have treated him at some
length and with considerable respect when the *Literary History of the
United States* appeared in 1948.[39] And the immense sales in 1947 and
1948 of the New American Library paperbacks of *Sanctuary*, *The Wild
Palms* (minus the "Old Man" chapters), and *Pylon*, cheaply priced and
with luridly suggestive covers, must surely have had a greater impact on
Faulkner's national visibility than the 20,000 copies of *The Portable* sold
over the 1946–1950 period.[40] Add the success in 1948 of *Intruder in the
Dust*, Faulkner's politically controversial yet appealingly Tom Sawyerish
new novel, and of the film version that promptly followed, and it becomes
reasonable to suspect that in 1945, whatever his protestations, Faulkner
had not in fact been deeply in need of *The Portable*'s assistance.

Faulkner's American reputation, recovered or not, had in any case little impact on the award of the Nobel Prize. Joseph Blotner's still indispensable biography indicates that in Sweden Faulkner was being talked
about in the context of the Nobel Prize as early as 1946,[41] but in 1950,
when the announcement of the 1949 prize was finally made, Faulkner
was still so far from being accepted as a "nationalist" writer in his own
country that the *New York Times* greeted the news with considerable
suspicion:

> His field of vision is concentrated on a society that is too often vicious, de-
> praved, decadent, corrupt. Americans must fervently hope that the award by a
> Swedish jury and the enormous vogue of Faulkner's works in Latin America

and on the European Continent, especially in France, does not mean that foreigners admire him because he gives them a picture of American life they believe to be typical and true. There has been too much of that feeling lately, again especially in France. Incest and rape may be common pastimes in Faulkner's "Jefferson, Miss." but they are not elsewhere in the United States.[42]

I'll leave you to ponder that last statement in silence and restrict myself to noting that the *Times* in its paranoia actually denies any American responsibility for the award, blaming it specifically on the "Swedish jury" and a miscellaneous bunch of other foreigners, most of them evidently French.

Faulkner did indeed win the Nobel Prize because of his high standing outside the United States, and there was, as always, plenty of anti-Americanism around, not least in France. But the choice of an American writer was scarcely in itself an anti-American gesture, and it was of course the case that from the early 1930s onwards European and especially French criticism—Larbaud, Malraux, Sartre, Camus, Coindreau—had recognized Faulkner as a major figure and praised him above all as a bold experimentalist working with such central modernist techniques as stream-of-consciousness, impersonal narration, time-shifts, structural counterpoint, and so on. In 1948 the Dutch critic Simon Vestdijk, dismissing *The Portable Faulkner* as a "shrewd hodge-podge" that reduced Faulkner to the status of an historical novelist, had praised instead Faulkner's "astonishing but undeniably subjective sense for dramatic-psychological conflict."[43] The Faulkner to whom the Nobel Committee awarded the prize was, to quote the presentation citation, "the greatest experimentalist among twentieth-century novelists" and the "unrivaled master of all living British and American novelists as a deep psychologist."[44] He was not, or not primarily, a regionalist or local colorist, and if young writers in France thought him a god, it was not because they were especially interested in him as the creator of Yoknapatawpha County.

4

It is arguable, indeed, not only that Yoknapatawpha County didn't help win Faulkner the Nobel Prize but that it hindered, and continues to hinder, the expansion of his international readership. Seen or heard from a distance, the name itself seems not just outlandish and impossible to spell or pronounce but more than a little fantastic, like C. S. Lewis's Narnia or Mervyn Peake's Gormenghast. I fear that when I did my own first desultory reading of Faulkner back in the early 1950s it was with the customary British sense—clearly shared by many of the transatlantic reviewers[45]—that he was writing with an almost perverse power and intensity about dangerous eccentrics living in a backward part of the world that I never expected to visit and didn't see why I needed to know about. At least, they seemed like eccentrics but might, worse still, be just typical inhabitants of that Yoknapatawpha that didn't exist and yet was still, confusingly, a part of Mississippi. In 1957 a first visit to this part of the world enabled me to clarify those impressions and even—under Evans Harrington's wise guidance—to gain a certain degree of reassurance, but I suspect that for many of Faulkner's readers and critics outside the United States Yoknapatawpha remains to some degree problematic.

I don't of course mean that international criticism of Faulkner has failed to respond to the social dimensions of Faulkner's work or to the importance of his settings. Among French critics Maurice-Edgar Coindreau and Claude-Edmonde Magny both wrote of Faulkner as a regionalist, Magny also comparing him to Balzac as a creator of a fictional world. More recently, one might point to Michel Gresset's attentiveness to Faulkner's Mississippian contexts in *A Faulkner Chronology*,[46] and to everything that André Bleikasten has written on *As I Lay Dying*. I would nevertheless suggest that international criticism has not, broadly speaking, been especially interested in Faulkner as a regional writer, in Yoknapatawpha as a topographical expression, or in Yoknapatawpha as a fictional world—a cosmos, whether owned by Faulkner himself or, as Philip Weinstein has recently insisted, by no one. Stanley Woodworth, in his *William Faulkner en France*, observed long ago that for French readers the South didn't translate—that Faulkner's Southernness, particularly as embodied in distinctive and dialectal speech patterns, simply didn't come across in French translations.[47] The existence of Michel Mohrt's *Jefferson, Mississippi* volume would seem to throw some doubt on that assertion, but Woodworth was evidently addressing a situation that he saw as requiring an explanation of some kind.

Nor do I mean to imply that *The Portable Faulkner*, by mapping and opening up the Yoknapatawpha territory, set off on this side of the Atlantic a universal stampede of academic Sooners. The very assertiveness of Cowley's thesis generated its own antitheses, and there were from the beginning those who felt that Cowley's ideas, influenced by George Marion O'Donnell's allegorical reading of *Sanctuary*,[48] were too abstract and schematic—and painted too romantic a portrait of the South itself—to be fully responsive to the dense, complex, and often deeply problematic character of Faulkner's novels. Olga W. Vickery's admirably independent study appeared in 1959,[49] and in the early 1960s James B. Meriwether preached against *The Portable* on several campuses, arguing with some vehemence that in representing Faulkner's work as an integrated sagalike totality it had distracted attention away from the distinctive qualities of the individual novels. Robert Penn Warren, in by far the most substantial of *The Portable*'s handful of contemporary reviews, suggested that Cowley's version of the Faulknerian "legend" was too insistently Southern and underplayed the extent to which Faulkner also dealt with wider issues: "The legend," said Warren, "is not merely a legend of the South, but is also a legend of our general plight and problem."[50]

Warren's elegant spin on Cowley's introduction—a contradiction embedded within an apparent endorsement—anticipated, and of course contributed to, the view of Faulkner as the pyschologist and prophet of the modern condition that became in the longer run increasingly prevalent. In the short run, however, American criticism, galvanized by the Prize, did for the most part follow in the directions Cowley had pointed. I think, for example, of Ward L. Miner's *The World of William Faulkner* and of Elizabeth Kerr's later and more extensively researched *Yoknapatawpha: Faulkner's "Little Postage Stamp of Native Soil."*[51] Then, from 1966 onwards, the critical foreground was massively occupied by Cleanth Brooks's *William Faulkner: The Yoknapatawpha Country*[52]—its exceptional authority deriving from Brooks's experience and prestige as a leader of the New Criticism, from his command of both the totality and the detail of Faulkner's work, and, by no means least, from his intimate knowledge, as a Southerner, of Faulkner's region. As the young British scholar I then was, acutely conscious of my limited knowledge of the South, I do not believe that I would have embarked upon *The Achievement of William Faulkner*, for all its differences in method and approach, had Brooks's work already appeared.

Much has happened over the last thirty years. We have learned, especially from Tom McHaney's important essay-review of 1979,[53] not so much to reject Brooks's work outright as to perceive with increasing clarity the inadequacies and distortions occasioned by his pervasive and sometimes intrusive insistence on the importance of "community" in Faulkner's fiction. As the New Criticism yielded ground to the many newer criticisms—its flags in the dust before innumerable intruders—Faulkner studies in America took, and continue to take, many different directions. Through all these changes, however, I see the importance of Yoknapatawpha as remaining from an American perspective essentially untouched.

I have rather more in mind here than the large support network on which Yoknapatawpha can currently depend: the Center for the Study of Southern Culture, the Yoknapatawpha Press (with a website so called), the Oxford Tourism Council, and so on. Nor do I allude simply to the presence of so many people here in this place this evening, to last year's publication of a handsome study of the architecture of Yoknapataphwa,[54] or to the conference paper, mentioned in Mark Royden Winchell's recent book on Cleanth Brooks, which sought "to determine the verisimilitude of Faulkner's world by comparing the average height of his characters with the available historical records."[55] (One wonders what height was assigned to the Tall Convict of *The Wild Palms*.) Clearly, *that* Yoknapatawpha is alive and well, as a kind of actualized virtuality, imposed on the visible, visitable topography of Lafayette County as Hardy's Wessex has become imposed upon the landscapes of southwest England.

My concern is rather with the conceptual Yoknapatawpha that serves as the reference point for Faulkner's regionalism and Southernness. Significant Faulkner criticism, in North America as elsewhere, is not now concerned with exploring topographical, sociological, or other parallels between a fictional Yoknapatawpha County and an actual Lafayette County. But when that criticism addresses, as it increasingly does, contemporary issues of race, gender, class, history, language, and cultural inherence it is still with the specifically Southern, Mississippian, regionalist, and in that sense Yoknapatawphan Faulkner that it must necessarily engage. As Richard C. Moreland has stressed, Faulkner consistently addressed such issues, and always from a Southern perspective—or several Southern perspectives.[56]

André Bleikasten, in a magisterial essay, has recently spoken of North American criticism of Faulkner as limited in its scope by an essentially parochial or at any rate provincial obsession with Faulkner as Southerner.[57] He believes, and passionately argues, that Faulkner's work should more often be set alongside that of his peers, the other great modernist novelists of his time. And he asks, rhetorically but very pertinently: "Instead of endlessly reading Faulkner *into* American contexts, why not read him out of them for a change?"[58] I'm much in sympathy with Bleikasten here, and I have myself insisted in the past on the importance of Faulkner's European literary roots and relationships. But we are neither of us Americans, and I suspect that our American colleagues may well feel that the issue raised is by no means a simple one. It isn't just that Americans remain somewhat self-conscious about a national literature that is, after all, still young—that was scarcely taught in American universities until after the Second World War. Canadians have more recently had occasion to begin thinking about their literature in similar nationalist terms. It's rather, I think, that confronting Faulkner in all his literary, personal, and sociopolitical complexity is for the seriously engaged American critic a burden as well as a privilege. That Faulkner has, by whatever routes, attained the status of a national, iconic figure, to come to terms with whose many and sometimes dark explorations and contradictions is indeed a complex fate, not to say a Faulknerian doom. I'm reminded of

John Gross's recent observation in the *New York Review of Books* that if American academics now feel more comfortable with F. R. Leavis's criticism than do their British colleagues it is perhaps because they haven't had to live with him.[59]

There is, perhaps, a further dimension to this national/international difference. Bleikasten, in the essay already mentioned, speaks of the international Faulkner canon as currently comprised of *The Sound and the Fury, As I Lay Dying, Sanctuary, Light in August, Absalom, Absalom!*, and *The Wild Palms*.[60] The American Faulkner canon, I suspect, would add *Go Down, Moses* certainly and *The Hamlet* probably, hesitate over *Sanctuary*, and make the serious mistake of relegating *The Wild Palms* to the minors. There's no disagreement, clearly, about the central core of major texts—*The Sound and the Fury, As I Lay Dying, Light in August*, and *Absalom, Absalom!*—and these are all, of course, classically modernist works set squarely in Yoknapatawpha, even if only *Absalom* is centrally concerned with the history of the region. But, if I'm at all correct in my assumptions, there's a clear split between the international standing of the modernist, non-Yoknapatawphan *Wild Palms* and the American preference for two centrally Yoknapatawphan but less distinctively modernist texts, *Go Down, Moses* and *The Hamlet*.

What's important here is not so much the increased exposure to Yoknapatawpha for its own sake that *Go Down, Moses* and *The Hamlet* provide but what they offer and demand in terms of confrontation with acute issues of race, gender, and class—and in terms, no less importantly, of sustained encounters with distinctive kinds of Faulknerian writing and construction. By which I mean simply that both books contain passages of singular beauty. The American approach to Faulkner may indeed include a peculiar obligation—even, as I suggested earlier, a doomed necessity—to engage with his texts not only intensively but widely, to keep the full range of his works continuously alive, and to do so within the acknowledged context of his regionalism.

Faulkner himself always insisted on his regional roots, preoccupations, and way of life, and it is, I think, clear that the entire post-*Portable* course of his career virtually demands interpretation as showing either that Cowley was right from the start about the importance, if not perhaps the role, of Yoknapatawpha in Faulkner's imagination or that Cowley's work was at least partly responsible for Faulkner's reassessing and reinstating that importance. As James E. Carothers has noted,[61] the familiar statements about "the little postage stamp of native soil" and so forth were all made in the latter half of the 1950s—after the Nobel Prize, of course, but after *The Portable* also. It's curious, even disturbing, that while the

currently canonical Faulkner texts all date from before the Prize, the
sanctified ex cathedra statements date from after it.

Such discontinuities, however, may have been more apparent than
real, more tactical than fundamental. If Faulkner sent such mixed messages to Cowley while *The Portable* was in preparation—co-operating
with the project but denying its surely unmistakable message—it was
perhaps because in 1945 he feared that categorization as a Southern regionalist would limit his appeal to the predominantly northern and urban
so-called national audience he had yet to consolidate and at the same
time compromise the international reputation he knew he already possessed. The supreme empowerment of the Nobel Prize, reinforced by the
associated evaporation of his financial anxieties, may then have progres-
sively emancipated him from concerns about audiences and sales and
allowed him to acknowledge—in interviews and political acts as well as
through his work—his fundamental, if deeply troubled, attachment to the
South in general and his own locality in particular. Those attachments,
after all, had always been integral to the self, or at any rate the self-
protective persona, which he chose to present to the world ("I'm just a
Mississippi farmer"), and integral also to the location, the material, and
the direction of his writing.

I have argued on a previous occasion[62] that while Faulkner was not
interested in constructing a Southern legend, a Yoknapatawpha saga, or
"a pageant of a county,"[63] he did seek the ultimate realization on paper
of his early and profoundly liberating conception of a distinctive, densely
interrelated, regional world. At some level, he always remained faithful
to that epiphanic moment when he "thought of the whole story at once
like a bolt of lightning lights up a landscape and you see everything."[64] It
was to his agent, Harold Ober, and not to Cowley that he spoke of "the
creation of my apocryphal country" as the labor of his life.[65] And the fact
that *The Sound and the Fury* and *Sartoris* were both published in the
same year of 1929 is nicely suggestive of the essential doubleness of
Faulkner's agenda, its combination of a radical post-Joycean experimen-
talism with an essentially conservative post-Hardyan regionalism—its realization, indeed, of each project through and in terms of the other.

Hardy is an obvious figure to invoke in this context. He has over the
years become in Britain a supremely representative "nationalist" figure
not despite but actually because of the rooted regional specificity of so
much of his work, reinforced by his insistence, like Faulkner, on living a
specifically regional life. Hardy is perhaps a little easier to live with than
Faulkner, his interlinked Wessex novels, though so often the vehicles of
tragic narratives, evoking with power and poignancy a vanished rural
England that becomes the more highly valued—and less authentically

imagined—the further it recedes in time. But he shares Faulkner's distinctive combination of instinctual conservatism and creative adventurousness; complex issues of gender and class arise in his work; and while he is still widely read around the world his iconic status within his own country inevitably demands from British and especially English readers and critics very much the kind of nationally conditioned response that I see Faulkner as extorting from his American readers and critics.

The Portable Faulkner in 1946 was already demanding some such response, its coordinated act of critical and textual conceptualization simultaneously challenging and enabling American critics and readers to think again about Faulkner, and to contemplate his work in its entirety virtually for the first time. Cowley had a thesis to advance and substantiate, and he was neither the first critic nor the last to choose occasional adaptation of evidence over impairment of the beauty of his original idea. It was precisely The Portable's consistency and integration—map, introduction, texts, appendix, map, each in its ordered place—that gave ballast to the thesis and thrust it out, so to speak, into the mainstream of literary history. Designed for and accepted by a general readership, it nonetheless set the terms for critical debate, its projection of a sharply defined position, so persuasive in the short term, generating over time a whole series of revisionist and rejectionist positions by successive critical generations.

As judged from this particular late twentieth-century moment, Cowley seems to have been sometimes right, if not always for the right reasons, and sometimes wrong, if not always for the wrong reasons. But he was right to celebrate Faulkner's achievement, right to demand that Faulkner's work be read, and right to offer his own understanding of how it might best be approached. By so emphasizing Yoknapatawpha and Yoknapatawphan texts he may even have contributed to Faulkner's deliberate shaping of the final stages of his career. And I submit, as a persistent if lonely admirer of those late novels, that it is a rare critic whose writings can lay claim to such momentous consequences.

NOTES

1. *Go Down, Moses and Other Stories* (New York: Random House, 1942), 362.
2. Cowley, *The Faulkner-Cowley File: Letters and Memories, 1944–1962* (New York: Viking Press, 1966), 24. Cowley quoted the same remark—though with "young writers" in place of "young people"—and another by André Gide in his "American Books Abroad" chapter in Robert E. Spiller et al., ed., *Literary History of the United States*, 2 vols. (New York: Macmillan, 1948), 2:1380.
3. *Faulkner-Cowley File*, 7.
4. Faulkner's letters to Cowley about *The Portable Faulkner* are available both in *The Faulkner-Cowley File* and (with the exception of a Cowley letter Faulkner simply annotated and returned) in Joseph Blotner, ed., *Selected Letters of William Faulkner* (New York: Ran-

dom House, 1977). Cowley's letters in *The Faulkner-Cowley File* have recently been supplemented by the reproduction of his letter to Faulkner of 20 June 1945 in Thomas M. Verich, *A Faulkner 100: The Centennial Exhibition* (University: University of Mississippi Libraries, 1997), fig. 31.

5. *The Portable Faulkner*, ed. Malcolm Cowley (New York: Viking Press, 1946), 2, 8.

6. It was actually titled "Appendix. Compson: 1699–1945," though Cowley in *The Portable* changed "Compson" to "The Compsons."

7. Donaldson, "Reading Faulkner Reading Cowley Reading Faulkner: Authority and Gender in the Compson Appendix," *Faulkner Journal* 7 (Fall 1991/Spring 1992): 27–39.

8. *Faulkner-Cowley File*, 14–15.

9. See my essay "Was Malcolm Cowley Right?: The Short Stories in Faulkner's Nonepisodic Novels," in Hans H. Skei, ed., *William Faulkner's Short Fiction: An International Symposium* (Oslo: Solum Verlag, 1997), 164–72.

10. The others were "Wash," "That Evening Sun," "Ad Astra," "A Rose for Emily," and "Death Drag."

11. *Portable Faulkner*, 8.

12. Two chapters were readily extracted from *The Unvanquished* and duly acknowledged on the "Contents" page, but since *Go Down, Moses* was then understood as a collection of short stories no source was given for "Was," "Delta Autumn," or indeed "The Bear."

13. *Portable Faulkner*, 26, 652.

14. *Faulkner-Cowley File*, 48.

15. Lester, "To Market, to Market: *The Portable Faulkner*," *Criticism* 29 (Summer 1987): 377.

16. Magny, *The Age of the American Novel*, trans. Eleanor Hochman (New York: Frederick Ungar, 1972), 214.

17. *Faulkner-Cowley File*, 37.

18. The "Courthouse" prologue from *Requiem for a Nun*.

19. The Compson Appendix was also present, as an attachment to *The Sound and the Fury*.

20. "Barn Burning," "Dry September," and "Shingles for the Lord."

21. E.g., "The world of William Faulkner, almost entirely concentrated within a county of his imagination, has become a commanding feature of the literary geography of America. In his twenty books he has portrayed the South in war and in peace, in reconstruction and regression, in novels and short stories, all interrelated to the cyclical life and history of the region of his creation."

22. London: Chatto & Windus, 1955. It substituted the intensely rural *As I Lay Dying* for the essentially urban *The Sound and the Fury* and omitted the non-Yoknapatawphan "Old Man" but inconsistently kept "Turnabout," the *Reader*'s one non-Yoknapatawphan addition, perhaps because of its romanticisation of British wartime gallantry.

23. Textual changes included the omission of the *Absalom* extract and the addition of the Nobel Prize address and two Yoknapatawphan prologues ("The Courthouse" and "The Jail") from *Requiem for a Nun*—not of course published when *The Portable* was originally compiled. An eighth subdivision, headed "The Undying Past," was introduced in order to accommodate "The Jail" and the Nobel Prize address and gather in the hitherto dangling Compson Appendix.

24. The text of the 1967 introduction is reprinted, as "William Faulkner: The Yoknapatawpha Story," in Cowley's *A Second Flowering: Works and Days of the Lost Generation* (New York: Viking Press, 1973), 130–55.

25. *Faulkner-Cowley File*, 22–23. The story had appeared in at least eight short story anthologies and in *A Rose for Emily and Other Stories*, the collection of eight Faulkner stories that Saxe Commins, Faulkner's editor at Random House, had edited as an Armed Services Edition in 1945. Cowley chose three more stories from among those selected by Commins.

26. *Selected Letters*, 228.

27. *Faulkner-Cowley File*, 31.

28. Meriwether, "William Faulkner: A Check List," *Princeton University Library Chronicle* 18 (Spring 1957): 144.

29. *Selected Letters*, 355.

30. Whit Burnett, ed., *This Is My Best* (New York: The Dial Press, 1942), xi, 522.

31. *The Portable Faulkner: Revised and Expanded Edition* (New York: Viking Press, 1967), xiii; *Second Flowering*, 136.

32. See *Portable Faulkner* (1946), 6–7, for Cowley's suggestion of possible Balzacian divisions for Faulkner's work as a whole. Cowley seems to have originated the idea of a collection of Faulkner's short stories, and it was in a letter to Cowley, written after a visit to him, that Faulkner first outlined the organization of *Collected Stories* itself (*Faulkner-Cowley File*, 34, 115–17).

33. See Joseph R. Urgo, *Faulkner's Apocrypha: "A Fable," "Snopes," and the Spirit of Human Rebellion* (Jackson: University Press of Mississippi, 1989), 97–105. For the textual history of *A Fable* see the introduction to Millgate, ed., *William Faulkner Manuscripts 20* (New York: Garland Publishing, 1986).

34. Schwartz, *Creating Faulkner's Reputation: The Politics of Modern Literary Criticism* (Knoxville: University of Tennessee Press, 1988). Schwartz's extensive research into Faulkner's situation in the 1940s is presented with equal fulness but a less sharply angled argument in two articles published ahead of his book: "Malcolm Cowley's Path to William Faulkner," *Journal of American Studies* 16 (August 1982): 229–42, and "Publishing William Faulkner: The 1940s," *Southern Quarterly* 22 (Winter 1984): 70–92.

35. Schwartz, *Creating Faulkner's Reputation*, 3.

36. *Lion in the Garden: Interviews with William Faulkner, 1926–1962*, ed. James B. Meriwether and Michael Millgate (New York: Random House, 1968).

37. See, e.g., *Faulkner-Cowley File*, 87, 88.

38. *Literary History of the United States*, 2:1119–34, 1263–72, 1374–91.

39. Ibid., 2:1304–6.

40. Schwartz, *Creating Faulkner's Reputation*, 58–59; "Publishing William Faulkner," 74.

41. Blotner, *Faulkner: A Biography*, 2 vols. (New York: Random House, 1974), 2:1207.

42. *New York Times*, 11 November 1950, 14. For Maurice-Edgar Coindreau's description in 1937 of similar American attitudes towards Faulkner and other contemporary novelists see his *The Time of William Faulkner*, ed. and trans. George McMillan Reeves (Columbia: University of South Carolina Press, 1971), 3.

43. Quoted in Hans Bak, "Simon Vestdijk: Dutch Critic of American Literature," in Rosemarijn Hoefte and Johanna C. Kardux, ed., *Connecting Cultures: The Netherlands in Five Centuries of Transatlantic Exchange* (Amsterdam: VU University Press, 1994), 266, 267.

44. Quoted in Blotner, *Faulkner: A Biography*, 2:1364.

45. The following passage is from an essentially favorable British review of *The Hamlet*: "The surface area covered by Mr. Faulkner's round dozen of novels . . . is small, and the same shoal of characters swim in and out, rapacious, cannibalistic, bulbous, or slimy, but always with their characteristics enlarged and faintly distorted by the intervening medium and myopic intensity of the recorder." Anonymous review, *Glasgow Herald*, 12 September 1940, quoted in Gordon Price-Stephens, "The British Reception of William Faulkner 1929–1962," *Mississippi Quarterly* 18 (Summer 1965): 148.

46. Gresset, *A Faulkner Chronology*, trans. Arthur B. Scharff (Jackson: University Press of Mississippi, 1985).

47. Stanley D. Woodworth, *William Faulkner en France, 1931–1952* (Paris: M. J. Minard, 1959), 30–31.

48. O'Donnell, "Faulkner's Mythology," *Kenyon Review* 1 (Summer 1939): 285–99.

49. Vickery, *The Novels of William Faulkner* (Baton Rouge: Louisiana State University Press, 1959).

50. Warren, "Cowley's Faulkner," *New Republic*, 12 August 1946, 177.

51. Published, respectively, by Duke University Press in 1952 and by Fordham University Press in 1969.

52. Published by Yale University Press in 1963.

53. McHaney, "Brooks on Faulkner: The End of the Long View," in *Review I: 1979*, ed. James O. Hoge and James L. W. West III (Charlottesville: University Press of Virginia, 1979), 29–45.

54. Thomas S. Hines, *William Faulkner and the Tangible Past: The Architecture of Yoknapatawpha* (Berkeley: University of California Press, 1996).

55. Winchell, *Cleanth Brooks and the Rise of Modern Criticism* (Charlottesville: University Press of Virginia, 1996), 451.

56. Moreland, "Faulkner and Modernism," in Philip M. Weinstein, ed., *The Cambridge Companion to William Faulkner* (Cambridge: Cambridge University Press, 1995), 23–28.

57. Bleikasten, "Faulkner from a European Perspective," in Weinstein, ed., *The Cambridge Companion to William Faulkner*, 75–95.

58. Bleikasten, 78.

59. Gross, "Lessons of an Immoderate Master," *New York Review of Books*, 26 June 1997, 37.

60. Bleikasten, 77.

61. Carothers, "The Rhetoric of Faulkner's Later Fiction, and of Its Critics," in Lothar Hönnighausen, ed., *Faulkner's Discourse: An International Symposium* (Tübingen: Max Niemeyer Verlag, 1989), 269–70.

62. Millgate, "William Faulkner: The Shape of a Career," in *New Directions in Faulkner Studies*, ed. Doreen Fowler and Ann J. Abadie (Jackson: University Press of Mississippi, 1984), 31.

63. Frederick L. Gwynn and Joseph L. Blotner, ed., *Faulkner in the University: Class Conferences at the University of Virginia, 1957–1958* (Charlottesville: University of Virginia Press, 1959), 3.

64. Ibid., 90.

65. *Selected Letters*, 199.

"A Sight-Draft Dated Yesterday": Faulkner's Uninsured Immortality

PHILIP M. WEINSTEIN

"Breathing is a sight-draft dated yesterday," says Will Varner in *The Hamlet*.[1] Webster defines a "sight draft" as a "draft payable upon presentation"; Varner is talking about the unpredictable moment of one's own death. He figures our uninsured breathing as a check already signed, a resource the gods have issued and can recall at any moment as of "yesterday." Mere "presentation"—or being in the present—threatens us utterly. I choose this passage in order to focus on *temporality* in three ways: as a central issue of this conference (Faulkner at 100), as a driving concern of modernism itself and of Faulkner's modernist practice, and finally as a core dimension of his appeal thirty-five years after his death.

Faulkner's uninsured immortality: the energy and anxiety that beset this year's conference stem from our awareness that his immortality is in fact mortal—that he lives in his posthumeity only so long as we continue to breathe life into him, that his currency itself is a check long since dated and always open to recall, liquidation. The man died in 1962, the writer has continued since then to flourish. He still flourishes, but there is no one in this room who does not know that he too can die. This year's conference, more than the earlier ones, is about the ratio between what is dead in his work, what still lives, and what has yet to live.

Why Faulkner? That is the topic of our panel, and I think it sets us apart from the other panels which—however critical they will be—begin by assuming his importance. Their business is more to analyze and reconceive that importance. Ours is to ask—or answer—why attend to him at all. To be sure, we are likely to read our topic less as a question (why Faulkner?) and more as an answer (why Faulkner). Don Kartiganer and his cohorts won't have been tempted to invite others among our colleagues—and their name is legion—for whom the answer to the question of "why Faulkner?" is: why indeed?

If that question is serious and not merely rhetorical, it could mean several things: Why Faulkner instead of other writers? Why Faulkner when his work has ceased to speak to a readership suspicious of canonical narratives of white male travail? Why Faulkner when his texts—no longer sheltered by a modernist commitment to formal innovation—seem to many readers to be willfully, perversely unreadable? Or, perhaps most insidious, why Faulkner in a postmodern climate in which reading itself has lost much of its prestige as a truth-discerning activity? This last meaning of "why Faulkner" could be reduced to: "what is the point of reading anything that difficult when, regardless of its contortions, it can never escape its ideological frame, can never represent the real?" Thanks to the past twenty years' success of poststructuralism and its sequel, cultural studies, we have reached something like a massive distrust of language itself as a vehicle reliably connecting writer and world. Why Faulkner indeed?[2]

Here is contemporary critic Jane Flax characterizing the poststructuralist stance toward the text: "The text is not the product of the consciousness of a singular author making present some aspect of experience, history, or thought. . . . The subject of writing is a 'system of relations between strata . . . the psyche, society, the world.' "[3] What professional Faulknerian here has not read such words—if not written them—in countless papers by students and colleagues? Yet who writes a line of poetry or prose in assent to these claims? Who would go to the trouble to write responsibly if this activity involved neither self nor experience nor thought, but instead the gassy vagueness of a "system of relations between strata"? Can there be writerly responsibility—not to mention other sorts of responsibility—without a concept of the minimally viable subject? This suspicion calls into question not only Faulkner's importance, but his very coherence.

I am impatient with the brittle insistence that, since you do not master your utterance entirely, you do not master it at all—and more, there is no "you" there in the first place. At a recent lecture on the revisionary moves of a medieval artist, I heard the speaker say that the artist's "intentions" were not only inscrutable but—citing a master critic—that "intention" was a term we should never use for human creativity. And I thought, if we can't speak of human creativity in terms of "intention," what realm—other than the pedestrian one of messages—does the term exist for? It seems to me a term we simply cannot do without, even though we cannot use it cleanly, just as subject and author are terms we cannot do without, even though we cannot use them cleanly. If we remove all trust from both the author who intends and the word that conveys, it is difficult to maintain that reading matters. If what Faulkner "means" lodges only minimally in what we may construe him to have intended his words to say, and maximally in larger cultural paradigms that predetermine him (the key to which, of course, the informed critic possesses, often in advance of reading him), how could the labor he spent to get his writing right matter?[4] Who in this hypersuspicious postmodern climate is willing to *credit*—to move *with*—the intricate twists and turns, the gorgeous arabesques, of Faulkner's prose?

When I was a teenager, my father warned me of the dangers of driving. You have to be totally alert, he said; otherwise you'll kill yourself and others. I believed this advice until I took my first long trip in the car. After about three hours of driving (with six more to follow), I realized that total alertness was not only impossible, it was bad advice. You must, at a certain point, submit to the vehicle if you want it to take you anywhere. We must revalidate the experience of submitting to the literary vehicle, learning all we can about the tricky and far from obvious moves it can make, yet granting it the power to take us somewhere. To know in advance, always and negatively, where it is going to take us is to foreclose the pleasure—let alone knowledge—such travel may afford. We former New Critics paid a huge price in not knowing the liabilities intrinsic to the vehicle—we were unforgivably innocent readers—but we did take trips. Let me return, now, to that "sight-draft dated yesterday."

Modernism itself may be generalized as a variously inflected understanding that "breathing is a sight-draft dated yesterday."[5] That is to say, an understanding that human life, because it is in time and destined for death, is radically groundless. Radically groundless: rootedly unrootable, the Latin root in "radical"suggests. How hard it is to make language give up its soothing message of groundedness, as Nietzsche knew when he said, "I am afraid we are not rid of God because we still have faith in grammar."[6] Lawful grammar suggests a lawful world being represented by that grammar. One of the most salient aspects of modernist practice is its insistence on innovative linguistic structures that shatter these inertial conventions, revealing that only our fictions—for better and for worse— sustain our sense of grounding. Our being-in-time is our central intolerable reality in need of fiction. Perhaps culture's dearest function is to provide credible fictions for humanizing time. The clichés we use to characterize different periods of history—the Medieval world view, the Enlightenment, Romanticism—could be seen as so many expressions of time made humanly meaningful: as medieval preparation for the afterlife, as enlightenment acquisition of humane reason, as romantic rebellion of the spirit against the slavishness of convention. All of these models provide "ends" to stave off our otherwise unbearable sense of the "end."

When modernism repudiates its culture's various models for domesticating temporality, it declares it alienation. "This abstract structure of temporality," writes Fredric Jameson, "clearly cannot emerge until the

older traditional activities, projects, rituals through which time was experienced, and from which it was indistinguishable, have broken down."[7]
In the unalienated realism of Balzac and Dickens and Tolstoy, time is the
medium in which human projects at first falter, then refine themselves,
and finally succeed—or if they fail, they fail reasonably. But time ceases
in modernism to be a familiar modality and becomes instead a cunning
and indecipherable puzzle, as in Joyce and Eliot, or a monster of oblivion
and redemption, as in Proust, or the perpetrator of a nightmarish bad
joke, as one wakes up to discover in Kafka. In Faulkner time rears its
head in a fashion that is humbler but no less terrifying: *Something is
going to happen to me.*"

"Something is going to happen to me": this signature Faulknerian
phrase emerges inside the heightened consciousness of Temple Drake in
Sanctuary, Joe Christmas in *Light in August*, and Harry Wilbourne in *If
I Forget Thee, Jerusalem*. All of these characters think this thought at the
moment of collapse of whatever protective codes of grounding they have
drawn on to sustain their sanity. They cease to be an "I" who acts and
become a "me" who is acted upon. Hurled into an encounter which dis-
ables their culturally trained defenses—their habitual ways of saying "I"
and thinking it means something—they discover their body going awry,
its rhythms of breathing (its "sight-draft dated yesterday") being called
in and liquidated. A moment of intolerable present time has decapitated
all preceding domesticated time; this decapitation registers on and
through the body.[8]

Faulkner had this insight as early as *Soldiers' Pay*; the speechlessly
wounded Donald Mahon is undone by encounters he can suffer without
ever subjectifying. Incapacity beyond the reach of therapy calls to Faulkner, shaping powerfully the incurable plights of Bayard and Horace and
Temple. But it is Benjy Compson in whom Faulkner first fully releases
the poetry of irreparable deracination. For Benjy is simultaneously so
many things: the literal defective offspring of a once-noble family whom
neither parent knows how to caretake, the symbolic fruit of an incestuous
twentieth-century South that has not yet learned to desire the other, the
uselessly poetic vessel of perception and feeling beyond the reach of
normative culture's contaminating codes, a wild child whose class rever-
berations Faulkner will later explore in Ike Snopes, whose race repercussions he will touch on in Jim Bond. Whatever figure Benjy transmutes
into, the plasma at his core remains the same: nonadaption, the rebuke
of all schemas of maturation and empowerment.

As Faulkner proceeds through his career, the ramifications of nonadap-
tation widen. Early on, such scandalous encounter between self and circumstance seems metaphysical: "As though the clotting which is you,"

Darl puts it in *As I Lay Dying*, "had dissolved into the original myriad motion."[9] Bundren projects, however stubbornly held, become subjected to forces that either fracture them or render them absurd. The most profound unselving force in that novel—and therefore the one most powerfully resisted by each character's system of defenses—is death itself, Addie Bundren's becoming, in time, not-Addie Bundren. In later novels the unraveling of subjectivity—the hallmark of Faulknerian plot—becomes less metaphysical and more cultural. Joe Christmas, Thomas Sutpen, Charles Etienne St. Valery Bon: when these figures shatter, they reveal—in the disarray that radiates into and out of them—an incoherence in the scheme of things that is manmade, not natural or metaphysical, indeed normative, not aberrant. At his diagnostic best, Faulkner shows the madness of the normative—shows, patiently and dizzingly, how long-sustained cultural structures of recognition and empowerment for some folks are simultaneously—for other folks—structures of nonacknowledgment and abuse. In Thomas Sutpen—he who is first the child abused, he who is later the adult abusing—it comes together as one: we end by seeing *Absalom, Absalom!* as an unbearable mapping of differential cultural positions (where you are on that map determines your fate)—a map that only a Southerner both outsider and insider could delineate in all its absurd and poignant contradictoriness.

No one has explored more movingly than Faulkner the cultural logic of such undoings. Kafka's parables of collapse and Joyce's immersion of the subject in his culture's constraints both come to mind, but it takes Faulkner to wed Kafka's sense of the uncanny with Joyce's familiarity with norms, with—if you will—the reasonableness of norms. Hugh Kenner once claimed that, for Faulknerian narrative to work, a region and a history and a multigenerational family all had to be in place. ("He needed inarticulate blood ties," Kenner wrote.[10]) In realism these familiar contours would produce the Balzacian canvas of moves and countermoves keyed to a set of recognizable cultural norms shared even when resisted, all of this unfolding within a domesticated temporality in which night follows day, maturity and old age follow childhood and youth. Perhaps this is what Faulkner desired with his Yoknapatawpha chronicles, but it is not what he achieved. A modernist sense of incapacitation holds him in its grip: time does not behave, the same event "abrupts" anew and "repercusses" again, people and things become uncanny, go awry.

The grip I speak of is trauma itself, and it registers insistently upon the Faulknerian body. "Breathing" is of the body, yet its being figured as a "sight-draft dated yesterday" places it in the social. Faulkner's drama is of breathing gone wrong because of social arrangements gone wrong. His achievement is less to summarize this disaster than to dramatize its "abruption" within the body and from body to body. He knew early on that his culture's most intractable contradictions operated within or beneath language, that language was a tool provided by culture, coopted by the psyche's defenses, and eloquent mainly for its evasions. Faulkner's greatness lodges in his decision not to judge but to *cite* this language in all its variety, pathos, and offensiveness. He thus gives us, in an unparalleled manner, an entire social text. Rather than attempt to master his culture's contradictions and indict them through his own voice or that of a delegated narrator, he arranges his memorable fictions architectonically, letting voice play against voice, no voice reliably his own. The benefit of this move is a capacity to say even the most outrageous things fearlessly, freshly, so long as they remain true to character. "I listen to the voices," Faulkner told Malcolm Cowley, "and when I put down what the voices say, it's right."[11] As Keats's Shakespeare "has as much delight in conceiving an Iago as an Imogen," so Faulkner is as drawn to Jason Compson as to Gavin Stevens.[12]

The Faulkner I summon to answer the question "why Faulkner?" is a writer who never pretended to domesticate time. In his great tragic work he writes of wounds that do not heal, encounters that repercuss rather than resolve. He is our supreme writer of the culturally unworkable. His fiction is not pedagogic: in the presence of can't matter and must matter he knows that both are true and that they cannot coherently coexist. He is our American witness who knows he is also witnessed—knows he is in history's gaze—but he does not pretend to know what he looks like witnessed, as on this day in 1997 when we are gazing at him. His work gathers an unparalleled authority in its generating of narrative structures that call authority into question: who better than Faulkner has shown us how men invent and enforce authority in the absence of authority's grounding? In short, he is the writer of pain radiated by the failure of culture's defenses rather than of wisdom garnered from the viability of culture's platitudes. The candor with which he accepts his own not-knowing—a not-knowing he turns into the most intricate fictional structures of delay and revision and reversal rather than temporal mastery—makes me think that the risk figured in a "sight-draft dated yesterday" is exactly how he would want his work's future to be viewed: "because it is your milk, sour or not," Tull thinks in *As I Lay Dying*, "because you would rather have milk that will sour than to have milk that wont."[13] The milk that matters is milk that can sour, go off in time; the mark on the paper that matters is, as Judith says in *Absalom, Absalom!*, the "mark on something that was once for the reason that it can die someday, while the block of stone cant be *is* because it never can become *was*."[14] Faulkner's immortality is not only uninsured but uninsurable—a mark that "is" and therefore at perpetual risk of becoming "was"—why would we defend it otherwise?

NOTES

1. William Faulkner, *The Hamlet*, in *Faulkner: Novels, 1936–1940* (New York: Library of America, 1990), 1019.

2. For a fuller meditation on our contemporary discontent with Faulkner's modernist commitments, see the final chapters of my *Faulkner's Subject: A Cosmos No One Owns* (New York: Cambridge University Press, 1992) and *What Else But Love? The Ordeal of Race in Faulkner and Morrison* (New York: Columbia University Press, 1996).

3. Jane Flax, *Thinking Fragments: Psychoanalysis, Feminism, and Postmodernism in the Contemporary West* (Berkeley: University of California Press, 1990), 197–98.

4. Arguments about intention are notoriously difficult, as my evasive wording reveals. To identify authorial intention is, necessarily, to move through readerly construal. It takes the critic's claim to "access" the writer's intentions, and such claims are always open to contestation. My point is not that we critics ever get the author's intentions right but that, rather, we do in fact make claims about them recurrently. We say (we even write) "Faulkner says," or "Faulkner sees": we posit the writer's shaping mind within the web of words. It seems that we cannot (at any rate we do not) characterize the manifold intelligence of works of art without some recourse to the concept of intention (a recourse we often "launder" by speaking, incoherently, about the "intentions of the text"—as though it had intentions of its own). At the least, I would propose that the author is a partner—and not just a dupe—of the structure of intentions we may discern in his or her text. One may of course choose to ignore this structure, but that leaves us, it seems to me, with an impoverished and conventional substitute-text in place of the complex and far-from-innocent one the author wrote. Obviously, this is not to say that writers know exactly what they are doing. It is to say that—in their endless acts of vision and revision—they know a great deal about it. I might close this speculative note by briefly articulating the relation of my argument to André Bleikasten's kindred argument (in this volume) about a "singular" Faulkner. I share with Bleikasten a commitment to Faulkner's texts as radically unpredicted by any of the cultural paradigms within which they are nevertheless inextricably immersed. But where Bleikasten tends to chastize current American commentary for ignoring Faulkner in favor of the larger paradigms that condition him, I would urge us to pursue his singularity precisely through his stunning ways of being caught up in his conditions. Creature and creator, complicit and inventive, he is never more compellingly William Faulkner than when he makes his singular way through the generic thickets of race, gender, class, culture, region.

5. For general commentary on literary modernism, see Peter Burger, *The Theory of the Avant-Garde*, trans. Michael Shaw (Minneapolis: University of Minnesota Press, 1984); Astradur Eysteinsson, *The Concept of Modernism* (Ithaca: Cornell University Press, 1990); Hugh Kenner, *A Homemade World* (New York: Knopf, 1975); Frank Kermode, *The Sense of an Ending: Studies in the Theory of Fiction* (New York: Oxford University Press, 1970); George Lukacs, *Realism in Our Time: Literature and the Class Struggle*, trans. John and Necke Mander (New York: Harper and Row, 1971); Judith Ryan, *The Vanishing Subject: Early Psychology and Literary Modernism* (Chicago: University of Chicago Press, 1991). Kermode explores modernist premises as a creative negotiation between the abstractions of myth and the formlessness of brute fact; Burger and Lukacs develop a general theory of alienation from a capitalist culture which modernist practice enacts; Eysteinsson lucidly distinguishes between kinds of modernism and the questions posed by each; Kenner and Ryan analyze specific modernist writers under the larger umbrella of shared modernist conventions.

6. Friedrich Nietzsche, *Twilight of the Idols*, in *The Portable Nietzsche*, ed. and trans. Walter Kaufman (New York: Viking Press, 1954), 483.

7. Fredric Jameson, *The Political Unconscious: Narrative as a Socially Symbolic Act* (Ithaca: Cornell University Press, 1981), 261.

8. The fullest studies of Faulknerian outrage are André Bleikasten's *The Ink of Melancholy: Faulkner's Novels from "The Sound and the Fury" to "Light in August"* (Bloomington: University of Indiana Press, 1990) and Warwick Wadlington's *Reading Faulknerian Tragedy* (Ithaca: Cornell University Press, 1987). For further probing of the conjunction of modernist norms and Faulknerian practice, see Richard Moreland's *Faulkner and Modernism: Rereading and Rewriting* (Madison: University of Wisconsin Press, 1990), as well as my *Faulkner's Subject* and the essays by Moreland, Bleikasten, and O'Donnell in my *Cambridge Companion to William Faulkner* (New York: Cambridge University Press, 1995).

9. William Faulkner, *As I Lay Dying*, in *Faulkner: Novels, 1930–1935* (New York: The Library of America, 1985), 156.

10. Kenner, 205–6.

11. Quoted in Stephen Ross, *Fiction's Inexhaustible Voice: Speech and Writing in Faulkner* (Athens: University of Georgia Press, 1989), 1.

12. John Keats, *Selected Poems and Letters*, ed. Douglas Bush (Boston: Houghton Mifflin, 1959), 279.

13. *As I Lay Dying*, 125.

14. William Faulkner, *Absalom, Absalom!* in *Faulkner: Novels, 1936–1940*, 105.

Faulkner's Playful Bestiary:
Seeing Gender through Ovidian Eyes

GAIL MORTIMER

Reading Faulkner is such an unquestioned and basic part of my life that it has undoubtedly been beneficial to me to be asked regularly, as my students do, why we are reading him. A woman, a Yankee, and a feminist, I am, at least in their view, an odd person to be fascinated with this Southerner whose fictive characters are so often eccentric or tormented, or both, and whose imagined world seems to them at times surreal. At first I have answered them by talking about my appreciation for Faulkner's understanding of the possibilities of language, his exploration of its rhythms and capacity to evoke a distinctive and compelling universe. Then, since some students—at least at the very beginning—have a difficult time appreciating language for its own sake, I also talk about how his fiction explores aspects of the American character that would otherwise seem strange or anachronistic, how we still live with the legacy of the frontier spirit, our exploitive attitude toward the land, our historic dismissal of the humanity of American Indians, and our national shame— racism. Faulkner shows us how to understand dimensions of ourselves which we are still struggling, and often not very insightfully, to overcome.

Students remain troubled, though, by particular aspects of Faulkner's stories, and recently they have challenged him on a matter I had never before thought about. Faulkner, they complain, regularly portrays violent scenes of animal abuse to which his narrators seem utterly indifferent. In the sheer number of such incidents, the students are certainly correct. Horses and mules in Faulkner's stories are regularly beaten or driven into raging rivers where they drown, dogs are viciously kicked, wild ponies are shackled together with barbed wire, one of them is killed when ropes stretched across its path cause it to break its neck, another is hit over the head with a washboard, and one poor horse is punctured with a fish hook and then inflated with a bicycle pump so it can be sold at a higher price. And all of this is without authorial comment.

One of the reasons I had never particularly noticed this recurrent vio-

lence toward animals is that such events typically appear within comic
contexts, in the midst of stories meant to display the folly or stupidity or
greed of human characters, or when cruelty to an animal is depicted as
just another instance of a character's general viciousness toward everyone in his world. Only rarely is our attention drawn to an animal's suffering, as in *Light in August* when Joe Christmas ruthlessly beats the horse
he steals when he runs away from the McEachern home, and even then
our sympathy is deflected onto a simile that emphasizes stasis rather than
feeling: "Save for the rise and fall of the stick and the groaning respira-
tions of the animal, they [horse and rider] might have been an equestrian
statue strayed from its pedestal and come to rest in an attitude of ultimate
exhaustion."[1] My focus in reading such passages, my students have
taught me, has perhaps been too exclusively drawn to the portrait of a
human character's desperation, fury, or sense of entrapment.

In *The Hamlet* my reading of the animals has entailed a different sort
of distancing, since I see them as embodying a type of Faulknerian allegory about the difficulty men and women have in understanding or loving
one another. Faulkner's imagination in this novel seems very like that of
Ovid in his *Metamorphoses*, where people are regularly transformed into
animals or plants that represent some salient feature of their personali-
ties. In Ovid's story of Philomela and her sister Procne, for example, the
villainous Tereus, who abducts and rapes his sister-in-law, is ultimately
transformed by the gods into a bird of prey in what may seem like a
punishment for his crimes, but in truth it only exposes what he has been
all along, as if to say that he has lost his humanity in yielding to his animal
lusts. Faulkner, similarly, does not hesitate to use animals as metaphors
to express one or another dimension of his characters, although it is important, as always, to recall that all of these perceptions are in fact *projections* of the masculine consciousnesses, both characters' and narrators',
that we regularly experience in his texts.

Faulkner has long attributed human traits to animals, just as he uses
analogies with animals to characterize humans, so that at times they seem
to displace one another in a given narrative. As Patrick Samway reminds
us,[2] Faulkner creates a virtual bestiary in *The Reivers*, where he ranks
horses at the very bottom of a hierarchy, followed by dogs, cats, mules,
and lastly, rats, which rate the highest place because they get everything
they need from humans without doing the least bit in return: A rat "lives
in your house without helping you to buy it or build it or repair it or keep
the taxes paid; he eats what you eat without helping you raise it or buy it
or even haul it into the house.[3] Cats are superior to dogs because while
both are parasites on humans, cats don't even pretend to love you. Dogs,
on the other hand, are incurable sycophants. Mules, who are wonderfully

apostrophized in *Flags in the Dust* as well as *The Reivers*, outrank horses, dogs, and cats because they are bright enough to put their own interests first and single-minded enough to work "patiently for ten years for the chance to kick [their owner] once" (*R* 92). Horses, at the very bottom of the list, are simply too stupid; Faulkner writes that if the horse "had only one gram of the intelligence of the most backward rat, he would be the rider" (*R* 92). Faulkner even placed himself within such an animal world in a fantasy he recorded in an interview: "you know that if I were reincarnated, I'd want to come back a buzzard. Nothing hates him or envies him or wants him or needs him. He is never bothered or in danger, and he can eat anything."[4]

Moreover, as I discovered last evening in a conversation with Faulkner's long-time friend, Joan Williams, he did not hesitate to use such distinctions to chastise someone dear who had disappointed him. During a period of frustration and anger with her, Faulkner expressed what Joseph Blotner has called "a flash of recrimination" in a letter he wrote to her in November 1953: "You take too much, and are willing to give too little. . . . People have attributes like animals; you are a mixture of cat and mule and possum—the cat's secretiveness and self-centeredness, the mule's stubbornness to get what it wants no matter who or what suffers, the possum's nature of playing dead—running into sleep or its pretence—whenever it is faced with a situation which it thinks it is not going to like."[5] Joan Williams was in the library this afternoon when I located this letter, which she had told me about, and her reaction upon rereading it conveyed her renewed sense of the unfairness of Faulkner's comments: "That's what *he* thinks!" she declared.

His playful admiration for scavengers like buzzards and rats, which scarcely at all disguises Faulkner's longing for what he sees as their autonomy and freedom from human responsibilities, is translated into appalled fascination in *The Hamlet*, where Faulkner's characters frequently comment on the rodentlike qualities of the Snopeses, particularly Flem and Mink. But as critics have noted, it is cows and horses that dominate this novel, where they serve as extended metaphors for how the male character/narrators view the Otherness of women, who are frequently likened to cows, as well as the masculinity in themselves that seems so precarious, which they see in the wildness and fragility of horses. You will recall that when Jack Houston marries Lucy Pate, he tries to hold on to that "bitless masculinity which he had relinquished" by buying a stallion.[6] The stallion, however, retaliates against the figure who signals Houston's domestication by killing her. Throughout *The Hamlet* males long to own horses, and they attempt to outwit one another through shady deals or lose their good sense at the sight of a herd of wild ponies.

The horses are emblems of the lost wildness of their unmarried youths, and they create havoc when the men even approach them, leaving several men maimed by the end of the novel.

Perhaps the more interesting displacement in this novel, however, and the one I want to focus on tonight, is the bovinity associated with such women in the novel as Ab Snopes's daughters, "two big absolutely static young women" with "broad expressionless faces" (H 21, 22) and, of course, with Eula Varner, very cowlike in her utter passivity, her constant chewing, her wide expanses of flesh, and her apparent indifference to others' motives toward her. Faulkner actually sees Eula in terms of several animals whose imperviousness to masculine influence mocks the males who long for her and wish to control her. She is described as being like "a blooded and contrary filly too young yet to be particularly valuable, though which in another year or so would be, and for which reason its raging and harried owner does not dare whip it" (H 109); she is a cat "sitting with veiled eyes against the sun" (H 125), and to her brother Jody she is like a bitch in heat, giving off something when she passes "anything in long pants" (H 110).

But mostly Eula is bovine, relentlessly female, mammalian, and she exudes a palpable threat to the peace of mind of her male observers. The men who follow and approach her are rendered helpless by their desire. They fall over themselves trying to be "the first" man in her life; they leave town, like Labove, when they are defeated, or when they think their leaving will cause the town to believe each of them was the one to take her virginity. Faulkner's narrator is explicit on the subject of their ineptitude, and, of course, the entire debacle is then paralleled by the narrative of Ike Snopes's successful courtship of Houston's cow. Noel Polk spoke this morning of Faulkner's "Afternoon of a Cow" as a text in which he portrays *himself* as the figure upon which a cow releases her frustration (by defecating) on this man who was only trying to help, in what Polk sees, intriguingly, as a Faulknerian allegory about himself as an artist struggling with his unwieldy subject. Ike Snopes's love affair with *his* cow is framed in language suggesting in a variety of ways the interchangeability as love objects of Eula and the cow, both "maiden[s] meditant" (H 193) as they retreat from their suitors. The analogies between Eula and Ike's cow signal one of Faulkner's more innovative narrative devices for addressing the elusive truths about the nature of men's encounter with the female gender and its attendant anxieties and bewilderment. The cow is not merely *like* Eula; it *replaces* her in this tale of the vicissitudes of masculine desire.

Faulkner's story of Ike and his cow explicitly refers to a figure in Roman mythology when Ike looks into his love's eyes and sees himself there "in twin miniature" as if he were looking into the eyes of Juno, the Roman goddess of women and marriage (*H* 201). This allusion recalls Ovid's story of Io, a maiden whom the god Jove seduces and then transforms into a milk-white cow in his unsuccessful attempt to keep his wife Juno from punishing the girl for the affair. The name "Io" is evident elsewhere in *The Hamlet* in the name of one of Ike Snopes's cousins, I. O., the schoolteacher, and when Ike tries to pronounce his own name, everything seems blurred but the two vowels: "Ike H-mope" (*H* 185). But it is Io's existence as a milk-white cow that makes her an emblem of female reproductive richness and creativity, and it is noteworthy that Eula Varner is given so many of the same epithets, both physical and mythological, as Ike's cow; she is not only "too much of mammalian female meat" (*H* 111) but able to make the very benches in the schoolroom where she attends classes "into a grove of Venus" (*H* 127), not only "the serene and usually steadily and constantly eating axis, center" of any group she is a part of (*H* 141) but a maiden whose body, as Labove the schoolteacher sees it, is "as fluid and muscleless as a miraculous *intact milk*" (*H* 134, emphasis added).[7] V. K. Ratliff, the sewing machine salesman, mourns the waste of Eula's splendor when she is married off to Flem Snopes by saying that it is like "baiting [a trap] with a freshened heifer to catch a rat" (*H* 176).

These characterizations of Eula vary from worshipful comparisons with ancient goddesses like Venus to debasing her into mere flesh, "galmeat," and thus expressing both extremes of masculine ambivalence toward this figure who too palpably embodies all that is female. Faulkner's males and the figurative language through which they try to think about Eula expose their fear and exasperation as well as their longing and awe. Yet, as if he cannot depict an average male encountering this apotheosis of femininity, Faulkner makes of Eula's suitors fawning and ineffectual adolescents, unable to approach her. It is she who chooses Hoake McCarron for her first lover and thereby makes of him a local legend.

To depict something approximating the best in human love and devotion, Faulkner turns from his normal, often cerebral, but troubled male characters to a retarded figure, Ike Snopes. Ike's very intellectual limitations mean that he is not bothered by thoughts of what his love represents, and so Faulkner is freed to make her utterly (excuse the pun) bovine, female, mammalian—a cow. Indeed, Ike grows through his love for his cow to having new capacities as a human being, unlike Eula's suitors, who seem diminished and enervated by their passion. Ike's adoration teaches him loyalty, tenderness, and how to care actively for her well-being. He even summons an extraordinary courage when he discovers she is in danger from a fire. He faces one of his greatest terrors by descending a staircase, an act that for him constitutes stepping off into sheer, empty space because he lacks depth perception. The world he moves through to reach her is full of obstacles that he faces straightforwardly in order to go to her rescue. Faulkner writes, somewhat ironically, that Ike "is learning fast now, who has learned success and then precaution and secrecy and how to steal and even providence; who has only lust and greed and bloodthirst and a moral conscience to keep him awake at night, yet to acquire" (*H* 202). Ike's intellectual limitations, then, free him from the anxieties about women that leave other men in *The Hamlet* defeated, and they become the source of his strengths as a lover. He has neither the imagination nor the cultural or personal memory to become a coward in this female's presence.

The passages indicating how different Ike is from nearly all men in Faulkner's fictive world who fall in love with women are explicit in showing his acceptance of, rather than anxiety about, the various dimensions of the feminine. At dawn one morning when he has escaped with the cow, Ike watches a sunrise that is replete with images of classic beauty associated with the arrival of Aurora, goddess of early morning, and an evocation of "Troy's Helen," and Ike's discovery that dawn "is not decanted onto earth from the sky," which might be seen as a kind of masculine act of impregnation, "but instead is from the earth itself suspired" (*H* 200), the earth being, of course, a symbol of the feminine. Thus, Ike has been brought on some level to an intuition about the power of what is female. Ike then pauses, "breathing in the reek, the odor of cows and mares as the successful lover does that of a room full of women, his the victor's drowsing rapport with all anonymous faceless female flesh capable of love walking the female earth" (*H* 200).

These to me are passages of such beauty that they transcend the offensive implications some have seen in Faulkner's treatment of women characters—and animals, as well. The fleshly correspondences between Eula and Ike's cow powerfully expose the source of masculine anxiety about the female in Faulkner's world: women are reminders of the flesh, of mortality and vulnerability, and of the helplessness that lingers in all of our psyches as a result of our dependency as infants on the nurturance of women. Males are not really alone—although Faulkner's stories might lead us to think so—in their awareness of this primary reliance on figures whose Otherness threatens us with a permanent sense of not being entirely at home in our physical worlds. Faulkner's stories are like Ovid's in using animals to echo and isolate salient features of our lives as humans and in reminding us thereby of our ineluctable participation in the physicality of our world.

NOTES

1. William Faulkner, *Light in August*. The Corrected Text (New York: Vintage International, 1990), 210.

2. Patrick Samway, S.J., "Narration and Naming in The Reivers," *Faulkner's Discourse: An International Symposium*, ed. Lothar Hönnighausen (Tübingen: Max Niemeyer Verlag, 1989), 254–62.

3. William Faulkner, *The Reivers: A Reminiscence* (New York: New American Library, Signet, 1969), 91. Hereafter cited parenthetically in the text as R.

4. William Faulkner, *Lion in the Garden: Interviews with William Faulkner, 1926–1962*, ed. James B. Meriwether and Michael Millgate (New York: Random House, 1968), 243.

5. Quoted in Joseph Blotner, *Faulkner: A Biography*, 2 vols. (New York: Random House, 1974), 2:1477.

6. William Faulkner, *The Hamlet*. The Corrected Text (New York: Vintage International, 1991), 238. Hereafter cited parenthetically in the text as H.

7. See also Karen R. Sass, "Rejection of the Maternal and the Polarization of Gender in *The Hamlet*," *Faulkner Journal* 4.1–2 (Fall 1988/Spring 1989: 127–38.

Faulkner's Continuing Education:
From Self-Reflection to Embarrassment

RICHARD C. MORELAND

The most common measure of Faulkner's importance has been his prob-ing literary critique of modern life, although the interpretation of that critique has changed and differed as his readers have. His formal and psychological experiments and their setting in a large social and historical context have made modern life in his fiction seem profoundly and perva-sively unfamiliar, unstable, unworkable, arbitrary, outrageous. His writ-ing questions the way we most conventionally perceive, think, write, speak, and act. It unsettles prevailing assumptions about time, space, language, loss, the self, the family, gender, culture, and history. The irony of his critique seems to cut in almost every direction, refusing its readers first this way out, then another and another. He has been important be-cause his critique is moving, extensive, and almost unrelenting. When Toni Morrison spoke at this conference in 1985, she described his work in terms of his refusal to look away, a phrase she also used to describe her character Sethe in *Beloved*, representing another vision of outrage and almost unrelenting critique.[1]

Another, somewhat different measure of Faulkner's importance, how-ever, is that the irony of his critique (somewhat like Sethe's) is pervasive and profound enough to turn also against itself, thereby making room for humor, tenderness, and a sometimes clumsy, embarrassing exposure of himself and his readers. I am not speaking of self-consciousness, but ac-tual embarrassment, clumsiness, impediments, as if he cannot foresee or control that exposure or the unexpected situations and perspective(s) to which he and his readers are thereby exposed. I want to acknowledge that this turning of irony against itself, this vulnerable candor, this poten-tial for clumsiness and embarrassment, is not the most flattering measure of Faulkner's importance. It can position and date his work, and it can sometimes look like a loss of nerve or a kind of compromise or a falling off in the intensity of his critique.[2] But I admire this candor in his writing, and I think this dimension of his writing has become more significant, and we have learned better how to discuss it, in the context of feminism and cultural studies, including what critics have been describing lately as a shift toward "border studies" in American criticism.[3] In the hybrid and cross-cultural setting of "border studies" and in the variously marked, located, interactive spaces described by feminism and cultural studies more generally, the unrelenting irony and critique with which Faulkner is often identified have become perhaps less important than a certain candor and self-exposure in his writing, as he tries to learn and write about what neither he nor his irony ever completely knows or controls. It is perhaps this less controllable dimension of his and others' writing that has helped us understand "the hybrid processes of cultural formation, deformation, and reformation" that take place where cultures, genders, races, classes, and different ways of understanding our experience conflict and overlap. It is in these interactive spaces—notably including the space of reading—that his writing opens itself in what Judith Butler has called "a certain linguistic vulnerability to reappropriation."[4] This vulnerability to reappropriation may account for some of his importance not only to cultural critics but also to writers like Ralph Ellison, Toni Morrison, Gabriel Garcia Marquez, Wilson Harris, and other writers around the world. In *Intruder in the Dust*, for example, a novel for which American Faulkner critics tend to apologize, Wilson Harris finds "a universe of unsuspected diversity, correspondence and potential"—a potential, especially, for "complex mutuality and a difficult creation of community."[5] It is no accident, I think, that this is a novel in which Faulkner's fiction comes closest to some of his most embarrassing public statements about current political controversies, statements about his taking a stand against federal civil rights legislation;[6] it is also a novel that attaches particular importance to an incident of clumsiness and embarrassment—twelve-year-old Chick Mallison's first encounter with Lucas Beauchamp when Chick has just fallen off a footlog into a frozen creek— "something a girl might have been expected and even excused for doing but nobody else."[7]

Faulkner critics such as my copanelists Gail Mortimer and Philip Weinstein—and too many others attending this conference for me to try to name—have written a dazzling body of criticism expanding on the psychological and philosophical implications of Faulkner's work.[8] These and other critics have also expanded and deepened the social critique embedded throughout his stories and novels. Criticism in this more social direction has increasingly stressed the "politics of location" in Faulkner. Philip Weinstein, for example, in his admirable recent book on Faulkner and Morrison, traces some of the broadest philosophical and social critiques in Faulkner's and others' modernist work back to "the drama of an innocent boy child outraged at his disinheritance. The failure of traditional culture," Weinstein writes, "to pass on to its sensitive young men (the writers [and] their protagonists) the materials out of which they might compose identity, project, and destiny, suggests the dysfunction of patriarchy itself—a dysfunction whose primary damage to white male sons, and secondarily to women and blacks, commands Faulkner's attention" (187). Weinstein goes on to position, as well, Faulkner's most compelled, if not compulsive readers: "The audience . . . to which modernism makes its most compelling invitations is university-trained, which is to say (until well into the twentieth century), almost always white and mainly male: an audience of elaborately educated sons who saw themselves cut off from the certainties of an earlier time" (187). I quote from Weinstein's book here not to position him or embarrass him but to call attention to the embarrassing social positioning of Faulkner's work that Weinstein rightly finds necessary in order to discuss Faulkner's work next to Morrison's. Moving back and forth between their works makes it especially clear how much even the most self-reflective ironies proceed from and keep returning to particular positions and orientations. (In deconstructive terms, any reversal also involves some kind of reinscription.) A Faulkner character such as Mr. Compson demonstrates repeatedly how an irony directed against his own position, without some sense of other potentially viable positions, does not necessarily change his position; nor does it allow him to learn much from anyone else. Instead, his irony often seems to excuse and preserve his own position from the more unpredictable criticism of others—and from riskier interactions with others.

This is how Paul Jay describes Richard Rorty's acknowledgment of his own "ethnocentric" position: he is ironic toward any philosophical grounds for privileging Western culture but then ironically privileges that culture nevertheless, because it is his (168–79). It is also the ironic result suggested by Walter Michaels's study of racial nativism and cultural pluralism in American modernist writing: an irony toward the racial purity of the nativist self and family leads to a series of ironic substitutes in figures of sterility, incest, homosexuality, suicide, and eventually a powerful new essentialist sense of cultural identities and cultural pluralism.[9] Michaels argues that this pluralism expresses "a commitment to the irrevocability of cultural differences and therefore to their basis in race." It is easy to recognize here the sometime tendency in Faulkner (who serves as Michaels's opening example) to move from an irony directed against the racism and sexism of white patriarchy toward the idea that African Americans and women are absolutely inscrutable except to those who share the same cultural or gender identity, as in the opening of "Pantaloon in Black" or the title story of *Go Down, Moses*. But again,

Faulkner's work does not always insist on giving the final word to his own ironic critique. In many such cases Faulkner seems acutely aware of the danger described by Wolfgang Iser, even if Faulkner doesn't always quite know how to avoid it, or perhaps whether he wants to avoid it: this danger with which Faulkner flirts is that "Instead of ironizing itself, irony becomes the sign of its own agony."[10] Mr. Compson is again an obvious example. Though Faulkner is not above dwelling on the un-healing wound of outraged innocence,[11] he and some of his characters also often take clumsier, more embarrassing chances, acknowledging their limitations, or trying to, but also trying to learn something from their experience, even their experience with people disturbingly differ-ent from themselves, without being sure of their success.

Faulkner's 1948 novel *Intruder in the Dust* includes more than its share of clumsiness and embarrassment. It dramatizes both the limita-tions of its own irony (and that of the culture it represents) and a some-what groping effort to move beyond that irony. It is perhaps Faulkner's most obviously dated and positioned novel; it wears its somewhat inco-herent politics on its sleeve. While it acknowledges a history of racial violence in the American South, it also features Gavin Stevens's argu-ments (in language that echoes some of Faulkner's public statements) against the civil rights legislation that was eventually signed in the year the novel was published. Gavin acknowledges more than once the irony of his defending the privilege of Southern whites to set Southern blacks free, but he defends it nonetheless. Although he insists on the "homoge-neity" of Southern whites and Southern blacks respectively, his argu-ments against the necessity of civil rights law also insist on the possibility of cross-cultural interaction and cultural change.[12] There is little in his speeches to explain how this interaction and change would work, but Faulkner explores one possibility at length in the novel's action, in what Chick Mallison and perhaps even Gavin Stevens might be understood to learn from Lucas Beauchamp. It is tempting to dismiss the apparent changes in Chick and the subtler changes in Lucas and Gavin during the course of the novel as lame and unrealistic justifications for Gavin's idea that civil rights legislation was unnecessary. But the kind of personal and cultural change that Faulkner is working here to imagine has been a sticking point throughout his career. As Weinstein puts it, although Faulkner knows that his culture's Oedipal/patriarchal model excludes women and blacks "in such a way as to dispossess the men as well[,] . . . he is incapable of revising it, for nothing in his culture's norms or in his relation to those norms positioned him to see his way past this disaster" (131). This is perhaps why the novel works so clumsily, and with such an embarrassing kind of hope, on Chick and Gavin's interaction with Lucas.

Weinstein discusses this novel in terms of two potential father figures for Chick, two figures between whom Weinstein sees little significant difference and from whom he sees Chick learning little, in another instance of the Oedipal patriarchy's repeated dysfunction. Lucas is described in terms of a masculine self-possession and impenetrability like that of his white grandfather, the old Carothers McCaslin, as well as Chick's own grandfather, yet Lucas is made "incapable of freeing himself" (125), and his self-possession is repeatedly undercut by his role as "Sambo" in Gavin's discussions of Southern history. Gavin is equally inept in his own realm of ideas and words, where his ideas of homogeneous and autonomous peoples or even persons is contradicted by the deep divisions he also acknowledges both between his class of Southern whites and those who want to lynch Lucas and between Lucas and other Southern blacks. Neither Lucas nor Gavin seems to offer a usable figure for Chick's identification. Weinstein finds much more significant and instructive differences in figures of manhood and paternity when he turns to Toni Morrison's later work. Whereas Lucas seemed "carefully lifted clear from his black culture" in Faulkner's novel (123), characters like Paul D, Stamp Paid, and Joe Trace seem to have learned from their own experience and from a culture schooled in slavery to relinquish white models of manhood and paternity and "to acknowledge a kind of radical interdependency of identity without which they would have perished" (127). Weinstein finds in Morrison's fiction a different model of identity beyond "the luxuries of innocence and outrage"—"an interdependency at the core of survival itself (for none of us makes it all alone) but one from which Western white males are still fleeing in numbers too vast for counting" (127). Weinstein's own lyricism here signals how valuable such a model of interdependent, communal identity can seem, not only to African American readers, but also how valuable it can seem to white male readers of Faulkner.

I realize that reading about a different model of manhood does not make for an instant transformation or conversion. It is not a question of mix and match identities or plug and play technologies of gender. There are larger histories, structures, and emotional forces at work. But I do believe we can learn something from reading about our interactions with each other, not just about who we are but also about who we might become, if only partly or temporarily, and about how we might interact differently with each other, if only imaginatively or experimentally. In reading we learn not just about our identities but also about the various, complex, and continuing acts of identification. Nor is this different model of gender identity, of course, a given throughout African American culture. Weinstein argues that Morrison has had to find her way into "this new vision of black manhood" in the course of writing several novels focused on characters who often fail to resist or reappropriate or find alternatives to the dominant white culture's dysfunctional models (127).

Looking back at *Intruder in the Dust* after such a reading of *Beloved* and *Jazz*, I begin to wonder how this different model of manhood in Morrison might change the feel of Faulkner's novel, as Faulkner's work is increasingly read in just such cross-cultural contexts. Insofar as this model in Morrison is indeed a cultural product that she has articulated and developed and not only an invention of her fiction, Faulkner's novel might be understood as reaching clumsily and hopefully in this cross-cultural direction. He may be trying to grasp a cultural and personal model some features of which he can appreciate and articulate from his position, but other features of which he may blur or distort under the pressure of his own needs or by imagining them in terms of more familiar models, models he might reject but cannot quite articulate his way beyond.

For example, Faulkner imagines Gavin and Chick as well as Lucas insisting on Lucas's independence and self-possession, on the model of the old white patriarchs. Faulkner has little trouble imagining Lucas ironically undercutting white stereotypes of blacks or white men's stereotypes of themselves by representing Lucas as a black patriarch, "not arrogant at all and not even scornful: just intolerant inflexible and composed" (292). It seems harder, however, for Faulkner to imagine or articulate for Lucas any more thorough reappropriation of the dominant culture's models and terms.[13] Yet what puzzles and fascinates Chick and Gavin is how Lucas manages somehow to maintain this kind of dignity even when he is seen as black by everyone around him and therefore unentitled to this kind of self-possession, and how he maintains that air of independence even when he comes to depend so crucially on the help of two teenage boys and an old woman friend of his late wife Molly's. His dependence on them and his other indignities in the novel may seem simply (and ironically) to undercut his supposed independence, but these impediments and embarrassments may also suggest a significant and fruitful contradiction in Chick and Gavin's and perhaps Faulkner's understanding of how a black man might manage his dignity differently than a white patriarch supposedly would. Without ever quite understanding how Lucas pulls this off, Chick does seem to identify more with Lucas's than with his uncle's or his own grandfather's example.

The novel traces Chick's identification with Lucas back to Chick's embarrassing but indelible memories of his first encounter with Lucas. Chick's actual father is a dim presence in the novel, mostly absent from the action except occasionally to prohibit, deny, or envy his son's becom-

ing "big enough to button his pants" (384). But the novel virtually begins
with Chick's detailed memory of an encounter in which Lucas begins to
play a more crucial role in Chick's growth, the role of a much more physically nurturing and tender father. Although in his speech Lucas seems,
like Chick's grandfather, "simply incapable of conceiving himself by a
child contradicted and defied" (288), Lucas leads Chick to the hearth fire
in his and Molly's bedroom and tells Chick twice to remove not just his
wet clothes but even his unionsuit so that he can be "enveloped in the
quilt like a cocoon" (291). Although Lucas is not present for the meal
Molly feeds Chick, it is Lucas who insists that Chick eat "of what obviously was to be Lucas' dinner" (292–93). And when Chick attempts to
translate his feelings about Lucas and Molly's intimate care and hospital-
ity into a token payment of seventy cents, Chick's body and affect contra-
dict and expose his more abstract gesture of payment—"standing with
the slow hot blood as slow as minutes themselves up his neck and face"
(294). Chick will continue to attempt throughout the novel to articulate
and discharge in his language and actions the kind of physical and emotional attachment to Lucas that Chick's own more familiar models of paternity, maternity, gender, and race work against.[14] Chick will act with a
growing sense that he will not discover or inherit his own manhood and
courage by virtue of his gender, race, or individual will, but that he must
somehow instead "draw [his] manhood up, quicklike," as a black father
in Morrison's *Jazz* explains impatiently to his white son.[15] He will have
to gather his manhood and courage not in spite of his physical circumstances and emotional attachments, but out of the depth and strength of
those same physical and emotional attachments. What Chick and to some
extent Gavin seem somewhat clumsily and fitfully to learn from Lucas,
as well as what Lucas seems to learn from his own situation in this novel,
is that none of them is the "self-contained virile subject who controls his
body and actions" (as white men are virtually promised by their culture),
the subject whose "self-identity is . . . necessarily bought through the
sacrifice, or abjection, of others."[16] All three are embarrassed into learning something about their own embodiment, their dependence on other
people, and their ability to learn something from each other.

To put this another way, this novel includes what Susan Donaldson
has described as a "semi-articulated" story. It is the story of an African
American man's recognition of his connection to the body and other supposedly feminine features of his experience, as well as his recognition of
his connection to African American history and culture (both of which
recognitions Weinstein finds in more developed form in later Morrison).[17]
Early in the novel Lucas scoffs at Molly's field slave "headrag"; later,
Chick is surprised at Lucas's grief at Molly's death, then Molly's presence

is felt again in Lucas and Chick's more or less acknowledged dependence on the loyalty and courage and resourcefulness of Molly's friend Miss Habersham. Although Chick describes the relationship of Molly and Miss Habersham in terms of their being "born in the same week and both suckled at Molly's mother's breast and grown up together almost inextricably like sisters, like twins" (349), their relationship does not remain associated only with the physical and the domestic. Like Chick, Miss Habersham acts on her physical and emotional attachments to Molly and Lucas not only in childhood or in the home but also in the more public, supposedly masculine realm of Lucas's near lynching. She not only helps Chick and Aleck Sander discover the proof of Lucas's innocence, she also consults with Gavin and the sheriff and helps guard the jail. Even Gavin's description of an African American "capacity to wait and endure and survive" (402), echoing Faulkner's comment on Dilsey Gibson in his Appendix to *The Sound and the Fury*, while it might be understood ironically as his unilateral lowering of others' deserts and expectations, might also represent his clumsy sense of valuable cultural lessons learned in African American history and culture. Waiting, enduring, and surviving beyond the failure of dominant cultural structures is what most of Faulkner's white male characters cannot quite learn how to do.

The novel's final scene dramatizes the clumsy, embarrassing courage and hope with which Faulkner tried to write his way beyond what he knew—and what his irony knew—out into the difficult but potentially rewarding spaces where identities and cultures overlap, again including the space of reading. Lucas has come to Gavin's office to acknowledge his debt to Gavin, Chick, and Miss Habersham, and he is willing to acknowledge that debt in Gavin's language of courtliness and business payments. When Gavin gives him his bill, however, Lucas does manage to reappropriate the phrase "none of my business" and the spirit of uninvolvement that phrase ordinarily signifies, by translating these into the different language of a blues song and into another challenge for Gavin to learn something despite himself from Lucas: "I'm a farming man and you're a lawing man and whether you know your business or not I reckon it aint none of my red wagon as the music box says to try to learn you different" (469). Lucas then counts out his money in such a way that the very personal nature of his money and his payment is almost unmistakable. Lucas knows only too well, however, that Gavin may miss such an observation by ironically throwing his hands in the air or throwing his pen to the floor. Lucas is supposedly paying now to replace the point in Gavin's pen that was broken when Gavin gave up making "sense" of Lucas's story in the language of the court (468). So after Lucas pays Gavin, he challenges Gavin to try again by writing him a receipt for what he has paid and what he has done. Ending his novel there, Faulkner may have recognized in Gavin's position something of his own tendency toward an inadequate, self-reflective irony along with his clumsy, embarrassing hopes of learning something nevertheless from trying to write about Lucas Beauchamp.

NOTES

1. Toni Morrison, "Faulkner and Women," *Faulkner and Women*, ed. Doreen Fowler and Ann J. Abadie (Jackson: University Press of Mississippi, 1986), 297. This connection was remarked by Doreen Fowler, "Reading for the 'Other Side': *Beloved* and *Requiem for a Nun*," in *Unflinching Gaze: Morrison and Faulkner Re-Envisioned*, ed. Carol A. Kolmerten, Stephen M. Ross, and Judith Bryant Wittenberg (Jackson: University Press of Mississippi, 1997), 139.

2. The valuable recent work of Faulkner critics such as Minrose Gwin, John T. Matthews, Philip Weinstein, and Karl Zender exemplified in their contributions to this volume, as well as the cautions sounded by André Bleikasten, have made me increasingly doubtful about the sometime suggestion in my *Faulkner and Modernism: Rereading and Rewriting* (Madison: University of Wisconsin Press, 1990) that Faulkner's interrogation of his own modernist irony in *Absalom, Absalom!* produced better writing thereafter in his career. I would prefer to suggest that this novel's interrogation of irony in a larger social and historical context was, first, part of a shift to another phase of Faulkner's career, different in many respects, but not necessarily better in any general sense, and second, Faulkner's way of focusing his own and others' critical attention on this dimension of his writing. Faulkner himself might have said in defense of his later work that he continued to reach beyond his grasp. Bleikasten has also questioned *Faulkner and Modernism's* tendency to reduce all "modernism" and "irony" to the melancholic, self-protective, and often politically conservative motivations and consequences that Faulkner often finds in the modernist irony of his own society and even his own work ("Faulkner and the New Ideologues," in *Faulkner and Ideology*, ed. Donald M. Kartiganer and Ann J. Abadie [Jackson: University Press of Mississippi, 1995], 20, n.19). This is also a fair objection. I would prefer to suggest not that all modernism or modernist irony is necessarily melancholic or conservative, but that understanding it as a purely negative critique can obscure its motivations and consequences in any particular instance. Faulkner's writing is candid enough to interrogate those more particular motivations and consequences in his fiction. Thus I would also argue not that *Absalom, Absalom!* is limited by its irony (as Judith Wittenberg's reference to *Faulkner and Modernism* suggests), but that it impressively elaborates its own irony's limitations and self-protectiveness: it ironizes its own irony.

3. A large body of feminist work on Faulkner is exemplified by the writing in this volume and previous work by Minrose Gwin, Susan Donaldson, Judith L. Sensibar, and Judith Bryant Wittenberg. Race and cultural studies in a broad sense would include the work in this volume and previous work by Thadious Davis, John T. Matthews, Carolyn Porter, Philip Weinstein, and Karl Zender. On the shift toward border studies in American literary criticism, see, for example, Paul Jay's *Contingency Blues: The Search for Foundations in American Criticism* (Madison: University of Wisconsin Press, 1997); Arnold Krupat's *Ethnocriticism: Ethnography, History, Literature* (Berkeley: University of California Press, 1992); Carolyn Porter's "What We Know that We Don't Know: Remapping American Literary Studies," *American Literary History* 6 (1994): 467–526; Gloria Anzaldua's *Borderlands / La Frontera: The New Mestiza* (San Francisco: Aunt Lute Books, 1987); and Jose David Saldivar's *The Dialectics of Our America: Genealogy, Cultural Critique, and Literary History* (Durham: Duke University Press, 1991).

4. Judith Butler, "Sovereign Performatives in the Contemporary Scene of Utterance," *Critical Inquiry* 23 (Winter 1997): 350–77.

5. Wilson Harris, "Reflection on William Faulkner's *Intruder in the Dust* in a Cross-cultural Complex," *World Literature Written in English* 22.1 (1983): 98, 106. See also André Bleikasten's discussion (in this volume) of Faulkner's international influence on other writers.

6. Gavin Stevens's lengthy remarks on the civil rights legislation that was signed by President Harry Truman in the same year the novel was published (1948) closely resemble Faulkner's notorious public statements against federal intervention in Southern racial conflicts. The question of the novel's place in current political debates is carefully examined in John Bassett, "Gradual Progress and *Intruder in the Dust*," *College Literature* 13.3 (Fall 1986): 207–16. The background of these debates in Southern politics is usefully summarized in Numan Bartley's "Politics and Ideology," *Encyclopedia of Southern Culture*, ed. Charles Reagan Wilson and William Ferris (Chapel Hill: University of North Carolina Press, 1989), 1151–58.

7. William Faulkner, *Intruder in the Dust* (1948), *William Faulkner: Novels 1942–1954* (New York: Library of America, 1994), 286. Other references to page numbers in the novel will appear in parentheses in the text.

8. Gail L. Mortimer, *Faulkner's Rhetoric of Loss: A Study in Perception and Meaning* (Austin: University of Texas Press, 1983); Philip M. Weinstein's *What Else But Love? The Ordeal of Race in Faulkner and Morrison* (New York: Columbia University Press, 1996).

9. Walter Benn Michaels, *Our America: Nativism, Modernism, and Pluralism* (Durham: Duke University Press, 1995), 146, n.26.

10. Wolfgang Iser, Review of Heide Ziegler, *Ironie ist Pflicht: John Barth und John Hawkes—Bewusstseinsformen des amerikanischen Gegenwartsromans*, *Modern Fiction Studies* 43.2 (Summer 1997): 490.

11. The figure of the unhealing wound is usefully explored by Weinstein, e.g., 117, 189.

12. "We—he and us—should confederate: swap him the rest of the economic and political and cultural privileges which are his right, for the reversion of his capacity to wait and endure and survive" (402).

13. Karl Zender's essay in this volume interprets such contradictions as signs of Faulkner's ambivalence about giving up male privilege and control. Faulkner's writing seems to me both defensive about this masculine control and often embarrassed about everything that sense of control ignores.

14. Chick's encounter with Lucas and Molly gestures toward what Kelly Oliver describes as a necessary reconception of paternity, maternity, and the family that would deconstruct oppositions in Western philosophy, phenomenology, psychoanalysis, and popular culture between the absent, disembodied father and the physical, nonsocial mother:

> If, however, in its beginnings parental love is not some abstract pleasure in reproducing oneself, but it is the pleasure in touching and smelling the infant—already a social pleasure, which becomes the pleasure of intersubjective interaction—then we can imagine a paternal Eros that is not the pleasure in reproducing the self or mastering or possessing the child. We can imagine a paternal Eros that is formed through touch and smells between father and infant which set up the loving relationship between father and son, between father and daughter. This paternal Eros is developed through the exchange of affective drives which sets up the possibility of the infant's *growth* into language and culture through affective attunement and the repetition of bodily dynamics rather than through threats and law."

Oliver's book is called *Family Values: Subjects Between Nature and Culture* (New York: Routledge, 1997), 230.

15. Toni Morrison, *Jazz* (New York: Knopf, 1992), 173.

16. Kelly Oliver, 231, 232.

17. Susan Donaldson, "Welty, Faulkner, and Southern Gothic," American Literature Association Symposium, Cancun, Mexico, 14 December 1996; Weinstein, 131.

Whose America? Faulkner, Modernism, and National Identity

JOHN T. MATTHEWS

"No spika."

—*The Sound and the Fury*

"You ain't heard nothin' yet."

—*The Jazz Singer*

A deracinated Quentin Compson drifts through *The Sound and the Fury*, no longer a Southerner, since the South he knows belongs to the past, and not yet a modern American, to whom regions hardly matter.[1] At moments, his usual gloom over the loss of place flares into the kind of social resentment more characteristic of his brother Jason. Quentin jokes bitterly, for example, that the ultimate consequence of ending Southern slavery is that blacks like Deacon, unlike "whitefolks," no longer have to work for a living.[2] Elsewhere he notes nastily that he can hear Julio, his immigrant accuser, "scratching himself" (144). Quentin recoils from the dirty dark ethnic "sister," whose refusal to disappear prompts her unwilling host to reword the future national anthem as "Land of the kike home of the wop" (125). Threatened with social befoulment, Quentin suffers the loss of purity in the corruption of his flesh-and-blood sister, whose departure organizes Quentin's experience of an entire way of life coming to grief.

In his recent reinterpretation of American modernism, Walter Benn Michaels takes these instances of Quentin's racial mourning as primary examples of "nativism," an outlook, according to Michaels, that distinguished the dominant culture of the American 1920s. American nativism was hostile to internal minorities on the basis of their foreign or un-American connections.[3] The murmurs about "durn furriners" in Quentin's section, or Jason's louder bigotry, put the novel in the context of post-World War I anxieties about defending the "purity" of American society. For nativists, American identity came to be understood as something one inherited by blood rather than acquired through citizenship. One supporter of the Johnson-Reed Immigration Act of 1924, which se-

70

verely reduced foreign influx, went so far as to argue that no immigrant could ever be truly "Americanized" because what made a person an American involved nature, not naturalization: American traits "must come to us with the mother's milk, the baby's lisping questions, and grow with our nerves and thews and sinews until they become part and parcel of our very being."[4]

As nativism prevailed in social and political matters between the wars, culture helped reshape the public imagination. In this view, a work like *The Sound and the Fury* attests to a strategic shift in the conceptualization of identity. If blood descent determines who belongs to America (and whom America belongs to), then the family gains primacy as the ultimate ground of national identity. Both race and nationality become functions of the family. For Michaels, Faulkner's very preoccupation with family goes far to establish the centrality of blood ties as the determinant of selfhood. Faulkner's characters cannot act properly until they know who they are; they do not know who they are until they know the mysteries of their ancestry. In *The Sound and the Fury*, Quentin's attraction to incest figures the desire for purity of lineage, just as Jason's anti-Semitism typifies a strategy for segregating "Americans" from those who retain ethnic characteristics. Recall that Jason claims not to hold a man's religion or appearance against him: " 'I have nothing against jews as an individual,' I says. 'It's just the race' " (116).

Michaels's important book, entitled *Our America*, assails nativist modernism for its alleged embrace of these racist tendencies. Since *Our America*'s roster of nativist modernists includes virtually all white canonical U.S. writers of the 1920s, as well as many writers of color who fail to imagine alternatives to nativist discourse, this book broadly indicts literary modernism for the spread of damaging notions about race and ethnicity. Moreover, Michaels extends his critique by arguing that when blood-based theories of racial difference lost scientific credibility, theories of *cultural* difference arose to accomplish the same ends. The principles of cultural relativism, by which all cultures are granted putative equality through their uniqueness, proved, according to Michaels, the inadvertent key to establishing culture as the basis of identity and ethnic distinctiveness. As a result, Michaels insists, multiculturalism conceals a pernicious form of racism at its core since it coerces individuals to accept their racial identity as a function of the culture into which they happen to be born. I shall return to this argument because it bears directly on the question of Faulkner's pertinence as a writer to our present society. First I want to explore an alternative account of race in modernist literature and the modernist Faulkner in order to challenge the reductivist position on modernism that *Our America* represents.

In one respect it is difficult to gainsay Michaels's identification of the *The Sound and the Fury*'s effects with the force of the characters' desires. Virtually all of the criticism that attempts to fathom the representation of race in *The Sound and the Fury* begins with the acknowledgment that it has been displaced to the margins or the unconscious of the text. John Irwin's landmark psychoanalytic study reads blackness as that which has been abjected by the psyche in process.[5] Thadious Davis patiently reconstructs the lives of the Gibsons against the neglect of their characterization, a neglect that mirrors the social subjugation of those permitted only to endure.[6] Eric Sundquist dismisses the way incest mystifies miscegenation in *The Sound and the Fury*, and impatiently awaits Faulkner's rendezvous in *Light in August* with his and the South's master problem: the burden of racial slavery.[7] Philip Weinstein admits that the representation of African Americans in the novel functions as pastoral background.[8] Even more direct efforts to read race interlinearly, like mine and Richard Godden's, depend on strategies for making matters of race present because the novel wishes them to remain absent.[9] We search *The Sound and the Fury* for the contours of the *subject* that commands so much of Faulkner's mature engagement with his native soil, the racialized history that so thoroughly organizes three of Faulkner's greatest novels over the next decade, *Light in August*, *Absalom, Absalom!*, and *Go Down, Moses*.

Yet there is a central anomaly in the apparent indifference of *The Sound and the Fury* to representing the inner lives and points of view of the African Americans who share the Compsons' world. Although Faulkner narrates the novel through the mentalities of declined white aristocrats, *The Sound and the Fury* unstintingly reproduces the *sounds* of African American vernacular. In Benjy's section, black voices are as common as white, and speak to him more familiarly than any but Caddy's. Likewise, Quentin's memories of childhood, which so pointedly depend on the recollection of spoken words, recall the copresence of black and white speech. Even the older Quentin remains within hailing distance of voices like Deacon's, or that of the black man in Virginia waiting for the train to pass. Jason must fend off the insult of all sorts of voices that refuse to silence themselves at his bidding, including those of his coworker Job, his house servants, and the young men he tries to hire, all of whom talk back black to the discredited master. The formal structure of *The Sound and the Fury*, moreover, directs the reader to see the Reverend Shegog's black vernacular sermon as the fulfillment of the balked efforts at communication preceding it. But what does it mean for Faulkner to locate in African American speech the heart of his aesthetic ambition? What does it mean that the Compson discourse, springing out of racial denial and evasion, opens itself to the sounds of racialized speech? And what does it mean that Faulkner's most experimental, most deliberately "artistic" and private novel is also the one most thoroughly saturated with dialect?

At one point in *The Sound and the Fury*, Quentin Compson wanders around suburban Boston and strikes up a conversation with some local boys. They comment on the oddness of his speech:

> "Are you a Canadian?" the third said. He had red hair.
> "Canadian?"
> "He dont talk like them," the second said. "I've heard them talk. He talks like they do in minstrel shows."
> "Say," the third said. "Aint you afraid he'll hit you?"
> "Hit me?"
> "You said he talks like a colored man." (73)

It is true, as several critics have noted, that the blacks in *The Sound and the Fury* speak like minstrel figures.[10] But in the exchange above, we are reminded that Faulkner's whitest of narrators also sounds like a black man, or at least like a minstrel show man. I want to argue that *The Sound and the Fury* is Faulkner's breakthrough novel in part because it realizes the relation between a (putatively) transregional modernism and racialized speech. That relation—between literary language and American dialect—itself proves dialectical because it points to the history of struggle between the races in the United States. A *social* dialectic of domination and resistance, of identification and subjugation, embeds the verbal oppositions between standard and dialect speech, between modernist textuality and the sounds of people speaking. Faulkner discovers his voice as a novelist, becomes "Faulkner," in the work of realizing the modernist sensibility as a function of his region's and nation's history. The interplay of dialects in Faulkner's writing marks how Faulkner's modernist voice comes to life as he accepts the obligation to tell about the South. Minority voices and subjects are not incidental to Faulkner's achievement; they are its foundation.

When Faulkner briefly fits Quentin with the minstrel mask, he indicates as well his own device as author for talking black. According to Michael North, such "vocal blackface" embodies much more than the familiar primitivist leanings of modernists like Conrad, Gertrude Stein, or Picasso.[11] Rather, the widespread practice of "racial ventriloquism" (i) among modern writers aims to challenge the authority of standard English and traditional literary forms. North describes several associated effects of dialect writing in prominent modernists. Eliot and Pound, for example, who incorporate vernacular speech in their early poems and adopt dialect masks like "Ol Possum" in their private correspondence about poetry, see dialect as a way to unsettle the dominance of iambic pentameter in verse. Conrad, himself a linguistic "outsider" to his chosen English, explores the links between the practice (and defense) of "standard" English and the racial solidarity upon which it is predicated. Conrad glimpses a future creolized world culture in which English splays into accepted dialects and foreign languages mix with the Queen's tongue. Claude McKay attempts to write dialect verse but discovers that he cannot extricate dialect from the significance and value already assigned it by the dominant culture, in which it serves as an emblem of "natural" speech. For these and other writers, according to North, "[m]odernism . . . mimicked the strategies of dialect and aspired to become a dialect itself"; "dialect became the prototype for the most radical representational strategies of English-language modernism" (i).

The use of dialect permitted modernist writers to signal their dissent from Victorian bourgeois mores, from the social privilege undergirding standard English, and from the imperialist power that employed it as the instrument of colonial subjugation. Conrad, one of the writers Faulkner repeatedly cited as a major influence, virtually announces the modernist project in the preface to his novella, *The Nigger of the "Narcissus."*[12] The novelist seeks to turn the text into a living experience for the reader: "My task which I am trying to achieve is, by the power of the written word, to make you hear, to make you feel—it is, before all, to make you *see*! That—and no more: and it is everything!"[13] Author and audience must share a good deal for writing to achieve this immediacy; it depends on "the subtle but invincible conviction of solidarity that knits together the loneliness of innumerable hearts" (Conrad 145–46, North 38). Conrad's intention might remind us of Faulkner's dream of transcending language altogether in Shegog's sermon, hearts "speaking to one another . . . beyond the need for words" (294), or of Faulkner's description of writing as arresting life's motion on the page so that it returns to living motion for the reader.

The modernist irony, as North elaborates it for Conrad, rests on the effort to transcend language through language. Hence Conrad's obsession with scenes of storytelling and written documents, as if he seeks to master the toils of language only to become encoiled in them. Such a position resembles Faulkner's despair at the "splendid failure" of writing *The Sound and the Fury*, and both reflect a widespread modernist frustration with the limitations of language to deliver the thing itself. Yet the obstacle to full intelligibility in the *Nigger of the "Narcissus,"* in North's account, proves to be less metaphysical than social. It inheres in the race of the title character. The Negro James Wait cannot be properly deciphered. The name entered for him on the ship's log has been smudged and cannot be made out. Wait's effort to identify himself goes awry when he calls out his last name, only to have it misunderstood by the crew as a command. The linguistic confusion introduced by Wait attests to a deeper racial incomprehension: the narrator describes the black man's face as "pathetic and brutal; the tragic, the mysterious, the repulsive mask of a nigger's soul" (Conrad 11, North 39). North concludes that "the title character of *The Nigger of the 'Narcissus'* thus seems to have entered the story only to be expelled, as if to illustrate the threat that racial and cultural difference pose to the solidarity on which successful reading and writing depend" (North 40). Conrad both identifies with the racial outsider—as in his relation to English or his critique of imperialism—and also confronts the danger to artistic success of linguistic chaos.

Conrad reduces Wait at the moment of his death to a gibbering "nigger," not the speaker of proper English he has been, but an example of what Conrad elsewhere called "the debased jargon of niggers" (North 40). Notice how the following description of Wait's final unintelligibility strikes a Shakespearean chord that Faulkner must have heard:

> James Wait rallied again. He lifted his head and turned bravely at Donkin, who saw a strange face, an unknown face, a fantastic and grimacing mask of despair and fury. Its lips moved rapidly; and hollow, moaning, whistling sounds filled the cabin with a vague mutter full of menace, complaint and desolation, like the far-off murmur of a rising wind. . . . It was incomprehensible and disturbing: a gibberish of emotions, a frantic dumb show of speech pleading for impossible things, promising a shadowy vengeance. (Conrad 93)

Here the "despair and fury," the "dumb show of speech," mark the racial status of "debased" utterance. The evocation of the English poetic tradition signals the very source of solidarity Wait's dialect endangers. When Faulkner glosses the Compson brothers' narratives of despair with the same passage from *Macbeth*, however, he reverses Conrad's racial polarity. In *The Sound and the Fury*, it is the erstwhile beneficiaries of a discredited social regime who tell tales signifying nothing. The "shadowy" meaning in the black man's "moaning" gains intelligibility in Faulkner's text. The principal of the dumbshow is a white man; the poet of grandeur, a black guest speaker.

Faulkner signifies on Conrad's initial confusion of proper name with command, of "Wait" with "wait." Benjy's famous mistaking of the golfer's call for his sister's name signals a kind of linguistic innocence; he does not know that aural signifiers may refer to more than one signified because such relations are conventional, not natural. But the semantic differences denoted by the two referents for "Caddy"/"caddie" also measure important social differences. Where Benjy only has ears for a proper name, the novel hears the designation of a social category. To the innocent "master," "Caddy" means a unique person, the unthinking solidarity of family, the promise of understanding. To the servant Luster, "caddie" means a generic function, the bond of blackness to service, and the promise of work. Faulkner offers his version of Conrad's verbal ambiguity in order to initiate the reader into "proper" and "common" ways of reading. He sets the stage for the novel's dialectical exploration of racial difference.

Faulkner strengthened his determination to perform "vocal blackface" in *The Sound and the Fury* by imagining elsewhere what it would mean to turn black voices away from his fiction.[14] In the short story "Black Music," Faulkner tells the tale of Wilfred Midgleston, an architect's draftsman in Manhattan who one day loses all his middle-class inhibitions, believes himself changed into a faun, scandalizes one of his female clients, and flees to a Latin American port city where he lives as an eccentric Anglo.[15]

One of "Black Music'"s important contributions to Faulkner's thinking about modernism and race involves the story's discrediting of any simple bourgeois primitivism. The protagonist leads an obscure middling life, envious with his wife of the better sort whose doings appear in society columns, and agog at the wealth enjoyed by his firm's clients. One of these, Mrs. William Van Dyming, undertakes to rebuild an estate in the Virginia countryside. Sent from New York to deliver the most recent drawings, Midgleston experiences an epiphany on the train; through the window a face stares back at him, a horned goatish image that he finally identifies as a satyr, or what he calls, in Faulkner's version I suppose of a Brooklyn accent, a "farn." Fortified by a good deal of whiskey forced on him by some concerned passengers, Midgleston disembarks, buys a tin whistle at the country store, disrobes, and makes a startling call on the Van Dyming party. Our poor man's Pan frightens Mrs. Van Dyming into a romp through the woods. Telling the story years later, Midgleston believes that his client felt the same release of natural impulses as her satyr pursuer. Somehow an escaped bull completes their *ménage*, and Midgleston reports that he could hear Mrs. Van Dyming "going wump-wump-wump inside like a dray horse."[16] Aroused, and afraid of that arousal, she barely whispers her husband's name to come help, "like she was afraid she would wake him up" (817).

Faulkner combines a criticism of upper class indulgent consumption with ridicule of an inadequate response to it. Van Dyming represents urban industrial capital, with "Park Avenue clothes and his banks and his railroads" (808). The mountain estate Mrs. Van Dyming designs will translate this wealth into a display of American imperial glory. The Van Dymings want one structure "built to look like the Coliseum and the community garage yonder made to look like it was a Acropolis" (807). Culture will be annexed and ornamentalized in this vision; the terraced hillside will become an outdoor theatre, where guests will stage their own plays. But the real point of the project—producing a spectacle of capital's power—appears at an intermediate stage, when Mrs. Van Dyming insists that the theater be built first "so the company could set and watch them building the Acropolises and Coliseums" (810).

Midgleston's effort to scandalize this embrace of imperial capitalism and official culture, however, amounts to little more than adolescent play-acting. Tin whistles are no more Pan's pipes than New York draftsmen are fauns. Midgleston's escape from his commonplace life leaves him pitifully isolated in Rincon. The very town functions as a reminder of the economic colonialism Midgleston flees since the Americans there work for a "Universal Oil Company." Midgleston's social death derives from his refusal to speak the actual language of the people whose marginalization corresponds to his own. Twenty-five years a resident of the town, "he hasn't learned more than ten words of Spanish" (799). The tension between English and Spanish clearly reflects the racial politics of Rincon. The Universal Americans loudly maintain "the superiority of the white race and their own sense of injustice and of outrage among the grave white teeth, the dark, courteous, fatal, speculative alien faces" (802). Catherine Kodat has shown that "Black Music" forecasts the importance of blackness in Faulkner's art; the dark faces embody the racial subject in Faulkner's later writing, a relation to blackness figured in Midgleston's sleeping each night in a roll of tarred roofing paper.

But the Midgleston of "Black Music" and "Carcassonne" prefers to let dark voices remain incomprehensible. Midgleston fails to recognize that his own dissatisfaction with American bourgeois life and his confinement to a service class put him in a position to identify with the alienated natives of Rincon. He might have seen this connection even earlier, when he becomes a faun in Virginia, since satyrs were part of the iconography of the myth of the "black beast rapist" (Godden 107). The satyr incapable of satisfaction acts like a racist projection of a free black man; Midgleston is called a "maniac at large" in the local Virginia newspaper, and Mrs. Van Dyming confuses her human pursuer with the rampaging bull, "with its glaring eyes and the shape of a huge beast with horns" (816). But the story refuses to racialize the draftsman's dissent. The fact that the Americans all talk in a rural Southern dialect suggests that Rincon is a lost corner of Yoknapatawpha.[17] The narrator's informants use expressions like "do you reckon," "got it stole," "durn fool," and so on. Rincon is a *strategically* displaced site since the story obliquely comes to terms with the South's material connection to racial exploitation, imperial mentality, and the silencing of minority speech. In mid-1927, three years before Faulkner was preparing "Black Music," his father had subdivided a plot of family land to allow a Standard Oil franchise and a service station to come to an Oxford streetcorner.[18]

If there is a black muse in *The Sound and the Fury*, it wears a minstrel mask. I am aware that identifying Faulkner's dialect effects in the novel with a form of minstrelsy may not break the critical cul de sac delimiting the work's representation of African American experience. But two recent major reconsiderations of blackface minstrelsy have complicated the meaning of one of America's earliest and most nationally characteristic popular arts. Eric Lott's *Love and Theft* (1993) and Michael Rogin's *Blackface, White Noise* (1996) each argues that blackface minstrelsy negotiates white culture's guilty indebtedness to black labor and culture.[19]

For Lott, minstrelsy's confused racial bearings seem most apparent in its first years, in the late 1820s and '30s, when white performers like T. D. Rice blacked up to dance Jim Crow in Northern cities. Lott insists that the peculiarly intense form of racial imitation involved in blackface constituted "a profound white investment in black culture," in which one may see in "early blackface minstrelsy the dialectical flickering of racial insult and racial envy" (18). Rogin, on the other hand, doubts the degree of racial envy in an expressive form so relentless and pointed in its ridicule of African Americans. However, he does not dispute Lott's contention that a surprising number of modern African Americans like W. E. B. Du Bois and James Weldon Johnson thought well of minstrelsy, counting it as authentic black culture deriving from plantation life (Lott 16). Rogin appreciates most the role of blackface in the movies, beginning with Al Jolson's *The Jazz Singer* and continuing through the blackface minstrel films of the thirties and forties. Muscials like *Dixie* or *Holiday Inn* (in which Bing Crosby appears in blackface) Rogin sees as crucial precursors to the race problem films of the late forties and fifties that helped prepare the way for the civil rights movement. (One of those films was Claude Brown's version of *Intruder in the Dust* in 1949.)

One pattern for the use of blackface governs its significance as much in the 1930s as the 1830s: newcomers or outsiders to the dominant culture resorted to blackface to stage the process of "Americanization." By masquerading as the disfranchised and despised, working class immigrants could imaginatively enact their own freedom to recreate themselves and accomplish assimilation. This is how blackface minstrelsy originated among the Irish of Northern cities, and it returned, according to Rogin, in the attraction of American Jews to blackface entertainment in the 1920s and '30s.

The path toward the modernization of minstrelsy led from live vaudeville to the movies, with Jewish performers prominent in both. According to Rogin, Jews were especially drawn to blackface because they saw their own ethnic alienation in the historical oppression of America's people of color. The landmark film in the tradition is *The Jazz Singer*, in which the Jewish Al Jolson plays a cantor's son, Jakie Rabinowitz, whose vocal gifts lean more toward the secular than the religious. Jakie's success singing pop carries him away from his family; his Old World father disowns him for being the first son in five generations not to serve as cantor. Eventually the prodigal returns on the eve of his father's death to sing the service for his congregation. The gesture reconciles him to his father, gratifies his mother, but does not interfere with the professional career of the rapidly assimilating "Jack Robinson," who goes on to musical stage stardom.

Rogin demonstrates that the Jewish son uses blackface to enact an Oedipal rebellion against the world of his ethnic fathers. Like any number of Hollywood moviemakers themselves, the Jolson character sets a course for assimilation and Americanization. He borrows blackface to do so, taking on the combined opprobrium and pleasure associated with the form. The black mask represents, in Rogin's reading, all that must be left behind in the passage into modern Americanized mass culture: ethnic religiosity, outdated stage forms like vaudeville, even the suddenly eclipsed silent movie. For as you know, *The Jazz Singer* is also notable for being the first sound film. When American cinema finds its voice in 1927, it turns out to be black. Through racial cross-dressing, or cross-speaking, movies like *The Jazz Singer* could suggest a route of white escape from traditional elite culture, could suggest a site for the formation of mass culture, could render the diversity of an ethnically "mongrelized" pluralistic society through the interplay of dialect and standard speech, could practice the ritual of self-making through assumed identity, and could dramatize the process of "whitening" necessary to the transformation of Old World ethnicity into New World Americanness.

When ethnic whites put on a version of African Amercian identity as a means to achieving American identity, we must worry that the transfer of cultural goods from black to white custody involves something more than mere borrowing. Isn't such impersonation and imitation also a kind of theft? In *The Jazz Singer*, Al Jolson resorts to blackface to gain a career, to kindle a romantic interest, to regain his mother, and finally to reconcile Gentile and Jew. Such expropriation of African American expressive means—and falsified stereoptyped means at that—consigned blacks only to deeper obscurity in the mass cultural imagination. Lott observes that minstrelsy's cultural borrowing mystifies the material dependency of whites on commandeered black labor. That is, minstrelsy disguises white indebtedness to black labor by making blackface figures ridiculous and helpless dependents on whites. But it also encodes white guilt by reenacting a cultural theft and placing whites in the position of dependent blacks.

In many similar ways, I wish to argue, Faulkner evokes the minstrel tradition to signal his own complex alienation from the South's dominant social and cultural traditions. The force of his disillusionment with Southern mythology makes him something of a native outsider, a kind of hypothetical person of color. One recalls his article for *Ebony* magazine entitled "If I Were a Negro," and in *Mosquitoes* Faulkner includes a brief self-portrait in which he casts himself as "a little kind of black man."[20] The character hearing this description wants clarification: "A nigger?" "No. He was a white man, except he was awful sunburned and kind of shabby dressed" (144–45). Thadious Davis rightly finds fault with the minstrel elements governing the physical descriptions and dialect speech of black characters in *The Sound and the Fury*; such stereotypes do betray limitations of imagination. But the limitations belong to an entire white culture that for more than a century spoke through and for blacks. As Eric Lott says, "after minstrelsy . . . there could be no simple restoration of black authenticity" (103). Faulkner reproduces minstrel and dialect forms partially and self-consciously because he senses the long history of cultural work they performed. Vocal blackface acknowledges the record of economic, social, and cultural robbery that conditions any attempt by whites in the Jim Crow South to comprehend black lives. Vocal blackface points to the lack whites sensed in themselves when they projected licentiousness and pleasure-taking onto blacks. *Blacks* in blackface, such as Luster, express the growing irreverence of a people learning to speak out. But blackface also measures the deep-seated artifice that helped disguise the repeated acts of dispossession, violence, denial, misrecognition, and contrition sustaining slavery and its aftermath. That "Jim Crow," the term for a system of apartheid, descends from the signature piece of minstrelsy suggests the persistence of a cultural mode laden with ideological investments. To be white is already to have entered a system of representation in which blacks are stolen from, subordinated, silenced, patronized, and then—perversely—envied; but to be self-consciously white, as Quentin and Faulkner learn, is to discover *within that identity* the denial of black labor, black nurture, black expression. When Faulkner finds his voice, the year after *The Jazz Singer*, he discovers it to be black, too. The voice of the white Southerner sounds like a black man sounds like a minstrel showman. *The Sound and the Fury* proves to be Faulkner's first talkie.

When Luster goes hunting for his missing quarter, he banters with some friends doing laundry in the branch. The patter and punchlines suggest a minstrel routine (Davis 79), a kind of comedic entr'acte, but several prominent themes of historical minstrelsy appear in this early episode. The tone of the bit makes Luster look like a slow-witted bumbler. He lets himself get tricked out of the golfball after carelessly losing the quarter he needs for the show. When he's asked "Where bouts you lose it?" he answers in classic simpleton fashion: "Right out this here hole in my pocket" (10). Against the broader backdrop of Luster's incessant search for missing assets, however, his exaggerated incompetence and dependence on white kindness serve to disguise serious disadvantages. The white golfer simply confiscates Luster's property, and his act confirms a whole system of unfair exchange: "White folks gives nigger money because know first white man comes along with a band going to get it all back, so nigger can go to work for some more" (10). Faulkner ventriloquizes an embarrassment over the material impoverishment of blacks by reproducing the double move of minstrelsy—to assign blame to the victim while reenacting the victimization.

Minstrelsy traditionally associates blackness with the indulgence of physical appetites. Such projections derive from the well-rehearsed pathology of white self-denial and hypocrisy among the slaveocracy, and the imagining of black bodies as sources of nurture and erotic satisfaction. Only the blacks in *The Sound and the Fury* seem to show any appetite. The whole black community is determined to indulge itself at the carnival. Luster's trips to the "getting place" mark the site of bodily satisfaction, as do the ribald exchanges over finding balls. Lott notes the "widespread preoccupation in minstrel acts with oral and genital amusement" (145). Luster threatens to eat Benjy's entire birthday cake himself, as if to illustrate the exaggerated mouths associated with blackface. (The showman tries to find room for fire in the mouth of the white spectator Benjy, but with no success.) When white performers applied blackening, they carefully avoided smearing grease around their mouths, perhaps to exaggerate the organ of laughter and ingestion associated with their models. The practice also highlights the site of vocal production, as if blacked up sound had to pass through the encircling trace of whiteness. You may recall Faulkner's own pen-and-ink sketch of a dancing couple framed by a jazz orchestra. The animated players appear to be black, but they have white lips, as if Faulkner was conceiving blackness as blackfacedness.

At the same time, this first minstrel-like routine in the novel also allows Faulkner to voice black indictment of an unjust society. When one laundress observes that nobody is making them go to the show, another answers ruefully: "Aint yet. Aint thought of it, I reckon" (10). Nothing, even entertainment, escapes the potential for coercion in the Jim Crow South.

As in post-Reconstruction blackface performed by African Americans, moreover, certain of the comedic passages in *The Sound and the Fury* ridicule white arrogance and stupidity. Luster inventively incorporates his charge into a running vaudeville bit. When a friend notices that Benjy won't be much help looking for the coin because "[h]e wouldn't know a quarter if he was to see it," Luster replies, "He can help look just the same" (10). Master Idiot Compson may as well get a taste of peremptory obedience and senseless work. Luster goes on to make his white man a dummy to his byplay. When Dilsey reminds him to do whatever Benjy wants, Luster calls for testimonial: "Dont I always does what he wants. Dont I, Benjy" (35). Has Luster broken Mr. Jason's window? "I never done hit. . . . Ask Benjy ef I did" (165). Luster gets the laughs, Benjy the comic abuse, in this reversal of white blackface prerogatives. For the Faulkner in vocal blackface who voices this scene, the minstrel elements permit complex feelings of identification, denial, guilt, surrender, and self-abuse.

Jason Compson's coworker at Earl's hardware store also plays a minstrel defense to the bigotry directed at him. Jason's narrative makes little room for black voices, and those we hear are heavier with dialect. But Job continues minstrelsy's work of turning black discomfiture into a source of amusement. Jason complains that if Job were a boll-weevil, he'd work himself to death waiting for the cotton that won't even be planted until Job finishes assembling the cultivators. Job picks up the conceit in tempo and wittily transforms it into a figure of economic futility, admitting that "nobody works much in dis country cep de boll-weevil" (115). Jason means to ridicule black laziness and dependency on white productivity, his constant themes, but Job sees his plight exactly in the boll-weevil's: forced to consume what others own, used to working "ev'y day in de week out in de hot sun, rain er shine," compelled to be tenants often on the move, and oddly thriving despite all-out opposition. Faulkner repeatedly authorizes Job's quick-witted putdowns of Jason, the best of which throws a snapper at Jim Crow injustice. When Jason calls Job a fool, he fires back: "I dont spute dat neither. Ef dat uz a crime, all chain-gangs wouldn't be black" (139).

Faulkner does not let us forget that the purpose of minstrelsy was to humiliate African Americans. The one moment Luster looks most like a minstrel figure—his "eyes backrolling for a white instant" (190)—he braces to receive a blow from his white master's hand. When Quentin evokes the plantation darky of minstrelsy, it is to ridicule the fatuous self-deception of modern racial abuse: "how Gerald throws his nigger downstairs and how the nigger plead to be allowed to matriculate in the divinity school to be near marster marse gerald" (65). Quentin—perhaps subvocalizing Shreve's mockery—affects black dialect here to satirize Southern white delusions about black people's childlike loyalty.

The layers of projection and artifice coloring one race's conception of the other govern the representational transactions of minstrelsy as a cultural form. Faulkner's pursuit of the "other" silenced dialects of his father's world leads him, in the case of African Americans, to the tradition of minstrelsy that had become inseparably associated with white production of black speech. The consequences of this association productively help Faulkner confront the obstacles to a white male Southerner's visitation of an historically plundered and defensive culture. The enormous richness of black folk culture, an imaginative wealth that many modernists recognized as the only legitimate source of cultural renewal and authenticity in the machine age, that richness could not be appropriated without triggering yet another round of thieving masquerade.[21]

Faulkner practices dialect writing as he deconstructs it, maintaining maximum self-critical awareness while reproducing what has not yet been entirely produced. Dialect in *The Sound and the Fury* appears not as itself but in opposition to "standard" English. The power of Shegog's sermon, for example, arises from its contrast to the superstandard style that frames it.[22] The opening paragraphs of the last section, with their artful alliteration and vertiginous suspended clauses, sets off the homely simplicity of the vernacular: "Dilsey" . . . "All right, here I is" (159–60). It is as if the shuttling between "white" and "black" language creates the only authenticity possible, a kind of dialectical artifice that acknowledges the means of production in the midst of reproduction.

Such scruple carries through to the climactic sermon as well, since the reader is never allowed to forget that the narrator remains outside the triumphal moment of communication. The edge of racial difference keeps the narrator's distance; his racial epithets for the "monkey"-like Shegog mark the interior spaces of a segregated social and cultural system. Shegog's own rhetorical effects arise from the *passage* between black and white forms. Faulkner here identifies the process of dissolving between whiteface and blackface that organizes dialect plurality in *The Sound and the Fury*. Shegog at first looks too black to the congregation because of his contrast with the coffee-colored home minister. Yet when he begins speaking, he sounds too white to be black at all—like Al Jolson in *The Jazz Singer*, who even in blackface sounds white. When Shegog pauses to adjust his address, he begins to blacken his voice in order to communicate more genuinely with his audience. Yet though his new sound seems as "different as day and dark from his former tone" (294), the sound of his dialect lags behind: "Brethren" is what the new sermon begins with, a word that remains standard in pronunciation and orthography. "Brethren and sisteren," Shegog continues, now nodding toward the grammatical forms of dialect ("sisteren") but not the aural. Not until *after* the congregation has experienced the transcendence of words in the direct communication of hearts, not until Shegog has already assumed the "attitude" of "a serene, tortured crucifix" does his "intonation, his pronunciation" become "negroid" (295).[23] And when the sounds of preaching in dialect finally may be "heard" in the novel's print, the narrator, like the reader, remains at a remove, not quite able to make out why the sermon moves its listeners so fully, nor of what exactly Dilsey has seen the first and the last. The only white man present—Benjy—sits "rapt" in a "gaze" of perfect incomprehension. Faulkner refuses to dodge the fundamental inauthenticity that laces this moment of indisputable eloquence, symbolic gravity, passion.

The discomfort of Shegog's sermon for many readers, I suspect, derives from Faulkner's deliberate attempt to incorporate the burden of representational and social history in the efforts to comprehend racial difference. Notice how stagily Quentin's man on the mule appears in the Virginia countryside:

> The train was stopped when I waked and I raised the shade and looked out. The car was blocking a road crossing, where two white fences came down a hill and then sprayed outward and downward like part of the skeleton of a horn, and there was a nigger on a mule in the middle of the stiff ruts, waiting for the train to move. How long he had been there I didn't know, but he sat straddle of the mule, his head wrapped in a piece of blanket. . . . (53)

Quentin must raise the shade, and later the window itself, before he can communicate with this figment, who himself must raise the curtain on his head. The lines of fence form the bell of a horn, an instrument that shows up again in the comparison of Shegog's voice to an alto horn, as if this black figure comes to Quentin theatrically outlined by the traces of black music. The image of a horn's "skeleton" marks the history of black mortality that binds land, labor, and song. Later, when Luster shows up for the church service, he wears a fancy new straw hat: "The hat seemed to isolate Luster's skull in the beholder's eye as a spotlight would, in all its individual planes and angles. So peculiarly individual was its shape that at first glance the hat appeared to be on the head of someone standing immediately behind Luster" (172). Like a minstrel player spotlighted on stage, Luster's individuality is delivered by a counterfeit presence concealed behind his face. His author?[24]

If Quentin were to follow Al Jolson's path to independence, he would sacrifice an identification with blacks in order to leave behind the world of his fathers and make himself a modern American. Quentin does head out on the path to Oedipal rebellion, of course, and it corresponds to an invitation to leave the South and join the nation. Not only does Harvard make him realize how the South differs from the rest of North America, it also prompts him to reform his sectional behavior in one key respect: "When I first came East I kept thinking You've got to remember to think of them as colored people not niggers" (53). Quentin's imaginative exploration of what it would be like to be Charles Bon, like Faulkner's experiment with blacking up a white man in *Light in August*, signals Quentin's alienation from his native views of race. Quentin narrates Bon's story in Boston; Faulkner writes some of *Light in August* in New York City. In part Quentin's Oedipal rebellion against the South leads him toward the realization that "the best way to take all people, black or white, is to take them for what they think they are" (86).

For this reason Quentin refuses to convert from Southerner to American if he must perform the sacrifice of blackness that in *The Jazz Singer* achieves ethnic assimilation. Quentin understands that "The Star-Spangled Banner" promises integration into the "land of the kike and the home of the wop" *because* such integration is withheld from blacks. With what fond dream of national pluralism must Deacon march in ethnic holiday parades, wearing a Yankee uniform and carrying an "Italian flag."[25] As ever, though, the dialect that augurs assimilation in *The Sound and the Fury* is spoken not by ex-slaves but by ex-Europeans. When Julio takes Quentin to court for damages, he demands the rights of a citizen. The dark complected Italian and his sooty sister resemble the Southern blacks Quentin is more familiar with. That Quentin experiences this episode partially as a reflection of his native predicament may be suggested by the dialect spoken by the officer and the squire who apprehend him. Beginning with the name Anse, and continuing with expressions like "Shet up" and "you durn furriner" and "Air you satisfied the gal aint took any hurt, you, there?" (85, 87), we appear to be at least in an aural flashback to Mississippi. Unlike Quentin's nostalgia-induced plantation darky, however, who sits and waits for white masters to toss him Christmas gift coins, Julio seeks legal indemnification for the theft of sister and loss of labor. At first "no spika," but soon American voice and rights. As a self-conscious Southerner, Quentin knows too well how Negroes were sacrificed to Americanization. The birth of the modern nation after Reconstruction lay through the crucifixion of blacks, as Thomas Dixon's novels helped envision. Quentin rejects that sacrifice, though he can imagine little more than identifying with their subjection—like joining his shadow by drowning, as the "niggers say."[26]

Walter Benn Michaels wishes to discredit modernist representations of race in America because, in my judgment, he prefers the postmodern solution of forgetting race by forgetting history altogether. "The real question," he writes, "is not *which* past should count as ours but why *any* past should count as ours" (128). The only freedom from racism turns out to be freedom from race as embodied in cultural difference. But Michaels takes the scientific refutation of any essential basis for race to an absurd conclusion by arguing that we should be free to choose and change our cultural affiliation on the basis of our behavior. The result of such freedom, as Michaels himself puts it, is the reduction of the concept of identity to nothing: "why does it matter who we are?" (128). Culture becomes one more commodity to be acquired and updated at the discretion of the postmodern consumer. Surely the achievement of Faulkner's writing is to defend against such historical disregard. Hardly complicit in any naive espousal of nativism, as Michaels would have it, Faulkner's texts plumb not only the history of relations between the races, but also the historical means for representing them. Michaels's reduction of literature to the simple reproduction of dominant ideas like nativism offends the power of literature to reflect critically. And by discounting the relevance of cultural history to individual action, it refutes itself. It is less new historicism than no historicism.[27]

Faulkner's investment in the complexities of minstrelsy and dialect writing reemerges most strikingly in *Go Down, Moses*. Especially in "The Fire and the Hearth" and "Pantaloon in Black," Faulkner again resorts to blackface material to highlight the misrecognitions that organize racial subordination. Faulkner maintains contact with the blackface tradition because through the 1940s it would keep the imagery of interracial fluidity, mixture, and pleasure alive in the popular imagination, particularly in the movies. According to Rogin, blackface musicals, however regressive in their own right, channelled useful material toward the serious race films of the late forties, such as *Home of the Brave*, *Pinky*, and, of course, Claude Brown's adaptation of Faulkner's *Intruder in the Dust*.

The title of "Pantaloon in Black," fusing European *commedia dell' arte* with rural black folkways, suggests a clash between mode of representation and subject matter. The pantalone story appears to offer an awkward analogue for the fate of one of Faulkner's humblest protagonists. Though Rider may be cuckolded in a way—by Death, he only distantly resembles the figure of the aging merchant more typically associated with the duped pantalone. The deputy does set out to turn Rider into the butt of his comedy, but even that account hesitates before the enigma of Rider's behavior.

Judith Sensibar has recently explained the *commedia* elements in the story as a resurgence of one of Faulkner's earliest masks for the artist, that of Pierrot.[28] In her important study of Faulkner's racial psychology,

Sensibar sees Rider as an embodiment of a Faulkner newly confronted with the obligation to acknowledge and mourn the maternal black contribution to his identity. In this view, Mannie's death approximates Mammie Callie Barr's, and both represent the lost physical nurture and pleasure located in the black female body. Adult Southern white males typically repress that loss; Faulkner's boldness in "Pantaloon" is to accompany Rider into the raw expression of grief over it.[29] Sensibar insightfully notes the structural parallel between Faulkner's early *commedia* Pierrot and that of the minstrels Eric Lott describes as creating an image of "mammy" out of unconscious racial guilt. The history of blackface minstrelsy suggests deep cultural roots as well for Faulkner's personal associations.

In a 1915 article for *Scribner's*, the literary scholar Brander Matthews first traced American blackface minstrelsy to antecedents in European popular culture, the *commedia* foremost among them.[30] Granting that familiar American performers like T. D. Rice and Dan Emmett gave distinctive form to the stage practices that became American Negro minstrelsy in the 1820s and '30s, Matthews argues that many of minstrelsy's standard bits derived from French and Italian street comedy. Later scholars have suggested origins for blackface characters in several *commedia* figures, especially the servant Harlequin, a clown who spoke a variety of dialects and wore a black mask considered African in its features.[31] These attributes of Harlequin fed into the evolution of the American Jim Crow, who is described in the following terms by one student of Rice's "Ethiopian Operas": Jim Crow is "irrepressible in his pursuit of pleasure and lazy and inefficient at work. . . . [H]is sexual passion is equally irrepressible; his loves always inconstant. His speech is marked by ludicrous malapropisms and incongruous usages. . . . He is . . . without ambition . . . and . . . immune to more than transitory troubles," though he possesses "child-like simplicity" and "eternal good humor."[32]

Rider is an abortive Harlequin Jim Crow in the deputy's story, a clown excused from his role by the irony of the white man's puzzlement. Rider actually does become Pantalone, however; several traditions of *commedia* portray Pantalone not only as virile, a lusty athletic lover of life like Rider, but also masked in black. Rider may be a pantaloon in black because the Jim Crow South steals his love; he becomes a cuckold to the lost prospect of belonging to a respectable black working class.[33]

I have been arguing that the minstrel tradition provides Faulkner with the means both to search for the long-suppressed black voices composing his world and also to register the kinds of historical interference that complicate the reproduction of speech and experience across a racial divide. Minstrelsy's European roots, embedded in the title of "Pantaloon in Black," point to the layers of recess through which blackness appears in white representations of it; even minstrelsy proves less a white imitation of black culture, or even a white projection of black culture, than a white-blackened descendant of white culture.[34]

Faulkner accidentally compounded this state of affairs in a reference he once made to the work of his younger contemporary Eudora Welty. On April 27, 1943, Welty received a fan note from a reader of her novel *The Robber Bridegroom*, one "Faulkner," whom she had never met: "Dear Welty," it reads, "You are doing fine. You are doing all right. I read THE GILDED SIX BITS, a friend loaned me THE ROBBER BRIDEGROOM, I have just bought the collection named GREEN something, haven't read it yet, expect nothing from it because I expect from you. You are doing very fine. Is there any way I can help you? How old are you?"[35] In misattributing "The Gilded Six-Bits" to Welty, Faulkner was recalling a short story actually written by Zora Neale Hurston. It appeared in the August 1933 issue of *Story* magazine, a volume Faulkner was sure to have seen since his own story "Artist at Home" was also published in it.

Hurston's story relates a marital crisis in which a black man discovers his wife to have cuckolded him. Joe and Missie May enjoy a simple life together, though it is marked by playful exuberance. One evening Joe takes his wife into town to visit the new ice cream parlor established by a sweet-talking man from Chicago named Otis Slemmons. Some weeks later Joe arrives home from his job earlier than usual on Saturday evening and surprises his wife in bed with Slemmons. Stunned, Joe withdraws into silence, until the couple eventually reconciles, largely around the birth of their son, who proves the "spittin' image" of Joe.

The resemblances to aspects of "The Fire and the Hearth" and "Pantaloon in Black" are remarkable. At the end of the story, Joe signals his reconciliation with Missie May by buying her a fifty-cent bag of candy kisses, a gesture echoed by Lucas when he buys Mollie a sack of candy after their divorce has been called off. Joe's anxiety about infidelity and paternity portend Lucas's outrage over Mollie's removal to Zack Edmonds's household. But it is the core problem of "The Gilded Six-Bits" that relates it to "Pantaloon in Black" since both stories detail black seduction by white attitudes toward money-making and advancement. Like Rider and Mannie, Joe and Missie May make a ritual out of payday. Saturdays, Missie May sweeps the yard earth into fresh patterns, its sidewalk carefully edged with bits of broken glass. Joe signals his return by tossing the week's silver coins through the open door: "there came the ring of singing metal on wood."[36] When Missie May's infidelity sends Joe into a kind of shock, he reacts much like Rider, with uncontrollable, unfathomable laughter: the caught philanderer Slemmons is so unnerved by this response that he "considered a surprise attack upon the big clown that stood there laughing like a chessy cat" (93). Again like Rider, Joe's deep feeling and complexly motivated behavior prove incomprehensible to whites. The clerk who sells Joe the candy marvels much like the deputy: "Wisht I could be like these darkies. Laughin' all the time. Nothin' worries 'em" (98).

Hurston's story unmasks two forms of inauthenticity. One involves this last reference to Joe's "darky" behavior; Hurston evokes the minstrel tradition pointedly so as to show its inadequacy to the anguish of her characters and the unexpected ways they defy stereotype. Hurston also casts doubt on the worth of white models of progress to African Americans. Joe first courts trouble when he decides to show off his wife to the sophisticated newcomer. Slemmons has dazzled the envious Joe with his slick "Chicago talk" (91), with his obvious prosperity, including a belly that makes him "look lak a rich white man" (89), and with two fantastic ornaments, a five-dollar gold piece for a stick-pin and a ten-dollar one on his watch chain (90). Missie May first falls in love with those coins, but when Slemmons flees the love couch and leaves behind his watch charm, Joe realizes that the ten dollar showpiece is nothing but a gilded fifty-cent piece. Slemmons's money resembles his talk, a false argot that represents the danger of playing white when white ways prove nothing but the gilt of falseface.

I want to read Faulkner's misattribution of this story as testimony to both the liabilities and liberties available to the writer's imagination. A decade after its appearance, "The Gilded-Six Bits" may have been on Faulkner's mind again at the time he was writing "Pantaloon in Black," about three years before the letter to Welty in 1943. If Faulkner assumes the story's author to be white, a plausible inference if *The Robber Bridegroom* is foremost on his mind, then he is implicitly acknowledging the shared premise that white writing about Southern blacks must accommodate a cultural history of (mis)representation. Both "Gilded Six-Bits" and "Pantaloon in Black" confront the ways in which white social and cultural forms interfere with black attempts at self-representation.[37] If, on the other hand, Faulkner assumes the author to be black, as hinted by the condescending terms of the offer to help, his recollection of Hurston's story suggests the grounds of a remarkable identification with black writing about Southern blacks. By resorting to Hurston's story at the moment of his deepest exploration of black vernacular culture, Faulkner practices a respectful, perhaps even redemptive, form of blackface, one fully apprehensive about the limits of racial comprehension. Either way, Faulkner, in an unguarded moment, poignantly echoes the contradictory impulses that organize the history of white representations of African Americans: impulses to appropriate, reap profit, gain inspiration, even envy; and impulses to repudiate, reverse dependence, forget, even humiliate. Faulkner's writing illuminates this agonizing exchange like no other white writer's because he so openly faces its history.

NOTES

1. See Philip Fisher on the pendulum swings between regionalism and national unification (Introduction, *The New American Studies: Essays from "Representations"* [Berkeley: University of California Press, 1991], xii). Fisher argues that the North and most of the rest of the country achieved national unity through the emergence of a consumer culture after the Civil War. A kind of regionalism reemerged in the twenties based on ethnicity, a regionalism of multiple cultures. Quentin suffers the loss of the "South" in both historical phases, first as the capitulation of the South to modernization, then as the irrelevance of geographical region to immigrant ethnic culture.

2. William Faulkner, *The Sound and the Fury*, ed. David Minter (New York: Norton Critical Edition, Second Edition, 1994), 82. William Faulkner, *The Sound and the Fury*, The Corrected Text (New York: Vintage International, 1987).

3. Walter Benn Michaels, *Our America: Nativism, Modernism, Pluralism* (Durham: Duke University Press, 1995), 2.

4. Charles W. Gould, *America, A Family Matter* (New York: Charles Scribner's Sons, 1922), 163 (as quoted in Michaels, 8).

5. John T. Irwin, *Doubling and Incest/Repetition and Revenge* (Baltimore: Johns Hopkins University Press, 1975).

6. Thadious M. Davis, *Faulkner's "Negro": Art and the Southern Context* (Baton Rouge: Louisiana State University Press, 1983).

7. Eric Sundquist, *Faulkner: The House Divided* (Baltimore: Johns Hopkins University Press, 1983).

8. Philip M. Weinstein, *Faulkner's Subject: A Cosmos No One Owns* (New York: Cambridge Univeristy Press, 1992).

9. John T. Matthews, "The Rhetoric of Containment in Faulkner," in *Faulkner's Discourse*, ed. Lothar Hönnighausen (Tubingen: Niemeyer, 1989), 55–67, and Richard Godden, "Quentin Compson: Tyrrhenian Vase or Crucible of Race?," in *New Essays on "The Sound and the Fury,"* ed. Noel Polk (New York: Cambridge University Press, 1993), 99–137.

10. See Davis, 78–79, and Catherine Gunther Kodat, "Modernism in Black and White" (Ph.D. diss., Boston University, 1993), 91.

11. Michael North, *Dialect of Modernism* (New York: Oxford University Press, 1994), 6.

12. Faulkner mentions Conrad's significance in an introduction he drafted for a reissue of the *The Sound and the Fury* planned for 1933: "After The Sound and The Fury [sic] and without heeding to open another book and in a series of delayed repercussions like summer thunder, I discovered the Flauberts and Dostoievskys and Conrads whose books I had read ten years ago" (William Faulkner, "An Introduction for *The Sound and the Fury*," ed. James B. Meriwether, *Southern Review* 8 (N.S., 1972): 708.

13. Joseph Conrad, *The Nigger of the "Narcissus"*, ed. Robert Kimbrough (New York, Norton, 1979), 147 (quoted in North, 38).

14. Kodat first proposed the important connection between the oblique thematic of race in "Black Music" and "Carcassone" and Faulkner's more direct efforts to depict the Gibsons in *The Sound and the Fury*. See particularly " 'The Ultimate Edge of the Flat Earth': Writing Blackness in *The Sound and the Fury*" (chapter 3, 69–98).

15. Joseph Blotner suggests that "Black Music," like its better-known companion story "Carcassonne," probably originated in Faulkner's New Orleans material and was revised

about the time in January 1930 that he began preparing his short story submission campaign (*Faulkner: A Biography*, 1-vol. ed. (New York: Random House, 1984), 253–54.

16. William Faulkner, *Collected Stories of William Faulkner* (New York: Random House, 1950), 816.

17. I wish to thank Noel Polk for pointing out to me that "Rincon" means "corner" in Spanish, and that there are many towns in South America so named.

18. Frederick J. Karl, *William Faulkner: American Writer* (New York: Weidenfeld & Nicolson, 1989), 313.

19. Eric Lott, *Love and Theft* (New York: Oxford University Press, 1993) and Michael Rogin, *Black Face, White Noise: Jewish Immigrants in the Hollywood Melting Pot* (Berkeley: University of California Press, 1996).

20. William Faulkner, *Mosquitoes* (New York: Liveright, 1927), 144.

21. Michael North says that dialect writing was popular in England and America in the early decades of the century in that it was held to be " 'purer' than the standard written language because it was less affected by printing, education, and 'elocution masters' " (North 19).

22. Stephen Ross, *Fiction's Inexhaustible Voice: Speech and Writing in Faulkner* (Athens: University of Georgia Press, 1989), 101–9.

23. Like most critics, Noel Polk credits Shegog's sermon with the achievement of "a direct, unmediated experience of the signified" (*Children of the Dark House: Text and Context in Faulkner* [Jackson: University Press of Mississippi, 1996], 135). In my reading, the moment never transcends the social frames that organize it as a white representation of black discourse. Polk is especially insightful on Faulkner's registration of class and race in the novel's use of dialect. Also see Mark W. Lencho, "Dialect Variation in *The Sound and the Fury*: A Study of Faulkner's Use of Black English," *Mississippi Quarterly* 41:3 (Summer 1988): 401–19, on Faulkner's aesthetic purposes in depicting significant variety of African American Southern dialect in *The Sound and the Fury*.

24. Kodat reads this scene differently, as marking the narrative's confrontation with the limits of representation that characterize all descriptive efforts, including those of the novel's first three monologues (95–98).

25. See Cedric Gael Bryant for an interpretation of Deacon as a trickster figure who employs the minstrel mask "to adapt to and exploit an environment that recognizes only the masks and not the individual behind them" ("Mirroring the Racial 'Other': The Deacon and Quentin Compson in William Faulkner's *The Sound and the Fury*," *Southern Review* 29 [Winter 1993], 37).

26. Godden argues that Quentin's entanglement with the Italian immigrants offers him a way to reimagine his obsession with Caddy's purity. Julio and his little sister introduce a new historical frame, one that shows how darkness, dirt, and promiscuity function as historically determined markers of class and labor. This new experience invites Quentin to revise the now outmoded Southern plantocractic narrative—racist and misogynistic—that has shaped him. Godden reduces Quentin's predicament to a matter subject to simple volition, as if Quentin could decide simply to repudiate one narrative and accept another. Godden's view seems mistaken on at least two counts: not only does Faulkner's writing exhaustively register the forces of historical conditioning, with their deep saturation of mental and even somatic structures of response, and with their capacities for disguise and self-deception, but Faulkner also grasps the collective and wide-ranging social efforts required to dismantle and replace a centuries-old institutions. That the immense social gains made during the civil rights movement have not delivered the U.S. from personal, institutional, and ideological racisms confirms just how prescient Faulkner was in detecting some fundamental incommensurablility when the immigrant narrative is attempted by African Americans. Quentin certainly does fail to commit himself to remaking the future, but he leaves that to others not because he denies its justness (as Jason does), but because he accepts the historical judgment of guilt, loss, doom.

27. Important challenges to Michaels's thesis have been swift to appear. Two of the most telling are by Charles Altieri, who disputes Michaels's assumptions about identity, culture, and authorial agency ["Whose America Is *Our America*: On Walter Benn Michaels' Charac-

terizations of Modernity in America"], and Marjorie Perloff, who faults Michaels's narrow range of examples ["Modernism without the Modernists: A Response to Walter Benn Michaels"]. Both essays appear in *Modernism/Modernity* 3.3 (1996): 107–13 and 99–105, respectively. See also Michaels's "Response," 121–26.

28. Judith Sensibar, "Who Wears the Mask? Memory, Desire, and Race in *Go Down, Moses*," in *New Essays on "Go Down, Moses*," ed. Linda Wagner-Martin (New York: Cambridge University Press, 1996), 101–27.

29. Sensibar's interpretation of Rider does not address two problems to seeing him as the author's representative: the story does not make Mannie a maternal figure in any way, nor does Faulkner suggest that "blackface" helps Rider express his grief. In the story, what is perceived as Rider's minstrel-like behavior remains the sign of white *incomprehension*.

30. Brander Matthews, "The Rise and Fall of Negro-Minstrelsy," *Scribner's* 57 (1915): 754–59.

31. George F. Rehin, "Harlequin Jim Crow: Continuity and Convergence in Blackface Clowning," *Journal of Popular Culture* 9:3 (Winter 1975): 691.

32. Rehin, 693, quoting James H. Dormon, "The Strange Career of Jim Crow Rice," *Journal of Social History* 3 (1969): 108–22. The habits of abuse associated with the Pantaloon figure more soberly forecast Rider's violent end: "Pantaloons . . . had to endure comic punishments and farcical indignities: they were exploded from mortars, dismembered, daubed with stove blacking, flung in the mud, laughed at, spurned, and left with the bill for others' entertainment" (David Mayer III, *Harlequin in His Element: The English Pantomime, 1806–1836* [Cambridge: Harvard University Press, 1969], 44.) Also see, Allardyce Nicholl, *The World of Harlequin: A Critical Study of the Commedia dell'Arte* (Cambridge: Cambridge University Press, 1963).

33. John T. Matthews, "Touching Race in *Go Down, Moses*," in *New Essays on "Go Down, Moses*," 21–47.

One scholar suggests that the name "pantaloon" derives from *pianta leone* ("to plant the lion"), a reference to the passion for profit that drove Venetian merchants to spread the flag of Venice—bearing the image of the Lion of St. Mark—around the world (Pierre Louis Duchartre, *The Italian Comedy: The Improvisation Scenarios Lives Attributes Portraits and Masks of the Illustrious Characters of the Commedia dell' Arte*, trans. Randolph T. Weaver [New York, 1966], 180).

34. No one has written more eloquently about the mutual distortions created by the self-masking of blacks, and the corresponding masking of whites by the falseness so imposed on blacks, than Ralph Ellison: "Here the 'darky' act makes brothers of us all. America is a land of masking jokers. We wear the mask for purposes of aggression as well as for defense, when we are projecting the future and preserving the past. In short, the motives hidden behind the mask are as numerous as the ambiguities the mask conceals" (*The Collected Essays of Ralph Ellison*, ed. John F. Callahan [New York: Modern Library, 1995], 109).

35. Joan St. C. Crane, "William Faulkner to Eudora Welty: A Letter," *Mississippi Quarterly* 42.3 (Summer 1989): 223–27.

36. Zora Neale Hurston, "The Gilded Six-Bits," *Complete Stories* (New York: Harper Perennial, 1995), 87.

37. Neil McMillen details the impediments to the emergence of a black bourgeoisie in post-Reconstruction Mississippi (*Dark Journey: Black Mississippians in the Age of Jim Crow* [Urbana: University of Illinois Press, 1990]). See chapter 5, "Black Labor / Black Capital."

"Faulkner before Faulkner":
The Early Career as a Construction in Retrospect

HANS H. SKEI

The early years of William Faulkner's literary career would be of little or no interest if they were not followed by the major years. It is inevitable and understandable that much energy has been devoted to an examination of the apprenticeship period in relation to the great novels and stories. It is valid and worthwhile to study the texts Faulkner wrote before *The Sound and the Fury*, but one does not have to look for signs of the later genius in any and all texts, and one should not expect regular and continuous growth from text to text or causal connection between early and later texts. The texts of the early years can only be given the significance we often see that they get because they are written by a writer who finally became the "Faulkner" created by such works as *As I Lay Dying*, *The Sound and the Fury*, *Light in August*, *Absalom, Absalom!*, *The Hamlet*, and *Go Down, Moses*.

This means that I am not accusing people of bad scholarship when I maintain that Faulkner's early years are always a construction in retrospect, and I accept that even the early career is a valid research area. It obviously commands our interest because of the later Faulkner, but if we concentrate on the texts of the period, a careful study of influences, relationships, and even growth is warranted.

The very concept of career is problematic, and seen in terms of the politics of modern literary criticism, it is anything but innocent. Faulkner is also a Dead White Male in the Western Canon, and even if the period I discuss most certainly is a precanonical phase in Faulkner's career, it has become what it is because of the steadily and at times rapidly growing reputation of Faulkner. Whether the New Critics or the New York intellectuals should be made responsible for certain revisions of Faulkner's career is not for me to say, but without Malcolm Cowley and numerous New Critics, among whom Cleanth Brooks must have been the most influential, the understanding of Faulkner's career would have developed in different ways.[1] As Faulkner scholars we *know* that his work is superb, but such knowledge should also be subject to scrutiny.

93

Faulkner's career does not amount to much before 1930, and in a certain sense his career begins and can be outlined—by reference to agents, publishers, correspondence, negotiations, serial rights, film rights, and so forth—only after 1929 or 1930. Yet we easily, if not inevitably, fall prey to one of the many career fallacies also for the other periods, if we think in terms of growth and development or look for an overall design in light of which most things can be explained.

Another aspect of the concept of career in a time of much debate about historiographical methods must be mentioned briefly. As I have already indicated, I think we should be very much on the alert and avoid all kinds of teleological thinking, of cause and effect, of historical or other types of contextualization which have as their aim to explain Faulkner's early or late work. Narrative history has its obvious role in biography and literary history and descriptions of literary careers. But we should—after Foucault, White, and Barthes—accept that a career is always created, shaped, formed in one mode or another, and coherence and continuity come as a result of our effort to explain and understand, and are not inherent in the material itself.[2]

In his book on *The Sound and the Fury*, André Bleikasten has called the period before Faulkner discovered his own turf and his own material "Faulkner before Faulkner."[3] This might indicate that we somehow know who or what Faulkner, the real one, the one we care about, is, but also that there is a different one who comes first. This may indeed be true, yet the complete transformation of Faulkner into the author of the 1929 novel cannot be fully explained, and one would be wrong in searching for the child of the father in his early and formative years. This is, of course, nonetheless what is done all the time, in literary histories, in biographies, in surveys of his career and its changing phases. What seems to be an almost instinctive and natural wish for coherency and continuity makes us look to the early period to find possible causes for the incredible and rapid change that took place. It is in this sense that my approach must be understood—and I do not think my understanding is radical or new, but fairly obvious: The early career is a construction made possible only by our understanding of the later parts of the career and the way it has been understood—or created, if you like. The promises we find in the early career are only there because Faulkner later kept them. The artificial pastoral elegies of his early poetry command our interest only because of Faulkner's extensive later use of the pastoral mode—in *Light in August* and *The Hamlet*, to mention only two novels. The early career is interesting and bewildering, and only in retrospect is it at all possible to find unity and continuity in it. Faulkner's themes, subjects, narrative methods went in many directions; changed abruptly, so that one really has to believe very strongly in natural growth and maturation in order to force a design on his early production. That he himself very deliberately chose to do many different things, and perhaps even knew what he was doing, does not imply that we can reconstruct his early career and find sources, influences, and certainly not causes for the many rather surprising directions his early writing took. The literary texts from the period are of little merit and seldom convincing; even in retrospect they show little more than talent and definitely not genius. The texts are given significance and studied in great detail because they were written by the young and uncertain hand of one who became a great story teller, which also means that in the history of Faulkner scholarship this interest came fairly late. Let me make it absolutely clear that I do not believe in cause and effect, in linear development, in unbroken continuity in literary history or in the works of an individual writer. Talking about literary history, literary biography, or literary careers we have to use concepts and terms that are really metaphorical, but I cannot see that we have other tools at our hand. What we should do then, perhaps, is to treat the time-honored concepts as being *hypothetical*,[4] and comment on their use and function as we write. Even a simple discussion of a phase of one writer's literary career must thus become metahistory. I make this point because we must be allowed to establish connections, for example, between texts from the apprenticeship years and the major works of the thirties and forties, but we do not have to think in terms of cause and effect, growth, and maturation.

The formative years of the 1920s deserve to be studied as closely as any other biographical or historical facts of Faulkner's life, and at some point theoretical observations must end and practical literary scholarship begin. All I ask is that the early years be studied with careful attention to the problems I have outlined, and that the construction of this phase of Faulkner's career become more than a search for early indications of later greatness.

The facts of Faulkner's life and literary output from its earliest beginning up to 1929 are well established in biographical and other life and work studies. The evaluation of the significance or value of individual texts may differ from critic to critic, but it does not differ seriously among seasoned critics. I shall not repeat the commonplaces about Faulkner the apprentice for this audience. Let me just mention that Faulkner's second prose sketch to be published, "The Hill" (1922), rightfully has been hailed by critics as Faulkner's most important early short story. It shows an author in complete control of his material and foreshadows many narrative techniques and themes in Faulkner's later fiction. There is little doubt, however, that even if the New Orleans sketches meant good writing practice and 1925 thus became the most decisive among Faulkner's "formative years," the most important "discovery" of the early years is that of Yoknapatawpha itself, meaning that *Flags in the Dust*, or *Sartoris* as the published novel was then called, marks a new direction, a new interest, perhaps even a new Faulkner. As he struggled against reluctant publishers, bad reviews, and low sales, Faulkner discovered his own "postage stamp of native soil"[5] the basis for his fictional Yoknapatawpha County. With *The Sound and the Fury* (1929) a complete transition seems to have occurred, but in both books he was, to different degrees, "rewriting the homeplace," to use Richard Gray's phrase.[6] In the early Yoknapatawpha texts, notably those dealing with the Sartorises and the Snopeses, Faulkner is less immersed in his fictional world than he is in later works, and the writing is too self-conscious. Also, the early novels are flawed by an almost narcissistic self-involvement and lack of distance from the fictional characters, whereas in *The Sound and the Fury* he has complete control of material and of narrative strategies.

If we do not think of a writer's career in sociological terms, including marketing, sale, publication, and if we do not think of it in terms of the politics of literary criticism, but rather, as literary scholars, concentrate on the literary or aesthetical quality of the texts, we may take a closer look at one particular text from this early period. This also means that I return to the question of what can be achieved by searching for similarities and sources and even early indications of later mastery in texts from the twenties which were reused in later works. My understanding of the early Faulkner, before *The Sound and the Fury*, has changed somewhat as a result of my work with early materials for *The Hamlet*. Accordingly, I shall end this brief presentation by a note on *Father Abraham* and *The Hamlet*, to indicate how far Faulkner had advanced in his rewriting of the homeplace, as early as in 1926, and also to demonstrate how much interpretive help there may be in a comparison of early and late approaches to the same story material. I am not trying to establish a continuous line of development from *Father Abraham* through numerous aborted attempts at a Snopes novel and the writing of a number of Snopes short stories. My aim is simply to show that the writer who created the earliest Snopes story was a fairly competent writer, and that there are textual connections that warrant an evolutionary study of the Snopes material, even if the development does not show continuous progress or growth. It shows relentless struggle, it reveals a writer of great talent, who, fortunately, did not get round to "pulling together" the Snopes material until he had reached a generous acceptance of the ways of the world and its strange people which he clearly did not possess as a young man.

Probably the best, and certainly the most ambitious story written in this period of Faulkner's career, *Father Abraham* (1984)[7] is the germ of the Snopes trilogy and Faulkner's first attempt with material that he would return to over and over again in the years ahead, until, in 1940, he brought the many loose ends together in *The Hamlet*. *Father Abraham* shows that the basic outline of the whole trilogy was there at a very early point, since Flem's position as a Jefferson banker is described briefly before the story moves backwards to its central concern: the auction of the spotted horses. The quality of this text proves that Faulkner was on the right track, having found "his" people and his kind of stories, whereas the awkwardness of parts of the early manuscript story proves that he was still not quite ready for the big leap into the chronicle of the Snopeses. The strength of the story material itself lends narrative power to the text and is clearly what makes this an efficient and convincing story, more so than the narrative voice, point of view, juxtaposition of character. In other words. *Father Abraham* is an accomplished and enter-taining and skillful story primarily because of a happy idea (the Snopes clan and the horse auction) and a material too rich for the limits of a short story, not because of the narrative handling. In order to move from *Father Abraham* to *The Hamlet*, Faulkner had to go far beyond the histor-ical and sociological reasons behind this new class of people. He had to make his transition from self-involvement to the dialogic use of voice and character, and in the long period between the early Snopes material and the first Snopes novel, Faulkner reached levels of formal mastery, rhetor-ical forcefulness and thematic complexities unparalleled in American lit-erature in the twentieth century. Accordingly, the Father Abraham material would be used with very different perspective and effect when *The Hamlet* was written, but my whole point from a career perspective is that the ground plan, the basic outline of the Snopes saga, did not change, even if attitudes and point of view did.

If *Father Abraham* shows Faulkner at his best in the early period, why then did he not pursue his master plan and write the Snopes novel? The final page of the twenty-five-page manuscript[8] indicates that Faulkner may have tried to carry the Snopes material further, but stopped short. Knowledge of other aspects of his career or biography, or an understand-ing of the textual complexities the Snopes material presented if it were to be transformed into a novel, may explain why, since I think it is fair to assume a close relationship in time between *Father Abraham* and *Flags in the Dust/Sartoris*. This is also a period when Faulkner wrote early versions of a large number of short stories to be published in revised form only after 1930.

The writing of *Flags in the Dust* and the later revisions, which also meant cutting down the length, followed by what certainly must have taken all of the author's time for a long period, the writing of his perhaps most complex, most ambitious, most experimental, and most heartbreaking novel, *The Sound and the Fury*, completed by October 1928, gave him no time at all to return to the Snopes novel. There is thus much evidence to indicate the impossibility of a Snopes novel at this time, but there is also textual evidence in *Father Abraham* as well as in *Sartoris* of a writer who had his material and handled it well, but was not yet quite the craftsman his abundant material required. Or maybe he was better equipped from the beginning than we tend to think, and that impatience and too many ideas and work in all directions left no time for one or a few concentrated efforts to bring parts of his rich material to completion. I do not wish to push this idea further, since even the very idea of an early apprenticeship period is arbitrary and a construction.

How does one conclude the presentation of an early and comparatively insignificant part of a great writer's career, a part that we have constructed in retrospect so that it ends nicely before the real career begins? Let me phrase it this way: The facts of a writer's life and career cannot explain how the works were written or what made it possible to write them, yet knowledge of the career may be of great help in understanding individual works better. And this is, after all, what is important: We study Faulkner's career because of the literature he wrote, and we should always concentrate more on the books he wrote than on his life and career. His writing may not always be for the uplifting of people's hearts, and it does little to brighten our everyday life. But in the intricacies of the narrative patterns, in the incessant murmuring of almost inaudible sounds and silences, in the pervasive and traumatic darkness of his tales, there are magical and profound moments of beauty and wisdom, reminding us of that which we did not know we had lost or forgotten. The study of a writer's career must help us understand the literary works better. After all, art, as Schopenhauer said, "has always reached its goal."[9]

NOTES

1. See Lawrence H. Schwartz, *Creating Faulkner's Reputation. The Politics of Modern Literary Criticism* (Knoxville: University of Tennessee Press, 1988).

2. See for instance Hayden White, "The Historical Text as Literary Artifact" in *Tropics of Discourse* (Baltimore: Johns Hopkins University Press, 1978). See also David Perkins, ed., *Theoretical Issues in Literary History* (Cambridge: Harvard University Press, 1991).

3. André Bleikasten, *The Most Splendid Failure: Faulkner's "The Sound and the Fury"* (Bloomington: Indiana University Press, 1976).

4. See Perkins's Introduction to *Theoretical Issues in Literary History*.

5. Faulkner's own phrase, in interview with Jean Stein. See *Lion in the Garden*, ed. James B. Meriwether and Michael Millgate (New York: Random House, 1968), 255.

6. Richard Gray, *The Life of William Faulkner* (Oxford: Blackwell, 1994). The phrase is the section heading for part 3 of the book.

7. *Father Abraham* was published as a book in an original, limited edition in 1983 by the Red Ozier Press, New York, and then by Random House in 1984. Edited and with an introduction by James B. Meriwether, the text is based upon a twenty-four-page manuscript (1–22, 24–25). Several closely related typescripts, some of them fragments, are in the University of Virginia collection, of which a carbon typescript of fifty-one pages carries the story as far as page 19 of the manuscript. One typescript fragment (pages 18,19, and 29) bears the title "Abraham's Children," but clearly belongs to the earliest attempts with the Snopes material, not to the reiterated attempts to make a marketable short story from this material, beginning late in 1928 with the submission of a story called "As I Lay Dying" to *Scribner's Magazine*.

8. See Thomas L. McHaney, ed,. *William Faulkner's Manuscripts*, 15 (vols. 1 & 2). *The Hamlet* (New York: Garland, 1987). Quoted from Introduction, xiv.

9. "So ist dagegen die Kunst überall am Ziel" is the German phrase, found in *Die Welt als Wille und Vorstellung*. Quoted by René Wellek near the end of "The Fall of Literary History" in *Geschichte—Ereignis und Erzählung* (Wilhelm Fink Verlag, 1973).

Absalom, Absalom! and the Challenges
of Career Design

JUDITH BRYANT WITTENBERG

In 1956, in a prelude to his now excessively quoted statement about finding his "own little postage-stamp of native soil" and learning to sublimate "the actual into [the] apocryphal," Faulkner told Jean Stein that, after completing his first novel, *Soldiers' Pay*, he discovered "that not only each book had to have a design but the whole output or sum of an artist's work had to have a design" and that he thus went on to create "a cosmos of my own."[1] Faulkner's late-life affirmation of the need for careful planning of individual novels is intriguing, given the limited evidence that he ever approached them in a truly methodical way. At the same time, although his assertion that after 1926 he was motivated by the vision of developing a well-wrought career may be equally open to question, it has made possible—as Donald Kartiganer noted[2]—the numerous attempts by critics in recent decades to articulate the nature of Faulkner's "grand design," his overarching metatext. Whether this putative design has been seen as consciously thematic[3] or aesthetically evolutionary,[4] or unconsciously psychobiographical,[5] it has been a compelling idea for many Faulkner scholars.

Yet if it is not too retrograde in this post-poststructuralist moment to consider the Barthesian and Foucauldian pronouncements of some years ago that the very notion of the author is problematic, a modern construction impelled by the desire to discern unifying principles, textual explanations, and the resolution of contradictions,[6] then it should follow that the concept of authorial career design becomes equally dubious. In adumbrating various tendencies in modernist writing, Edward Said has suggested that the idea of "career" itself is a modern creation, permitting one "to see a sequence of intelligible development" as opposed to a group of "scattered occasions," a "miscellany of writings." For the writer as for the critic, says Said, "the notion of career as statement becomes privileged."[7]

Certainly some Faulkner scholars have questioned the appropriateness of discerning "a sequence of intelligible development" in the forty years of Faulkner's literary productions. André Bleikasten has provided us with one caveat in noting that "critical inspection is inevitably retrospection," and thus "the temptation is almost irresistible to read [an author's works] as the necessary fulfillments of a pre-established design." While such readings satisfy our hunger for consistency, order, and significance, says Bleikasten, they also lead us to ignore significant discontinuities in the work of a writer like Faulkner.[8] Indeed, Michael Millgate suggested at this conference some years ago that, because we do not know whether in the late 1920s and the 1930s Faulkner was directing his energies toward preconceived goals or simply giving those energies their head, perhaps we should apply the term "career" to Faulkner primarily in its earlier usage as meaning "a short gallop at full speed." Millgate said that it is entirely possible much of the impulse behind Faulkner's corpus emanated from a single visionary moment in the middle 1920s when he "thought of the whole story at once," conceiving not of specific tales but the possibility of narrative production on a grand scale, and added that the pattern of Faulkner's fiction reveals, not unity, but two quite divergent creative agendas.[9]

If such commentary by theorists and critics makes it difficult to proffer a vision of Faulkner's career grounded in decidability and linear development, it is perhaps also impossible to provide any synoptic sense of "the major phase," my assignment for this morning's discussion. "The major phase" is another concept under interrogation, most recently by Noel Polk, who calls it a "deleterious ideological construct" that prevents us from taking Faulkner's late works seriously.[10] Hence it may be more useful—certainly it appears a more manageable undertaking—to consider briefly one of Faulkner's own fictions from the so-called great period that rather explicitly dramatizes an unresolved struggle with both the concept and the implementation of career design. The tensions that inform Faulkner's major novels have been variously described—Philip Weinstein recently defined them as the clash between the desire for self-ratification and a series of subversive differential forces[11]—and I would suggest that in *Absalom, Absalom!* these tensions also coalesce quite distinctively around the issue of career.

However much one might dispute the issue of artistic progression, it is difficult not to see *Absalom, Absalom!* as a culminating text not only in Faulkner's own corpus but in American literary modernism and in twentieth-century literature generally. To be sure, Richard Moreland has argued that *Absalom* is limited in fundamental ways by its own adherence to modernist tenets,[12] but its combination of unusual narrative scope and sophisticated artistry has for several decades assured the novel a place in the front ranks of the literary pantheon, and should continue to do so. What is also notable about *Absalom* is the way in which it—perhaps more than any of Faulkner's previous novels—both celebrates and profoundly questions the feasibility of a career that proceeds by conscious design.

Sutpen and his grand design were the point of origin of the novel, according to Faulkner's public statements about its inception, and also serve as its compelling and endlessly interpreted center. Thanks to the available West Point concordances, we can tell that Faulkner rarely had used the word "design" in earlier novels of this period, and had never mentioned "career." Though he sometimes depicted working artists or artist-surrogates—one thinks, for example, of Gordon and other figures in *Mosquitoes* or Cash Bundren of *As I Lay Dying*—he did not explore the consequences of a lifelong dedication to a clearly conceived and ardently pursued vocational project. By contrast, in *Absalom, Absalom!* "design" appears at least thirty times and there is a reference to "the career of Thomas Sutpen," the story of the latter covering the entire sixty-two years of his life span and the nature of his design that serves as the obsessive focus of the multiple narrators.[13] Moreover, in his revisions to the manuscript, Faulkner added the word "design" at least three times.[14] How preoccupying a motif was "design" in particular reveals itself in the fact that, in a few instances, "design" appears many times on a single page of the novel—so frequently, in some instances, that it begins to sound almost meaningless, repetition without alteration, becoming at the last self-deconstructive.

Despite the prevalence of the term inside the text and the manner in which it is there thematized and interrogated, we have external evidence that Faulkner's own design for the novel, if in fact there was one, proved difficult to fulfill. (I might add here parenthetically that, somewhat sardonically, an early reviewer of *Absalom* described Faulkner as "not operat[ing] by filling in some design . . . constructed by the rational mind," and in 1936 even Malcolm Cowley used terms like "confused" and "partial failure" to characterize the novel.[15]) In at least one respect, Faulkner's conception of it altered and expanded over time; in early descriptions of *Absalom* to his editor, he called it the story of "a man who outraged the land, and the land then turned and destroyed the man's family"; a few months later he presented it as the tale of "a man who wanted a son through pride, and got too many of them and they destroyed him."[16] The addition of dynastic ambitions to Sutpen's territorial enterprise gave the final work a greater scope, but was perhaps partly responsible for Faulkner's problems in completing the novel. He later said that *Absalom* was, among all his work, the "hardest" to write, next to *The Sound and the Fury*,[17] and his letters of the early 1930s record some of his difficulties with it, including a worrisome sense at one point that "the book is not quite ripe yet," frequent interruptions to "boil the pot" by writing short stories, trips back and forth to Hollywood, and a period when he "got in trouble" with *Absalom* and so set it aside entirely to work on *Pylon*.[18] When asked in 1947 about his "best work," he mentioned three other novels and omitted the one most critics now regard as his greatest achievement and perhaps the finest American novel of the twentieth century.[19]

Absalom's demonstration of the almost inevitable failure of a design like Sutpen's—and, by implication, perhaps any rigidly methodical and intensely focused design—has been a subject for critical discussion over the years,[20] and the disastrous nature of Sutpen's grandiose project, in both its conceptualization and outcome, is too familiar to all of you to warrant further rehearsal here. What I might suggest is that in terms of authoriality, if you will, Sutpen could well have functioned as an important tutelary figure for Faulkner, embodying both the hazards and the splendors of visionary planning and intense commitment at a pivotal moment in his own career as a writer. Just why he might have chosen that particular time in the mid-1930s for such a consideration remains a matter of sheer speculation; its origin may have been, on the one hand, his "astonishment" to discover, not long after the publication of *Sanctuary*, that to at least some New Yorkers "I am now the most important figure in American letters,"[21] and, on the other, his awareness that he remained a minority writer notorious for his "difficulty" and fondness for "violence," and hence likely always to generate only a modest literary income.

Making allowance for the considerable differences involved, there is much about Sutpen's career, at least insofar as it appears to one of the fascinated observers who attempt to explain and tacitly memorialize him, that is reminiscent of certain characteristics of Faulkner's. According to Mr. Compson, Sutpen has a mind "at once visionary and alert," and apparently had a "fixed goal" in mind from an early age.[22] Prior to the Civil War, as a result of Sutpen's "singleminded unflagging effort" and his "secret and furious impatience" (25, 56), he manages to accomplish a great deal, clearing the virgin land to create an enormous plantation and acquiring a family, his second. Sutpen is, in these prewar years, impressive in his productivity, his thorough-going pursuit of both professional and personal fulfillment. Still, there is a "fate working behind the scenes," which eventually reveals itself in the form of uncontrollable external forces, such as the Civil War and its devastation of the South, and profound personal errors, such as his misunderstanding and mistreatment of the human beings in his own private cosmos. Though Sutpen manages resiliently and against all odds to recoup some of his losses in the postwar years, he is ultimately destroyed, largely by those one could describe as his own creations: his sons, his racially mixed daughter who burns down his house, and the poor white, elevated to the status of comrade, who murders him. Authorship proves no guarantee of immortality, and by the time-present of the novel there is little tangible trace of Sutpen.

Faulkner spoke at times of wishing to be, as a private individual, "abolished and voided from history,"[23] but he expressed eagerness at other times to be recognized for his artistic accomplishments, particularly after another American war had interrupted his work and the vagaries of critical reception and book publishing had almost eradicated him from the literary domain. Faulkner's difficulties with "fate" diverged sharply from those of Sutpen, to be sure, but in the period just before Malcolm Cowley's "rescue" of him in the 1940s, Sutpen must have seemed like a prophetic creation. Faulkner wrote somewhat plaintively to Cowley in 1944 that "I have worked too hard at my (elected or doomed, I don't know which) trade, with pride but I believe not vanity, with plenty of ego but with humility too . . . to leave no better mark on this our pointless chronicle than I seem to be about to leave,"[24] and one thinks of Sutpen, whose ultimate legacy is a burned-out shell of a house and a retarded great-grandson whose whereabouts are unknown.

The various observers who attempt, with some futility, to comprehend and evaluate Sutpen—or even to provide a cogent summary of his tale—tantalizingly evoke, at least in some of their rhetoric, the phrasing of certain of Faulkner's reviewers in the years preceding his completion of *Absalom, Absalom!* Some of them sound like Miss Rosa in her demonizing portrait of Sutpen that surrounds him with "sulphur-reek" (4): in the 1930s, Edwin Muir wrote of the "sulphurous and overcharged atmosphere" of Faulkner's novels, Henry Canby of the sadism of *Sanctuary*, Granville Hicks of the disease and violence of Faulkner's fictional world.[25] Still others, most importantly Evelyn Scott, used language similar to that of another Sutpen observer, Mr. Compson: in her long essay on *The Sound and the Fury*, Scott compared the 1929 novel to a "tragedy" with "the spacious proportions of Greek art," described the story as "the fall of a house," deemed Jason "a completely rational human being" who fails to consider emotional factors and thus "annihilates himself," and called the book's depiction of innocence "terrible" as well as "terrifying."[26] This is not to suggest, of course, that Faulkner took ideas for his great novel from his reviewers, but there are certainly intriguing parallels between their divergent evaluations of his earlier work and the divergent language and approaches of Sutpen's observers to the enigmatic figure at *Absalom*'s center.

The thematizing of language and communication in the novel enhances the authorial implications of the depictions. The role of language is foregrounded by the memorable passage describing it as that "fragile thread" by which the "corners and edges of men's secret and solitary lives may be joined for an instant now and then" (202). Although the event that precipitates Sutpen's obsession with his design is a "fall" into a world riven by economic and class divisions, it also involves what one might call the horror of the undelivered message and causes Sutpen to repeat with anguish, *"He never even gave me a chance to say it. Not even to tell it, say it"* (192). Sutpen's status as an author-surrogate is further suggested by the way he talks compulsively to his rare listeners, articulating the *"compelling dream"* that drove him to relentless hard work and repeated efforts to fulfill his design (134), and by his appearance at one moment as *"a madman who creates within his very coffin walls his fabulous immeasurable Camelots and Carcassonnes"* (129). That his only surviving legacy is a moaning and inarticulate great-grandson underscores the enormity of what has been lost linguistically.

Neither Sutpen's ultimate failure to realize his grand design nor the inability of his various appraisers to reach closure about either its nature or value fully subverts its haunting power. Faulkner's splendid novel manages to celebrate the power of that impelling vision as well as to critique it. Indeed, there is something almost Sutpenesque about one of the auxiliary apparatuses Faulkner prepared for the first edition of *Absalom, Absalom!* I refer of course to the map found among the endpapers to the novel, which names locales, characters, and events from Faulkner's past, present, and future fiction, and designates himself, the undersigned, as "sole owner & proprietor" of the imaginative world of Jefferson and Yoknapatawpha County. This may be a masculine ideal, as Philip Weinstein has suggested,[27] but it is powerfully affirming and generative, and Faulkner's fictive universe, as depicted at this time, is considerably larger than Sutpen's Hundred. Faulkner's growing sense of pride in his artistic accomplishment appears, in this volume, to be accompanied by an awareness of the needs of his prospective audience, for the ancillary materials to this complex literary production also include a chronology of events in the novel and a genealogy consisting of brief biographical sketches of all the characters. It would be ten more years before Faulkner would again attempt to make one of his difficult modernist texts more accessible to the reading public, when he prepared his appendix to *The Sound and the Fury*.

Thus the apparatus external to *Absalom, Absalom!* evinces Faulkner's proprietary pride in his fictional oeuvre as well as a growing sense of his potential consumers, both perhaps signs of a consciousness that he was fashioning a career, not simply discrete literary works, a career, more-over, that he was attempting with some success to move in the right direction. In addition, the narrative itself highlights the process of artistic creation in a celebratory way. Much has already been written by Faulk-ner critics about *Absalom*'s status as perhaps the most important metafic-tion in his corpus. Despite the bleak trajectory of the plot line, other factors such as what John Matthews has described as the "playful lan-guage that disseminates meaning,"[28] and also the "happy marriage of speaking and hearing" represented by the various narrators and their listeners—and by implication, the readers—serve as tribute to the plea-sures of the creative process and to the jouissance of encountering the writerly text.

Moreover, several aspects of the text serve either literally or metaphor-ically as indices to the metafictional nature of *Absalom, Absalom!*, from actual artifacts—such as the lawyer's ledger, the letters by Charles Bon and Mr. Compson, Sutpen's stone monuments, Rosa's odes to Confeder-ate soldiers and Bon's portrait—to suggestive elements such as the motif of architecture and the role of the French architect, whom General Com-pson describes as "an artist," and whose task it is in the planning of the mansion to serve as a "curb" to the excesses of Sutpen's "dream of grim and castlelike magnificence" (29) and yet bring the project effectively to fruition. The metafictional theme becomes even more explicit with Rosa's comment to Quentin that "maybe you will enter the literary profession" and some day "remember this and write about it" (5), and with Judith's commentary on the need to "weave [one's] own pattern into the rug," to make "at least a scratch . . . a mark" (101). The latter is couched in terms intriguingly similar to Faulkner's later public statements about his own personal goal as a writer, "to leave a scratch on that wall [of oblivion]" or to "leave a decipherable scar," a "scratch" on "the face of the supreme Obliteration."[29]

Pursuing a little further the notion that, in terms of Faulkner's own career design, Sutpen was both an admonitory and triumphal figure and that *Absalom* itself can be seen as a complex meditation on the subject, let me conclude by noting the provocative parallels between Sutpen's ambitious plans and certain of Faulkner's undertakings. Sutpen's design is striking in both its literal and visionary geography—the enormous ac-tual land mass and the Sutpen's Hundred project—and it is also similar to Faulkner's ventures in this domain. Faulkner's acquisition of land in the Oxford area during the 1930s was considerable, and included the property on which Rowan Oak sat, the twenty-four acres of Bailey's

Woods, and a three-hundred-and-twenty-acre farm outside of town, complete with tenant farmers and a commissary; by 1940 Faulkner was asserting somewhat boastfully that "I own a larger parcel of it than anybody else in town."[30] Faulkner also had a solidly geographical vision of his fictional enterprise, as represented by the map appended to *Absalom* and his later references to the "Golden Book" of "my apocryphal county," which Cowley described as his "inner kingdom."[31] Although Sutpen is finally defeated, in part by his own deficiencies, commentators inside the text testify to his "courage and shrewdness," and Faulkner himself later spoke rather approvingly of Sutpen's "grand design" and of the fact that he not only "dreamed so high," but "had the force and strength to have failed so grandly."[32] These latter phrases bear echoes of Faulkner's subsequent comments on other writers, whom he rated "on the basis of their splendid failure to do the impossible," and on his own work, which was impelled by the desire to write "one perfect book" but which "never matche[d] the dream of perfection."[33] However much *Absalom* may have allowed him to contemplate the "demon-driven" necessity of his writing career and to consider proleptically its risks, within ten years he was able to look back with pride and proprietorship and say, "By God, I didn't know myself what I had tried to do, and how much I had succeeded."[34]

NOTES

1. *Lion in the Garden: Interviews with William Faulkner, 1926–62*, ed. James B. Meriwether and Michael Millgate (New York: Random House, 1968), 255.

2. Donald Kartiganer, *The Fragile Thread: The Meaning of Form in Faulkner's Novels* (Amherst: University of Massachusetts Press, 1979), xiv.

3. See, e.g., Karl F. Zender, *The Crossing of the Ways: William Faulkner, the South, and the Modern World* (New Brunswick: Rutgers University Press, 1989); Walter Taylor, *Faulkner's Search for a South* (Urbana: University of Illinois Press, 1983).

4. See, e.g., Gary Stonum, *Faulkner's Career: An Internal Literary History* (Ithaca: Cornell University Press, 1979), Judith L. Sensibar, *The Origins of Faulkner's Art* (Austin: University of Texas Press, 1984).

5. See, e.g., David Minter, *William Faulkner: His Life and Work* (Baltimore: Johns Hopkins University Press, 1980); Judith Bryant Wittenberg, *Faulkner: The Transfiguration of Biography* (Lincoln: University of Nebraska Press, 1979).

6. Roland Barthes, "The Death of the Author," *Image, Music, Text* (Paris: Editions du Seuil, 1968); Michel Foucault, "What Is an Author?" *Language, Counter-Memory, Practice*, ed. Donald Bouchard (Ithaca: Cornell University Press, 1977).

7. Edward Said, *Beginnings: Intention and Method* (New York: Columbia University Press, 1985), 227, 234–35.

8. André Bleikasten, *The Most Splendid Failure* (Bloomington: Indiana University Press, 1976), 3–5.

9. Michael Millgate, "William Faulkner: The Shape of a Career," in *New Directions in Faulkner Studies*, ed. Doreen Fowler and Ann J. Abadie (Jackson: University Press of Mississippi, 1984).

10. Noel Polk, *Children of the Dark House* (Jackson: University Press of Mississippi, 1996), 248.

11. Philip M. Weinstein, *Faulkner's Subject: A Cosmos No One Owns* (New York: Cambridge University Press, 1992), 2.

12. Richard C. Moreland, *Faulkner and Modernism* (Madison: University of Wisconsin Press, 1990), 7–8.

13. Noel Polk, ed., *"Absalom, Absalom!": A Concordance to the Novel* (Ann Arbor: UMI Press, 1989).

14. Gerald Langford, *Faulkner's Revisions of "Absalom, Absalom!"* (Austin: University of Texas Press, 1971).

15. *William Faulkner: The Critical Heritage*, ed. John Bassett (London: Routledge & Kegal Paul, 1975), 196, 207.

16. *Selected Letters of William Faulkner*, ed. Joseph Blotner (New York: Random House, 1977), 79, 84.

17. *Faulkner in the University*, ed. Frederick L. Gwynn and Joseph L. Blotner (Charlottesville: University Press of Virginia, 1959), 281.

18. *Selected Letters*, 83–84, 92, 93; *Faulkner in the University*, 36.

19. *Lion in the Garden*, 53–54.

20. See, e.g., James Guetti, *The Limits of Metaphor* (Ithaca: Cornell University Press, 1967), Donald Kartiganer, *The Fragile Thread*.

21. *Selected Letters*, 53.

22. William Faulkner, *Absalom, Absalom!*: The Corrected Text (New York: Vintage International, 1986), 24, 40. All subsequent page references are included in the text.

23. *The Faulkner-Cowley File*, ed. and comp. Malcolm Cowley (New York: Viking, 1966), 126.

24. Ibid., 7.

25. *The Critical Heritage*, 100, 108, 120.

26. Ibid., 77–80.

27. Philip Weinstein, *Faulkner's Subject*, 1.

28. John T. Matthews, *The Play of Faulkner's Language* (Ithaca: Cornell University Press, 1982), 119.

29. *Faulkner in the University*, 61; *Selected Letters*, 125.

30. *Selected Letters*, 128; Joseph Blotner, *Faulkner: A Biography*, 2 vols. (New York: Random House, 1974), 986–1069.

31. *Faulkner-Cowley File*, 25, 166.

32. Ibid., 15; *Faulkner in the University*, 97.

33. *Lion in the Garden*, 81; *Faulkner in the University*, 65.

34. *Faulkner-Cowley File*, 91.

Faulkner's Career: Concept and Practice

Karl F. Zender

What do we mean when we speak of a writer's career? I first became aware of this question as an issue for contemplation some twenty years ago, when reading Gary Lee Stonum's *Faulkner's Career: An Internal Literary History*. "Does the term [career]," Stonum asks, "actually name some phenomenon that may become a specific object of study?" In common usage, the answer seems to be no. "Modern criticism," Stonum says, "employs the word 'career' regularly and innocuously, but only rarely asks what is meant in saying that writers have such things. In fact, the term does not usually designate a concept . . . noticeably distinct from the writer's life . . . , from his works . . . , or from both of them together."[1] Against such usage, Stonum proposes a more focused alternative. Viewing "career" dynamically, Stonum argues for an understanding of the concept "as the relation between the results of a course of writing and the furtherance of that course, that is, between the texts a writer has already written and the writing of new texts." Viewed this way, Stonum says, "[c]areer as past output becomes an active force in shaping career as continuing production" (15–16).

This approach to the idea of career has proven enormously useful when applied to William Faulkner's fiction. Stonum's book, Martin Kreiswirth's *William Faulkner: The Making of a Novelist*, Eric Sundquist's *Faulkner: The House Divided*—these are only a few of the works of criticism that have approached Faulkner's fiction as a conversation with itself, in the sense of tracing its representations of recurrent situations, themes, and motifs. And speaking personally, such contribution as I myself have made to the interpretation of Faulkner's fiction has arisen largely under the aegis of "career studies" as here defined; it has been a source of fascination to me to follow the arc of Faulkner's development, discovering how later manifestations of a fictional element arise out of and modify earlier ones. In the time allotted to me today, I wish to summarize a study of this sort that I have been engaged in for some time, centered on Faulkner's use of the incest motif. In so doing, I hope to add to our understanding of one of the central transitions of Faulkner's career—his shift from an early fiction of self, libido, and family to a later fiction of history, race, and region.[2]

So how does our interpretation of the incest motif change, if approached from a career studies perspective? The dominant tradition in Faulkner studies interprets the motif in either religious or psychoanalytic terms. In the words of Cleanth Brooks, the most persuasive exponent of a religious interpretation, Quentin Compson's obsession with incest in *The Sound and the Fury* expresses "alarm at the breakdown of sexual morality," by attempting to define a "point beyond which surely no one would venture to transgress." For John Irwin, the reigning psychoanalytic interpreter of the motif, incest joins with doubling, repetition, and revenge to enact a doomed Oedipal struggle against the priority of the father over the son and of the past over the present and the future. In its fullest extension, it expresses "the inability of the ego to break out of the circle of the self and of the individual to break out of the ring of the family," and it becomes a symbol "of the state of the South after the Civil War, . . . of a region turned in upon itself."[3]

Few would dispute the explanatory power of these approaches to the incest motif. But each also displays a tyrannizing unity, to borrow a phrase David Wyatt applied to Irwin's *Doubling and Incest* some years ago. Rather than seeing Faulkner's use of the motif as evolving as his career advances, both interpretations assert the existence of a single global meaning, repetitively enacted. Whether the characters involved in the act or fantasy of incest are Josh and Patricia Robyn, Horace and Narcissa Benbow, Quentin and Caddy Compson, Charles Bon and Judith Sutpen, or the various members of the McCaslin and Beauchamp families, its meaning remains essentially unchanged. Similarly, the complex equivocality of incest as a literary and historical phenomenon is compressed by these interpretations into a single Procrustean shape. Marc Shell begins a provocative recent interpretation of the motif by speaking of incest as located at either "the perverse periphery or . . . the holy center of human life."[4] But this sense of doubleness, of incest as a site of fascination as well as of taboo, is largely absent in interpretations of the motif in Faulkner's fiction.

An alternative to the prevailing approaches is to explore the developmental logic underlying Faulkner's uses of the incest motif, seeking to attach this logic to the larger history of incest as trope, fantasy, and fact. A fruitful place to begin, as so often in the study of Faulkner, is with his romantic forebears. Exploring depictions of incest among the romantic poets—particularly those in Shelley's poetry—reveals the importance of a distinction, frequently occluded in discussions of the motif, between parent-child and sibling incest; for among the romantic poets, parent-child and sibling incest are assigned directly opposite moral valences. As Peter Thorslev says in a study of romantic representations of incest, "parent-child incest is universally condemned . . . ; sibling incest, on the other hand, is invariably made sympathetic, is sometimes exonerated, and, in Byron's and Shelley's works, is definitely idealized."[5]

This contrast between negatively and positively valued images of incest invites interpretation in political terms. In *The End of Kinship*, his broad-ranging study of the incest motif, Marc Shell argues that throughout postclassical western history, the Christian cloistral orders embodied an ideal of egalitarian "universal siblinghood," as opposed to the hierarchical and patriarchal structures of episcopal and secular authority; and he argues also that this opposition was expressed metaphorically as a contrast between sibling incest on the one hand and parent-child (specifically father-daughter) incest on the other. In the romantic era, Shell argues further, the ideal of universal siblinghood reconstituted itself in secular terms, as the revolutionary ideal of fraternity. As this change occurred, images of father-daughter incest came to be used to express the tyrannical power of the *ancien régime*; while images of brother-sister incest shadowed forth the new, "fatherless," egalitarian social order that the French and American revolutions were struggling to articulate.

This argument is entirely consistent with the moral and political valuation placed on imagined acts of incest by Shelley and Byron in their poetry—most particularly by Shelley in *The Cenci* and "Laon and Cythna" (the original, unexpurgated form of "The Revolt of Islam"). In Count Francesco Cenci's forced incestuous coupling with his daughter, Beatrice, Shelley depicts, as Earl Wasserman says, "not only a domestic but a political and religious tyranny as well, the three modes being implicated in each other."[6] In the earlier, optimistic "Laon and Cythna," by contrast, Shelley depicts brother-sister incest as a metaphor for human perfectibility. Viewing the incest taboo as an example of "those outworn opinions on which established institutions depend," Shelley envisions its defiance as a way of struggling against "the Anarch Custom's reign." And projecting this struggle along an historical axis, he presents Laon and Cythna's union as a trope for the way history will ultimately overcome the setback dealt to the struggle for liberty by the Reign of Terror and the ascendancy of Napoleon Bonaparte. Beginning with a narrator filled with "visions of despair" because "the last hope of trampled France had failed," Shelley arrives finally at a vision of egalitarian incestuous love, reborn in "a People mighty in its youth, / A land beyond the Oceans of the West, / . . . / Nay, start not at the name—America!"[7]

In his early reading of Shelley, Faulkner would have had access to a more politicized understanding of the incest metaphor than the ones advanced in most current readings of his fiction. He also could have arrived at such an understanding from within the intellectual culture of his own age, for the sexual liberationism of the 1920s carried forward into the modern era the romantic challenge to the incest taboo. But a further factor, deriving from Faulkner's identity as a Southerner, complicated enormously his relation to both the romantic and modernist interpretations of the motif. I refer here to the attitude toward incest found in the early-twentieth-century literature of social reform, particularly in works reflecting the assumptions of the then-popular eugenics movement.

Untroubled by romantic and modernist interpretations of incest as a social convention, fated to wither away, writers in this tradition depict incest as the most striking of a variety of threats posted by lower-class immorality to the maintenance of a healthy American gene pool. In depictions of "the degenerate hillbilly family . . . spawning endless generations of paupers, criminals, and imbeciles," as Nicole Hahn Rafter says, these writers create a lurid argument in support of programs for sterilization or long-term incarceration of the genetically "unfit."[8] And while their studies focus on Northern as well as Southern instances of inbreeding and hereditary degeneracy, they are particularly vehement in their depictions of the Southern instances—presumably because in the South the possibility of inbreeding combined with the possibility of miscegenation to compound the geneticists' fears of a lower-class assault on American racial integrity.

Faulkner's regional pride is nowhere more evident than in his rejection of this lurid view of rural Southern incest. In 1933, for example, he dismissed as "perhaps . . . the most sentimental" of Southern writers "the ones who write bitterly of the incest in clayfloored cabins."[9] But the popular view nonetheless possessed a complicating power relative to the depictions Faulkner *did* choose to present; it is the tacit counterimage that his aristocratic images of Southern incest attempt to deny. Furthermore, Faulkner's regional pride limited his direct access to the romantic and modernist interpretations outlined above; for to accept those interpretations without qualification would imply acceptance as well of a more general egalitarian (and hence anti-Southern) political and social agenda. This he was unwilling to do. Instead, by a logic resembling the one that permitted Southern apologists for slavery to speak of the War Between the States as the "Second American Revolution," Faulkner began his career by standing romantic and modernist sexual views on their head. He used sibling incest as a trope in support of, rather than in rejection of, regionalism and political reaction. And by a similar logic, he avoided for a long time assigning any meaning whatsoever to images of father-daughter incest.

Once these contexts have been brought to mind, the direction of Faulkner's development relative to the incest motif becomes clear. It consists of a movement away from Southern conservatism and toward liberalism—toward, that is, a reactivation of a Shelleyean opposition between father-daughter and brother-sister incest as political metaphors. It consists also of a steady increase in the complexity of his treatment of the motif—an increase in his awareness that the causes (and costs) of sexual inhibition are social and historical as well as psychological. This line of development occurs in three stages, the first consisting of the series of early depictions culminating in the Quentin Compson section of *The Sound and the Fury*, the second of the linking of incest with race and history in *Absalom, Absalom!*, the third of the politicized depictions of father-daughter and sibling incest in *Go Down, Moses*.

If we ask what is new about Faulkner's use of the incest motif in *The Sound and the Fury*, as compared to its immediate predecessor, *Flags in the Dust*, a partial answer is that Quentin Compson is Horace Benbow "placed," in the sense that Horace's quasi-incestuous longing for his sister is depicted essentially without irony, whereas Quentin's is not. A fuller answer is that in *The Sound and the Fury* Faulkner begins to subject to critical scrutiny the reactionary implications of his earlier uses of the motif. Like Horace, Quentin uses fantasies of sibling incest as a way of *not* experiencing life as subject to time and change and therefore as inherently political. But Quentin's attempt to use incest in this way is shadowed (as Horace's is not) by an alternative interpretation, in which incestuous yearnings are associated less with resistance to time than with immersion in it. Quentin may believe that his incest fantasy arises exclusively from his wish to rescind Caddy's sexual initiation; but Faulkner shows us the desire for a similar maturation that this belief conceals. And he reveals as well, if only fleetingly, a link between the desire for sexual maturation and a wish to break free of Southern insularity. "[H]es crossed all the oceans all around the world," Caddy says of Dalton Ames, as if geographical and sexual adventuring were somehow linked.[10]

Yet if in *The Sound and the Fury* Faulkner begins to question his earlier uses of the incest motif, the intense subjectivity of the novel's narrative method causes this questioning to remain tentative and incomplete. As John Matthews says in a study of narrative "frames" in the novel, "the text behaves as if it has no context. . . . History makes itself felt in *The Sound and the Fury* by being forgotten, by making itself into a background blur."[11] Faulkner's labor over the next dozen years—his labor in

Absalom, Absalom! and *Go Down, Moses*—is to turn this background into foreground, to implicate the incest motif in culture and history.

In *Absalom, Absalom!* this labor takes the form of a direct repudiation of the construction Quentin had earlier attempted to place on sibling incest. The stories that Quentin hears from Rosa Coldfield first compel his attention when she speaks of Henry Sutpen's murder of Charles Bon—an act Quentin initially understands as a version of his own relation to Caddy and her lovers, conducted to the conclusion for which his incest fantasy was a symbolic substitute. In the second half of the novel, though, as Quentin and Shreve struggle to create their own version of the Sutpen story, this *Sound-and-the-Fury*-like understanding of the meaning of the murder of Charles Bon (and of sibling incest) is replaced by its opposite. As Quentin and Shreve's attention shifts from Thomas Sutpen to Charles Bon, the issue ceases to be whether Henry will serve his father's interests by preventing Charles from committing incest with Judith and becomes instead whether he will find some excuse—in the fact that "kings have done it! Even dukes!"—for defying his father and aligning himself with his brother.[12] And once he succeeds in doing so, the issue alters still further, becoming an exploration of whether Henry can maintain this allegiance in the face of his father's revelation that Bon is part black.

As with Henry, so with Quentin. Quentin and Shreve's sympathetic identification with Henry and Charles first aligns itself as *The Sound and the Fury* would predict, with Quentin paired with the Puritanical Henry and Shreve paired with the "outlander" Charles. But as the novel advances, these pairings blur, until finally "both of them were Henry Sutpen and both of them were Bon, compounded each of both yet either neither" (280). Because this blurring occurs immediately after Henry has given Charles permission to marry Judith, it suggests that Quentin here discovers an alternative to his own earlier use of the incest fantasy; it suggests that he sees in Henry's allegiance to Charles a model for the integration of the censorious and desiring halves of his own personality. But for Quentin, as for Henry, this integration can no longer remain confined within psychological limits. Just as the revelation of Bon's black ancestry raises the question of whether "it's the miscegenation, not the incest, which [Henry] cant bear" (285; italics omitted), so also for Quentin. How far will his defiance of his backward-looking suicidal melancholy extend? Will it consist only of a private effort to free the fantasy of sibling incest from the regressive meaning assigned to it in *The Sound and the Fury*? Or will it expand outward, politically and socially, into an attempt to repudiate as well the taboo against miscegenation?

The significance of these questions for Faulkner's depiction of Southern history has been explored by a number of commentators. Less frequently explored, because more abstractly presented, is their relation to the political tensions of the mid-1930s, the period in which the novel was written. Viewed in this context, the telling and retelling of the Sutpen story can be construed as a struggle between right- and left-wing ideologies, figured forth, as they were the mid-1930s, as a rhetoric of fatherhood on the one hand and of brotherhood on the other. In the sixth and seventh chapters of the novel, when Quentin and Shreve retell the Sutpen story in a fashion consistent with Mr. Compson's earlier narrative, Quentin says that Shreve "*sounds just like Father*" and that "*[m]aybe nothing ever happens once and is finished*" (147, 210). But when they turn in the eighth chapter to creating their own version of the story, a voice clearly distinguishable from Mr. Compson's emerges. In its "protective coloring of levity" (225), the voice is identifiably Shreve's. But it is more than his voice alone, for it speaks "the heart and blood of youth . . . strong enough and willing enough for two, for two thousand, for all" (236). It seeks to express, as Shreve says of Charles Bon, a vision of human possibility in which the "ambiguous . . . dark fatherhead" could be "eluded" and "all boy flesh" could be "brothered perennial and ubiquitous everywhere under the sun" (240).

The vision of universal brotherhood that Quentin and Shreve strive to create frees the incest motif from the merely private meaning that had dominated its appearances in Faulkner's earlier fiction. Beyond the struggle for sexual competence of *The Sound and the Fury*, yet implicated within it, lies the struggle for political competence of *Absalom, Absalom!* In *Go Down, Moses*, in his last significant use of the incest motif, Faulkner extends this meaning further, by linking the incest trope ever more explicitly to Southern history and to America's political situation on the eve of World War II.

The distance Faulkner had travelled between his early understanding of the motif and *Go Down, Moses* can be measured by his innovations in its use in the later novel. In *Go Down, Moses*, for the first time in his fiction, Faulkner concerns himself with father-daughter as well as sibling incest, and with incest as an overt, not just an imagined, act. Also, he assigns political meanings to father-daughter and sibling incest echoing the ones Shelley had used in *The Cenci* and "Laon and Cythna." He depicts L. Q. C. McCaslin's incestuous coupling with his daughter Tomasina as an act of sexual tyranny parallel in meaning to the "curse" of possession, by which Southern plantation owners had imposed a structure of domination on an "earth" meant to be held "mutual and intact in the communal anonymity of brotherhood."[13] And in "Delta Autumn," he poises against this *Cenci*-like meaning a liberationist view similar to Shelley's in "Laon and Cythna," by depicting in the affair between Roth Edmonds and his black cousin an attenuated form of sibling incest, in which taboos of race, region, and class are defied (at least temporarily) in the service of egalitarian love.

The climax of the conflict between these meanings is the meeting between Isaac McCaslin and Roth Edmonds's lover at the end of "Delta Autumn." It has long been recognized that Isaac is a descendant of Quentin Compson—that in the short story originals out of which *Go Down, Moses* was formed, Isaac's role is occupied by Quentin. In the terms pursued here, this filiation reveals itself in Ike's devotion to the ideal of fraternity, as in the phrase quoted above about an Edenic South held "mutual and intact in the communal anonymity of brotherhood." He returns to this ideal often, always as a fantasized alternative to the world of racial inequality and economic competition in which he actually lives. When he thinks of conversations in the hunting camp as "the best of all talking," for example, he describes them as egalitarian, the talk of men, "not white nor black nor red but men"; and when he looks up at the commissary ledgers as a child, he imagines that they will tell a benign story of "the land which they had all held and used in common . . . without regard to color or titular ownership" (184, 256).

Isaac's encounter with Roth Edmonds's lover tests this dream of universal brotherhood in the real world. It offers Ike an image of egalitarian social relations not just as a fantasized alternative to life in time but as its goal. When he touches the nameless young woman's hand after learning that she is Tennie's Jim's granddaughter, he senses their kinship, feeling how "the strong old blood ran after its long lost journey back to home" (345). This journey back is more than a rapprochement between the black and white descendants of L. Q. C. McCaslin, significant as this is; implicit in it as well is the hope that the Edenic promise of America can be renewed, in the form Shelley had imagined, of egalitarian sexual relations. Further, the journey back broaches the possibility of an even more general bonding between the sexes, for it is the first instance in Faulkner's contemplation of the incest motif in which the ideal of "brotherhood" broadens into the ideal of "siblinghood." Black, Northern, well-educated, the young woman offers Isaac—"Uncle Isaac," as she calls him—the possibility of "kinship" across the barriers of sexual and gender and racial taboo and regional chauvinism.

But working against these possibilities is a wide array of circumstances—not only slavery's legacy of sexual and racial and economic inequality but the destruction of the Southern wilderness and the political stresses of the early 1940s—all of which create in the novel's characters an extreme pessimism about the future of America as a nation. So it is scarcely surprising that Isaac fails to step across the gulf separating himself from the larger "kinship" expressed in Roth's lover's touch. Declining that touch's implicit utopian promise, he instead descends into sexual and racial hysteria, envisioning miscegenetic sexual relations nightmarishly, as "*Chinese and African and Aryan and Jew, all breed[ing] and spawn[ing] together until no man has time to say which one is which nor cares*" (347). "*Maybe in a thousand or two thousand years in America,*" he says, in an inadvertent parody of the liberal dream of progress, "*But not now! Not now!*" (344).

Why the evolution of Faulkner's use of the incest motif stops with his depiction of Ike's hysteria—and, more generally, with the writing of *Go Down, Moses*—is a question beyond the scope of this essay to explore. But an approach to an answer can be suggested if we consider for a moment directions taken by thought about incest in recent years. The sexual radicalism of the 1920s clearly still continues (even if often in debased forms), with the emergence in the last twenty years of what Benjamin Demott has called a "pro-incest lobby," whose members range from scholars investigating sexual behavior to letter-writers to men's magazines to (most recently) anonymous fantasists on the Internet.[14] But the last twenty years have also seen the emergence of a strong countervoice, in the form of feminist critiques of male-centered developmental scenarios. Ranging from objections to Freud's dismissal of childhood incest as female fantasy to confessional accounts of real-life experiences, this countervoice seeks to recenter the story of incest on the female rather than the male participant and to emphasize its costs over its putative benefits.

A number of recent commentators—John Duvall, Minrose Gwin, Richard Moreland, Joseph Urgo—have sought to align Faulkner's fiction with this newly emergent voice.[15] Moreland argues, for example, that in extending imaginative sympathy to poor whites in *The Hamlet*, blacks in *Go Down, Moses*, and women in *Requiem for a Nun*, Faulkner anticipates a decentered postmodern politics of class, ethnic, and gender inclusiveness. This is an attractive line of argument, if only because it encourages positive and generous readings of Faulkner's late fiction. But it has largely left unexamined the question of what model for psychic development is to replace the male-centered Oedipal model that Faulkner so exhaustively explores. And it verges at times on special pleading in Faulkner's defense, as it seeks to discover a postmodern politics in what Minrose Gwin has rightly described, quoting Teresa De Lauretis, as "the chinks and cracks of masculinity, the fissures of male identity or the repressed of phallic discourse" ("Feminism and Faulkner" 64).

A tragedy at the heart of Faulkner's fiction—at the heart, one is tempted to say, of his anger—is the suspicion that all male development

is a form of psychic imperialism, a cooptation of some "other" (generational, sexual, racial) in the service of the self. Construed more broadly,
this tragedy is a doubt about liberalism as a political ideology—about
the structural contradiction between liberalism's advocacy of an ever-
expanding political inclusiveness and its tacit commitment to maintaining
white male privilege and power. Beyond each level of achieved empathy
in Faulkner's fiction stands a further level of exclusion and marginalization. Beyond the aristocratic Charles Bon stands the déclassé Jim Bond, a
person also deserving (yet not receiving) Quentin and Shreve's sympathy;
beyond Charles Bon as well stands Judith Sutpen, no less than Charles a
victim of her father's dynastic ambitions, yet never the center of Quentin
and Shreve's sympathetic attention; beyond Judith stands Roth's lover,
nameless, the daughter of a washerwoman, the last of *Go Down, Moses*'s
long line of black female victims. Where, Faulkner's fiction seems to ask,
does the expansionist economy of liberalism end? How far can its quest
for inclusiveness extend, if its center in a male-dominated social order—
and in the white male psyche—is still to hold?

Contemplating the evolution of Faulkner's use of the incest motif has
carried us a considerable distance away from the question I posed at the
outset of this talk, of what we mean when we speak of a writer's career.
But the distance may be more illusory than real. In *Keywords: A Vocabulary of Culture and Society*, Raymond Williams observes that the word
"career" is normally used with "some conscious [or] unconscious class
distinction." We use the word, he suggests, to designate forms of labor
more dignified—with more promise of "explicit internal development"—
than those designated with words like "work" or "job."[16] I wonder if the
word does not carry as well an affiliation with a rather old-fashioned idea
of personal identity, as integral and continuous, and with an historically
defined range of political possibilities.

The burden of my argument has been that Faulkner's journey into
liberalism ends where a decentered postmodern politics begins. Because
my own political development has been toward, rather than beyond, liberalism, I do not find this an unattractive concluding point for Faulkner
to have reached. But what of those who read Faulkner from a postmodern
perspective, who seek in his fiction, in Philip Weinstein's words, a decentered subject and a cosmos no one owns?[17] Will they find in "career"
a concept helpful to the reading of Faulkner in the next millennium? Or
will developmental readings give way before the tendency to call into
question the authority of the author and of the centered self?

NOTES

1. Gary Lee Stonum, *Faulkner's Career: An Internal Literary History* (Ithaca: Cornell University Press, 1979), 14–15. All multiple references in this essay are to the edition first cited.

2. The argument synopsized here appears in full form in Karl Zender, "Faulkner and the Politics of Incest," *American Literature* 70 (1998): 739–65.

3. Cleanth Brooks, *William Faulkner: The Yoknapatawpha Country* (New Haven: Yale University Press, 1963), 331; John T. Irwin, *Doubling and Incest / Repetition and Revenge: A Speculative Reading of Faulkner* (Baltimore: Johns Hopkins University Press, 1975), 59.

4. Marc Shell, *The End of Kinship: "Measure for Measure," Incest, and the Ideal of Universal Siblinghood* (Stanford: Stanford University Press, 1988), xi.

5. Peter L. Thorslev Jr., "Incest as Romantic Symbol," *Comparative Literature Studies* 2 (1965): 41–58.

6. Earl R. Wasserman, *Shelley: A Critical Reading* (Baltimore: Johns Hopkins University Press, 1971), 86.

7. Percy Bysshe Shelley, "Laon and Cythna," in *The Complete Poetical Works of Percy Bysshe Shelley*, ed. Neville Rogers, 4 vols. (Oxford: The Clarendon Press, 1975), 2: 99–273. The quoted phrases appear in the Dedication (l. 86) and Canto XI, Stanza XXXIV (l.4439).

8. Nicole Hahn Rafter, *White Trash: The Eugenic Family Studies, 1877–1915* (Boston: Northeastern University Press, 1988), 2.

9. William Faulkner, "An Introduction to *The Sound and the Fury*" [I], in *Critical Essays on William Faulkner: The Compson Family*, ed. Arthur F. Kinney (Boston: G. K. Hall, 1982), 71.

10. William Faulkner, *The Sound and the Fury* (New York: Vintage International, 1990), 150.

11. John T. Matthews, "The Rhetoric of Containment in Faulkner," in *Faulkner's Discourse: An International Symposium*, ed. Lothar Hönnighausen (Tübingen: Max Niemeyer Verlag, 1989), 55, 67.

12. William Faulkner, *Absalom, Absalom!* (New York: Vintage International, 1990), 273.

13. William Faulkner, *Go Down, Moses* (New York: Vintage International, 1990), 246.

14. Benjamin Demott, "The Pro-Incest Lobby," *Psychology Today* 13 (March 1980): 11–12, 15–16.

15. John N. Duvall, *Faulkner's Marginal Couple: Invisible, Outlaw, and Unspeakable Communities* (Austin: University of Texas Press, 1990); Minrose C. Gwin, *The Feminine and Faulkner: Reading (Beyond) Sexual Difference* (Knoxville: University of Tennessee Press, 1990); Minrose C. Gwin, "Feminism and Faulkner: Second Thoughts or, What's a Radical Feminist Doing with a Canonical Male Text Anyway?" *Faulkner Journal* 4 (1988–89): 55–65; Richard C. Moreland, *Faulkner and Modernism: Rereading and Rewriting* (Madison: University of Wisconsin Press, 1990); Joseph R. Urgo, *Faulkner's Apocrypha: "A Fable," Snopes, and the Spirit of Human Rebellion* (Jackson: University Press of Mississippi, 1989).

16. Raymond Williams, *Keywords: A Vocabulary of Culture and Society*, rev. ed. (New York: Oxford University Press, 1983), 53.

17. Philip M. Weinstein, *Faulkner's Subject: A Cosmos No One Owns* (Cambridge: Cambridge University Press, 1992).

Faulkner's Grim Sires

CAROLYN PORTER

I have been at work for some time on a manuscript whose working title is "Grim Sires and Spectral Mothers: The Family in Faulkner." I am trying to comprehend the unfolding problematic of gender in Faulkner's work from *The Sound and the Fury* through *Go Down, Moses*, understanding "gender" not only as the cultural institutionalization of sexual difference, but further, and alongside race and class, as a major historical predicate for both social power and cultural dysfunction. The story has led me up to and into *Absalom, Absalom!*, from whence I still hope someday to emerge—no doubt grim, and probably spectral myself. The argument so far goes something like this.

The thematic nexus of gender in Faulkner's major novels from *The Sound and the Fury* through *Go Down, Moses* is the family, the original locus of individual psychic struggles as well as the central social structure that both provokes and contains them. It is little wonder, then, that critics concerned with gender have so far drawn heavily on psychoanalysis, since it affords some indispensable theoretical tools and models for understanding the modern, Anglo-European family as a major site and vehicle for the construction of gender identity. Feminist psychoanalytic criticism has proven particularly effective in pursuing the questions raised by Faulkner's complex treatment of motherhood, especially in *The Sound and the Fury* and *As I Lay Dying*, where by any accounting the mother—whether dead or alive, woefully absent or dolefully present—figures centrally in the family economy of loss and desire. But as Faulkner's social canvas broadens with *Light in August*, and as his historical focus deepens with *Absalom, Absalom!*, the critical pressure of his attention to the family gradually, and then decisively, shifts to the father. Recall, for example that the Quentin Compson of *The Sound and the Fury* who laments, *"If I could say Mother. Mother,"* returns in *Absalom* to meditate, obsessively, on fathers: *"Yes, we are both Father, or maybe Father and I are both Shreve, maybe it took Father and me both to make Shreve or Shreve and me both to make Father or maybe Thomas Sutpen to make all of us."*[1]

I am not suggesting that fathers displace mothers, as if in a fit of premature political correctness, Faulkner had decided to give their roles equal time. Rather, I mean that the question of the status and function of fatherhood, which *The Sound and the Fury* poses and which *Light in August* begins to address more fully with its elaborated array of fathers and grandfathers, leads finally in *Absalom, Absalom!* to a concerted interrogation of fatherhood as the enigmatic source and vehicle of social identity and political sovereignty—the "grim sire," as Melville says in *Moby-Dick*, who harbors "the old State-secret."[2] From what Quentin and Shreve imagine as the vantage point of the delegitimized son, Charles Bon, "no man had a father," that is "no one personal" father. Rather, "all boy flesh that walked and breathed stem[s] from that one ambiguous eluded dark fatherhead" (*AA* 239–40). Like the "young exiled royalties" whom Melville's Ishmael enjoins to seek out their "grim sire," Quentin and Shreve are launched on a quest to discover that "ambiguous eluded dark fatherhead" represented by Thomas Sutpen, a man who appears to Quentin at the novel's very outset as God, enunciator of the *"Be Sutpen's Hundred* like the oldtime *Be Light"* (*AA* 4). Once it is recognized that this "state-secret" belongs not to any particular father, living or dead, but to the patriarchal social system on which Anglo-American fatherhood itself depends, it seems no accident that Faulkner should focus more insistently on the father as he broadens his social perspective from the "nuclear" families of *The Sound and the Fury* and *As I Lay Dying* to the genealogical histories unfolded in *Absalom* and *Go Down, Moses*.

More specifically, Faulkner's most ambitious exploration of motherhood, *As I Lay Dying*, produces in Addie Bundren a portrait of maternal subjectivity at the same time that it delivers an excoriating critique of fathers and the language of patriarchy.[3] (In Lacanian terms, patriarchy is here revealed as a kind of machine fueled by the denial of lack.) *As I Lay Dying* then opens the way for the multiple registers in which fatherhood is explored in *Light in August*. From Old Doc Hines and Calvin Burden through MacEachern, fatherhood is repeatedly inflected as the site of a punitive social discipline fueled by religious fanaticism and racial hatred. But in *Absalom, Absalom!*, Faulkner addresses the authority of patriarchy itself, that authority on which an Anse Bundren no less than a Doc Hines relies.

The narrative excavation here conducted to unearth the story of Thomas Sutpen, a "grim sire" indeed, exposes the structure of patriarchy itself to a corrosive critical scrutiny—one that is far more ambitious than anything Faulkner had attempted before. Consider that in *Light in August*, as in *The Sound and the Fury*, it still makes sense to talk about "bad" fathers and "good" ones. Mr. Compson, as John Irwin has demonstrated,[4] is a distinctly bad father, and Byron Bunch, we may safely infer, will be a good one to Lena's child. But much as Addie Bundren differs from the loathsome Mrs. Compson of *The Sound and the Fury*—whether Addie Bundren is a bad mother becomes less important than the question "What is a Mother?"—Thomas Sutpen's story definitively raises the stakes on the father. That is, whether Sutpen is a good or a bad father is virtually irrelevant to the question implicit in Quentin's effort to hypothesize a patrilineal line—the question of what *makes* a father. It is to this question that Sutpen's story provides an answer, even if an all too unsatisfying one.

Sutpen is not just a would-be father, he is a would-be patriarch. Faulkner repeatedly described Sutpen as a man who "wanted a son," wanted to "establish a dynasty," to "make himself a king and raise a line of princes."[5] As I have argued elsewhere,[6] what makes a dynastic father is a son, more specifically a son who can both bear and pass on the father's name, generating what Sutpen envisions as "the fine grandsons and great grandsons springing as far as the eye could reach" (*AA* 218). That is, dynastic fatherhood depends upon and is constituted by, an infinite and self-reiterative signifying process. Every father, to be a father, must reiterate the name of his father in order to become a father himself.

What difference does it make, then, to understand Thomas Sutpen in these terms? The answer begins to emerge in a response Faulkner made to a question posed by a student at the University of Virginia, where Faulkner visited in the late 1950s. Asked whether Sutpen ever acknowledged Clytie as his daughter, Faulkner explained that "it would not have mattered" whether he did so or not, since she was "female," and Sutpen would "have to have a male descendant," if he was "going to create a dukedom" (*FU* 272). So much for daughters. What about wives and mothers?

"I had a design," Sutpen tells Grandfather Compson. "To accomplish it I should require money, a house, a plantation, slaves, a family— *incidentally* of course, a wife" (emphasis added, *AA* 212). If daughters are irrelevant, mothers and wives are only slightly less so. Clearly enough, the natural domain in which both mothers and children are "made" is physically necessary, but nonetheless "incidental" in the dynastic register where both sons and fathers are made. Of slightly more consequence, though still, as it turns out, "incidental," is the legal sanction of marriage on which the legitimacy of those children, sons included, depends. As Sutpen eventually comes to realize, to Rosa's horror, the legitimacy conferred by marriage can if necessary be retroactively effected without terminal damage to the dynastic line. Thus, if Rosa bears Sutpen a son, he can then *confer* his name on both her and that son after the fact; if not, he can withhold it. It is, after all, by the same token that he has already *denied* his name to his first wife and son. In other words, conferring and denying his name is the father's prerogative. As General Compson says, at the time Sutpen put aside Eulalia and Charles, he "would not permit the child, since it was a boy, to bear either his name or that of its maternal grandfather," and yet neither would he "do the customary and provide a quick husband for the discarded woman and so give his son an authentic name" (*AA* 214). Charles Bon's putative "marriage" to the octoroon mother of *his* son rephrases the same point by marking the degree to which the legal sanction of marriage is flexible. Under certain conditions, we might put it, a first wife can be put aside if a man wishes to marry someone else. Under certain conditions, a father can choose to deny his name to his own son.

Those conditions, of course, are racially defined and historically specific to the slaveowning South. It is after all the "peculiar institution" of slavery that makes racial identity the ground for abrogating the legal sanctions of marriage as well as the legal recognition by fathers of their own children. More specifically, it is the legacy of slavery which specifically dictates that the child follow the so-called condition of the mother. Accordingly, Sutpen's behavior both mirrors and repeats that of the slaveowning white planter who rapes the black slave women he "owns," and thereby spawns children he can automatically *dis*own. In this regard, Sutpen's story re-presents a distinctive Southern social pattern of familial cruelty, exploitation, and abuse. Just as this "peculiar" institution was extended and even amplified in the postbellum era by means of the "one-drop rule," Sutpen's design fetishizes it, so that even in 1909, Jim Bond remains in bondage.

But it is critical to understand that what particularizes Sutpen's case also serves to foreground its generalizable implications for patriarchy. In this sense, the "black blood" assigned to Eulalia and her son Charles, far from *particularizing* Sutpen's story, makes it *representative*. For after all, the "peculiar institution" dictated that, according to the matrilineal rule of Roman slavery, the black mother, in becoming a mother, erased—blotted out—the name of the father, thereby reducing any and all of her sons (whether their fathers were black or white) to the status of "boys," that is, men legally incapable of becoming fathers. Consequently, as Shreve puts it, the black son of a white father inevitably "inherited what he was from his mother and only what he could never have been from his father" (*AA* 174). What enables Faulkner to excavate the "grim sire," in other words, is the racial discourse of "blood" that a black son introduces into the dynastic line. If what makes a father is a son—the basic rule of dynastic patriarchy—what blocks Charles Bon from being that son is his legal inability to bear and pass on the name of the father. Once assigned to the eldest son in a dynastic line, "black blood" leads to a serial catastrophe that not only dooms Sutpen's design but also fractures and lays bare patriarchy's social structure.

What is peculiar about the South, I am suggesting, is also and precisely what enables it to serve as a highly sensitized social register for representing what is by no means peculiar to it. As Faulkner remarked to Malcolm Cowley, "I'm inclined to think that my material, the South, is not very important to me. I just happen to know it, and don't have time in one life to learn another one and write at the same time. Though the one I know is probably as good as another, life is a phenomenon but not a novelty, the same frantic steeplechase toward nothing everywhere and man stinks the same stink no matter where in time."[7] Among those who "stink the same stink," for example is Abraham, who puts aside the slave Hagar and her son Ishmael, and who is ready to obey God's command to kill his only remaining son, Isaac. Indeed the Bible is full of this "stink." For instance, when the boy Sutpen responds to his rejection at the planter's front door, he at once confronts and violently repudiates his own impotence, an impotence whose discovery immediately produces the phallic monument in which it is at once disavowed and enshrined. That monument recalls the "Pillar of Absalom," which Absalom had erected in the Valley of the King. "I have no son," he said, "to preserve the memory of my name."[8] So he had given the pillar itself his name.

I have elsewhere outlined some of the revelations regarding patriarchy that emerge from Faulkner's scrutiny of the grim sire.[9] Let me here adduce only one kind of example—that of the women, or at least a couple of them, before turning to the issue of sons and brothers.

Consider Rosa. Sutpen's infamous "proposal" to Rosa in effect blurts out what the woman's function under patriarchy really is, "to become a womb to bring forth men children," as Deborah Clarke puts it.[10] As feminist theory from Gayle Rubin to Luce Irigaray has made clear, the patriarchal economy requires the exchange of women by men, and the only social positions its structure accords women are those of wife and mother, virgin, or prostitute. Rosa's refusal to accept the terms of patriarchy's proposition leads her to become, as she puts it in the course of her lascivious tribute to the sensual in the novel's fifth chapter, "*all polymath love's androgynous advocate*" (AA 117). Just as Rosa's exclusion from the role of wife enables her to enunciate the sexual body on behalf of all those denied its pleasures by a patriarchal regime, her exclusion from the role of mother enables her to wage a campaign of revenge that both speaks for, and acts on behalf of, Ellen Coldfield and Eulalia Bon as well as

Milly Jones—the mothers whose failure to meet Sutpen's genealogical demands document the truth his proposal blurts out.

Sutpen's proposal to Rosa expresses clearly, if scandalously, what patriarchy demands of women. Luce Irigaray's classing of women (into wife and mother, virgin or prostitute)[11] recalls Mr. Compson's infamous division of women into "ladies, women, females," or more specifically, "virgins . . . courtesans . . . and "slavegirls and women" (AA 87). Mr. Compson ostensibly omits mothers altogether, but the omission turns out to be a repression. That is, the mother is repressed here because if she were included in the list, she would have to show up in at least two places: as the (black) slave and as the (white) wife. But once this is acknowledged, the mother's real status as a broodmare is revealed. And, I am suggesting, Sutpen's career as would-be father makes this irresistibly clear. The effective nullification of women as human is after all presupposed by his design, and thus inevitably reenacted in his career as both husband and nothusband, from Eulalia Bon through Milly Jones. As you may recall, riding out one fine morning to check on his mare Penelope's new colt, Sutpen rides on to find Milly has had their baby. "Well, Milly," he says, standing over her with his horsewhip still in hand, "too bad you're not a mare too. Then I could give you a decent stall in the stable" (AA 229). It is this kind of behavior that repeatedly provokes outcries of astonishment, as when General Compson responds to Sutpen's bewilderment at Eulalia's apparent refusal to lie still and suffer: "Good God, man, what else did you expect? Didn't the very affinity and instinct for misfortune of a man who had spent that much time in a monastery even, let alone one who had lived that many years as you lived them, tell you better than that? didn't the dread and fear of females which you must have drawn in with the primary mammalian milk teach you better? What kind of abysmal and purblind innocence could that have been which someone told you to call virginity? what conscience to trade with which would have warranted you in the belief that you could have bought immunity from her for no other coin but justice?" (AA 213).

General Compson invokes a "dread and fear of females" as a natural male trait. But such stereotypical expressions of masculine defensiveness are just as baffling to Sutpen as the ostensibly hysterical responses of Rosa and Eulalia. And he remains baffled even when his behavior provokes his murder.

I want now to turn to the sons in the novel. They fare little better than do their mothers and sisters and aunts. Most obviously, Bon's strategy for forcing the question of paternal recognition reflects the demands made on men entailed by the same system whose structure Sutpen's proposition to Rosa reveals. That is, by threatening to marry Judith, Charles Bon insists on his rights as a man under patriarchy, viz., to participate "equally" with other men in the exchange of women.[12] Because his "black blood" denies him this right (the same right that Sutpen enjoyed when he exchanged his mastery over the rebellious slaves in Haiti with Eulalia Bon's father for his daughter's "hand," or again, when he made the mysterious exchange for Ellen with Goodhue Coldfield), Charles Bon's access to a legal, recognized fatherhood is blocked. The same "black blood" of course blocks his access to Sutpen's paternal recognition, which is why he has resorted to the threat of marrying Judith. In effect, to become a father in this system, one must first be recognized either as a son or as a son-in-law. Once displaced into what Juliet Flower-MacConnell has called "the regime of the brother"[13] and made visible by the racist discourse of blood, the dilemma of the son in patriarchy is itself blurted out in the final confrontation between Bon and Henry. In forcing Henry to choose between regarding him either as his brother or as *"the nigger who's going to sleep with your sister,"* Charles is insisting, even unto death, upon the recognition necessary for him to enter the patriarchal social economy, and thus exposing the fundamental terms on which that economy operates (*AA* 286).

But it is important to note that this scene signals a double catastrophe, one that points forward as well as backward in history. In the context of patriarchy, Henry's murder of Bon is a displaced filicide, but in the context of modern liberal society, it is a fratricide.

To take patriarchy first, when Henry recognizes Bon as his brother, he tries at once to repudiate his father and to become him, that is, to assume the father's positive function as He who can recognize the son. But this effort fails, because Henry cannot meet Charles Bon's demand for paternal recognition. Instead, Henry can only exercise the negative, vengeful father's role. Once Thomas Sutpen reveals Bon's "black blood" to Henry, that is, Henry is forced to carry out the Oedipal threat. In the patriarchal economy here anatomized, Bon can only be recognized by being killed (that is, recognized *as* the son). That Henry does so in the "name of the father" signals once more the pervasive irony with which obedience to the law of the father not only undermines Sutpen's dynastic reign, but lays bare the very structure on which it depends.

A similar order of revelations awaits us on the "distaff" side. Like Rosa, Judith is excluded from the patriarchal exchange system, at least once Charles Bon has been murdered. Recall the scene where Judith, having asked Charles Bon's son to call her "Aunt Judith," proceeds to suggest that they tell the world that he is Henry's son, rather than Bon's (*AA* 168). His "coal-black" son Jim Bond *"does not,"* as Judith puts it, *"need to have any name,"* but Charles Etienne St. Valery can assume the name Sutpen from his putative father Henry (*AA* 168–69). But of course, Judith is in no position to impose the Sutpen name on Bon's son. Only the father can do that. Yet in her effort to restore a patrilineal line of Sutpens, she mimics and thereby foregrounds, the patriarch's behavior. Of course, the irony here points up the distortions of actual blood lines by the demands of patriarchy. When she asks Bon's son to call her "Aunt," Judith doesn't know that in biological fact, she *is* his aunt. In the dizzying domain of Sutpenland, sons are not sons, husbands are "nothusbands," and women are widowed without ever being brides.

But, to return to the boys.

The final confrontation between Charles and Henry signals a modern, as well as a patriarchal, catastrophe. If Henry's murder of Bon is a displaced filicide, it is also a prophetic fratricide. As Juliet Flower-MacConnell has argued, the Oedipal drama that Freud portrayed was already, even as he wrote, being displaced by "the regime of the brother."

To see how Falkner addresses these issues, we need to recall the way Freud tried to account for a comparable shift from the rule of the fathers to that of the brothers. In *Totem and Taboo*, Freud spins a mythic story in which he imagines that the sons band together and kill the father, effecting a primal murder that collectively grounds civilization in the father's name. (Lacan's revision of this story locates the Symbolic father in the place of this dead father.) In what Mikkel Borch-Jacobson calls a "Freudian version of Hegel's struggle for pure prestige," the phantom of the Father rises up to attack the guilty sons, demanding their love and submission.[14] In Freud's as in MacConnell's version, "the regime of the brother" is fueled by the authority it has appropriated from the father, but unlike Freud's, this regime tries to exercise that authority not in the father's name, but rather in the name of fraternity, brotherhood, and social equality.

But, as Carol Pateman has demonstrated, the move from status to contract, from monarchy to democracy, from a sovereignty located in the immortal one of the king's two bodies to a sovereignty distributed evenly among free and equal individuals, fails to fulfill its promise since, for one thing, it falls short of assigning full equality to women. That is, for women, the "social contract" turns out, whether in Lockean theory or in American practice, to be a "sexual contract," as Pateman calls it.[15] For another thing, it turns out that fraternal democracy depends as well on a different order of difference than was provided by patriarchy. Indeed, it turns out in America, at least, that democracy requires racism. If racial discourse serves to unravel and reveal patriarchy, it also returns to provide a basis for social difference, one both more fundamental and more

flexible than class. *"You are my brother,"* says Henry. *"No, I'm not,"* says
Charles, *"I'm the nigger that's going to sleep with your sister. Unless you
stop me, Henry"* (AA 286). The racial discourse of "blood," which enables
Faulkner to excavate the "grim sire's" "state secrets," also serves to foreground the new, modern, and foundational difference between black and
white. In the time remaining, then, I want to sketch out a way of understanding how the issue of recognition figures centrally in Faulkner's evis-
ceration of *both* traditional patriarchy and modern fraternity.

Recognition is, of course, central to the boy Sutpen's experience at the
planter's front door. Indeed, it is fair to say that the novel as a whole is
organized by a series of scenes in which recognition is demanded and
denied: Sutpen turned away by the black butler at the front door, Wash
Jones turned away by the black Clytie at the back door, Rosa confronted
by Clytie at the foot of the stairs, Quentin paralyzed at the door to Henry's room, Henry stopping Bon at the front gate to their father's house.
If we were to pursue the issue of recognition fully, we might begin with
Charles Taylor's account. As Taylor puts it, "what has come about with
the modern age is not the *need* for recognition but the conditions in
which the attempt to be recognized can *fail*. That is why the need is now
acknowledged for the first time."[16] Under these conditions, identity
based on recognition is severely compromised, to put it mildly. One well
known feature of this problem is that in which Taylor is primarily interested: if everyone is formally recognized as equal, then recognition is
itself empty—everyone is simply recognized as the same. (This is the
future that Shreve invokes when he pompously concludes that "the Jim
Bonds . . . will bleach out again like the rabbits and the birds do, so they
won't show up so sharp against the snow" [AA 302]).
    Another, and perhaps less discussed, feature of the vexed relation be-
tween identity and recognition emerges when we situate Charles Bon's
dilemma in relation to that of Joe Christmas. That is, *Light in August*
obviously addresses the condition of unrecognizability, demonstrating
that to be unrecognizable is intolerable—both for the self that repudiates
the available terms of social identity and for the society whose members
insist upon imposing them. In *Absalom, Absalom!*, by contrast, the question of identity is not only one of being/not being recognized, but as well
of who, or more specifically, what, has the authority to recognize a human
subject. For after all, as Gertrude Stein put it, if "I am I because my little
dog knows me," neither I nor my recognition can count for much.[17] By
contrast, as Louis Althusser put it, if God says to Moses, "Moses!" and
Moses replies "It is I," Moses's identity is secured through a recognition
that counts for a great deal.[18] In other words, the question raised most

famously by Ralph Ellison's *Invisible Man*—am I unrecognizable or merely unrecognized?—speaks to the contrast we could draw between Joe Christmas and Charles Bon. Christmas, that is, is unrecognizable—he fails to fit into any category, and thus his presence establishes a limit, a boundary, a margin on which he moves. Bon, on the other hand, is in *principle* recognizable, but in *fact* unrecognized. That is, there is something or someone vested with the authority required to recognize Bon—as son, brother, father, husband. For Joe Christmas there is no such authority. On the contrary, indeed, anyone claiming to be able to recognize him, to ascribe to him some given and reliable status or identity—is forthwith repudiated. (One is reminded of Marlon Brando in *The Wild Ones*: asked "What are you rebelling against," he replies "What you got?")

Bon, on the other hand, is always potentially recognizable as any or all of a set of identities socially defined by patriarchy, but he is in fact denied and negated by his father's refusal to recognize him. In other words, because there is in his world a potential source of recognition, an authority whose repudiation of him can itself be recognized and attacked, Bon—unlike Christmas—does not simply move round a fated circle, one that emblematizes the boundary formed by the unrecognizable self on its margin. Instead of refusing an identity, Bon insists upon one.

In both instances, however, death is the price of recognition.

Which is perhaps one way of signalling why Faulkner's *Absalom, Absalom!* finally is—as its title suggests, and as mine is meant to remind us—a lament. Under patriarchy, there is no real filial, much less familial, connection. Quentin and Shreve try for page after page to find some thread of love in the story they are retelling, but they can't. On the other hand, the dream of equality is doomed as well, as the final outcry of Wash Jones may serve to indicate: *"Better if his kind and mine too had never drawn the breath of life on this earth. Better that all who remain of us be blasted from the face of it than that another Wash Jones should see his whole life shredded from him and shrivel away like a dried shuck thrown in to the fire"* (*AA* 233).

Lest it be thought that I am arguing for Faulkner's enlightened disavoval of patriarchy, I should note that, in *Go Down, Moses*, he sets out rather desperately to recuperate it—by assigning the "black blood" to the fathers themselves—both Sam Fathers and Lucas Beauchamp. Displacing fatherhood almost wholly from white to black families, he presents us, on the one hand, with Uncle Ike—"Uncle to half a county, but father to no one"—and Lucas Beachaump on the other: *"Both heir and prototype simultaneously of all the geography and climate and biology which sired old Carothers and all the rest of us and our kind, myriad, countless, faceless, even nameless now except himself who fathered himself, intact and complete, contemptuous as old Carothers must have been of all blood black white yellow or red, including his own.*"[19] Here, Faulkner works hard to resuscitate the patriarchal ideal, but now using the discourse of blood to redefine the father in terms that aim to exorcise racial difference altogether. It doesn't work, in my view, but it serves to close the interrogation of the fathers that opened in *The Sound and the Fury*.

And so, I want to close with a passage from the Quentin section of *The Sound and the Fury* where I think the essence of Faulkner's lament is already expressed.

> It used to be I thought of death as a man something like Grandfather a friend of his a kind of private and particular friend like we used to think of Grandfather's desk not to touch it not even to talk loud in the room where it was I always thought of them as being together somewhere all the time waiting for old Colonel Sartoris to come down and sit with them waiting on a high place beyond cedar trees Colonel Sartoris was on a still higher place looking out across at something and they were waiting for him to get done looking at it and come down Grandfather wore his uniform and we could hear the murmur of their voices from beyond the cedars they were always talking and Grandfather was always right. (*SF* 107)

Through a process of splitting and doubling, Quentin's imagination here personifies death, first as a "man something like Grandfather," and then, as "a friend of his"—indeed, a "private and particular friend" who sits talking with him. (The scene, itself often repeated in Faulkner's work, echoes that in Exodus 33:11, where God goes into the tent with Moses, and talks with him "as a man speaketh unto his friend.")

The fact that the two old men "waiting on a high place" are waiting for the old Colonel "to come down and sit with them" renders their position not only subordinate, but analogous to that of the child forbidden to "touch" his grandfather's desk, or to "talk loud" in the room "where it was." Note how the fearful respect of the child forbidden to intrude upon his grandfather's hallowed office is subliminally attached to the patience a child is called upon to display as he waits for the grown-ups to "get done" with their mysterious business and listen to him. Fear and wish are fused. Patriarchal authority descends from above, the child's wish for recognition from the man who wields it ascends from below, but they never actually meet, connect, transact any business. Instead, the desire for recognition is arrested, put on hold, made to wait—stymied by the very awe that such authority inspires. Meanwhile, there is nothing for these old men to do but talk.

NOTES

1. *The Sound and the Fury*, ed. David L. Minter (New York: Norton, 1987), 58; *Absalom, Absalom!* (New York: Vintage International, 1990), 210.) All subsequent references are to these editions and will be given in the text.

2. "Wind ye down there, ye prouder, sadder souls! Question that proud, sad king! A family likeness! aye, he did beget ye, ye young exiled royalties; and from your grim sire only will the old State-secret come." *Moby-Dick* (New York: Houghton Mifflin, 1956), 155.

3. See Carolyn Porter, "Symbolic Fathers and Dead Mothers: A Feminist Approach to Faulkner," in *Faulkner and Psychology*, ed. Donald M.Kartiganer and Ann J. Abadie (Jackson: University of Mississippi Press, 1994), 78–122.

4. See John T. Irwin, *Doubling and Incest, Repetition and Revenge* (Baltimore: Johns Hopkins Press, 1975).

5. *Faulkner in the University*, ed. Frederick Gwynn and Joseph L. Blotner (New York: Vintage, 1965), 98. All subsequent references are to this edition and will be given in the text.

6. See "*Absalom, Absalom!*: (Un)Making the Father," *The Cambridge Companion to William Faulkner*, ed. Philip M. Weinstein (Cambridge: Cambridge University Press, 1995), 168–96.

7. *The Faulkner-Cowley File*, ed. Malcolm Cowley (New York: The Viking Press, 1966), 185.

8. See II Samuel XVIII, 18.

9. See Porter, "Symbolic Fathers and Dead Mothers," in *Faulkner and Psychology*, and "*Absalom, Absalom!*" in *Cambridge Companion to Faulkner*.

10. "Familiar and Fantastic: Women in *Absalom, Absalom!*," *Faulkner Journal* 2 (1986), 64.

11. *This Sex Which Is Not One*, trans. Catherine Porter (Ithaca: Cornell University Press, 1981), 185–86.

12. For a different interpretation of what is at stake in Bon's threat, one in which "manhood" is the issue, but its relation to the exchange system is not regarded as pertinent, see Irwin, *Doubling and Incest*, 49.

13. *The Regime of the Brother: After the Patriarchy* (New York, Routledge, 1991).

14. "The Freudian Subject: From Politics to Ethics," *Who Comes After the Subject?*, ed. Eduardo Cadava, Peter Connor, Jean-Luc Nancy (New York: Routledge, 1991).

15. *The Sexual Contract* (Stanford: Stanford University Press, 1988).

16. "The Politics of Recognition," *Multiculturalism*, ed. Amy Gutman (Princeton: Princeton University Press, 1994), 37.

17. See "Identity: A Poem," *A Stein Reader*, ed. Ulla E. Dydo (Evanston, Illinois: Northwestern University Press, 1993), 588. (Of course, Stein herself would not agree with this reading of her line.)

18. "Ideology and Ideological State Apparatuses," *Lenin and Philosophy*, trans. Ben Brewster (New York: Monthly Review Press, 1972), 179.

19. *Go Down, Moses* (New York: Vintage International, 1990), 114–15.

Reading the Absences: Race and Narration in Faulkner's *Absalom, Absalom!*

DOREEN FOWLER

The African American, Quentin Compson observes, is "a sort of obverse reflection of the white people he lives among."[1] With startling candor, Quentin names the object status that Euro-Americans have conferred on African Americans. African Americans, Quentin says, have been assigned the role of facing a mirror in which a white can locate a self-image. Black has been constructed as what white is not, the other that makes possible the normative. From Quentin's mirror-image we can infer that the African American is denied the subject position and relegated to the shadowy role of marginalized other.

In *Playing in the Dark*, Toni Morrison reflects on the racial divide that white America has invented so as to constitute what she calls "the dominant cultural body": "Deep within the word 'American' is its association with race. . . . American means white, and Africanist people struggle to make the term applicable to themselves with ethnicity and hyphen after hyphen after hyphen. . . . The American nation negotiated both its disdain and envy [of Africanist people] . . . through a self-reflexive contemplation of fabricated, mythological Africanism. For the settlers and for American writers generally, this Africanist other became the means of thinking about body, mind, chaos, kindness, and love."[2] Morrison goes on to challenge literary scholars to investigate "the ways in which a non-white Africanist presence and personae have been constructed—invented—in the United States, and . . . the literary uses this fabricated presence has served."[3] Her purpose, she writes, "is an effort to avert the critical gaze from the racial object to the racial subject; from the described and imagined to the describers and imaginers; from the serving to the served."[4] I propose that in *Absalom, Absalom!* Faulkner engages in precisely the project that Morrison outlines; that is, in *Absalom* Faulkner shifts the gaze from, in Morrison's words, "the described and imagined to the describers and imaginers"; and narration itself is the subject. Faulkner turns over the narration to character narrators, Miss Rosa, Mr.

Compson, Quentin, and Shreve; and the focus of the novel is their construction of meaning, in particular, their construction of racial meanings.
In this way, Faulkner negotiates the insidious myth of racial otherness
by focusing on the mythmakers and their articulation of racial identity.[5]

Other critics, notably Thadious Davis and James Snead, have sensi-
tively analyzed the way disparaging terms—what Snead calls "figures of
division"—are used in *Absalom* to construct a racial divide.[6] I propose
to look closely at another strategy employed to foster a myth of racial
otherness—a cultural erasure of the visible signs that white inheres
within black and black within white.

This form of cultural censorship has been documented by a number of
nineteenth-century Southern witnesses. For example, in her account of
her life as a slave, Harriet Jacobs writes that it was common practice in
the South to dispose quickly of the evidence of racial merging. The master who was also the father of a slave would, in Jacobs's words, "pass . . .
[the mother and the child] into the slave trader's hands as soon as possible, . . . thus getting them out of . . . sight."[7] Moreover, as Jacobs records,
Southern laws were written so as to enable white men to deny the paternity of racially mixed children. "[I]t was a crime," Jacobs writes, "for a
slave to tell who was the father of her child."[8] Another antebellum observer, Mary Chesnut, also remarks this cultural denial of racial mixing.
She writes: "the mulattoes one sees in every family exactly resemble the
white children—and every lady tells you who is the father of all the mulatto children in everybody's household, but those in her own she seems
to think drop from the clouds, or pretends so to think."[9]

Arguably this denial of blurred racial boundaries, to which Jacobs and
Chesnut bear witness, persists in the present. In fact, Faulkner may have
had firsthand knowledge of a cultural blindness to interracial alliances.
In *William Faulkner and Southern History*, Joel Williamson locates evidence that Faulkner's paternal great-grandfather, William Clark Falkner,
had a shadow family. Descendants of Emeline Lacy Falkner, whom the
Old Colonel took to live in his yard in 1858, claim that her daughter,
Fannie Forrest Falkner, born between 1864 and 1866, was the Old Colonel's daughter. Williamson interviewed members of Fannie's family who
say that the Old Colonel paid for her education at Rust College and visited her in Holly Springs.[10] However, if Fannie was the Old Colonel's
daughter, she was, as Williamson describes her, "a shadow daughter,"
since, in the words of Williamson, "the Colonel seemingly never publicly
claimed blood kin" with Fannie.[11] On the maternal side of the family, it
appears that Faulkner's mother's father, Charles Butler, disappeared
from Oxford to elope with a beautiful octoroon woman, the companion
of Mrs. Jacob Thompson. Joseph Blotner, in his 1974 biography, records

that Butler's disappearance coincided with the departure of Mrs. Thompson's companion,[12] and Williamson traces Blotner's knowledge to reliable sources, Dorothy Oldham, Estelle Faulkner's sister, who, in turn, had her information from Mamie Lewis Slate, the niece of Jacob Thompson.[13] However, despite the testimony of witnesses like the descendants of Fannie Forrest Falkner and Mamie Slate, these interracial relationships are difficult to verify because, to my knowledge, they have never been acknowledged by members of the Faulkner family.[14]

I propose to show that in *Absalom, Absalom!* Faulkner exposes this same blindness to the collapse of culturally fabricated black-white distinctions. Toni Morrison, perhaps America's leading authority on racial ideology, has observed that a form of racial censorship characterizes the novel. In a 1993 interview in the *Paris Review*, Morrison points out that "Faulkner in *Absalom, Absalom!* spends the entire book tracing race, and you can't find it. No one can see it, even the character who is black can't see it. I did this lecture for my students that took me forever, which was tracking all the moments of withheld, partial or disinformation, when a racial fact or clue *sort* of comes out but doesn't quite arrive. I just wanted to chart it. I listed its appearance, disguise and disappearance on every page, I mean every phrase!"[15] The reason "you can't find [race]" in *Absalom, Absalom!*, as Morrison astutely remarks, is because the narrators are the unconscious exponents of a racial ideology that mandates black-white separation. More specifically, this racial ideology dictates that they erase from their narration any Africanist presence that cannot be presented as utterly other. Race does appear in their narrations but only when they can represent black as unbridgeably different from white. For example, Miss Rosa allows into her narration the slaves that Sutpen brings with him from Haiti to Mississippi, but notice that she constructs these slaves as "wild men."[16] Similarly, Quentin and Shreve focus on the butler who turns young Tom Sutpen away from the front door of the big white house, but in their construction of him, the man is reduced to a "monkey-nigger" (189). However, when an Africanist presence threatens racial binary oppositions, when a link between black and white surfaces, the narrators, without conscious awareness, suppress that link. Accordingly, Henry kills Bon; and the narratives of Miss Rosa, Mr. Compson, and, for a time, Quentin and Shreve are censored. Charles Bon's murder is rehearsed over and over again in *Absalom*, but the reason why he must die is not explained until the final pages of the novel because the narrators conform to the same racial code that dictates Bon's death. Like Thomas Sutpen who will not say "my son" to Charles Bon, the narrators, until just before the novel's conclusion, withhold that Charles Bon bridges the distance between white Sutpen and racial other.

Lost in the maze of Miss Rosa's fulminations and Mr. Compson's rambling rhetoric, we may overlook significant absences. Missing from Miss Rosa's account is any reference that might tie Charles Bon to those whom she constructs as other. Because she unconsciously adheres to a code that mandates racial separation, she herself performs this separation; inserted in her narrative are gaps that separate black from white. She does not acknowledge what Quentin and Shreve ultimately recognize—that Bon is Thomas Sutpen's racially mixed son. She withholds from her account and apparently from herself any reference to Bon's one-eighth African wife and their son, who figure so prominently in Mr. Compson's narration. General Compson knows of the existence of Bon's wife and child; he even observed the woman weeping beside Bon's grave. He knows that after Bon's death Judith and Clytie bring Bon's racially mixed son to live with them. Étienne Bon's tragic life story is known to General Compson, to Quentin's father, to Quentin, and apparently to other citizens of Jefferson. But Miss Rosa, who loved Bon, never betrays any knowledge of the boy who is raised by Judith and Clytie. Miss Rosa's blindness, when we look for it, is truly remarkable. How could she fail to know that Judith died of yellow fever contracted while nursing Étienne Bon? How could Miss Rosa, who secured the headstone for Judith's grave, willfully ignore for twenty-five years the headstone beside Charles Bon's that reads "Charles Étienne Saint-Valery Bon. 1859–1884" (155)? But Miss Rosa never gives any sign of knowing that Charles Bon has a son who is not entirely white.

Because, without conscious awareness, Miss Rosa erases every trace of the other woman and the child, she does not acknowledge that Charles Bon substituted a photograph of his wife and son for Judith's photograph.[17] According to Mr. Compson, Judith finds on Charles's dead body the metal case that she had given him containing her photograph, but which now holds a picture of the octoroon wife and the racially mixed child. In Miss Rosa's account, the pictures have not been exchanged. She recalls running up the stairs to the second floor of the Sutpen house and finding Judith standing outside a closed bedroom door holding "something in one hanging hand" (114). A few sentences later she identifies this "something" in Judith's hand as "the picture of herself in its metal case which she had given [Bon]" (114). In Miss Rosa's version, Judith's picture is not displaced by the picture of the other woman and the child because Miss Rosa unconsciously erases all traces of a connection between Bon and those whom she constructs as other. In this way, by exclusion, otherness is fabricated.

The full measure of Miss Rosa's unconscious erasure of racial mixing is spoken at the novel's conclusion, when finally Quentin discloses what

happened when he and Miss Rosa went out to the old Sutpen place on
that September night in 1909. Even at this climactic moment in the
novel, after she has been out to the Sutpen place and has seen Henry,
still she clings to tropes of alienation. Walking back down the rutted path
to her carriage escorted by Jim Bond, son of Étienne Bon, grandson of
Charles Bon, and great-grandson of Thomas Sutpen, Miss Rosa stumbles
and falls. Turning to Jim Bond she says: "You aint any Sutpen. You dont
have to leave me lying in the dirt" (297). With these words, a repressed
meaning surfaces disguised.[18] In his essay, "On Negation," Freud explains that a repressed image or idea can make its way into consciousness
if it is negated. "Negation," Freud writes, "is a way of taking cognizance
of what is repressed; indeed it is already a lifting of repression, though
not, of course, an acceptance of what is repressed."[19] In other words, we
can utter a repressed meaning so long as we simultaneously disavow it
by negating it.[20] Accordingly, when Miss Rosa says to Jim Bond, "You
aint any Sutpen," she is simultaneously uttering and disavowing an unconscious meaning—that Jim Bond and Thomas Sutpen are related, that
black is not separate, not different from white.[21]

While it is not until the final pages of the novel that Charles Bon's full
identity is acknowledged, disguised allusions to his resolution of racial
difference sometimes slip past unconscious censors. For example, as Mr.
Compson attributes to Bon a shadowy quality, he goes on to add a phrase,
in which forbidden meanings surface undetected. Bon, Mr. Compson
says, is "an impenetrable and shadowy character. Yes, shadowy: a myth,
a phantom: something which they engendered and created whole themselves" (82). At one level, Compson appears to say that the Sutpens
wholly created Bon; but, alternatively, Compson's phrase, "created whole
themselves," can be read to mean that Charles created them whole; that
is, that he is their missing part, their missing son and brother, whom they
have alienated, and whose return will render them whole again.

Near the end of Mr. Compson's account, forbidden subliminal meanings again appear in a disguised form.[22] On the surface, he appears to
dismiss his own interpretation of the Sutpen tragedy. After all that rea-
soning and rhetoric, all those invented scenes, Compson admits his account "does not explain." But he quickly revises his assessment to
suggest not incomprehensibility but cultural interdiction: "Or perhaps
that's it: they dont explain and we are not supposed to know" (80). As he
continues to muse on the failure of his narrative, he identifies a lack: "Yes,
Judith, Bon, Henry, Sutpen: all of them. They are there, yet something is
missing" (80). With these words Mr. Compson strikes on precisely the
problem with not only his narration but also Miss Rosa's and, until nearly
the end of the novel, Quentin and Shreve's. "Something is missing" from

these versions of the Sutpen story because the narrators unconsciously censor their accounts. "Something is missing" because they have wrenched apart black from white and opened up a gap. It is noteworthy, I think, that, as Mr. Compson continues to reflect on the shortcomings of his interpretation, he repeatedly underscores the word, "nothing": "they are like a chemical formula exhumed along with the letters from that forgotten chest . . . ; you bring them together in the proportions called for, but nothing happens; you re-read, tedious and intent, poring, making sure that you have forgotten nothing . . . ; you bring them together again and again nothing happens" (80). Compson's emphatic reiteration of the word "nothing" is a clue, a disguised meaning out of the unconscious mind. "Nothing" is what the narrators introduce into the narrative as they erase evidence of racial fusion. "Nothing" is what they make of Charles Bon. Bon is a "shadowy, almost substanceless" (74) figure in the narrative because they have rendered him so. Because what he is cannot be accounted for within their racial ideology, because in him black and white fuse, they blot him out. Like Thomas Sutpen who will not acknowledge Bon, and Henry who kills him, the narrators make a cipher of Charles Bon and censor his story.

This essay has traced a pattern of racial repression. In conclusion, I want to make clear that I am not accusing Faulkner of racial censorship. Rather, I contend that, like Harriet Jacobs and Mary Chesnut, Faulkner, through a different medium, is challenging and exposing racial censorship. Faulkner represented a world that held as its first principle that black must be separate from white, for, if black is not separate from white, then whiteness itself is undermined. Faulkner accurately renders this world, but even as he transcribes the perspectives of those who cling to notions of racial difference, he reveals that racial identity, like all identity, is constructed through language. Faulkner structures *Absalom, Absalom!* so that the reader struggles through wave after wave of language to reach a long withheld denouement. When that denouement finally arrives, it is all the more powerfully evoked because it is so hard-won. At the novel's conclusion, Quentin and Shreve at last disclose that Charles Bon resolves notions of racial difference, that he effaces the difference between white Sutpen and racial other; and this revelation opens upon another—that it is not race but social prohibition, as enforced by language, that separates father from son and brother from brother.

NOTES

1. William Faulkner, *The Sound and the Fury.* The Corrected Text (1929; New York: Vintage, 1987), 106.

2. Toni Morrison, *Playing in the Dark: Whiteness and the Literary Imagination* (New York: Vintage, 1992), 47–48.

3. Ibid., 90.

4. Ibid., 91.

5. My interpretation owes a debt to the work of other scholars. It owes much to Donald M. Kartiganer's pathbreaking chapter in *The Fragile Thread: The Meaning of Form in Faulkner's Novels* (Amherst: University of Massachusetts Press, 1979), which first taught us that the needs and desires of the tellers shape their tale. I am indebted as well to John T. Irwin's *Doubling and Incest/Repetition and Revenge* (Baltimore: Johns Hopkins University Press, 1975), which brilliantly argues that *Absalom, Absalom!* maps repression. Another work that helped me to form my own interpretation is Richard C. Moreland's *Faulkner and Modernism: Reading and Rewriting* (Madison: University of Wisconsin Press, 1990). In his critical study, Moreland demonstrates that Miss Rosa and Mr. Compson cling to the stance of a Southern modernist; that is, they view the Sutpen tragedy either with nostalgia or irony and both aesthetic devices seek to distance and to protect, to reify distinctions of class, race, and gender.

6. See Thadious M. Davis, *Faulkner's "Negro": Art in Southern Context* (Baton Rouge: Louisiana State University Press, 1983), 179–238; and James A. Snead, *Figures of Division: William Faulkner's Major Novels* (New York: Methuen, 1986), 101–39.

7. Harriet A. Jacobs, *Incidents in the Life of a Slave Girl*, ed. Jean Fagan Yellin (1861; Cambridge: Harvard University Press, 1987), 36.

8. Ibid., 13.

9. *Mary Chesnut's Civil War*, ed. C. Vann Woodward (New Haven: Yale University Press, 1981), 30.

10. Joel Williamson, *William Faulkner and Southern History* (New York: Oxford University Press, 1993), 64–67.

11. Ibid., 64.

12. Joseph Blotner, *Faulkner: A Biography*, 2 vols. (New York: Random House, 1974), 57. It is noteworthy, I think, that in his 1984 one-volume version of Faulkner's biography, Blotner deletes the reference to the simultaneous departure from Oxford of Mrs. Thompson's beautiful octoroon companion.

13. Williamson, 123–24.

14. In an interview with me on 4 February 1991, James Murry Faulkner, William Faulkner's nephew, denied that Charles Butler eloped with Mrs. Thompson's companion.

15. Toni Morrison, "The Art of Fiction CXXXIV," Interview with Elissa Schappell, *Paris Review* 129 (1993): 101.

16. William Faulkner, *Absalom, Absalom!* The Corrected Text (1936; New York: Vintage International, 1990), 27. All further citations to this text will refer to this edition.

17. For an interpretation of the switched pictures, see Elisabeth Muhlenfeld, " 'We have waited long enough': *Judith Sutpen and Charles Bon*," *Southern Review* 14 (1978): 66–80.

18. Minrose Gwin has astutely observed that the repressed returns in Miss Rosa's narrative. Gwin writes that Miss Rosa is the uncanny hysteric; that is, in her text, there erupts "all that the symbolic order must repress in order to speak" (71). See *The Feminine and Faulkner: Reading Beyond Sexual Difference* (Knoxville: University of Tennessee Press, 1990).

19. Sigmund Freud, *The Standard Edition of the Complete Psychological Works of Freud*, ed. and trans. James Strachey, 24 vols. (London: Hogarth Press, 1961), 19:235–36.

20. See also François Pitavy, "Some Remarks on Negation and Denegation in William Faulkner's *Absalom, Absalom!*," in *Faulkner's Discourse*, ed. Lothar Hönnighausen (Tubingen: Max Niemeyer Verlag, 1989), 25–32.

21. Eric J. Sundquist also identifies signs that Miss Rosa may subliminally know that Charles Bon is Sutpen's black son. Sundquist points to the moment in the novel when Miss Rosa, stopped by Clytie from ascending the stairs of Sutpen's house, exclaims, "And you too? And you too, sister, sister?" (112–13). According to Sundquist, this scene between Clytie and Rosa intimates that "Rosa herself, perhaps vicariously, understands the full di-

mensions of Bon's tragedy as well as Sutpen's" (114). See *Faulkner: The House Divided* (Baltimore: Johns Hopkins University Press, 1983), 111–17.

22. Whereas I interpret inconsistencies and contradictions in the three narrations in terms of unconscious censorship and the disguised return of repressed meanings, other critics, noting contrary tendencies in the text of *Absalom, Absalom!*, have offered alternative interpretations. For example, Floyd C. Watkins suggests that the bewildering divergence of meanings in *Absalom* may reflect "the impossibility of knowing history and the past fully and accurately, and perhaps even the method of development of myth" (86). See "What Happens in *Absalom, Absalom!?*," *Modern Fiction Studies* 13 (1967): 79–87. In his collation of the manuscript of *Absalom* with the Modern Library published text, Gerald Langford identifies passages that plainly state Mr. Compson's ignorance of Bon's ancestry and others that signal Mr. Compson's awareness. Faced with such inconsistency, Langford concludes that Faulkner repeatedly altered the plan of his novel, writing at some time with the intention that Mr. Compson should know and at other times with the intention that he should not. Langford's conclusion proceeds from the assumption that either Mr. Compson knows or does not know. Langford does not allow for the possibility that Mr. Compson may be consciously unaware even as traces of disavowed meanings leak into his narrative. See *Faulkner's Revisions of "Absalom, Absalom!": A Collation of the Manuscript and the Published Book* (Austin: University of Texas Press, 1971), 8–12.

The Strange, Double-Edged
Gift of Faulkner's Fiction

DAVID MINTER

In this brief essay, I want to focus on two scenes from Faulkner's fiction, one from *Absalom, Absalom!* (1936), and one from *Sanctuary* (1931), hoping that we can revisit them with eyes slightly altered by two quotations, one from M. M. Bakhtin's *The Dialogic Imagination* (1981), the other from W. H. Auden's *The Dyer's Hand* (1962). The statement from Bakhtin deals with the dynamic relations that define and situate literary texts:

> we may call this world the world that *creates* the text, for all its aspects—the reality reflected in the text, the authors creating the text, the performers of the text (if they exist) and finally the listeners or readers who recreate and in so doing renew the text—participate equally in the creation of the represented world in the text. Out of the actual chronotopes of our world (which serve as the source of representation) emerge the reflected and *created* chronotopes of the world represented in the work.[1]

Auden's statement, even more than Bakhtin's, goes over ground that would have seemed like native ground to Faulkner, in part because it bears in interesting ways on conflicting interpretations of American culture that were prominent during the years in which Faulkner emerged as a writer, though, as I shall later make clear, the value of this statement for us depends on our success in modifying the absolute line it draws between the "sacred" and the "profane." The quotation is as follows:

> The value of a profane thing lies in what it usefully does, the value of a sacred thing lies in what it *is*; a sacred thing may also have a function but it does not have to. . . .
> Great changes in artistic style always reflect some alteration in the frontier between the sacred and profane in the imagination of a society. Thus, to take an architectural example, a seventeenth-century monarch had the same function as that of a modern State official—he had to govern. But in designing his palace, the Baroque architect did not aim, as a modern architect aims when designing a government building, at making an office in which the king could govern as easily and efficiently as possible; he was trying to make a fit home

for God's earthly representative to inhabit; in so far as he thought at all about what the king would do in it as a ruler, he thought of his ceremonial not his practical actions.[2]

With these quotations in mind, I want to state the central contentions of this paper—first, that without his ever having put it to himself in these terms, Faulkner somehow recognized (or sensed so deeply as to make it tantamount to imaginative recognition) that the kinds of texts he was most interested in and had the most talent for creating were texts that drew readers into active, re-creative roles of the kind that Bakhtin delineates; second, that one of the things that he drew his readers into was the process of understanding and imaginatively revising two contradictory views of American history, one allied with the North, the other with the South, both of which redefined both its status and that of the other by surreptitiously redrawing the line between the "sacred" and the "profane," each implicitly claiming for itself traits associated with the "sacred" while assigning to the other traits associated with the "profane"; and third, that he also drew his readers into the process of recognizing that the traditional cultural authority of these terms and the claims based on them were changing.

Although the two views of American history that I have in mind are familiar, I want briefly to recall them by borrowing observations from C. Vann Woodward's *The Burden of Southern History*. The North regarded the South as deviating from "the national pattern" that it associated with moral rectitude and thought of as justifying unparalleled success, a pattern that centered on habits of industry which were easily adapted to industrialism and were allied not only with habits of the heart but also with "urbanity" in two different senses of the term—that is, becoming increasingly urban and also increasingly urbane. In short, the North regarded the South as deviating from what Woodward calls the "National myths, American myths" associated with "the American Way of Life"—big concepts that he defines in terms "of the uniquely American experience of success," gauged primarily in terms of achieving unparalleled economic abundance and avoiding ever "being on the losing side in a war." The nation's actual experience of economic abundance and military success, Woodward goes on to suggest, fostered a sense of self-righteousness, and with it "the legend of American innocence," in terms that set the South's continuing economic, social, and cultural backwardness, together with its history of failure, defeat, and guilt, apart, making it a source of embarrassment to the nation as a whole and also making it defensive in ways that Woodward directly associates with the twelve Southern "agrarians" (or "fugitives," as they also called themselves) who wrote *I'll Take My Stand* (1930).[3]

One sign of the depth of the nation's sense of the South's backwardness and decadence can be seen in the way that it turned up at unexpected times, in unexpected places—in, for example, the *New York Times*'s defensive response to announcement of Faulkner's being named winner of the Nobel Prize. For the logic of the *Times*'s editorial was to dissociate the larger nation from the "too often vicious, depraved, decadent, corrupt" society represented in Faulkner's fiction, where "Incest and rape [were] common pastimes"[4]—a move no one had thought necessary for earlier U. S. recipients of the prize, beginning with the satirically minded, fault-finding Sinclair Lewis in 1930. The nation's sense of the South also found expression in jokes about and parodies of its speech patterns, cooking, climate, manners, and mores—in short, its "culture." Southern views of the North, on the other hand, some of them codified by the Agrarians, tended to center on condemnations of the North's desertion of the land and the rhythms and folkways—"the way of life"—associated with its cultivation, in pursuit of a "godless" industrialism and a profane worship of money as well as its unholy "war of aggression" against the South. At times, furthermore, the South's defense of itself also included a defense of the institutions of slavery and segregation, couched in Biblical terms or in appeals to the cultures of Greece and Rome, that were clearly designed to contrast the South's "traditional," "agrarian," "Christian" "way of life" with the North's vulgar, "godless" industrialism and capitalism.[5]

The views of American history embedded in the North's sense both of itself and of the South, and of the South's sense both of itself and of the North, have, I think, interesting ties to conflicting interpretations of other episodes in modern history, including clashes and wars not fought on this continent. For present purposes, however, I want simply to note that they possessed considerable currency and force during the years in which Faulkner emerged as a writer. For, although Faulkner had limited and even strained relations with the Southern Agrarians and seems to have given little if any credence to their diagnoses or prescriptions, there was at least one way in which he shared a need resolutely felt and either disguised or obliquely expressed by them—namely, the need for a sense of aesthetic form that seemed somehow allied, if not with a sense of the sacred, at least with considerable nostalgia for it. Strangely, however, his solution to this need seems to me to have more in common with that of the Northern poet Wallace Stevens, as worked out in poems like "The Idea of Order at Key West," "Notes Toward a Supreme Fiction," "The Rock," "The Poem That Took the Place of a Mountain," and "Sunday Morning," to name a few, or, put another way, with literary "modernism," than with Southern Agrarianism. And it found expression in his effort to salvage at least a sense of some absolute, or, put another way, a sense of certitude that went with a sense of the sacred, or to borrow from Stevens, a sense of "some imperishable bliss," if only as an impossible possibility. For Faulkner knew, I think, what Stevens knew, and what Stevens's heroine in "Sunday Morning" learns—namely, that evocations and approximations ("ambiguous undulations," to use another of Stevens's phrases) that echoed old reports (or "old tales and talking," to use a familiar phrase of Faulkner's), which were in turn based on old texts that could be evoked but could not be reconstituted or replaced, were as much as he could hope to create, and further, that they would suffice. For he clearly sensed that one implication of needing terms like "sacred" and "profane" in the twilight of their useful lives as terms of authority was that writers and their readers would have to make do with a sense of beginnings, a sense of endings, and, thus, a sense of narrative—which, I would argue, is one way of describing what we as readers must labor to gather from fractured, discontinuous novels and stories. And he sensed, further, that just as this cultural predicament brought with it invitations to creativity, it also brought temptations of the kind of improvisation that, as I hope to show, we see played out in *Sanctuary*, where, among other things, the term *sacred* is profaned.

By way of further clarifying the implications of the interrelated contentions that I have stated as a thesis, let me suggest, first, that one of Faulkner's hopes had to do, not with redrawing the line between the sacred and the profane, but rather with finding new ways of coping with the continuing diminishment and corruption of these terms as interpretive and even foundational concepts. For it is at least in part his revisionary stance in these matters that accounts both for the complexities of his fiction and for the resistance that his fiction initially provoked, including, to take three very different examples, the *New York Times*'s editorial, the early silence and neglect of most of the Southern Agrarians, and, more surprisingly, what we might call the taming efforts of the "New Critics" and their heirs, some of whom were, of course, also Southern Agrarians.

There are, of course, different ways of looking at the writings of the third of these groups—the Southern Agrarians who were also "New Critics"; and they clearly included many valuable, pioneering efforts that dramatically extended our understanding of Faulkner's fiction. Yet it seems to me clear that a part of what the "New Critics" sought was a way of saving the notion of the "sacred" in what they viewed, with alarm, as an increasingly "profane" world, and, further, that they sought to achieve this by reclaiming it for "art."[6] For there are clearly important ties between the formal qualities that the New Critics "discovered" and then celebrated in poetry and the cultural qualities that the Agrarians discovered and then celebrated in the history of the South. This suggests, as it seems to me, that it was not incidental but telling, first, that a surprising number of the most important New Critics were Southern; second, that they employed terms that had clear religious associations, including, for example, Robert Penn Warren's essay called "Pure and Impure Poetry" (1943); Allen Tate's essay called "The Angelic Imagination" (1951); and Cleanth Brooks's essays called "Criticism, History, and Critical Relativism," "The Heresy of Paraphrase," and "The Problem of Belief and the Problem of Cognition," all included in *The Well Wrought Urn* (1947); third, that they employed interpretive tools and strategies perfected in Biblical studies, including those associated with "exegesis" and with what in Biblical studies were referred to as "form criticism" and the "higher criticism"; and fourth, that they spent much time and energy separating sheep from goats, as it were, by conferring upon a select group of poets and poems something that we have learned to recognize as "canonical" status, thus collapsing into a decade or two their version of the much longer process by which some texts had been brought into the Bible and others had been left out. Moves such as these stemmed, we need to recognize, from deeply felt needs, some of them overtly secular; but they included a desire to save the concept of the "sacred" for the world they saw emerging around them. With this in mind, furthermore, we can better appreciate the significance of a series of interrelated developments, including, first, the widening gap between "canonical" and "noncanonical" works; second, the attention lavished on problems having to do with "intent"; third, the line drawn between scholars whose tasks lay in "establishing texts" and critics whose tasks lay in "interpreting" them; and fourth, the widespread assumption that poetry, by virtue of being "purer" than drama and fiction, was superior to them. In short, in several ways the roles of the "New Critics" became almost priestlike—in particular, they became keepers of texts on which they lavished attention and to which, in some ways, they controlled access, as priests had once controlled access to the sacraments, and they became practitioners of things that resembled sacramental rites.

2

But what have such things as these to do either with "National Myths, American Myths,"[7] even when broadened, as I propose here, to include new directions in literary criticism, or with Faulkner's innovative fiction? A full answer to these questions, which I hope someday to provide, would take more space than I have in this paper. As a start, however, I want to examine, first, the scene in *Absalom, Absalom!* in which the young

Thomas Sutpen first encounters the institution of private property as represented by the Southern plantation system, and with it also encounters both the caste system of slavery that defined black slaves as property and the class system that empowered large landholders to subjugate and exploit poor, landless white families like the Sutpens; and second, the trial scene in *Sanctuary*, which ostensibly unfolds both as a championing of the "sacred" concept of "womanhood"[8] and as a search for justice that will vindicate Temple Drake by offering her the protection of the court, by restoring her to the loving arms of her father, and by properly and legally punishing those who have terrorized and raped her.

The first of these scenes is from chapter 7 of *Absalom, Absalom!*, where Quentin recounts for Shreve what Sutpen reputedly has told Quentin's grandfather during their pursuit of the French architect when he is trying to get "back to New Orleans or wherever it was" that he was going.[9] It is here that we learn that Sutpen had been born in 1808 in the unnamed territory that later became West Virginia, "where what few other people he knew lived in log cabins boiling with children like the one he was born in," and where the "men and grown boys" hunted or lay

> on the floor while the women and older girls stepped back and forth across them to reach the fire to cook, where the only colored people were Indians and you only looked down at them over your rifle sights, where he had never even heard of, never imagined, a place, a land divided neatly up and actually owned by men who did nothing but ride over it on fine horses or sit in fine clothes on the galleries of big houses while other people worked for them; he did not even imagine then that there was any such way to live or to want to live, or that there existed all the objects to be wanted which there were, or that the ones who owned the objects not only could look down on the ones that didn't, but could be supported in the down-looking not only by the others who owned objects too but by the very ones that were looked down on that didn't own objects and knew that they never would. Because where he lived the land belonged to anybody and everybody. . . . So he didn't even know there was a country all divided and fixed and neat with a people living on it all divided and fixed and neat because of what color their skins happened to be and what they happened to own, and where a certain few men not only had the power of life and death and barter and sale over others, they had living human men to perform the endless repetitive personal offices . . . that all men have had to do for themselves since time began. . . . (179–80)

Like those that surround it, this passage comes to us as a series of revelations, as only the greatest writing can. Its concentrated audacity epitomizes both the chapter in which it appears and the novel of which it is a part. For present purposes, however, I first want to note that it presents basic possessions—food, clothing, shelter, simple dishes, tools, and weapons—as well as a shared sense of territoriality and a collective will to defend one's territory against other claimants to it as "natural," and thus as present even in simple, "primitive" communities. In short, such things come to us as, if not "natural," direct and more or less inevitable human extensions of nature. In addition, it presents gender-based differentiations of tasks and prerogatives in much the same way, which is to say as also "natural." By contrast, it presents all differentiations based on class and caste, together with all more elaborate forms of social organization and arrangement and with the desire for all other kinds of possessions and privilege—indeed, all knowledge of their existence and all desire for or "need" of such possessions and privilege, as well as all hope for or ambition associated with acquiring them, and thus all concern with status—under the aspect of the institution of property and the power, prerogatives, and transformations of human life that accompany it. In short, all of these things—our knowledge of their existence, our sense of needing or desiring them, our habit of judging ourselves and others on the basis of "success" in acquiring them, and our habit of organizing social life on the basis of their possession—become in *Absalom, Absalom!* lessons, not of nature but of society. Finally, in keeping both with this and with his depiction of the "fall" of the Sutpens into Tidewater Virginia, Faulkner presents the young Thomas Sutpen's learning of these things as a loss of "innocence" that he had not even known he possessed (see 178–79, 183–88).

In the pages that follow, Faulkner elaborates and glosses the distinctions he has drawn—namely, those between a world where the land "belonged to anybody and everybody" and where the people, except for lines drawn by a clear sense of gender and a hazy sense of age (see 184, 185, 189), all did the same things, sharing work and leisure, and one where the land is "property" and thus is "divided and fixed and neat," and where, as a result, the "people living on it" also become "all divided and fixed and neat," separated and organized by boundary lines, or by distinctions that function as boundary lines. As a result, the family's descent from their simple mountain community into the "splendor" of Tidewater Virginia comes more and more resoundingly to resemble the "fall," like "the oldentime" fall into sin, to borrow a phrase that occurs in the first chapter of the novel (see 4). "That's how it was," Faulkner writes. "They fell into it, the whole family" (222).

This fall takes the young Thomas Sutpen and his family into a patriarchal world in which "work" becomes "labor"—that is, where familiar tasks and chores once performed to benefit a family and a small community are now performed for wages or for credit at the plantation store—a change that fundamentally alters the tasks themselves and their relations to the people who perform them. Gender differentiations, including those having to do with labor, become even sharper; and both the men and the women who, possessing no property and having no exalted social standing, undergo a transformation in which they begin to resemble the domesticated beasts they work with. Having less to express, they show less expression—the one exception being a new emotion that Faulkner describes as "a kind of speculative antagonism" (186), which they feel toward other people but feel free to express only toward the black slaves whom they encounter for the first time. Like the transformation of their lives, furthermore, this new antagonism is in considerable measure economic in its origins. For it is based in part on the meager wages they receive for the labor they perform; in part on the exorbitant prices and exorbitant credit they are charged at the store that is also owned by the plantation owner; in part on their sense that they live less well even than the black slaves; and in part on their sense that they neither have nor have any hope of acquiring any part in the leisure, the privileges, and the luxury enjoyed by the family of the powerful man who owns "all the land and the niggers and apparently the white men" too (184). For, unlike both the poor whites and the enslaved blacks, whose lives are defined by labor and want that increase antagonism among and between them, none of the family of the owner wants for anything, and none does any work. They live "in the biggest house" the Sutpens have "ever seen." Playing a clearly ornamental role, the women and children ride around in a fancy carriage, wearing fancy clothes, and crowding lesser people off the roads (see 187), while the master of the plantation, far from working or even supervising the work of others, spends his days lying in a hammock under the trees with a servant who does "nothing but fan him and bring him drinks" (184).

Faulkner presents Thomas Sutpen's awakening to the realities of the world into which he and his family have fallen as recognition that the society of Tidewater Virginia is founded on an institutionalized conviction that there are crucial differences "not only between white men and black ones, but . . . between white men and white men" and, further, that the majority must be degraded so that a few can be exalted (see 183). At one point, we see Sutpen recalling the sight of "his sister pumping rhythmic up and down above a washtub in the yard, her back toward him, shapeless in a calico dress and a pair of the old man's shoes unlaced and flapping about her ankles and broad in the beam as a cow, the very labor she was doing brutish and stupidly out of all proportion to its reward: the very primary essence of labor, toil, reduced to its crude absolute which only a beast could and would endure" (191). At another, we see him "seeing his own father and sisters and brothers as the owner, the rich man . . . must have been seeing them all the time—as cattle, crea-tures heavy and without grace, brutely evacuated into a world without hope or purpose for them" (190). As a result, the remote, virtually invisi-ble owner, whose life is defined by leisure, luxury, and indulgence, comes to us wrapped in a totally unearned sense of privilege made possi-ble by socially sanctioned abuses of the institution of property that result in the degradation of a large majority of the white people as well as all of the black people for the benefit of a few.

We know, of course, that Faulkner aspired to ownership of property and that, over time, he managed to acquire a considerable amount of it. So, lest I be misunderstood, let me hasten to add that it is not my inten-tion to suggest that Faulkner ever became, even in the 1930s, the United States' so-called red or radical decade, during which he wrote both *Absa-lom, Absalom!* and *Sanctuary*, anything like a concerted reformer, let alone any kind of revolutionary. He clearly did not. But in dealing with a writer like Faulkner, and especially in dealing with scenes like those we encounter in *Absalom, Absalom!*, as well as those that lead up to and culminate in Ike McCaslin's renunciation of property in *Go Down, Moses* (1942)—where property, including human beings as well as land and other "possessions," as recorded in old family and plantation store led-gers, comes to us as a basis for establishing and exacerbating unjust dis-tinctions regarding gender as well as class and race—it is important to keep actively in mind W. B. Yeats's admonition: that it is of our quarrels with others that we make rhetoric and of our quarrels with ourselves that we make poetry. Which is to say that it is important that we take seriously the possibility that Faulkner was deeply self-conflicted about many things of importance to him, including the worship of success, the fear of failure, and the values of a culture that attaches ultimate importance to materialistic definitions and measures of both of these things.

Ostensibly, the second scene that I want to examine, the trial scene that begins in the closing pages of chapter 27 and continues through chapters 28 and 29 of *Sanctuary*, is staged in the name of achieving "jus-tice," defending Temple Drake's "honor," and offering her "sanctuary," in an apparently sympathetic, protective court and in the strong, caring arms of her father, both of which present themselves as champions of the concept of "womanhood"—the "most sacred thing in life," (284). But as the trial unfolds, it becomes yet another painful violation of Temple and, then, precipitates a public "lynching," which is to say a ritual sacrifice, of a poor white man named Lee Goodwin, who is wrongfully accused of the crimes committed against Temple. In this process, the hypocrisy both of Temple's father and of the court and its officers is exposed, for, acting in consort, they betray the concepts of "womanhood" and "justice" that they purport to honor. Acting, we surmise, at the behest of Temple's father, the officers of the court make a mockery of the trial by turning it into a carefully staged scene dedicated to reestablishing and celebrating not only his paternal authority over Temple's body and her story but also his social-political authority over the meaning of "justice" and the force of "public opinion." Here, even more than in the scene we examined in *Absalom, Absalom!*, issues having to do with abuses of power, privilege, and class are brought under the aspect of gender, or more specifically of paternalism and patriarchy, in their manifold forms and expressions. For what we witness is Judge Drake's successful effort to bend both the law, as represented by the District Attorney, the judge, and the jury, and public sentiment, as represented by a lawless mob, to the task of reestablishing his power and authority, even at the expense of betraying justice and inflicting further pain on his daughter.

The trial in question, which is staged in the "honorable Circuit Court of Yoknapatawpha county" (282), purports to be a disinterested search for truth, designed to vindicate Temple Drake, who has been terrorized as well as repeatedly and brutally raped, by properly charging, trying, convicting, and punishing the man or men responsible for what has happened to her. Ironically, however, despite the lip service paid to "womanhood," both the dominant players in the courtroom—the judge, the jury, the District Attorney, the defense attorney—and the most conspicuous members of the audience are male. "Speak out. No one will hurt you. Let these good men, these fathers and husbands, hear what you have to say, and right your wrong for you," the male District Attorney tells Temple—who sits "in an attitude at once detached and cringing, her gaze fixed on some thing at the back of the room" and her mouth fixed "like something both symbolical and cryptic" (284). Furthermore, since by this time we know a great deal about Temple's story, we soon realize that the story that unfolds in the courtroom has been fabricated, presumably by the men who dominate the courtroom, for purposes other than those recited by the District Attorney. Certainly, it bears highly problematical relations to what we as readers know has happened to Temple. To Faulkner's readers, therefore, fall two crucial tasks: first, that of tracking the many ways in which what passes for truth in the courtroom is false and; second, that of discerning whose interests the lies serve. For the "parrot-like answers" (286) that Temple gives during her testimony are not only obviously rehearsed and perjured; they also have three important effects: they successfully convict an innocent man in whom neither the court nor Temple's father nor the folk of Jefferson nor the Memphis underworld has much interest, though he is in fact a war hero; they publicly reestablish the power and authority of her father, Judge Drake, over Temple's

life and story; and they make it possible for the District Attorney to insti-
gate a lynching of the man they have conspired to convict.

The actions, if not the conspiracy, that achieve these ends involve the
presiding judge and the District Attorney, both of whom defer to and
take their cues from "Judge Drake," Temple's white-haired, immacu-
lately dressed, obviously wealthy, powerful father who carries a Panama
hat in one hand and a slender black stick in the other and manages to
dominate the courtroom with a minimum of effort. "Yes, sir, Judge," the
Court answers to the only words that Judge Drake speaks ("is the Court
done with this witness?" he asks), as he approaches Temple, who sits "in
her attitude of childish immobility, gazing like a drugged person above
the faces, toward the rear of the room" where the four young soldierlike
men who accompany her father and obey his almost invisible commands
stand "stiffly erect near the exit," waiting to escort both the girl and "the
old man erect beside her" from the courtroom (288–90).

In this scene, in which Temple's childlike helplessness and dependence are stressed repeatedly, along with her excruciating discomfort,
Faulkner repeats details (the "blank eyes," "the savage spots of rouge,"
"her blank face rigid," and especially her tortured, arching, and writhing
body) that evoke the rape scenes that have occurred earlier in the novel.
Twice on her way down the aisle, after her perjured testimony has been
completed, Temple stops. The second time she begins "to cringe back,
her body arching slowly, her arm tautening in the old man's grasp."
Nearer the door, she moves "again, in that shrinking and rapt abasement"
that we have seen earlier. Finally, after she is surrounded by the four
young, erect soldierlike men who accompany her erect father, we see
her, once again, "shrunk against the wall just inside the door, her body
arched again . . . clinging there," in what proves to be her last, futile act
of resistance and surrender before her father and the four young men
close around her arched body and take her away (289–90).

In this scene, I think, as much as any scene in Faulkner's fiction, terms
purportedly having to do with truth and justice, as Foucault might put it,
are casually traded in for terms having to do with power and authority
that are exclusively male and paternal. Working together, the men in
charge of the court contrive for the town of Jefferson a show in which
the authority of Temple's father over public opinion and public action as
well as Temple, her story, and her body are reestablished. Just as the
court acts at the behest of Temple's father, so, too, does the mob of drum-
mers who rape, mutilate, and burn Lee Goodwin, follow the explicit suggestion of one of her father's deputies, namely, the District Attorney.
This is "no longer a matter for the hangman, but for a bonfire of gaso-
line———," says Yoknapatawpha's honorable District Attorney in his

summation, just after he has reminded the court and its spectators that "womanhood" is the "most sacred thing in life" (284).

Whether we think of "the sacred," as Auden suggests, primarily in terms of what it *is* or primarily in terms of its function, it seems clear that in the fallen world of *Sanctuary* it has become a wholly honorific concept dedicated to reinforcing, enhancing, and ornamenting patriarchal authority. Temple, you will recall, is eighteen years old at the time of her trial, and she has done, as the young sometimes do, several foolishly reckless things. And it is in part as a result of some of them that she has suffered terribly. Yet, the court's interests do not lie primarily with Temple at all; they lie with her father, which means, as it turns out, that they have much to do with his status and power, little to do with vindicating his daughter, and nothing to do with truth or justice. Preempting the court's declared purposes, Judge Drake's ends culminate in three interrelated developments—the public reestablishment of his control over Temple, her story, and her cringing, writhing body; second, the public humiliation of Horace Benbow who persists despite warnings in his bumbling yet well-intentioned effort to defend Lee Goodwin;[10] and third, the public reestablishment of his and the court's control, as upper-class white men, over the pent-up anger and frustration—or the "speculative antagonism," to borrow a phrase from *Absalom, Absalom!*—of lower-class white men who are encouraged to mutilate and murder one of their own. In short, *Sanctuary*, perhaps the angriest of Faulkner's novels, is also the bleakest and most disillusioned. Its world, to borrow again from Yeats, this time from "The Second Coming," is one where the best lack hope as well as all conviction, while the worst are full of what passes for "passionate intensity" and also possess a shrewd sense of power. Finally, let me suggest that one source of our resistance to "reading" this novel, our disease with it, almost certainly stems from our sense that in our roles as readers we too are being manipulated into sharing the crowd's prurient, voyeuristic interests both in the repeated rapes of Temple and of the rape and burning of Lee Goodwin. " 'Git on home now. . . . Show's over,' " the night marshal says. " 'She was some baby,' " one of the men in the crowd says to another. " 'Jeez. I wouldn't have used no cob' " (294).[11]

These two very different scenes seem to me to represent Faulkner's angry, conflicted, iconoclastic imagination at its most daring. Together they subject to profound interrogation several treasured assumptions about both the United States and the American South. The scene from *Absalom, Absalom!* takes us back to what we might call the prehistory of Yoknapatawpha County. It recalls for us the cultural authority that Tidewater Virginia had for North Mississippi as well as the rest of the South. And it not only revises, it explodes the South's favored version of the plantation system as based on a supportive, caring form of paternalism rather than the remote and callous ownership of Northern capitalism. It thus calls into question the South's sense of itself as made more humane, gentle, and caring, indeed, more "natural," by virtue of its agricultural economy and way of life—as seen, for example, in the celebration of attachment to the "land" seen not only in novels like *Gone with the Wind* but also in many works of the Agrarians, which often seem to assume that simply being closer to the land made people more humane. Certainly, it is hard to imagine how any absentee capitalist owner could have been farther removed from or more indifferent to the workers dependent on him, or more complacent in his assumption-conviction that he had a right to exploit them and their labor for his profit and comfort, than Faulkner's Virginia gentleman-planter-plantation-store-owner. Furthermore, by bringing both the class system introduced by the plantation system and the caste system introduced by the institution of slavery under the aspect of the institution of private property, and thus under the aspect of modern capitalism, Faulkner created scenes that, read with care, were virtually certain to disturb and even offend Northerners and Southerners alike. The scene from *Sanctuary* presents legal institutions in general and courts in particular, not as institutions dedicated to ensuring justice by punishing the guilty and protecting the innocent, but as institutions cynically committed to serving the interests, shoring up the egos, and protecting and even enlarging the power of rich, arrogant men whose overriding concern is with themselves and their status. Together, in one way or another, scenes such as these challenge all of us. "Whose myths and whose history?" they seem to ask in all but words, as they draw us into perilous versions of what Bakhtin calls active participation and, indeed, complicity "in the creation of the represented world in the text."[12]

By looking back into the past in novels like *Absalom, Absalom!* and out into the world around him in novels like *Sanctuary*, Faulkner was able to create participatory texts that remind us that the human need for community is born of a need for order as well as a need for relatedness, and further, that the writing and reading of novels are, among other things, expressions of both of these needs. At the same time, however, and in the same motion, he also reminds us that people fully drawn into such ventures—whether they begin with little fear of order or much fear of it—soon find themselves moving in harm's way. For there is no sanctuary in any active relationship with the worlds of either of these novels. Once the reader's role is raised to an active pitch, it becomes not only challenging but also perilous. That, as it turns out, is Faulkner's strange, double-edged gift to all of us, even now, one hundred years after his birth. To adapt a line borrowed from another great writer, the texts that constitute that gift might well be marked with some such warning as this: "Beware, ye who enter here."[13]

NOTES

1. M. M. Bakhtin, *The Dialogic Imagination: Four Essays*, ed. Michael Holquist, trans. Caryl Emerson and Michael Holquist (Austin: University of Texas Press, 1981), 253.

2. W. H. Auden, *The Dyer's Hand and Other Essays* (New York: Random House, 1962), 58–59.

3. C. Vann Woodward, *The Burden of Southern History* (Baton Rouge: Louisiana State University Press, 1960), 3, 8–9, 13–14, 18–19, 21–22. For an excellent discussion of the Southern Agrarians, see Richard H. King, *A Southern Renaissance: The Cultural Awakening of the American South, 1930–1955* (New York: Oxford University Press, 1980), 51–60.

4. The statement from the *New York Times* is quoted in the introduction by Robert Penn Warren, ed., *Faulkner: A Collection of Critical Essays* (Englewood Cliffs, N. J.: Prentice Hall, Inc., 1966), 6.

5. See Woodward and King as cited in note 3 above.

6. See King, 63–76.

7. See Woodward, 13; cf., 8.

8. See *Sanctuary*, The Corrected Text (New York: Vintage International, 1993), 284. All parenthetical page citations to *Sanctuary* are to this edition.

9. See *Absalom, Absalom!*, The Corrected Text (New York: Vintage International, 1990), 177. All parenthetical page citations to *Absalom, Absalom!* are to this edition.

10. I owe this observation to a comment made by a participant at the Faulkner and Yoknapatawpha Conference in Oxford, Mississippi, 1997. I regret having lost track of his name.

11. Given the importance of the "lynching" scene to my discusssion of *Sanctuary*, I want to provide additional information that may be helpful. During the nineteenth century, lynching remained a weapon of choice of vigilantes across the United States, and it continued to be used against whites as well as blacks. In 1885, for example, of 185 victims of lynchings, 111 (60%) were white and 74 (40%) were black. By 1900, however, lynching was a weapon used principally in the South, and the ratio of white to black victims had changed dramatically: of the 115 victims, 9 (7.8%) were white and 106 (92.2%) were black. As the twentieth century progressed, both the decline in number of incidents and the shift in the racial identity of victims continued. In 1920, 53 blacks and 5 whites were lynched; in 1930, a year before *Sanctuary* was published, 21 people were lynched, 20 (95%) blacks and 1 (5%) white. Furthermore, like Faulkner's depiction of the lynching of Lee Goodwin, lynchings often became public spectacles: instigated by a handful of people, they were carried out by a larger group of exuberant volunteer vigilantes and were witnessed by an even larger crowd, some of whom joined in the humiliation and mutilation of the victim. Meanwhile officers of the law and other public officials tended either to avert their eyes or, on occasion, to applaud the event. See John Boles, *The South Through Time* (Englewood Cliffs, N. J.: Prentice Hall, Inc., 1995), 419–21, as well as works cited therein.

12. Cf. Woodward, 13 and 7–9; King, 63–76; and Bakhtin, 253.

13. This line is freely translated, or more precisely, is adapted, from Dante's *Divine Comedy: Inferno*, iii. 9, which reads as follows: "Lasciate ogni speranza voi ch'entrate!" More strictly translated, the line reads "Abandon all hope, ye who enter here."

Not the Having but the Wanting:
Faulkner's Lost Loves

JOHN T. IRWIN

Let me speak for a moment about a recurring aspect of Faulkner's life and art, namely, his affinity for a type of romantic attachment best characterized as "troubadouresque," an attachment in which the love object is idealized and often unattainable, or is ultimately denied to the lover (because he is rejected), an amorous involvement in which the lover's devotion is absolute, the measure of his love the suffering it causes, and the ultimate form of this love a consummation that is death, a *Liebestod*. Critics have pointed out the influence of the Decadent poets (especially Swinburne), of Walter Pater, and James Branch Cabell, on Faulkner's "troubadouresque" love affairs. And yet Faulkner came by his interest in this type of romantic involvement in his own right. As a young man he had proposed to Estelle Oldham and been rejected, and she had subsequently married someone else. Then in 1925 he met Helen Baird, courted her in New Orleans and Pascagoula through 1926, felt that her interest didn't match his, but nevertheless proposed marriage, and was once again rejected. And the next year she too married someone else.

We know that Faulkner's love for Helen left a mark on at least five of his works—*Mayday, Helen: A Courtship, Mosquitoes* (1927), *The Sound and the Fury* (1929), and *The Wild Palms* (1939). The first two of these were gift booklets whose unique copies were presented to Helen Baird in 1926. Both booklets were hand-lettered, and *Mayday* was also illustrated by Faulkner's own color drawings. *Mayday* is an Arthurian quest-romance in which a young knight named Sir Galwyn, after seeing the image of a beautiful woman in a magical stream, goes in search of her in the company of two companions, Hunger and Pain. What Galwyn finds is three other beautiful women: the Princess Yseult, with whom he holds a lengthy conversation while she is bathing naked in a stream, the Princess Elys and the Princess Aelia, both of whom Galwyn physically possesses. The latter two ladies are associated with the evening and the morning stars respectively, and Galwyn notes that once he has enjoyed

the ladies' favors these two romantic symbols of unattainable desire van-
ish from the sky. What Galwyn ultimately learns from his quest is "that
it is not the thing itself that man wants, so much as the wanting of it."[1]

Indeed, the theme of *Mayday* is that the possession of the beloved is
the death of love, and that the true romantic must find a way to keep
desire always in a state of wanting, never of having. Finally Galwyn
comes back to the stream in which he had originally seen the beautiful
maiden, engages in a conversation with the Lord of Sleep (*Mayday* 86),
sees the image of the maiden again, then descends into the stream, presumably to drown himself, the maiden being identified by Saint Francis
as "Little sister Death" (*Mayday* 87). Certainly, *Mayday* seems like a
strange kind of present for a woman one is courting. Critics, particularly
Carvel Collins, have pointed out that the story's ironic tone owes a debt
to Cabell's *Jurgen*, and perhaps Faulkner's point in presenting it to Helen
Baird was to make her understand the way he felt about love or to give
her some sense of how little he valued any object of desire in comparison
to the practice of his art.

At any rate, *Helen: A Courtship*, a booklet of sixteen poems, was a
much more appropriate gift for a woman to whom he ultimately proposed
marriage. Interestingly enough, in the second of these poems, entitled
"Bill" and dated "PASCAGOULA-JUNE-1925," he describes her as "a
flame/ Of starlight."[2] Collins notes in this connection that Helen Baird's
aunt had told him that Faulkner had paid her a visit in 1926, during
which he had avowed his love for her niece and had said that he always
thought of Helen "as an amber flame" (*Helen: A Courtship* 92). Collins
reads this as an image meant to evoke Helen's zest for living in terms of
Pater's famous dictum that "To burn always with this hard, gem-like
flame . . . is success in life."[3] Certainly, an interesting and persuasive
interpretation, but one should also note that one of the most striking
physical features of Helen Baird was that she bore the scars on her body
of a massive burn. As Blotner phrases it, "She did not hesitate to put on
a bathing suit or evening dress even though they revealed the scars of a
terrible accident. 'I was burned,' she would say offhandedly."[4] And in the
poem immediately preceding the one in which Faulkner refers to Helen
as "a flame of starlight," a poem entitled *TO HELEN, SWIMMING* and
also dated PASCAGOULA-JUNE-1925, he describes her as having a
"boy's breast and the plain flanks of a boy" and speaks of "the brown and
simple music of her knees" (*Helen: A Courtship* 111), which is to say, he
describes Helen attired in a bathing suit, the garb in which, as Blotner
says, her burn scars would have been most visible. One wonders, then,
whether in the next poem in the sequence, Faulkner's image of Helen as
"a flame/ Of Starlight" represents the refiguration of the burn-scarred

body of the beloved as the metaphorically burn-producing flame of love, indeed, wonders, if Helen had, as Blotner suggests, treated the burn scar as a kind of perverse beauty mark, as a kind of blemish accenting by contrast her attractiveness and vivacity, whether Faulkner continued this metaphor by making her scar a symbol of passion and its effects on both lover and beloved alike, a possibility that we shall want to consider again later when we examine Faulkner's decision to give this striking physical feature of Helen to the character of Charlotte Rittenmeyer in *The Wild Palms*.

Faulkner of course dedicated his second novel, *Mosquitoes*, to Helen Baird and modeled the character of Patricia Robyn on her. He gave Patricia a brother with the same nickname (Josh) as Helen's own brother, but he also made Patricia and Josh twins, sharing an incestuous attraction. I have dealt with *Mosquitoes* and the figure of Patricia Robyn at some length in *Doubling and Incest/ Repetition and Revenge*, and I would only recall here that when in *The Sound and the Fury* the motif of brother-sister incest comes back, it is linked not so much to *Mosquitoes* as to *Mayday*, the gift booklet that Faulkner presented to Helen Baird in 1926. At the very beginning of Quentin's section of *The Sound and the Fury*, he awakens to the ticking of his grandfather's watch and thinks, "Like Father said down the long and lonely lightrays you might see Jesus walking, like. And the good Saint Francis that said Little Sister Death, that never had a sister."[5] The recurrence of the image of Little Sister Death links Quentin's suicide by drowning with Sir Galwyn's apparent suicide at the end of *Mayday* and also links Quentin's sister Candace, with whom he is obsessed, with the maiden (identified with death) whose image Galwyn sees in the stream and pursues to his own destruction.

Now consider the number of structures and images that, by the time of *The Sound and the Fury*'s publication in 1929, had become associated in Faulkner's mind with the "troubadouresque," unattainable love object: first, an incestuous attraction, usually between brother and sister; second, the structure or imagery of narcissism, sometimes involving twinning, always involving doubling, and probably relying on the classical story of Narcissus as told by Pausanias in which Narcissus has a dead, beloved, twin sister of whom he is reminded whenever he looks at his own image in the pool, a detail that accounts for the gender difference that cuts across Faulkner's narcissistic pairs; third, the fact that this gender difference, annexed to the structure of narcissism, involves as well a blurring or reversal of gender, in Faulkner's words, a kind of "emotional bisexuality"[6] or hermaphroditism; fourth, a sense of the narcissistic love object as potentially death-dealing because suicide-inducing; and fifth, a sense of art as a means of creating a substitute, narcissistic love-object in the work, a work that captures and holds forever the otherwise unattainable beloved in the artist's life.

Taking into account the various elements in this complex it seems clear that though Faulkner may have been influenced by Swinburne, Pater, and Cabell as Collins suggests, he was primarily operating in an American gothic tradition, a tradition whose major nineteenth-century exponent, Edgar Allan Poe, had experienced the same interplay between real-life love-objects and his own fiction writing that Faulkner was to experience later. Indeed, Poe had married his own version of Little Sister Death, his thirteen-year-old first cousin Virginia whom he called "Sis" and who, six years into their marriage, contracted tuberculosis and spent the next five years dying by degrees before her husband's eyes. And in what can only be described as a series of prophetic short stories published between 1835 and 1841 that included "Berenice," "Morella," "Ligeia," "The Fall of the House of Usher," and "Eleonora," Poe returned again and again to the image of a beautiful dying woman whose physical deterioration mirrors and to some extent accelerates the mental and emotional deterioration of her male companion, who is often both spouse and close blood relation. Indeed, in "The Fall of the House of Usher" he combines the motifs of an incestuous attraction between brother and sister, twinning, narcissistic mirroring, and a suicidal *Liebestod*. Given Poe's influence, it is easy to see why Faulkner, by the time of his first full-blown use of these linked motifs in *The Sound and the Fury*, opted for an incestuous attachment between brother and sister, because the familial resemblance between siblings aligns so closely with the mirror-image resemblance of narcissism, and because the *forbidden* character of the *incestuous* love-object aligns with the *impossible* character of the *narcissistic* love-object (one's reflected image as other). This last alignment associates the suicidal consummation of narcissism (in which one enters the water like Sir Galwyn to possess the object of one's desire only to drown) with the consummation of incest and by extension with that type of "troubadouresque" attachment to an unattainable object whose idealized consummation is a love-death and, by further extension still, with that more worldly wise version of romantic love in which the possession of the object of desire immediately causes the death of desire and the need for artistic possession as a saving alternative.

All of which brings us to *The Wild Palms*, the last of the five works touched in some way by Faulkner's feelings for Helen Baird. When Charlotte Rittenmeyer first meets Harry Wilbourne at a party in a New Orleans artist's studio, she immediately makes a series of intimate revelations about herself:

"I've got two children, both girls," she said. "That's funny, because all my family were brothers except me. I liked my oldest brother the best but you cant sleep with your brother and he and Rat roomed together in school so I married Rat and now I've got two girls, and when I was seven years old I fell in the fire place, my brother and I were fighting, and that's the scar. It's on my shoulder and side and hip too and I got in the habit of telling people about it before they would have time not to ask and I still do it even when it doesn't matter anymore."

"Do you tell everybody like this? At first?"

"About the brothers or about the scar?"

"Both. Maybe the scar."

"No. That's funny too. I had forgotten. I haven't told anybody in years. Five years."

"But you told me."[7]

As we noted, Faulkner gives Charlotte Helen Baird's most striking physical feature, the extensive burn scar, but where we had earlier suggested that this feature had been transformed and metaphorized in the image of the beloved as flame in one of Faulkner's poems to Helen, in the case of Charlotte Rittenmeyer, the burn gotten in a struggle with her favorite brother is literal and untransformed and meant to suggest the way she has been scarred by her forbidden love for her sibling. Yet what is most interesting about Faulkner's giving Helen Baird's distinctive physical trait to Charlotte is that at the time he was writing *The Wild Palms* he was deeply involved with another woman, indeed, the third great love of his life, a woman who, like Helen, ultimately rejected Faulkner and married someone else. Faulkner had begun an intense love affair, probably as early as 1935, with Meta Carpenter, a woman who, like Faulkner at that period, worked for the film director Howard Hawks in Hollywood. By 1937 when it had become clear that no matter how much Faulkner loved Meta, he was not going to divorce Estelle and risk losing his daughter for her, Meta married the pianist Wolfgang Rebner. Her rejection left Faulkner heartbroken, and he threw himself back into working on *The Wild Palms*, saying later that he wrote the book "to stave off what I thought was heartbreak" (Blotner 2:978).

But the pain of Meta's leaving was to become more physical and more intense in the fall of 1937 when Faulkner on a trip to New York met her and Wolfgang Rebner, recently returned from their honeymoon. The encounter with Meta was apparently so emotionally wrenching that Faulkner went on an enormous bender, passed out in his hotel room at the Algonquin with his bare back against a radiator steam pipe, and suffered third-degree burns. According to Carvel Collins, Meta remembered that when Faulkner invited her and her husband to have dinner at the Algonquin, "they arrived to find him bedridden because of that burn, and in such pain that they left quickly to give him rest" (*Helen: A Courtship* 89). The severe pain of the burn continued during the months it took Faulkner to complete *The Wild Palms*.

Now it seems almost certain that Faulkner's rejection in 1937 by Meta brought back memories of, and added a further emotional dimension to, his 1927 rejection by Helen, but in *The Wild Palms* the image of a woman's burn-scarred body has not been suppressed in favor of the image of a flame of passion, rather what is explicitly mentioned in the text is the burn on Charlotte's face, shoulder, side, and hip, a fictive burn that screens and refigures the real burn on the body not of a beloved woman but of her male lover, the novel's author scarred in the wake of seeing Meta again in New York. Charlotte Rittenmeyer merges in one person then the images of Faulkner's two lost loves, Helen and Meta, as well as that of their scarred lover.

Obviously, the story of Harry and Charlotte in *The Wild Palms* was written not only to stave off Faulkner's heartbreak at being rejected by Meta but also to serve as an examination or expression of his own feelings about her and about marriage. Although Faulkner clearly loved Meta, and theirs had been by all accounts an exceptionally passionate and romantic affair, he would not divorce his wife to marry her because he had come to believe from his own experience that marriage and domesticity spelled the inevitable death of love. He seems to have wanted Meta as a mistress but not as a wife. Certainly, the whole point of the affair between Charlotte Rittenmeyer and Harry Wilbourne—their being attracted to each other at first sight, Charlotte's leaving her husband and children to run away with Harry, Harry's throwing over his career, and their passionate odyssey across country—is that it represents a foredoomed attempt to maintain not only the existence but also the power of romantic desire in the face of the quotidian and the domestic. At one point during their long journey, Charlotte tells Harry, "My God, I never in my life saw anybody try as hard to be a husband as you do. Listen to me, you lug. If it was just a successful husband and food and a bed I wanted, why the hell do you think I am here instead of back there where I had them?" (*The Wild Palms* 99). That aspect of Faulkner's "troubadouresque" attachments that we noted earlier in *Mayday*, the sense that romantic love is killed by the physical possession of the beloved and that "it is not the thing itself that man wants, so much as the wanting of it," undergoes a further, naturalistic progression in *The Wild Palms*, where it is the prolonged physical possession and the day-to-day tedium of marriage that kills love. Harry says at one point that he and Charlotte had come to be "about money the way some unlucky people were about alcohol" (*The*

Wild Palms 107) and that as a result he had become "the Complete Householder" (*The Wild Palms* 113). This condition of worrying about money and respectability was the way, he says, that the powers-that-be forced people to "conform to the pattern of human life which has now evolved to do without love—to conform or die" (*The Wild Palms* 118). But what Charlotte had shown him when they ran away together was how "to live for the short time you are loaned breath, to be alive and know it" (*The Wild Palms* 113), and it is that passionate love they both wish to preserve. Indeed, the reason Charlotte seeks the abortion that ultimately costs her her life is that the intrusion of a third person, a child, would spell the end of their affair. She tells Harry, "It's not us now. That's why: don't you see? I want it to be us again, quick, quick. We have so little time. In twenty years I cant anymore and in fifty years we'll both be dead. So hurry. Hurry" (*The Wild Palms* 177).

Indeed, it is precisely the illicit character of their love that constitutes its attraction. When Charlotte first introduces herself to Harry, she says she liked her oldest brother best but that you can't sleep with your brother so she married his college roommate and that in a childhood struggle with that brother she had been badly burned. Clearly, what Charlotte had tried to do by marrying the man who slept in the same room with her brother was to find a socially acceptable relationship that would take the place of her forbidden love for her sibling, the kind of substitute that Narcissa Benbow, for example, finds in *Flags in the Dust* when she marries a man coded as a brother, a man more than half in love with death (since the death of his twin in the war), a man who, in effect, stands in place of Narcissa's brother Horace. But the problem for Charlotte is that her love for her brother is not only socially forbidden but associated with pain, with the burn she received struggling with him, and thus her respectable, boring marriage is unable to serve as a substitute in two important respects for this incestuous attraction. I would suggest that the reason she is immediately drawn to Harry is not just that he offers an illicit (i.e., adulterous) love for a forbidden (i.e., incestuous) one but also that he offers a love shadowed with the prospect of pain. After all when Harry's friend Flint introduces him to the crowd at the party where he meets Charlotte, he describes him as someone who has "a scalpel in his sleeve" (*The Wild Palms* 33). And Charlotte tells Harry that the second time she saw him she learned "that love and suffering are the same thing and that the value of love is the sum of what you have to pay for it and anytime you get it cheap you have cheated yourself" (*The Wild Palms* 41). Of course the culmination of their affair involves Harry's actually using a scalpel on Charlotte when he performs the abortion, an operation Charlotte evokes as a kind of perverse sexual intercourse when she says, "We've done this lots of ways but not with knives, have we?" (*The Wild Palms* 186). And she continues, "It's all right. We know how. What was it you told me nigger women say? Ride me down, Harry" (*The Wild Palms* 186). Earlier when she had made him promise to perform the abortion, she had told him to kiss her, and Faulkner tells us that they had kissed "as brother and sister might" (*The Wild Palms* 184). Indeed, one is reminded of another brother and sister in Faulkner and of the scene in which Candace has been lying on her back in the stream and Quentin uses his knife as a kind of substitute penis in an attempted *Liebestod*, offering to kill her and then himself as a way of insuring that they will be joined forever only to find that her repeated exhortations to "push it" finally unman him.

Yet when Harry finally loses his beloved as a result of the abortion he has performed, he doesn't kill himself like Sir Galwyn or Quentin Compson; indeed, he explicitly rejects the possibility of suicide with the most memorable line in the book, and in this regard Faulkner seemed to turn, in the wake of his rejection by Meta, back to strategies he had employed after being rejected by Helen. In *Mosquitoes*, Julius Kaufmann says, "You don't commit suicide when you are disappointed in love. You write a book" (*Mosquitoes* 228). Faulkner had rendered Helen in the character of Pat Robyn and then explained in some detail what he had done by having the sculptor Gordon tell Pat about Cyrano, who had tried to capture a girl and hold her forever in a book: "he was in love with her. She couldn't leave him, either. Couldn't go away from him at all. . . . He had her locked up. In a book" (*Mosquitoes* 269). But as Julius Kaufmann also says, "Lucky he who believes that his heart is broken: he can immediately write a book and so take revenge" (*Mosquitoes* 228). Certainly, Faulkner's portrayal of Helen as Pat Robyn involved some measure of revenge for her indifference to his proposal of marriage, but Meta had been far from indifferent; if anything, she had loved Faulkner too much, wanting him not just as lover but as husband, and clearly his writing of *The Wild Palms* had served to memorialize their passionate love affair in the doomed affair of Charlotte and Harry. But Faulkner had also memorialized, in what Charlotte and Harry have to say about marriage, money, and respectability, the first great love of his life, who had also rejected him, married someone else, divorced him, and then married Faulkner, a marriage that soon proved to be extremely unhappy for both parties.

Faulkner concludes Charlotte and Harry's cross-country odyssey by bringing them back to a beach cottage on the Gulf coast of Mississippi, a spot ressembling Pascagoula, and to an encounter with an old married couple, the doctor and his wife, who represent everything Charlotte and Harry have been trying to avoid in their relationship and everything

Faulkner had been trying to flee in his marriage. Indeed to the extent that Pascagoula is the model for the Gulf coast beach where Charlotte and Harry end their affair, this setting imports into the novel a dual resonance, for Pascagoula was the place where Faulkner courted Helen Baird in the summer of 1926, and it was also, strangely enough, the place where he took his wife Estelle on their wedding trip in 1929, strange because Estelle by all accounts was not a person who particularly liked the beach and because she may well have known that this site held for Faulkner memories of another woman. At any rate it was here on their wedding trip that Estelle tried to drown herself by walking into the Gulf of Mexico. And it is here that Faulkner brings Charlotte and Harry, Charlotte to die from Harry's use of the phallic scalpel in an abortion evoked as a kind of dangerous sexual intercourse, and Harry to resolutely refuse suicide after his love's death, almost as if following the dictum from *Mosquitoes* that "you don't commit suicide when you are disappointed in love. You write a book," though in this case it wasn't Harry who wrote the book but Faulkner. What being disappointed in love means here is being rejected by, is losing, the beloved, yet in this very same setting on the Gulf coast Faulkner had known someone to attempt suicide whose disappointment in love resulted not from losing but from gaining a spouse and certainly that attempted suicide resonates beneath the contrast between the unmarried Charlotte and Harry on the one hand and the old doctor and his wife on the other, and between the unmarried Faulkner and Helen at Pascagoula in the summer of '26 and the married Faulkner and Estelle in the summer of '29.

If the Stanislavsky method of acting involves using emotions associated with events in one's own life to understand and portray the emotions of a character one is playing, even though events in that character's life may bear little resemblance to events in one's own, then we could say that Faulkner practiced something like the Stanislavsky method of writing, using recurring incidents and emotions in his own life not just to create characters in his fiction but also to fuel the writing of various works from gift booklets to novels, and none of the recurring scenarios in Faulkner's life seems to have been more productive, and dare one say, more sought after, than that type of troubadouresque attachment that sprang from his being rejected by an idealized woman. This scenario of an unfulfilled love, of an unattainable or lost love-object, entered into Faulkner's fiction again and again, wearing, I would suggest, always the same mask, that of a forbidden, incestuous attachment between brother and sister—Josh and Pat Robyn, Narcissa and Horace Benbow, Quentin and Candace Compson, Darl and Dewey Dell Bundren, Charles Bon and Judith Sutpen, Charlotte Rittenmeyer and her oldest brother, Gavin Stevens and his sister Margaret.

But if it is the case that when you are disappointed in love you don't commit suicide, you write a book, then any great, failed love affair always holds within itself the potential for at least two books. Which is to say that if the Faulkner-Meta Carpenter affair fueled the writing of *The Wild Palms* as a means of staving off Faulkner's heartbreak, then their romance was also to produce, some thirty-five years later, Meta's nonfiction account *A Loving Gentleman: The Love Story of William Faulkner and Meta Carpenter*. Putting aside the Harlequin-romance quality of some of the prose, one is struck most by Carpenter's interpretation of Faulkner's reason for finally refusing to seek a divorce. She recounts how Faulkner had told Estelle about their love affair and asked to be set free, and that Estelle had replied that she would seek not only custody of their daughter but also a financial settlement of such size that Faulkner would be a pauper for the rest of his life. Carpenter says that while Faulkner might have been able to accept giving up custody of his daughter or giving up her (Meta), he would never "permit Estelle to wipe out the years of serious writing that were left to him. . . . To pay that price was unthinkable."[8] Such a punitive financial settlement would have meant that Faulkner would've had to spend the rest of his life working as a scriptwriter in Hollywood, exhausting his talent. As Carpenter says, "Had he gone the other way, paid the price of his freedom, *A Fable*, the Snopes trilogy, *The Unvanquished*, *Requiem for a Nun*, *Intruder in the Dust*, and the later short stories would never have been written" (Carpenter 185). This interpretation, with its sense of the clear disparity in value between love and art, recalls the type of comment made by several of Faulkner's characters in *Mosquitoes*. But Carpenter's version also raises the possibility that in rejecting Faulkner and thus releasing him from having to seek a financially disastrous divorce, she had in some way facilitated Faulkner's later works, works that would never have been written if her lover had sought his freedom and Estelle pursued her vow to ruin him. On one occasion after Meta's marriage to Wolfgang Rebner, Faulkner, in describing his emotional situation to her, had quoted what he said was a line spoken by one of his characters: "Between grief and nothing I will take grief" (Carpenter 230). Perhaps Faulkner would have been more truthful if he had said that between art and love he would always take art. Indeed, almost from the first, there was never any real contest between them, and if on the odd occasion Faulkner did choose love, he preferred the kind that was unattainable, hopeless, irrecoverably lost, the kind that broke the heart but fueled the imagination, the kind of love that always turned back into art.

NOTES

1. William Faulkner, *Mayday* (Notre Dame: University of Notre Dame Press, 1977), 71. All multiple references in this essay are to the edition first cited.

2. William Faulkner, *Helen: A Courtship and Mississippi Poems* (Oxford and New Orleans: Yoknapatawpha Press and Tulane University Press, 1981), 112.

3. Walter Pater, *The Renaissance* (Chicago: Academy Press, 1982), 236.

4. Joseph Blotner, *Faulkner: A Biography*, 2 vols. (New York: Random House, 1974), 1:438.

5. William Faulkner, *The Sound and the Fury* (New York: Vintage Books, 1956), 96.

6. William Faulkner, *Mosquitoes* (New York: Liveright, 1955), 251.

7. William Faulkner, *The Wild Palms* (New York: Vintage, 1995), 35.

8. Meta Carpenter and Orin Borsten, *A Loving Gentleman: The Love Story of William Faulkner and Meta Carpenter* (New York: Simon and Schuster, 1976), 185.

Race Cards: Trumping and Troping in Constructing Whiteness

THADIOUS M. DAVIS

1

Trump: N. 1. Card Games a) often plural. A suit the cards of which are declared as outranking all other cards for the duration of the hand. b) A card of such a suit. 2. A key resource to be used at the opportune moment. 3. Informal. A reliable or admirable person. V.—tr. To take (a card or trick) with a trump. intr. To play a trump card.

—American Heritage Dictionary

For many years, I resisted what seemed to be mandatory attention to *Go Down, Moses* for Faulkner scholars who addressed issues of race. My sense of that text was that its overwhelmingly self-conscious sermonizing and cobbling together of disparate parts made it somewhat suspect and clearly problematic. I valued the text precisely because of its instability, permutations, uncertainties, and fissures, basically for its modernist aesthetic and intellectual stance, so none of the claims for unity or coherence ever seemed compelling to me, but beyond that, as a reader with a particular social identity (black, female, Southern), I found the representation of blacks, from Tomey's Turl in "Was" to Butch Beauchamp in "Go Down, Moses," reactionary, perhaps most particularly so the ciphered black women—Tennie, Mannie, Molly, Nat, Fonsiba, Eunice, Tomasina. In fact, even one of the celebrated textual creations seemed to me most retrograde; every time I read "The Old People" and "The Bear," I configured Old Ben, the bear, with a black man's face. In my interactive participation with the narrative and in my interpretation of its deep structural level, Old Ben loomed as that mighty abstraction, "The Negro," the trope *par excellence* of endurance and sufferance. Descriptive, symbolic language, and emblematic passages pushed the association and, concomitantly, distanced me as a black reader from the text.[1] Ensconced in the margins, I read against the grain of received critical thinking about both "The Bear" and *Go Down, Moses*.

More recently, I began my own retrospective—a rereading and rethinking of Faulkner's novels—still largely from the margins, a space that has grown increasingly familiar if not comfortable in the past twenty years. *Go Down, Moses* remains as problematic for me as ever, but with some differences. I understand it as modernist historical fiction, an exploration of a time that Faulkner represents as mid-nineteenth and early twentieth century, and I also understand it as a book written half a century ago and from both of these temporal frames it becomes for me an effort to make comprehensible a shifting world by holding a space from which to contemplate, interrogate, and evaluate one's own material and experiential world. Indeed, I worry less over the visible figure of the bear playing nature as a trope of blackness and more over what happens to the text when I exercise my authority as a reader and locate Tomey's Turl at the center of a reading of *Go Down, Moses*.[2] Surely she must be joking, those of you who have contemplated every page of that book must be thinking. Tomey's Turl—surely she can't mean Tomey's Turl, but rather Isaac McCaslin or perhaps even Ike's black kinsman, Lucas Beauchamp. And those of you less familiar with *Moses* are probably wondering who or what is Tomey's Turl. But yes, I am serious about situating Tomey's Turl, the comic stereotyped slave who appears only in the wildly slapstick opening section, "Was," at the center of a reading of the text. From that radical repositioning, Tomey's Turl functions to transgress and disrupt the power and authority of whites over both lives and stories. After much struggling with *Go Down, Moses* from the position of my own raced and gendered readerly identity, and with an appreciation for Faulkner's raced and gendered writerly identity, which we, neither of us, can escape, I have come to Tomey's Turl from the legal perspective of critical race theory as a "righted" and "willful" black subject resistant to subjugation, domination, and oppression. By centering Tomey's Turl as trope and trump, referencing both black rights and will, I have also come to a different appreciation for the pleasures and possibilities of the text, though I am not yet convinced that its ideology, or its structure is unproblematic or that the cultural work of decentering textual spheres of influence and strongholds of power will displace cultural hegemony and racial supremacy. Nevertheless, I know that necessarily inscribed within my attention to *Go Down, Moses* is my own continued stake in the power of literature and the efficacy of words.

2

"Who dealt these cards, Amodeus?" Only he didn't wait to be answered. He reached out and tilted the lamp-shade, the light moving

up Tomey's Turl's arms that were supposed to be black but were not
quite white. . . .

—"Was," *Go Down, Moses*

Tomey's Turl, the active dealer in the card game, who is coincidently
also the passive object of the wager, when put under the light, confounds
the observer's expectations: his arms "were supposed to be black but
were not quite white." I read Tomey's Turl in this moment as a racial
trope of hybridity that calls into question a black/white binary, but also
as the signifier of the whiteness of the observer and card player, Hubert
Beauchamp. Tomey's Turl disrupts the visual component of normative
whiteness, but the observation of his difference constitutes at the same
time a reminder of the presence of the card players as racially defined,
as white men. Hubert also constructs Turl visually as "that damn white
half-McCaslin" (6), but socially and culturally as "a nigger," in order to
make Turl's social condition perform as a more favorable comment on
Hubert's precarious one. That is, for Hubert being white though without
money is infinitely better that being black and slave. In foregrounding a
racial concern with discontinuity, instability, and disjuncture, I am suggesting that the moment can be understood as ancillary to a concern with
how to represent "whiteness" within the social, historical, and literary
narrativity magnified by moving, shifting light.

The light on Tomey's Turl extends out to the card players, the two in
this second poker game, Amodeus (Buddy) McCaslin and Hubert Beauchamp, and the one in the first game, Theophilus (Buck) McCaslin, all
three white men and all three slaveholders, active in the white social,
political, and economic world of the Antebellum South. In the first game
of draw poker between Hubert and Buck the stakes are Tennie and Turl,
the slaves and a white woman, Sophonsiba Beauchamp: "The lowest
hand wins Sibbey and buys the niggers" Hubert states in waging his
sister.[3] In the second game of five card stud poker, the wager is "Buck
McCaslin against the land and niggers," promised as Sophonsiba's dowry
(25). What is at stake is race continuity in either game, and whether Buck,
Buddy, or Hubert wins, it is all the same: the white men against the
land, the slaves, and the white woman. Here the card games are not only
gendered masculine, but racialized "white," because they are a means of
maintaining hegemony and of exerting social control.

In the two poker games between first Buck and then Buddy McCaslin
and Hubert Beauchamp is a contest for the possession of blacks and
women—for blacks in the legal bondage of slavery and for women in the
legal institution of marriage. The black dealer and the white card players
can be understood as significations of the mutually defining aspects of

race in Faulkner's text. In lighting Turl, Hubert Beauchamp unmasks whiteness's hidden neutrality, though he also opens up the latent threat of the black dealer to determine the winning hand and to undo the power resident within the white players. In the end, Hubert merely can say "I pass" to his white opponent (28). As Cornell West has remarked, "Without the presence of black people in America, European-Americans would not be 'white'—they would be only Irish, Italian, Poles, Welsh, and others engaged in class, ethnic, and gender struggles over resources and identity. What made America distinctly American for them was not simply the presence of unprecedented opportunities, but the struggle for seizing these opportunities in a new land in which black slavery and racial caste served as the floor upon which white class, ethnic, and gender struggles could be diffused and diverted. In other words, white poverty could be ignored and whites' paranoia of each other could be overlooked primarily owing to the distinctive American feature: the basic racial divide of black and white peoples."[4]

Faulkner's characters in the tableau at the card game are raced subjects. While race is not self-evident, without the mediating presence of an other, the dichotomous black/white racial divide clearly dictates the terms for being white and not black. Race is always an unstable category of analysis, but it can be understood as a relationally derived construct. White raciality for Hubert, Buddy, and Buck is inherent in the solidification of their white social identities, in owning and bequeathing property, in legitimating matrimony and patrimony, they exercise their difference from black others, just as they do in casting an ironic eye on the staged performances of Turl, from whom the trope of minstrelsy is never far. Yet we come to know the social identities of the white twins because of Tomey's Turl. In general, his moves challenge the power and authority of whites over him. In particular, his moves challenge one key aspect of his containment in slavery: his right to sexual expression, which has been excluded from the eccentric world of the McCaslin place under the ownership of the twins Buck and Buddy. As such Tomey's Turl's challenge is to the right of his McCaslin owners not only to restrict his will to court Tennie, denying his desire for a wife, but also to enforce his conformity to their refusal of sexuality.

Read from the perspective of Tomey's Turl as a race for full expression of a mature, sexual self within society, running away is a periodic reminder that despite attempts to reduce slaves to children without will, enslavement does not necessarily produce simplistic objects of property. Tomey's Turl asserts that sexual desire is resident within the black male body and that, despite stereotypical representations or caricatures of excessive black male sexuality, sexual expression cannot be summarily denied him.

Unlike Buck and, in particular, Buddy, Tomey's Turl is not content to remain in an unattached social condition. He desires and wills, and thus separates himself from the undifferentiated middle-aged boys, his twin brothers at the McCaslin place. Buck and Buddy are constructed within the social roles designated as masculine and feminine, but they play off the expectations for gender formation and gender boundaries within their society. Buck drinks, wears a tie, farms the land, and socializes outside of the confines of his property; Buddy cooks, does not drink, and remains at home in an unconventional domestic space, but is the poker player. Buck resists courting Sophonsiba Beauchamp because the twins exist within a space where "ladies were so damn seldom thank God that a man could ride for days in a straight line without having to dodge a single one" (7), and within that space they can behave without acknowledging their sexuality, or the misogyny implicated in their descriptions of women.

Like Buck and Buddy, Tomey's Turl does not escape the cultural formation of roles. He is labeled "nigger" (9, 10), and objectified outside of the expected code of behavior of (white) men, whose racialization is assumed: "Because, being a nigger, Tomey's Turl should have jumped down and run for it afoot as soon as he saw them. But he didn't; maybe Tomey's Turl had been running off from Uncle Buck for so long that he had even got used to running away like a white man would do it" (8–9). The boundary of race is an already existing social condition in the cultural logic upon which the narrative depends, in the binary oppositional of freedom, and in the social interactions among the players. The frequency with which Buck refers to Tomey's Turl as "my nigger" fixes Turl's racialization within the economy of slavery and establishes his subordination to his owner's legal authority over him, but more significantly here, it defines Buck as white by means of ownership and his own articulation of a racial hierarchy, and this despite Tomey's Turl's being visually white and Buck's brother.

Tomey's Turl's strategy allows for the development of responses to his actions. For example, Buck can court Sophonsiba Beauchamp as a result of, and in response to, Tomey's Turl's running, which redefines the social life of the McCaslins to include interdependence and interaction, and forces the McCaslins to enter into white society and white cultural mandates. Buck's reluctant courtship is an indirect and evasive tactic that functions in cooperation with Tomey's Turl's strategy. In instigating Buck's courtship of Sophonisba as "protection" (12) for his own courtship of Tennie, Tomey's Turl impacts both his future and that of his white owners.

Tomey's Turl dons his white Sunday shirt before beginning his run. In this act of dressing up, of dressing "free" and "white," of transforming himself into a "gentleman," he announces that different rules are in motion from those that obtain on the McCaslin place. In producing an image through clothing of himself that is different from his everyday asexual, subjugated self, Tomey's Turl suspends the boundaries and codes of that life, and rewrites the script for the black male body. Concomitantly, he initiates the ritual that forces Buck into a similar transformation: "The only time he wore the necktie was on Tomey's Turl's account" (7), which is another way of stating his participation in the social world of whites. And, therefore, in going after Tomey's Turl, Buck allows himself to become a necktied "suitor" and a white man, and Sophonsiba Beauchamp to become the object of his sexual interest and offhand courtship. Buck and Sophonsiba both then can participate in and become white cultural scripts: the marriage game, the husband and the wife roles, the squire and landed-gentry conventions. Racial formation, as Michael Omni and Howard Winant remind us, "is always historically situated," and thus "our understanding of the significance of race, and of the way race structures society, has changed enormously over time."[5] Indeed, the danger in using race as a category of analysis remains its fluidity. Henry Louis Gates Jr., states that "The sense of difference defined in popular usages of the term 'race' has both described and *inscribed* differences of language, belief system, artistic tradition, and gene pool, as well as all sorts of supposedly natural attributes such as rhythm, athletic ability, cerebration, usury, fidelity, and so forth."[6] Without falling into the traps Gates outlines, or essentializing race and promulgating biological determinism, it is possible to consider race a significant category of analysis, albeit a slippery one.

Go Down, Moses, given its social, structural, and historical context, provides a window for entering into, for observing, race and a discourse on whiteness. And what does *Go Down, Moses* representing race discursively allow us to observe? For one thing, how insistently Faulkner uses "white" as a designation of race. Throughout the text, "white" is the adjective of choice; it is an insistent marker of identity. For example, in "The Fire and the Hearth," white is the loaded and determining trope for Zack Edmonds and his family: "And Molly, a young woman then and nursing their own first child, wakened at midnight by the *white* man himself and they followed then the *white* man through the streaming darkness to his house"; "Molly delivered the *white* child"; Lucas returns to find "the *white* man's wife dead and his own wife already established in the *white* man's house"; and "It was as though the *white* woman had not only never quitted the house, she had never existed" (my italics, 45–46).

Beginning with the representation of white angst in an Ike McCaslin immobilized by inherited power and privilege, the text plays off Ike's refusal to exercise skin privilege and white power, while also examining his unwillingness to give up his assumptions of white racial superiority, as the narrative of "Delta Autumn" suggests. The Christian symbolism linking Ike's monklike appearance and existence to his response to ownership and domination may also be read through the lens of Gilles Deleuze and Felix Guattari's analysis of race and racism. Deleuze and Guattari argue that the visible face of a Christ racialized as white has come to be identified with "the White Man" and with being able to claim a white racial identity: "If the face is in fact Christ, in other words, your average ordinary White Man, then the first deviances, the first divergence-types are racial: yellow . . . black."[7] What they observe as "the degrees of deviance" from the representative Christlike, "White-Man face," are codified into "non-conforming traits" that are considered not merely racial difference but racial deformity, and that lead ultimately to the racist perception that "there is no exterior, there are no people on the outside. There are only people who should be like us and whose crime is not to be."[8]

The opening of *Go Down, Moses* with its focus on the angst of Old Ike McCaslin, a Christlike figure "who owned no property and never desired to" (3), fixes the narrative historically, and culturally defines Ike's whiteness—his prerogative to own property, land or slaves—his skin privilege that enables his right to inherit and to reject his inheritance: "his was the name in which the title to the land had first been granted from the Indian patent and which some of the descendants of his father's slaves still bore to the land" (3). Because of the racial marking of Indians and slaves, Ike's own race can go unmarked but nonetheless pronounced and visible. In part 4 of "The Bear," the same originary land acquisition names and racializes: "the tamed land which was to have been his heritage, the land which old Carothers McCaslin his grandfather had bought with white man's money from the wild men . . . and tamed and ordered . . . it for the reason that the human beings he held in bondage and in the power of life and death had removed the forest from it" (243). The formation of the plantation in the nineteenth century coincides with the consolidation of race theories, and thus, Ike's refusal of patrimony and ownership because of their connection to the slavery and white privilege resonates against a widespread acceptance of scientific racism. Ike's father and uncle, Buck and Buddy, before him also attempt to resist the ideology

and practice of racial hierarchies when they refuse residence in the Big
House, the home begun by their father, Old Carothers, as the seat of his
power and progeny. Buck and Buddy vacate their inherited Big House,
but in a conflicted gesture similar to Ike's in the next generation, they do
not renounce their claim to it or ownership of the slaves who subsequently inhabit it.

The encoded incest committed by Old Carothers and deciphered by
Ike grounds a discourse on the whiteness of the McCaslin men (e.g., their
relation to the land and to slavery, their exercise of power or repudiation
of it, their subjugation of blacks and women). This white-male centered
focus is a way of reading identity, familial, or cultural formation and disin-
tegration in the text, but it is also a way of encoding the McCaslins as
white within the political economy and social order representing whiteness in the text. Faulkner represents Ike McCaslin in the boundedness
of his existence: walled off, violating nobody's rights, protecting no one,
and convinced of his own righteousness. His repudiation of property,
inheritance, enables his sense of righteousness and white racial difference. Thus self-constituted as "righteous," Ike rejects identification with
negative formations in his external world (slavery, economic exploitation,
sexual aggression, incest, ownership, and consumerism). Patently antiso-
cial, except in the closed society of hunters, he consciously rejects the
white social world into which he was born and initially socialized; however, he ultimately recognizes that he has been able to escape neither
the defining, race-marked social world not its informing racial ideologies.

Ike cannot racially reinvent himself. He is a white man, a subject constituted out of a specific social world and its ideologies. His move to
negate his history merely reinscribes that history into the text for it is the
always- already-remembered and to-be-remembered point of entry into
his subjectivity. He does nothing to challenge directly the cultural integrity resonating in the present. The meditative strategy of the first part,
"Was," recurs in "The Bear" certainly, but even more so in "Delta Autumn," in which Ike's passive conciliatory memory conflicts with his con-
testatory, agitated, and aggressive actions. There he would seem to be
policing fixed boundaries between the races when he bequeaths memo-
rabilia from the game of hunt (horn), and offers property (money) to erase
culpability and negate complicity, but in so doing, he resorts to the same
legal codes that protect property and the propertied, and that make some
men white and whiteness the measure of civilization and culture.

The ultimate act of ownership is bodily control. For enslaved women
like Tomasina and Eunice who are so controlled by their masters, to reproduce is not just to duplicate themselves as property, but to reproduce
the image of the owner. "Reproduction," master-slave intercourse lead-

ing to reproduction, is a narcissistic act in addition to being a declaration of legal authority of not merely patriarchy (the law of the father), but also the law of the land. "The power of the master must be absolute to render the submission of the slave perfect," as *State vs. Mann* ruled in 1829.[9] Incest both guarantees the exclusive right to property and manifests the absolute power of the master. In the father-daughter incest that Ike Mc-Caslin deduces in his familial history, old Carothers McCaslin legally possessed the body of his daughter. Her body is marked incest victim, and is re-marked a second time as doubly the property of the father. Carothers McCaslin's sexual conquest of Tomasina is an act of staving off competition for property already owned and marked as owned, an act of claiming territory and policing or enforcing that claim. In marking his daughter Tomasina's body as his exclusive property, Carothers violates not legal codes regarding the right to own property and to protect property from seizure by trespassers or transgressors, but the religious, moral, ethical, cultural, and societal codes of individual and communal conduct or behavior. And he successfully staves off all competitors for his "property" Tomasina and reproduces yet more property (Tomasina's son, Tomey's Turl)—property that in its "white" maleness is even more the image of the owner-father Carothers than Tomasina could ever be in her femaleness. But ultimately, Tomasina's trauma, or that of her son, merely figures the project at the center of the discourse on ownership: Ike Mc-Caslin's trauma, which is thus sexual as much as social.

Ike "reads" into the plantation commissary ledger the homosocialities of whiteness within a slaveholding society. The text of the ledger, multiply inscribed by Carothers and both of his twin sons Buck and Buddy, may be deciphered as the ultimate homosocial act—the incestuous right of the father-owner over life and body, and thus Ike's rejection of his own inherited right (by virtue of his white, male, son positionality) to land (and the legal and commercial traditions of the plantation) is also a rejection of his right to the masculinity and the heterosexual prerogatives that figure in Carothers's sexual domination of his daughter.

Within *Go Down, Moses*, Ike's choice of the society of men, Sam Fathers, and the hunters is not necessarily a displacement of male heterosexual erotic desire, but it can be read as homoerotic attraction to the "other" of Tomasina, or Eunice; that is to say, it is an attraction to the other as reconfigured by a Sam Fathers outside of race and, ultimately, by the men of the big woods. Foucalt theorizes: "It is through sex—in fact, an imaginary point determined by the deployment of sexuality—that each individual has to pass in order to have access to his own intelligibility . . . to the whole of his body . . . to his identity."[10] That Ike textualizes the "sin" as sexual inscribes into the ledgers his own sexual awakening and his "fear" of a biological danger implicit in any recognition of self as a sexual being. I read it as a fear not unlike Buck's and Buddy's of being fully socialized as white—given the implications of whiteness within their culture. Foucault concludes that "Sex is worth dying for. It is in this (strictly historical) sense that sex is indeed imbued with a death instinct"; however, he suggests that in the West, death became more acceptable because of the high value placed on love.[11]

When in "Delta Autumn" the young woman descendant of Tomey's Turl asks whether Ike has lived so long that he has forgotten how to love (346), her words may be read in relation to the higher value placed on love (with the attendant suggestion of the transcending spiritual) as a way of ameliorating the necessary sexual (bodily and material) component of the intercourse that produced yet another biracial Edmonds-McCaslin-Beauchamp child. She exerts on the scene a reconfiguration of Tomey's Turl: a configuration of Ike's own absent and long vacated desire for either love or sex; each has been replaced by a desire for death.

In deciphering a homosocial message in the ledgers, I locate a potential double assault against property, ownership, and the laws protecting both, in order to reinvent a white social identity. Ike, however, capitulates to the "will" of old Carothers when he attempts to disperse to Tomey's Turl's children their monetary legacies, and his racial self remains indebted to biology, psychology, and law. To circumvent the authority of Carothers's legal will, to break its binding contract, would be a transgression of the expected order and the rationale behind that order. To vacate a will is to disrupt patriarchy in the site of patrimony and property. But, when Ike relinquishes his claim to a paternal inheritance, he does not deny the authority of Carothers's will and its assertion of right over his black progeny. The questions of property and the dispersal of property, and proprietary rights linked to paternal rights, that Ike raises, are, from the outset of the narrative, embedded in the attention to race and to racial difference, and to economic and social power particularly relevant to whites.

In the midsection of "The Bear," the white father-black daughter incest and the sexual domination figured as the defining trope of both the slave economy and its economic legacy, tenancy, magnify race and racial difference in the systemic imbalance of power. In particular, it argues that whiteness within this historical and economic condition is impervious to any attempted constraints on its desires and appetites. Such a discourse answers the need Toni Morrison identified for studies "in which an Africanist character is used to limn out and enforce the invention and implication of whiteness."[12]

Of course, it is fast becoming not merely trendy but clichéd to formulate discourses on whiteness as a long overlooked racial category. But some redress corrective is necessary—for the time being—because literary studies and Faulkner studies, as they were conventionally practiced, though not articulated as such, as an all-white aesthetic enterprise, as a primarily white cultural project, could not adequately contain or accommodate racial difference when that difference was not erased in the creative product or silenced in the critical methodology of a person maintaining a racially marked identity as intricately informing the project. "Society is suffused," Omni and Winant conclude, "with racial projects, large and small, to which all are subjected. This racial 'subjection' is quintessentially idealized. Everybody learns some combination, some version of the rules of social classification, and of [his] or her own racial identity, often without obvious teaching or conscious inculcation."[13] For example, in "The Fire and the Hearth," when the white boy Carothers moves into his white male adulthood: "Then one day the old curse of his fathers, the old haughty ancestral pride [read: race-pride] based not on any value but on an accident of geography, stemmed not from courage and honor but from wrong and shame, descended to him" (107). Inserted into and inserting himself into a social structure that is comprehensively and rigidly racialized, young Carothers becomes *white*. Lost to him is the interchangeability of two houses, two families, and an expansive occupation of a nonhistorical world, the one represented in the text as "the two houses had become interchangeable: himself and his foster-brother sleeping on the same pallet in the white man's house or in the same bed in the negro's and eating of the same food at the same table in either" (107). A *white* racial identity becomes "common sense" for Carothers, what Omni and Winant term "a way of comprehending, explaining, and acting in the world. A vast web of social projects mediates between the discursive or representational means in which race is identified and signified on the one hand, and the institutional and organizational forms in which it is routinized and standardized on the other."[14] In his particular moment of racial acculturation, Carothers "knew, without wondering or remembering when or how he had learned that either, that the black woman was not his mother, and did not regret it; he knew that his own mother was dead and did not grieve. There was still the black woman, constant, steadfast" (107). More than a distancing from the maternal, the knowledge conveyed here is a necessary removal from blackness constructed as mother because, historically, the issue of slaves followed the legal condition of their mothers. Carothers must sever identification with Molly as mother so that he can become white. Without this racial separation, he cannot enter into his racial identity.

Faulkner's construction of whiteness in response to the dispersal of

Tomey's Turl's descendants functions to insert him into the cultural conversations of the late 1930s and early 1940s. The lure of cities and the promise of the North destablilized the fixity of white and black people in the South and the rigidity of caste and class position. This destabilization not only undermined the economic, social, and political life of an as yet premodern Mississippi, but it also undermined the production of texts based on a racially polarized and bifurcated land, culture, heritage. In the aftermath of *Go Down, Moses*, except for its polemical rewriting and rediscovery in *Intruder in the Dust*, Faulkner turned from the race binary in the construction of whiteness, to class dynamics as it inscribes white raciality. This shift is anticipated by *The Hamlet* and the Snopeses, by Sutpen and Wash Jones in *Absalom, Absalom!* This shift is prefigured in Faulkner's discursive practice toward the end of *Go Down, Moses*. There one of the hunters observes in "Delta Autumn": " 'And what have you got left. . . . Half the people without jobs and half the factories closed by strikes. Half the people on public dole that wont work and half that couldn't work even if they would. Too much cotton and corn and hogs, and not enough for people to eat and wear. The country full of people to tell a man how he cant raise his own cotton whether he will or wont, and Sally Rand with a sergeant's stripes and not even the fan couldn't fill the army rolls' " (323). The "people" here designates "white people," working-class white people; the racial determinant is apparent in the reference to white fan dancer Sally Rand, because no black man could in safety be linked to such a textual reference—the sexual taboos, fears, and fantasies would be too great. Thus, "people" is a term demarking a group distinguished race, that is, "whiteness."

I am not suggesting that, by reading the construction of whiteness as a significant enterprise in *Go Down, Moses*, we also remake Faulkner as a race traitor, to use the term currently associated with one part of the whiteness movement in the United States, although I suspect that Ike McCaslin, despite his lapses and failures to move beyond his cultural conditioning, for a brief moment when renouncing his patrimony of ownership and aggression, comes close to being a race traitor. In fighting against the mandates of racial supremacy, Mab Segrest, for instance, Southern, white, activist, and lesbian, entitled her political autobiography, *Memoir of a Race Traitor*, in order to subvert the negative meaning assigned the term by white nationalists and white supremacists. The periodical *Race Traitor*, founded by Noel Ignatiev, whose research for *How the Irish Became White* helped initiate "white studies," attempts to foster a widespread rejection of white privilege and encourages activist racial stances under the watchword "Treason to whiteness is loyalty to humanity." However, the periodical is not unproblematical in the work that

Ignatiev terms "New Abolitionist"; *Race Traitor* has published interviews with neo-Nazis and projected that white militias can become allies in overturning the race system.[15] Yet Ignatiev has worried over the potential for whiteness studies to become apolitical, narcissistic, and nationalistic; both he and David Roediger, *The Wages of Whiteness: Race and the Making of the American Working Class*, have distanced themselves from the potential excesses implicitly validated by the concept of whiteness and the elevation of the category of whiteness. Roediger's title plays off the conceptual frame W. E. B. Du Bois presented in *Black Reconstruction* (1935); Du Bois pointed out that low-wage earning white workers received an additional compensation, a type of public and psychological wage for being white, and that the wage of whiteness placed them in a superior position to all blacks, no matter the wage category to which blacks belonged.[16]

Nor, when I raise the issue of whiteness in Faulkner's canon, am I suggesting that an outpost of Jeff Hitchcock's Cambridge-based Center for the Study of White American Culture be set up in Oxford, Mississippi, or based at the annual Faulkner conference. Manifestations of neo-white nationalism can after all achieve the reverse of the political call for leveling racial hierarchies. As West puts it, "enforced social hierarchy dooms us as a nation to collective paranoia and hysteria," insofar as "the paradox of race in America is that our common destiny is more pronounced and imperiled precisely when our divisions are deeper."[17]

I am suggesting that one measure of Faulkner's enormous literary achievement is his construction of race as central to his fiction, to his representation of characters, specifically his construction of white characters and whiteness, and to the metaphorical power of his language struggling with an interrogation of what it means to be white. That achievement is remarkable for its insistent race-consciousness, for enabling discourses on race and racial transgressions and transactions not merely in the South but in the United States as a whole. This particular aspect of his achievement is not usually acknowledged primarily because most attention has been devoted to his construction of racial others, the African Americans and to a lesser extent the Native Americans, who populate his texts. I am especially interested in this discourse not merely because it disturbs the notion that race only applies to people of color in Faulkner's writing, but also because it constitutes one of the possibilities for fresh conversations about Faulkner's particular achievement and the potential for future Faulkner scholarship, particularly on the occasion of his one hundredth birthday. In fact, my working title for this paper, "Thirteen Black Birds and One Hundred White Doves: A Birthday Gift," acknowledges that texts, of course, are multiply interpretable. They occupy political, social, moral, philosophical, aesthetic, and cultural spaces, and perform multiple forms of work, and are endlessly elastic.

3

> Then one morning Isaac was at home, looking at a newspaper . . .
> when he realized what it was and why. It was the date. *It's some-*
> *body's birthday,* he thought.
> —"The Fire and the Hearth," *Go Down, Moses*

I wanted to be a nature poet and write hauntingly of Southern landscapes lush with brilliant birds, animals green framed in hanging moss, musky magnolia floral curtains, under spiraling hot, blue white moon spaces, wisteria and lemon-scented verbena, luminous sunscapes of bayous, rigolettes, rivers. I forgot "Poplar trees bear a Strange Fruit," and Billie Holliday's real blues, deep roots, blood red leaves, strong limbs, flexing, spreading North and South, charred black bodies, burnt fruit on the bitter vines. And coming of age in the 1960s, I did not forget that within the boundary of Mississippi a symbolic condition exists as signification of the threat to black rights and freedom within the state: Mississippi did not ratify the Thirteenth Amendment to the Constitution until 16 March 1995. In 1865, that amendment outlawed slavery, but Mississippi alone of the states refused to endorse the amendment. While that technicality bascially had no impact on the end of slavery either within the United States or within the State of Mississippi, it is a legal legacy that speaks to the recalcitrance of the state and its legal system in the treatment of blacks. In part, the material reality of conditions for blacks in the state and the consensus white perception of the subservience of blacks can be read as giving rise to the cultural logic and ideologies infusing Faulkner's *Go Down, Moses.* Not to know this misses an opportunity to understand how the past can inform the present, and how race matters for whites—even under the most absurdly futile circumstances.

And so, I could not be a nature poet. Instead, I turned the remnants of my poetic eye to the multiple worlds of the many-layered South, to Faulkner and his images, his discourses, his people, his Tomey's Turls, and I am sometimes comforted, sometimes not, by the intellectual property I claim there.

NOTES

1. See my initial reading of Old Ben as "The Negro," Thadious M. Davis, *Faulkner's "Negro": Art and the Southern Context* (Baton Rouge: Louisiana State University Press, 1983), 244–46.

2. See my beginning formulation of that reading in Thadious M. Davis, "The Game of Courts: *Go Down, Moses*, Arbitrary Legalities, and Compensatory Boundaries," in *New Essays on "Go Down, Moses*," ed. Linda Wagner Martin (New York: Cambridge University Press, 1996), 129–54.

3. William Faulkner, *Go Down, Moses* (1942; New York: Vintage International Edition, 1990), 23. Further references will appear in the text.

4. Cornell West, Epilogue to the Vintage Edition, *Race Matters* (New York: Vintage, 1994), 156–57.

5. Michael Omni and Howard Winant, *Racial Formation in the U. S.: From the 1960s to the 1990s* (New York: Routledge, 1994), 61.

6. Henry Louis Gates Jr., "Writing 'Race' and the Difference It Makes," in *"Race," Writing, and Difference*, ed. Henry Louis Gates Jr. (Chicago: University of Chicago Press, 1985), 5.

7. Gilles Deleuze and Felix Guattari, *A Thousand Plateaus: Capitalism and Schizophrenia*, vol. 2 (London: Athlone, 1988), 178. See also Roland Young, *Colonial Desire: Hybridity in Theory, Culture, and Race* (New York: Routledge, 1995), 180.

8. Deleuze and Guattari, 178.

9. *State v. Mann*, 13 North Carolina 266 (1829).

10. Michel Foucault, *The History of Sexuality*, vol. 1: *An Introduction* (New York: Vintage Books, 1990), 156.

11. Ibid.

12. Toni Morrison, *Playing in the Dark: Whiteness and the Literary Imagination* (Cambridge: Harvard University Press, 1992), 53.

13. Omni and Winant, 60.

14. Ibid.

15. See Ellen Barry's informative article, "White Like Me," *The Providence Phoenix*, 11 July 1997, 8–12.

16. The aim to racialize whiteness and deconstruct the term and its function in power relations is evident currently in numerous books and special issues of periodicals: Vron Ware's *Beyond the Pale: White Women, Racism, and History* (London: Verso, 1992), Ruth Frankenberg's *White Women, Race Matters: The Social Construction of Whiteness* (Minneapolis: University of Minnesota Press, 1994), and Matt Wray's *White Trash: Race and Class in America* (New York: Routledge, 1997), all share in formulating the current discourses on whiteness. In part white responses to Cornell West's *Race Matters*, these recent discourses on white raciality also take their impetus from Morrison's *Playing in the Dark: Whiteness and the Literary Imagination*.

17. West, 8.

What Faulkner Read at the P. O.

THOMAS L. MCHANEY

Chief among the matters Faulknerian that remain untapped is his intellectual life, especially the development of Faulkner's mind as he made
his way into the culture of writing. This is difficult, if not impossible, to
document with precision, but what I would recommend is closer looks at
the general intellectual ambience during short periods of his life that we
suspect were particularly stimulating: the years 1914 to 1918, when the
World War and the initial tutelage of Phil Stone were both extremely
important; the months in New Haven in 1918; the months in Toronto in
1918–1919; the initial postwar period in Oxford and on the University of
Mississippi campus, 1919–1921; the very short trip to New York and New
Haven in 1921; the post office years; the year in New Orleans; the time
in Paris and Europe and its brief twilight back in New Orleans and Pascagoula; the years back in Oxford before his marriage to Estelle in 1929.
With no family responsibilities, no demanding jobs—and often no jobs
at all—Faulkner was, in different ways in each of these different periods,
listening, reading in both the popular and literary press, and thereby
discovering through essays, reviews, anecdotes, and conversations not
only what books to read but why he should be reading them. As his
artistic ambitions changed, and especially as they became increasingly
focussed upon the very difficult matter of writing serious fiction, his reading, his own later remarks indicate, took on new importance and meaning
both in the current moment and retrospectively. I feel especially strongly
that we have as yet nothing like a full exploration of the role in Faulkner's
intellectual development played by his activities and acquaintances at the
University of Mississippi. For this occasion, I have narrowed my topic to
a speculation upon "What Faulkner Read at the P.O."

Like many of the episodes of Faulkner's life, his tenure at the University Post Office at Ole Miss is treated as a diversion on his way to a
writing career. None of his biographers devotes much space to it, and I
suspect the impression of many people is that it was not only an intermis-
sion and a debacle, but also of short duration. Its dominant representation, like what passed for years as the basic representation of Faulkner's

long and complex tenure in Hollywood, takes the form of a couple of humorous anecdotes with a couple of punch lines: If you have a fourth class post office, you get a fourth-class postmaster, or, Now I won't have to be at the beck and call of every son of a bitch who has two cents for a stamp.

As with so many of the jokes about his life, however, the self-desparaging summaries of the post office interlude were created by Faulkner himself for his own purposes. What does the joking hide? As usual, it hides his intellect.

Faulkner spent his days in that little post office for almost three years. Three years is a long time in the life of an ambitious young writer who would be accused by complaining patrons that he was neglectful of his duties because he was a "habitual reader of books and magazines."[1] He does not appear to have been displeased with the job, himself, until it was over. If we suppose that he was sometimes busy, this was relatively easy and undemanding work that did not go home with him. He had assistants to meet the two northbound and two southbound trains twice a day and haul the mail up the hill from the nearby station to the campus. It would have been the practice for the sales and general delivery call window to be closed while the mail was put up, even if his assistants did much of that work too. Faulkner, who had trained as a bookkeeper in his grandfather's bank and practiced similar skills as an accounting clerk with the Winchester Repeating Arms Company in New Haven in 1918, kept the books, ordered supplies, and handled other paperwork for postal transactions while managing the distribution of incoming mail and the sending out of both private and official university mail. This he did for three years without too much challenge to his competence or authority until the last few months. Despite his final relief when he lost the job,[2] for thirty-six months he had the kind of undemanding position Poe, Hawthorne, and Melville would have killed for in their own time.

If Faulkner held back some of his patron's magazines, then, as it is said, in order to read the ones that interested him before they were picked up, three years adds up to a lot of exposure to monthly and weekly magazines. Recall, as well, that his postal customers were not only students but University of Mississippi professors (many of whom lived in housing on campus not far from the post office) and the university library (where he was obviously quite welcome to go and pick up magazines that eluded him as they passed through the post office). What magazines, and what reading?

Of course, we don't know. So the best I can do at the moment, and in the space alotted, is to sketch for you what the medium of the magazine might have brought into Faulkner's ken from December 1921 through

October 1924. Already, Faulkner had absorbed a great deal of nine-teenth- and twentieth-century writing, both fiction and poetry, and even applied it for his own purposes. He had published imitations of Mallarmé and Villon, as well as drawings, reviews of contemporary fiction and the-ater, early examples of ironic prose fiction, and had begun making elegant little hand-lettered volumes of his unpublished work. A mind so engaged had plenty of reason to dip into the magazine literature of the day. There is a traditon, but no hard evidence, that Faulkner and his tutor Phil Stone read *The Dial* and *The Little Review* at this time, with the implication that Stone put these magazines in Faulkner's hands just as he did the dozens of books from the Brick Row Book Shop in New Haven he sud-denly, in 1922, began ordering out of his father's law office in Oxford, where the records of the transactions remained on file and were copied in the late 1950s by James B. Meriwether.[3] As it happened, these orders from Oxford are coincident with Stone's return to Oxford from a three-year assignment at the family's branch practice fifty miles away in Charleston, Mississippi, in Tallahatchie County on the edge of the Delta. (It's intriguing to suppose that the files of the Charleston office might have had records of earlier transactions that helped build Stone's li-brary—and Faulkner's education—during the previous three years, since even while working in the Delta, Stone returned on week ends to Oxford and saw his young protégé and other friends.)

But *The Dial*, at least, Faulkner could have read in the University Post Office, if he intercepted the copies bound for the Ole Miss library, and perhaps it was he, in this case, and not Stone, who called attention to *The Waste Land* in the November 1922 issue, Edmund Wilson's essay about the poem, "The Poetry of Drouth" (December 1922), or Eliot's provocative review of *Ulysses*, "Ulysses, Order, and Myth," the following year (November 1923). In those three years at the post office, *The Dial* alone would have represented a remarkable curriculum. In 1922 it pub-lished, among much else, stories by Conrad Aiken, Sherwood Anderson, and D. H. Lawrence; essays by Kenneth Burke, Malcolm Cowley, Eliot, Pound, Yeats, Herman Hesse on *The Brothers Karamazov*; Amy Lowell on E. A. Robinson (who was one of Stone's favorite poets); reproductions of art by Matisse, Picasso, Lachaise, Demuth, and others. Among the many reviews of new books were some that focussed on those that Faulk-ner himself would review or later imitate. Regarding Huxley's *Crome Yellow*—which definitely inspired Faulkner's *Mosquitoes* a year or two later—the reviewer noted that the inhabitants of the country estate, Crome, were not living characters but "*fantoches*," a term that might have jumped at Faulkner, who had published his poem with that title at Ole Miss two years before.[4]

The 1922 *Dial* had plenty of modern poetry to go with all the excitement about Eliot, winner of the magazine's annual $2000 prize for *The Waste Land*, including Cummings, Hart Crane, Marianne Moore, Sandburg, William Carlos Williams. A fine little comment on Joyce's new novel quoted Valery Larbaud on the variety and complexity, rather than the linearity, of Joyce's play upon Homer's *Odyssey* in *Ulysses* (June 1922: 662–63), and Paul Rosenfield observed that Sherwood Anderson "has to face himself where Freud and Lawrence, Stieglitz and Picasso, and every other great artist of the time, have faced themselves" in order to add a " 'phallic Chekhov' to [those who] remind an age that it is in the nucleus of sex that all the lights and confusions have their centre."[5] Kenneth Burke's essay on Flaubert's correspondence draws attention to the French writer's observations that he seemed to attract the attention and trust of "animals and the insane," including the "imbecile daughter" of a tenant on his father's farm—a poignant note of identification for the young Faulkner, whose solicitude for Margaret Brown, the afflicted daughter of one of his friends on the university faculty, would lead to "The Wishing Tree" and *The Sound and the Fury*. In that regard, Burke also quotes Flaubert's ambition to write "a book about nothing . . . which would sustain itself by the internal force of its style . . . [and] an invisible subject."[6] In the following year, 1923, of course, would come "Ulysses, Order and Myth" by T. S. Eliot (November: 480–83), as important an expression of the hegemony of the modern as *The Waste Land* itself. On it goes, until in the spring of his final year in the post office Faulkner might have read in *The Dial* a brilliant appreciation of Emily Dickinson by Conrad Aiken and Thomas Mann's "Death in Venice" (March 1924) or a cautionary review of the "faked folklore and faked Magic" of James Branch Cabell's *Jurgen* that nonetheless quoted, with praise, the kind of purple passage that Faulkner himself would still be putting in his early novels (April 1924: 363). I find it intriguing that the month following Faulkner's dismissal from the postmastership, one Charles K. Trueblood wrote in *The Dial* of a now forgotten novel that "the book should be found well done by professors of the art of fiction" (November 1924: 429). Could the author and his piece foreshadow the professorial Ernest V. Trueblood whose careful diction and style in "Afternoon of a Cow" contrast so sharply with that of his intemperate employer, Mr. Faulkner, whose novels and stories Trueblood has been writing for years?[7]

But Faulkner's literary inclinations may well have obtained considerable sustenance from magazines far more general and less provocative than *The Dial* or *The Little Review* (which had had its own problems with the postal service and which the university library apparently did not receive). General magazines received by the university library, and probably in some instances by faculty or student postal patrons, carried material about nineteenth- and early twentieth-century writers who were as attractive and important to Faulkner as were the avant-garde of the twenties, but they also often promoted the avant-garde. The very first issue of *Time Magazine*, for example, March 3, 1923, has, alongside a very favorable review of Gertrude Atherton's daring novel *The Black Oxen*, a column headed "Shantih Shantih Shantih / Has the Reader Any Right Before the Bar of Literature," an acknowledgement of *The Dial* award for the clearly difficult poem *The Waste Land*.[8] Just below is the recommendation for the magazine's readers to get their hands on a dozen books including *Babbitt*, *Jurgen*, Housman's *Last Poems*, Sherwood Anderson's *Many Marriages*, the aforementioned *Black Oxen*, and Hergesheimer's *The Bright Shawl*, which Faulkner had reviewed not long before in *The Mississippian*. The June 1922 *Atlantic* carried a long and witty, yet serious, essay entitled "Flapper Americana Novissima," written by the psychologist G. Stanley Hall; Hall was the author of a standard work on adolescence as well as *Jesus, the Christ, in the Light of Psychology*, which came out the year before his death in 1924. Could Faulkner, whose interest in flappers, adolescence, and Jesus would meld in more than one book, have missed completely the man who brought Freud to Massachusetts during the fall Quentin Compson matriculated at Harvard?[9]

Other high quality popular magazines were publishing essays and features on subjects in which the young writer had an interest, and some of these even appeared amidst the work of writers whom he actually knew. For example, during this three-year period, Stark Young, who sometimes visited his kin in Oxford and on whom Faulkner had depended for shelter and employment advice during the brief and unsuccesful assault on New York City in 1921, published nearly one hundred pieces—poems, stories, essays, and reviews—in a variety of magazines. William Alexander Percy of Greenville, whom Faulkner knew through both Stone and his younger Ole Miss friend Ben Wasson, published more than a dozen poems in several magazines. Stephen Vincent Benet, whom Faulkner had met at Yale while staying with Stone in 1918, published an equal number in several, and his brother William Rose Benet and sister-in-law, Elinor Wylie, whose poetry Faulkner demonstrably liked, appeared more often. The uniqueness of our young postmaster is such that he could hardly pick up a magazine of the day that didn't have someone or something specifically attracting his attention.

If Faulkner saw only *American Mercury*, the *Nation*, the *New Republic*, *North American Review*, and the *Yale Review*, for example, all of which the University of Mississippi Library apparently received (and where the work of writers he knew appeared), he found the writing of his acquaintances collected with essays and reviews about other writers in whom he was taking increasing artistic interest: Balzac, Bergson, Conrad, Dostoevsky, Flaubert, James G. Frazer, Freud, Joyce, Thomas Mann, Nietzsche, and Proust. In May of 1922, the *Nation* proved especially interesting in Oxford, and elsewhere in Mississippi, because of a very critical view of the state by a woman named Beulah Amidon Ratliff. One of a series of essays on American states by the likes of H. L. Mencken (Maryland), William Allen White (Kansas), and Dorothy Canfield Fisher (Vermont), "Mississippi: Heart of Dixie" provoked dozens of critical replies from Mississippians published the following weeks, including one— responded to in the magazine by Ms. Ratliff, the author—from the grandmother of Richard Howorth, who owns Square Books.[10]

Not long after Faulkner assumed his duties in the post office, *North American Review* printed a European sketch from Stark Young reflecting the trip he had taken in 1921 when Faulkner first failed to find him at home in New York City. Close by was a piece on Dostoevsky comparing him to Baudelaire and Nietzsche and discussing the annihilation of time in his narrative, a condition created, the article's author supposed, by Dostoevsky's epileptic seizures, before which he was said to have moments filled with thoughts and emotions that a lifetime is insufficient to narrate.[11] At about the same time, in the *New Republic*, where Faulkner himself had published "L'pre midi d'une faune" in 1919, and where Stark Young and Will Percy published regularly, he could have read a review of James G. Frazer's *The Golden Bough*—just out in the one-volume abridgement that Faulkner would read—under the title "A Dangerous Book," and Conrad Aiken's excellent review of *The Waste Land* that *The Dial* itself recommended.[12]

It was Faulkner's good fortune, then, I think, to have this position in the period when he had the greatest need, and probably the greatest receptivity, to explore and absorb the information, the language, and the recommendations for further reading that came in so many American magazines of his day. It was likewise good fortune for this to occur not in some far and alien place but in a world he took for granted, surrounded by family and friends. Education, we know, is unpredictable. It doesn't always happen when or where or how we expect it to. Three years of reading other people's mail, and borrowing other people's books, on a university campus, was, after all, for a man who'd trained in an RAF ground school, done some college work, and undergone a personal tutorial with a man who had four college degrees and a splendid library, enough to complete a postgraduate program. We might be reminded of Ishmael's remark in *Moby-Dick* (a book Phil Stone bought Faulkner in 1922) that a whaling ship was his Yale College and his Harvard. Much later, in *Go Down, Moses* (1942), Faulkner has the past-haunted woodsman Isaac McCaslin think that, in turn, the woods have been his kindergarten and the great bear his alma mater. Faulkner himself might have said with justice that Phil Stone was his Yale College, and the Post Office his Harvard.

Several years after Faulkner published *The Sound and the Fury*, he was invited to write a preface for a new limited edition of the novel. This 1933 project never came off, and the drafts of a preface Faulkner wrote for the volume did not surface for another two decades. In one draft preface written in 1933, he says that the writing of *The Sound and the Fury* changed his own consciousness, and "without heeding to open another book and in a series of delayed repercussions like summer thunder, I discovered the Flauberts and Dostoievskys [*sic*] and Conrads whose books I read ten years ago."[13] Faulkner was notoriously casual about dates, but I am tempted to interpret "ten years ago," penned in 1933, as applying to the post office years: that is, specifically, to 1923 and '24, the culmination of Faulkner's three years of habitual reading and study on the Ole Miss campus, not as a registered student but as a member of the staff. The postmaster who read his patrons' or the university's magazines, experiencing what the art critic Robert Hughes has called "the shock of the new," also read the novels by writers who were repeatedly featured, reviewed, explicated, and recommended in those magazines.

After he came into his own as a writer and mastered the influences and techniques that he had absorbed during his apprenticeship, after he had created a fictional cosmos that put him on a world stage in Stockholm, Faulkner would call Yoknapatawpha County "my own little postage stamp of native soil."[14] For all his jokes about being postmaster, I do not think he had forgotten what the responsibility of selling a few stamps to a few sons of bitches had allowed him to achieve.

NOTES

1. Joseph Blotner, *Faulkner: A Life*, 2 vols. (New York: Random House, 1974), 1:363. More circumstantial treatments of the official "case" of Faulkner's conduct in the post office are in Joan St. C. Crane, " 'Case No. 13733-C': The Inspector's Letter to Postmaster William Faulkner," *Mississippi Quarterly* 42 (Summer 1989): 229–45, and Gerald Walton, "William C. Falkner, Postmaster: Some Correspondence," *Journal of Mississippi History* 51 (February 1989): 1–15.

2. Philip Cohen has recently published a letter from Faulkner to his friend Ben Wasson that expresses his relief that he is "free again": "My God, I didn't know how I did hate that Post Office until this morning." " 'This Hand Holds Genius': Three Unpublished Faulkner Letters," *Mississippi Quarterly* 46 (Summer 1993): 479–83.

3. Joseph Blotner, *William Faulkner's Library: A Catalogue* (Charlottesville: Bibliographical Society of the University of Virginia and University Press of Virginia, 1964): 6.

4. *The Dial* (January 1922): 632. "Fantoches" is reprinted in *William Faulkner: Early*

Prose and Poetry, ed. Carvel Collins (Boston: Atlantic / Little Brown, 1962). Stone ordered *Crome Yellow* in April 1922 (Blotner, *Catalogue*, 125).

5. *The Dial* (January 1922): 35.

6. *The Dial* (January 1922): 154.

7. *Uncollected Stories of William Faulkner*, ed. Joseph Blotner (New York: Random House, 1979), 424.

8. *Time* 1 (March 3, 1923): 12.

9. G. Stanley Hall, *Adolescence; Its Psychology and Its Relations to Physiology, Anthropology, Sociology, Sex, Crime, Religion and Education* (New York: D. Appleton, 1905) and *Jesus, the Christ, in the Light of Psychology* (New York: Appleton, 1924). He was also editor of *The American Journal of Psychology*.

10. *Nation* (17 May 1922); responses on 2 August and 23 August.

11. *North American Review* (January 1922).

12. *New Republic* (23 February 1923).

13. "An Introduction for *The Sound and the Fury*," ed. James B. Meriwether, *Southern Review* 8 (Autumn 1972): 708; another draft of the introduction, published in *Mississippi Quarterly* 26 (Summer 1973), has the phrase "Flauberts and Conrads and Turgenievs which as much as ten years before I had consumed whole and without assimilating at all, as a moth or a goat might" (414). In the *Southern Review* version he also speaks of measuring his choices as a writer "by the scale of the Jameses and Conrads and Balzacs" (709).

14. "Interview with Jean Stein Vanden Heuvel," *Lion in the Garden: Interviews with William Faulkner, 1926–1962*, ed. James B. Meriwether and Michael Millgate (New York: Random House, 1968), 255.

Faulkner and Love: The Question of Collaboration

JUDITH L. SENSIBAR

Today I will talk about work in progress. This summer I've been revising some chapters of my book project, "Faulkner and Love: A Family Narrative." This paper is about the process of trying to piece together the complicated intellectual and emotional relationship that existed between Estelle Oldham and William Faulkner during one of the most crucial periods in Faulkner's imaginative development, the years 1921–25. An essay drawn from these chapters and focusing on one of Oldham's short stories and the story itself, which is called "Star-Spangled Banner Stuff," will be published in *Prospects: An Annual of American Cultural Studies* (1997). Part of what I'll say here previews those publications.

But first, to provide context, I'll briefly summarize the subject of these chapters I've been revising. It concerns the centrality of William's and Estelle's erotic and intellectual relationship to Faulkner's creative development. Estelle Oldham is most commonly portrayed as a stupid, spoiled, hysterical Southern Belle. William's marriage is judged a tragic mistake. This narrative has a long genealogy. My favorite description is Joel Williamson's image of Estelle: "wrist-cutting, self-drowning, window-jumping Estelle, already with two children when he married her and a body threatening death if she attempted a third."[1]

Critics speculate at length on Estelle's mental instability, moral lapses, physical illnesses, alcohol and drug abuse, and her role as millstone around the great author's neck. Yet few have acknowledged and none have explained the existence of her fiction, and no one has explored Faulkner's professional interest in and highly productive use of it, which includes the interplay of their imaginations that editing, rewriting, coauthorship, and shared readings entail. My chapters use their collaboration, Estelle Oldham's fiction, and the stories and novels Faulkner made from some of it as significant sources of information about both Faulkner and the woman with whom he had an intense and highly complicated relationship, one that lasted from his childhood until his death. For it was her creativity that William Faulkner engaged in dialogue, delighted in, and profited from. I suggest that when we read the short stories Oldham wrote in the context of Faulkner's apprenticeship work and his major fiction, we can clearly perceive the shaping effect she had on his creative vision, especially in regard to the erotics of human desire in the context of those historically bound terms, race and gender.

Many modern literary artists seem to thrive on a desire for sexual and racial indeterminacy and multiple identities that can be, at different moments (and for differing reasons), either suffocating or liberating to their creativity. I think of Sherwood Anderson mentally donning "black-face" as he sat at the typewriter in his sweltering New Orleans apartment the summer of 1924, writing what he hoped would be the next Great American Novel, or of Faulkner in the teens and early twenties experimenting endlessly with the various poet identities (wounded war hero, ragged bohemian, fin de siècle dandy, good ole boy) that comprised the artistic persona of his decade long self-apprenticeship to poetry.[2]

As part of their desire for multiple identities, many great artists also seem to need friends, but better, lovers who will play parts or roles with them. Best are lovers who, while not great artists themselves, are creative enough to participate meaningfully in a critical dialogue. Such dialogue, as we know from Faulkner's fiction, most famously *Absalom, Absalom!*, is a way of entering and being entered by the other's mind. That blending, too, I'm convinced, can prove immensely rewarding. Certainly it was for Faulkner.[3]

But let me speak specifically about Estelle, William, and "Star-Spangled Banner Stuff." On the 17th of November 1924, Estelle Oldham Franklin and her two young children made a sudden and unplanned departure from Shanghai on the T.K.K. *Shinyo Maru*. She was bound for Oxford, Mississippi. All evidence indicates that she had no intention of returning to her husband, Cornell.[4] In her baggage she carried longhand versions of a novel and the short stories that she had written during the past three years. Among these manuscripts was "Star-Spangled Banner Stuff." In the trans-Pacific mail to her was the announcement of William Faulkner's first book of poems, *The Marble Faun*, which Faulkner had ordered sent earlier that month.

Although William Faulkner collaborated in revising and then submitted at least one of her stories under their joint byline, and later (under his own name) published it and several other stories that were originally Estelle Oldham's, none of her fiction was ever published. And, as far as is currently known, none of her original manuscripts survive. However, as Joseph Blotner notes, there are extant versions of three of the stories that Faulkner is known to have revised and/or rewritten with Estelle and tried to publish ("Selvage"/"Elly," "Idyll in the Desert," and "A Letter"). There are also typescript versions of three other stories, two of which Faulkner also typed for Oldham, probably shortly after she arrived home in December 1924. "Star-Spangled Banner Stuff" is included in the latter group.

This story has been available to scholars since the mid-nineteen sixties. A note on its provenance states that "Mrs. William Faulkner, then the wife of Judge (Cornell) Franklin" wrote "Star-Spangled Banner Stuff" "ca. 1924 in Shanghai. William Faulkner subsequently read the story in Oxford, Miss., and, according to Mrs. Faulkner, offered suggestions regarding its construction—The story was never published."[5]

The mixture of carbons and original typescript pages that comprise the Alderman Library version of "Star-Spangled Banner Stuff" indicates that it is a revision of an earlier, now missing typescript. While the majority of pages are carbons, there are also original typescript pages preceded or followed by large page breaks indicating portions that were significantly rewritten. Both William and Estelle made ink autograph corrections throughout this entire typescript, providing readers with a rare holograph example of their collaborative work. Both have made minor substantive revisions.

Estelle's extant stories resemble contemporaneous popular colonial romance stories published in venues like the Shanghai English language newspapers, American and British short story collections, and mass circulation magazines like *Scribner's*, the *Saturday Evening Post, McCall's,* and *Freeman*. "Star-Spangled Banner Stuff" is, in this sense, a period piece and should be read as such. Stylistically, Estelle was no modernist revolutionary. It was her sensibility that was subversive. While her contemporaries wrote about their host country's barbaric practice of buying and selling its women and children, she wrote about her contemporaries' marketing of their own women. The narcissism of her bratty heroine, her sly portrayals of her fellow colonials' sexism, and her exposure of the shallowness of their devotion to democratic ideals, highlighted in her title "Star-Spangled Banner Stuff," give her story an edge not found in most East-West encounter fiction then appearing in the popular press. Her often campy tone mocks the very genre she has chosen.

Oldham's fiction is of interest to us because of its interest to and obvious importance for Faulkner. In writing about Faulkner's decade-long self-apprenticeship to poetry (1915–1925), I concluded that until the would-be writer renounced his poetic persona—the Pierrot mask with all its crippling implications—he remained essentially stuck in other poets' voices. As long as he refused to translate his beloved *pierrotiste* persona's dreams, to dare to divine their meanings for himself, and so transform them into art, he could never be more than a mediocre, highly imitative poet. In the final movement of his symphonic sequence, *Vision in Spring*, finished and given to Estelle just before the Franklins moved to Shanghai in 1921, he had begun to do this.[6] Since then, his progress had slowed to a virtual standstill.

As both Joseph Blotner and Susan Snell have carefully documented, for the next three years, during which Estelle Franklin lived in Shanghai, Faulkner wrote very little that was new.[7] Instead, he worked on revisions of his major poem sequences, *The Marble Faun* and *Vision in Spring*.[8] Blotner writes that William had been showing Estelle his poetry and asking her to critique it since they were teenagers.[9] Apparently he continued to do so during her marriage to Cornell Franklin and colonial sojourn, first in the Hawaiian Territories (as they were then called) and later in Shanghai (1918–1924). Manuscript evidence indicates that when William gave *Vision in Spring* to Estelle, he asked her to comment on it. She marked it and mailed it back to him from Shanghai.[10] In 1923, he submitted the revised sequence, which he retitled *Orpheus, and Other Poems*, to the Four Seas Company. In 1924, he sent them the revised *Marble Faun*, which he had essentially completed in 1920. Meanwhile, in Shanghai, Estelle had been doing some writing of her own. To summarize then: in early December 1924 when Estelle first showed William the fiction she had completed during their three year separation, he was still writing poetry almost exclusively, the same poetry he had been writing when she left. Yet shortly after her return—in the space of weeks— Faulkner moves first from poetry to prose sketches which were published almost as soon as he wrote them. And then, remarkably, in early March, Faulkner begins his first novel which he finishes by mid-May 1925.[11] What internal and external circumstances help to account for the massive and almost instantaneous shift of direction in Faulkner's imaginative development at this particular point in time?

Although he would leave for an extended stay in New Orleans shortly after the New Year, William Faulkner and Estelle Franklin were together during her first month at home in December 1924. And, while she and her children went to Columbus to visit her mother-in-law shortly after Faulkner left for New Orleans in January, her return to Oxford coincided with Faulkner's week-long trip to Oxford at the end of February, shortly before he began writing his first novel, *Soldiers' Pay*.[12] All previous accounts have given Faulkner's brief and intense friendship and his tutorial with Sherwood Anderson that began in March 1925 as the immediate impetus for Faulkner's extraordinary burst of creativity during the first six months of 1925 and, most importantly for his sudden and so seemingly magical transformation from poet to novelist. I suggest a rather less dramatic, more obvious, and simpler explanation: one much closer to home and deeply rooted in Faulkner's own history. Estelle's return to Oxford where she and William could resume their relationship, which included their comfortable intellectual exchange, was probably a more significant factor than his new and short-lived friendship with Anderson. To say this in no way minimizes the contributions of Faulkner's other mentors. However, introducing Estelle's actual presence and the fact of her fiction add a human and psychic dimension that was there in life, and so provide a more accurate and nuanced portrait of this moment. While Blotner documents the pattern of William and Estelle's intellectual dialogue, his and all subsequent biographical accounts, Thomas Moser's recent sensitive essay on Estelle as muse excepted, ignore its implications.[13] As one of Faulkner's brothers writes about their childhood, "with her listening, he found that he could talk."[14] But she was much more than a passive listener. William wanted her opinion; discussion of his work had always been part of their relationship.

Related and equally important to their relationship in adolescence was William's interest in imitating Estelle's appearance. Most adolescents are preoccupied with their looks. But for Faulkner, whose fiction would be defined in part by its passionate exploration of the terrors and pleasures of masking, mirroring, and merging—especially as these relate to those slippery matters, racial and sexual identities—the ability to manipulate his own appearance and imitate and emulate others became inseparable from his creative persona. That humans emulate and imitate the objects of their desire is a commonplace. One of the people Faulkner both sought and feared to merge with was Estelle. Faulkner played with his desire in various imaginative ways. Joseph Blotner writes that "there was a kind of dandyism" in Faulkner's adolescent appearance (155). Faulkner's brother is more direct noting that his brother had "an almost foppish taste in clothes" and that he spent most of his bank bookkeeper's salary "adorning himself."[15]

Like Estelle, William "had a graceful slim figure that the tight clothes flattered." Not content with a store-bought look, William had his mother alter a dress-suit so that the pants were so tight "that by the time . . . the image in the mirror suited her son, they were close to skin-tight" (Blotner 180). Like Estelle, he spent excessive amounts on dress clothes and, again according to Blotner, "was very much the fashion plate" (157, 175). Furthermore, Blotner writes, William's "predisposition to slightness was augmented by the fact that now, in emulation of Estelle, he took only toast and black coffee for breakfast."[16]

William's inclusion of Estelle's voice in his writing process, his fascination with clothes and with altering his body image to mirror hers, these had taken many permutations during the course of what was already a long relationship by December of 1924 when Estelle returned to Oxford from Shanghai. But, by then, collaboration with her (and others) and masking as a form of collaboration were clearly parts of Faulkner's creative process. Yet, until this point, as far as is known, William identified himself as a poet, not a fiction writer. As a poet he had made no recognizable advance since 1921.

One can only speculate about Faulkner's response to Estelle Oldham's fiction. But informed speculation based on prior history suggests that it would have been profound. Importantly, her extant stories show that, while they originated in her own imagination and experiences, they often responded to and offered alternative readings of major themes and characters in the books of poems he had given and dedicated to her. In short, by effecting a role and gender reversal—she as writer and he as reader—her stories expanded the terms of their dialogue. I suggest that when Estelle arrived in Oxford in December 1924 and showed William her work and he offered to type it for her, the act of taking over her words, entering into and assuming the mask of her imagination—of becoming in this way a fiction writer rather than a poet—was a defining moment in his transformation from poet to novelist. Typing her novel and her stories, entering and merging with her voice in the very physical way in which typing and perhaps, at times, editing or revising another's words permits, gave him access to a voice and identity or self he had never reached before.

In October 1926 Faulkner would offer Estelle Franklin a private commemoration marking the moment of his transformation from poet into novelist. As with other handmade books he had given her, he dated and dedicated *Royal Street*, a handprinted collection of all but one of the eleven short sketches he had published in the January-February 1925 issue of the New Orleans *Double Dealer*, to Estelle. Significantly he added an additional sketch called "Hong-Li," his extension of their continuing literary dialogue and tribute to the wealth of imaginative material present for him in the fictional voices Estelle brought home from Shanghai.[17] We might also speculate that Faulkner again commemorated this moment in 1935 when he imagined the transaction between the poet laureate of Jefferson County, Rosa Coldfield, and Quentin Compson, the might-be short story writer in his opening chapter of *Absalom, Absalom!* Here fiction triumphs over life, as it always did for Faulkner, and the artist's identity as man or woman becomes indeterminate: the failed and ridiculed poet is a woman but her overwrought and hyperbolic language acts as a constant touchstone for the incredible tales that Quentin and other men will then attempt to tell.

NOTES

1. Joel Williamson, *William Faulkner and Southern History* (New York: Oxford University Press, 1993), 250 and passim.

2. For a discussion of Faulkner's apprenticeship to poetry and its impact on his mature fiction see Sensibar, *The Origins of Faulkner's Art* (Austin: University of Texas Press, 1984).

3. The best known of such friends are Phil Stone and Sherwood Anderson. For a fuller account of Estelle's role in this capacity see Sensibar, " 'Drowsing Maidenhead Symbol's Self': Faulkner and the Fictions of Love," in *Faulkner and the Craft of Fiction*, ed. Doreen Fowler and Ann J. Abadie (Jackson: University Press of Mississippi, 1989), 124–47.

4. Almost a year later, under extreme pressure from her family and her husband who had by then followed her to Mississippi, Estelle did go back Shanghai. Yet in less than two months, probably by mid-January 1926, she and her children left Shanghai again—this time for good.

5. The Linton Massey Faulkner Collection, The Alderman Library, Charlottesville, Virginia.

6. For a discussion of the importance of this sequence to the development of Faulkner's creative imagination see *The Origins of Faulkner's Art*, 196–207.

7. See Blotner's *Faulkner: A Biography*, vols. 1 and 2 (New York: Random House, 1974) and Susan Snell, *Phil Stone of Oxford: A Vicarious Life* (Athens: University of Georgia Press, 1991).

8. As he wrote in a 1924 biographical sketch prepared for his publishers, The Four Seas, " 'The Marble Faun' was written in the spring of 1919." See Blotner, *Faulkner: A Biography* 1-vol. ed. (New York: Random House, 1984), 117.

9. *Faulkner: A Biography* (1974), 140, 142, 152, 155.

10. See Sensibar, *Origins*, 238–39, n. 32. Joseph Blotner thinks that Faulkner "gave Estelle a carbon of the collection of poems, bound it and titled it *Vision in Spring*, asked her for her comments, then used the ribbon copies to make up *Orpheus, and Other Poems*, which he then sent to Four Seas. It's not impossible that when they sent it back he destroyed it, or kept it and cannibalized it. You noticed all the pencil markings on *Vision in Spring* I'm sure. And they clearly aren't his. I'm sure they are Estelle's" (Joseph Blotner, letter to the author, 4 June 1983).

11. See James G. Watson, ed., *Thinking of Home: William Faulkner's Letters to His Mother and Father, 1918–1925* (New York: Norton, 1992), 167–231 and Hans H. Skei, *William Faulkner: The Novelist as Short Story Writer* (Oslo: Universitetsforlaget, Publications of the American Institute, University of Oslo, 1985), 31–51.

12. See *Oxford Eagle*, 19 and 22 January and 24 February 1925; *Thinking of Home*, 178, 184, 220, 228; Murry Falkner's journal quoted in Blotner, *Faulkner: A Biography* (1984), 132; Snell, *Phil Stone of Oxford*, 173.

13. Blotner, 1974, 140, 142, 152, 155, 160, 162. See Thomas C. Moser's persuasive and beautifully written "Faulkner's Muse: Speculations on the Genesis of *The Sound and the Fury*," in *Critical Reconstructions: The Relationship of Fiction and Life*, ed. Robert M. Polhemus and Roger B. Henkle (Stanford: Stanford University Press, 1994), 187–211. Although my understanding of the nature of Faulkner's erotic life differs somewhat from Moser's, his careful interpretive reconstruction of the relation between Faulkner's creativity and Estelle's and William's unions and separations has been essential to my own reading.

14. John Faulkner, *My Brother Bill: An Affectionate Reminiscence* (New York: Trident Press, 1963), 122.

15. Ibid., 130. Since John was notoriously unsympathetic to Estelle, this statement is especially meaningful.

16. Blotner, 1974, 157.

17. "Hong-Li" is published in Noel Polk's " 'Hong-Li' and *Royal Street: The New Orleans Sketches* in Manuscript" in *A Faulkner Miscellany*, ed. James B. Meriwether (Jackson: University Press of Mississippi, 1974), 143–44. See also his "William Faulkner's 'Hong Li' and *Royal Street*," *The Library Chronicle of the University of Texas at Austin* (N.S. 13, 1980), 27–30.

Faulkner's Other Others

ARTHUR F. KINNEY

I think the ghost of . . . ravishment lingers in the land, that the land is inimical to the white man because of the unjust way in which it was taken from Ikkemotubbe and his people. That happened by treaty, which President Jackson established with the Chickasaws and the Choctaws, in which they would take land in Oklahoma in exchange for their Mississippi land, and they were paid for it, but they were compelled to leave it, either to leave on—to follow a chimera in the West or to stay there in a condition even worse than the Negro slave, in isolation.

The Indians held the land communally, a few of them that were wise enough to see which way the wind was blowing would get government patents for the land. There was one of them, a Choctaw chief, was one of the wealthiest men in Mississippi, Greenwood Leflore, he was wise enough to get a patented deed to his land and to take up the white man's ways, he was a cotton planter, he'd built a tremendous mansion and imported the furnishings from France, and he was quite wealthy.

—William Faulkner at the University of Virginia
9 March 1957

"The Indians are the neglected people in Faulkner," Lewis M. Dabney wrote in 1974. "They are the first phase of his Yoknapatawpha legend, the point of departure of his novels, and they have even been called his most successful creations, yet their world has never been explored."[1] This is still largely true, although Indian mounds, still scattered around northeastern Mississippi, appear in *If I forget thee, Jerusalem* and are important features in "Gold Is Not Always" and *Go Down, Moses*; they are discussed in Calvin S. Brown's book on *Archaeology of Mississippi*, a book that Faulkner owned. Occasionally Faulkner's knowledge and use of native Americans has been questioned, as in the description of Issetibbeha's death in "Red Leaves": "the grave was dug, and for twelve hours now the People had been coming in wagons and carriages and on horseback and afoot, to eat the baked dog and the succotash and the yams cooked in ashes and to attend the funeral,"[2] yet every detail is accurate historically and ethnologically. Indeed, Faulkner included in a letter to Malcolm Cowley in 1945 a rough map which showed the Chickasaw-Choctaw boundary, the Choctaw agency, Colbert's Ferry the Indians took over the Tennessee River, and the Indian trail used by Chickasaws long before 1801 when it become the main route into Mississippi for white settlers. The forgotten red race in Faulkner—the truly other others—remains a potentially highly charged if largely untapped resource in his work in part because we have taken less time to interpret them.

This was surely not the case with Faulkner himself. He resurrected four Indian stories to compose "The Wilderness," an entire section of his *Collected Stories* published in 1950. The earliest of the four chronologically, "Lo!," is at first reading the funniest. It was first published in *Story* magazine in November 1934 and is perhaps the first American fiction about a political sit-in. The Chickasaws—man, woman, and child—have trekked in unrelenting crowds some 1,500 miles to Washington, some even to President Jackson's White House itself, to determine the guilt or innocence of Frank Weddel's nephew. He has been charged with the murder of an unnamed white settler who bought a small piece of land, which just happened to be at the only ford in their river and built a tollgate on it. When Frank Weddel's nephew gambled to win back the land for the Indians, he lost. According to the white federal agent's report, the white settler then " 'died' " of " 'the white man's disease [that] seemed to be a split skull.' "[3]

Now some of them squat in the President's bedroom corridor, wearing "the beaver hats, the formal coats, the solid legs clad from thigh to ankle in woolen drawers," their underwear substituting for pantaloons rolled up and kept tightly at their sides (385). They mock the white man by wearing only a portion of his clothing. On the surface, their action supports the simplicity and naiveté thought to characterize the Indians; at the same time, however, it displays contempt for the white man's clothing. (Historically, white men's trousers were found to be too binding to men used to loin cloths.) Mockery fuses with parody and satire, but not for long. A few pages later the omniscient narrator comments that the uncle of the accused, "the soft, paunchy man facing them with his soft, bland, inscrutable face" has behind his face and manner "something else: something willful, shrewd, unpredictable and despotic" (394–95). What the narrator finally observes is the canny use of intimidation that this action and others embody. But in the context of the story, this use of intimidation, like the use of clothes, parodies and extends the white man's behavior and turns it back against him.

Under the high humor of "Lo!," then, there is a serious struggle for racial dominance. But "Lo!" is not simply Faulkner's tall tale. As the historian of the Chickasaws, Arrell M. Gibson, has shown, many such "ugly incidents" were occurring and he cites one that lies behind a story like "Lo!": "Two white men opened a store in the Chickasaw Nation in defiance of treaty proscriptions and federal law. Chief Tishomingo, principal full-blood leader in the tribe next to Ishtehotopa, the Chickasaw king, seized and sold the traders' goods. The traders brought charges under Mississippi law. Chief Tishomingo was thrown in jail, and a Mississippi court rendered a judgement against him for nearly $500."[4] Embedded in "Lo!," then, are fear and force, struggle, battle, and survival.

That a humorous Indian story is meant to encode something far more serious and dangerous is confirmed in the next one chronologically, "A Courtship." Ostensibly, the competition of Ikkemotubbe, an Indian, and David Hogganbeck, a white settler, for the sister of Herman Basket, we are nevertheless told even before the contest begins, in a flash forward, what will happen years later: "Moketubbe was the Man when Ikkemotubbe returned, named Doom now, with the white friend called the Chevalier Soeur-Blonde de Vitry and the eight new slaves which we did not need either, and his gold-laced hat and cloak and the little gold box of strong salt and the wicker wine hamper containing the four other puppies which were still alive, and within two days Moketubbe's little son was dead and within three Ikkemotubbe whose name was Doom now was himself the Man."[5] The apparently happy contest of young men who both lose has customarily been seen as a courtship of the two men for each other, but the real story is that their humiliation will lead, in the case of Ikkemotubbe, to the birth of Doom the despot. The fine white man's clothes and the white man's poison with which he returns to seize control of the tribe where he was embarrassed make this contest too a struggle that in time will use intimidation to achieve dominance. The white man supplied the doom of the Indian by inspiring Doom himself to employ the white man's values and ways. Faulkner's stories about Indians, then, use Indians to comment on something else.

2

What is really going on in the relatively untapped Indian stories of Faulkner has been discussed in one of the most significant books to be written in the last decade about American culture and American fiction, explicitly including Faulkner's. In *Playing in the Dark*, Toni Morrison proposes that "Race has become metaphorical—a way of referring to and disguising forces, events, classes, and expression of social decay and economic division far more threatening to the body politic than biological 'race' ever was."[6] She is speaking here exclusively of African Americans, but in Faulkner's deployment of Indians, such metaphors can fracture the narratives in which they appear, interrupt them, and jolt us through forceful unexpectation, as in this passage in the hitherto quiet, humorous story of "A Bear Hunt," published first in the *Saturday Evening Post* in 1934 but reprinted in *Collected Stories* in 1950 and again in *Big Woods* in 1955: "Five miles farther down the river from Major de Spain's camp, and in an even wilder part of the river's jungle of cane and gum and pin oak, there is an Indian mound. Aboriginal, it rises profoundly and darkly enigmatic, the only elevation of any kind in the wild, flat jungle of river bottom. Even to some of us—children though we were, yet we were descended of literate, town-bred people—it possessed inferences of secret and violent blood, of savage and sudden destruction."[7] This passage occurs early in the story, just after we hear of a prank—less violent, less savage but in its way no less aggressive—when the Provine gang interrupted a Negro church picnic and "with drawn pistols and freshly lit cigars . . . held the burning cigar ends to the popular celluloid collars of the day, leaving each victim's neck ringed with an abrupt and faint and painless ring of carbon" (147). The upshot in what otherwise seems a tall tale about Ratliff besting Luke Provine through a hoax played with Indian help, is underlined by the narrator: "When we grew older we realized that they were no wilder or more illiterate than the white people" (148) and this parallel is again reinforced at the end when we learn that Ash, Ratliff's black accomplice in his prank with the Indians, was himself one of the humiliated persons at the church picnic. "Literature redistributes and mutates in figurative language," Morrison tells us (66); here a black man mediated crime and punishment with Indian aid. It is a subtle matter—necessary in a story which works through high humor—but it is clearly a basis of the work; "A writer's response to American Africanism," says Morrison, "often provides a subtext that either sabotages the surface text's expressed intentions or escapes them through a language that mystifies what it cannot bring itself to articulate but still attempts to register" (66). Elsewhere she calls "black surrogacy"—to which we may now add Indian surrogacy—"an informing, stabilizing, and disturbing element" (13).

The arrangement of such narrative forces in "Red Leaves" is more open and so has been frequently observed. Ostensibly, this is the story of the Indians' pursuit and capture of Issetibbeha's personal black slave who by tribal ritual should be buried with his master, who has just died, along with the Indian chief's horse, dog, and other personal possessions. We learn this only after we learn about the racial division at the Indian camp and the way the Indians treat black slaves on what they call their plantation, an imitation of white slaveholders. They are put to all the hard labor, live in tighter quarters, and are often demeaned as "the men who like to sweat." But this is one tragic register seen through another: the

Indians "cleared the land with the Negroes and planted it in grain. Up to that time the slaves had lived in a huge pen with a lean-to roof over one corner, like a pen for pigs. But now they began to build quarters, cabins, putting the young Negroes in the cabins in pairs to mate; five years later Issetibbeha sold forty head to a Memphis trader, and he took the money and went abroad upon it."[8] As the white men provide a model of slavery—and of the slave market—for the red man, so Issetibbeha's journey to Paris for clothes provides the model for Doom who, like his uncle, will extend personal rule into personal despotism. "Red Leaves" is not just about the tragic fate of an unnamed black slave; it is also about white despotism imitated by the Indian.

The Indians did own slaves; a federal census of the Chickasaw nation in 1827 listed approximately 4,000 Indians and 1,000 black slaves; moreover, Dabney reports, the Indians insisted on racial purity (9) and " 'in 1838 the Choctaw National Council passes a law prohibiting the cohabitation of any member of the nation with a Negro slave,' "[9] making miscegenation illegal. "One likely reason for the paucity of critical material on this large and compelling subject," Morrison contends, "is that, in matters of race, silence and evasion have historically ruled literary discourse. Evasion has fostered another, substitute language in which the issues are encoded, foreclosing open debate"(9). Faulkner tips his hand, though, by substituting the red man's treatment for the white man's. Red men stand in for white men, but they can also stand in for black men, too, as in the case of Sam Fathers.

When we first meet Sam he is a blacksmith recounting his ancestry (and his odd name) to young Quentin Compson in "A Justice." According to Quentin, Sam "talked like a nigger—that is, he said his words like niggers do, but he didn't say the same words—and his hair was nigger hair."[10] So the case stood in 1931 in *These 13*. Sam's grandfather is Ikkemotubbe and his grandmother and mother presumably all-black slaves, making Sam one-quarter Indian and three-quarters African American. Sam's father, not Sam, had two fathers—red and black. By the time of "The Old People" and "The Bear" in *Go Down, Moses* (1942), however, Sam is himself named Two Fathers, the son of the Indian Doom and his quadroon mistress so that he has a more acceptable heritage for young Isaac McCaslin: he is now half-Indian, three-eighths white, and only one-eighth black. This gives quite another meaning to John T. Matthews's observations that " 'The Old People' feigns innocence. . . . 'The Old People' is founded on a duplicity."[11] So in "The Old People" Sam is described by young Isaac as

a man not tall, squat rather, almost sedentary, flabby-looking though he actually was not, with hair like a horses mane [a distinctive feature of the Choctaws] which even at seventy showed no trace of white and a face which showed no age until he smiled, whose only visible trace of negro blood was a slight dullness of the hair and the fingernails, and something else which you did notice about the eyes, which you noticed because it was not always there, only in repose and not always then—something not in their shape nor pigments but in their expression, and the boy's cousin McCaslin told him what that was: not the heritage of Ham, not the mark of servitude but of bondage.[12]

Doubtless to their relief, Cass tells Ike, " 'He [Sam] probably never held it against old Doom for selling him and his mother into slavery, because he probably believed the damage was already done before then and it was the same warriors' and chiefs' blood in him and Doom that was betrayed through the black blood which his mother gave him' "(162).

Sam's birthright is a double bondage. An inherited slave with Indian blood, he is given special privileges on the plantation. But he has enough black blood not to be truly Indian, as Boon is: Sam kills bears with a rifle, Boon with a knife. Sam is also contrasted to Jobaker, a full-blooded Chickasaw who lives alone in the woods while Sam lives on the farm, supported by the Edmondses. As an Indian, Jobaker is naturally alone, free and self-reliant. By contrast Sam, with his black blood, was once owned by slave owners and has to be freed. Ike later learns Sam knew this: *for seventy years now he had had to be a negro.* Sam thus teaches young Isaac how to slice the throat of a deer in much the same way Joe Christmas is thought to have sliced the throat of Joanna Burden and Rider killed the night foreman at the lumber mill. If we look to Africanist encodings that Morrison would alert us to, we will see that the religiosity about nature, and especially about the bear as a totem, is not only a Chickasaw belief, but an Africanist one,[13] a part of the West African myth already rooted in the New World. And the burial ground for Sam—where Faulkner has been thought to substitute mistakenly a Choctaw rite for a Chickasaw one—is also an African burial custom. The subtle mysteries in "The Bear" draw heavily on Africanist belief and associate Sam with his once predominant black ancestry, so that his sacrificial death resonates with that of Rider and Butch Beauchamp. "A writer's response to American Africanism often provides a subtext that either sabotages the surface text's expressed intentions or escapes them through a language that mystifies what it cannot bring itself to articulate but still attempts to register" (Morrison, 66).

3

"Knowledge," writes Morrison, "however mundane and utilitarian, plays about in linguistic images and forms cultural practice" (49). We have already seen how Sam's method of killing deer is described by Faulkner in almost precisely the terms he associates with African American cultural practice in *Go Down, Moses, Light in August*, and refers to in "That Evening Sun." Morrison's implied principle here is substitution—that is, the work metaphor does. But she also develops substitution by way of reversal. This would read Faulkner's works racially from the margin, so that, in discussing "A Courtship," for instance, we would see that while all the men are named, their object alone is not—she remains nameless, objectified as "Herman Basket's sister." This happens with other Indians, implying statements of race and gender in Southern cultural practice in Faulkner's fiction. In 1830 President Andrew Jackson bribed a minority of Choctaw Indians into signing the Treaty of Dancing Rabbit Creek, thus seizing all the remaining Choctaw land in Mississippi for white settlers—forcing out the founders and residents for centuries—while the white William Ward, "arbitrary, tyrannical, and insulting,"[14] allowed only sixty-nine families to remain on newly held white territory. Faulkner gives us this moment bifocally in *Requiem for a Nun*. We are given two portraits of the last royal Indian's departure from Yoknapatawpha in "The Jail." Mohataha is "the fat shapeless old matriarch in the regal sweat-stained purple silk and the plumed hat, barefoot too of course but, being a queen, with another slave to carry her slippers, putting her cross to the paper and then driving on";[15] on the same page, we see "the wagon, the mules, the rigid shapeless old Indian woman and the nine heads which surrounded her—like a float or a piece of stage property dragged rapidly into the wings across the very backdrop and amid the very bustle of the property-men setting up for the next scene and act before the curtain had even had time to fall" (190–91). The marginalized Indian queen is moved to stage center and given a name only to be pushed back off to the side and marginalized once again.[16] This passing presence (or the deliberate but comprehensible absence) of such marginal persons and attitudes is also a part of Morrison's sense of substitution and reversal, "effort[s] to talk . . . with a vocabulary designed to disguise the subject" (50).

With all of this in mind, I want to look briefly at one last example in another Indian story, although never labeled as such by Faulkner, in which the other other—the Indian—is made to comment on both white men and black. The title of the story is "Mountain Victory," like "A Courtship" and "A Justice" a title that is ironic. The protagonist is Saucier Weddel, a Confederate major of Choctaw and French ancestry. He identifies himself with justifiable pride to his accidental hosts, Tennessee mountaineer abolitionists with whom he has sought shelter for himself and his black servant Jubal on their trip home at the end of the War Between the States. " 'My name is Saucier Weddel, I am a Mississippian. I live at a place named Contalmaison. My father built it and named it.

He was a Choctaw chief named Francis Weddel, of whom you have probably not heard. He was the son of a Choctaw woman and a French émigré
of New Orleans, a general of Napoleon's and a knight of the Legion of
Honor. His name was Francois Vidal.' "[17] Weddel is kind to Jubal, and
risks his life remaining with him overnight in the mountaineer's barn
because Jubal is too drunk to leave before dawn. When the two attempt
to leave with one of the mountaineer's sons at dawn, they are all three
ambushed and killed by the father and the other son. The reason for the
killing is not that Weddel was travelling with an African American but
that it appeared the abolitionist's daughter was attracted to Weddel despite his mixed ancestry and might leave with him. The reason the abolitionists kill the Confederate, then, is fear of miscegenation: a Confederate
attitude, not the Unionist one to which they lay claim. The Indian is
made analogous to the African American in the mountaineer's mind.
Through the other other, Faulkner encodes the depravity of the white
man and here of the Unionist sympathizer.

"Through significant and underscored omissions, startling contradictions, heavily nuanced conflicts," Morrison argues, "through the way
writers peopled their work with the signs and bodies of this presence—
one can see that a real or fabricated Africanist presence was crucial to
their sense of Americanness. And it shows" (6). In Faulkner, I would
suggest, meaning resides not just in the white protagonist or the other,
the African American, but also in the relatively untapped other other—
the Indian. The Indian fiction in *Collected Stories* is called "The Wilderness" because it is the wilderness they occupied for centuries before the
white man made himself the native American. The wilderness is also
the unknown and unsettled land where they are consigned by President
Jackson and his administration. The wilderness in *Collected Stories* and
elsewhere is a metonymy which playing in the dark illuminates. Here too
actual and apocryphal meaningly, metaphorically, meet.

NOTES

1. Lewis M. Dabney, *The Indians of Yoknapatawpha: A Study in Literature and History*
(Baton Rouge: Louisiana State University Press, 1974), 3.
2. "Red Leaves," in *Collected Stories of William Faulkner* (New York: Vintage Books,
1977), 322. Cf. Arrell M. Gibson's account of *The Chickasaws* (Norman: University of Oklahoma Press, 1971): "They washed the corpse, anointed the head with oil, painted the face
red, and dressed him in his best clothes. His gun, ammunition, pipe, tobacco, and a supply
of corn were buried with him" (11). This is for any man of the tribe. Such burial rites are
also implied for Sam Fathers in *Go Down, Moses.*
3. "Lo!" in *Collected Stories*, 392–93.
4. Gibson, 174–75.
5. "A Courtship" in *Collected Stories*, 363. "Chickasaw fishermen collected and pulver-

ized wild plants, such as devil's shoestring, and nuts, such as buckeyes and walnuts, to create natural poisons" by which they trapped fish. Duane K. Hale and Arrell M. Gibson, *The Chickasaw* (New York: Chelsea House, 1991), 15–16.

6. Toni Morrison, *Playing in the Dark: Whiteness and the Literary Imagination* (New York: Vintage Books, 1993), 63.

7. "A Bear Hunt" in William Faulkner, *Big Woods* (New York: Random House, 1955), 147–48.

8. "Red Leaves," in *Collected Stories*, 320.

9. Dabney, 86, quoting from Wyatt F. Jeltz, "The Relations of Negroes and Choctaw and Chickasaw Indians," *Journal of Negro History* 33 (January 1948): 31.

10. "A Justice," in *Collected Stories*, 344.

11. John T. Matthews, *The Play of Faulkner's Language* (Ithaca: Cornell University Press, 1982), 244.

12. *Go Down, Moses* (New York: Vintage International, 1990), 160–61.

13. Dabney, 144.

14. Charles Hudson, *The Southeastern Indians* (Knoxville: University of Tennessee Press, 1976, 1992), 455.

15. William Faulkner, *Requiem for a Nun* (New York: Vintage, 1975), 190. Mohataha may be a fictional representation of that last king of the Chickasaw nation, Ishtehotopah, who was the last to leave for Oklahoma; his land is marked two miles south of New Albany. Lochnivar, in Pontotoc, also lays claim to being the last Indian-occupied land in Northern Mississippi.

16. Her portrait gains resonance if held against actual departures. Jesse Burt and Robert B. Ferguson tell us of "Chickasaw Billy and another youth, Kapia, both fine athletes who lived near Ripley in Tippah County, [and] had many friendships among white youths. They asked T. J. Young, a friend with whom they ran footraces and wrestled, to go with them when they left, and even offered him money if he would, but Young did not go." *Indians of the Southeast: Then and Now* (Nashville and New York: Abingdon Press, 1973), 173. In a far more frequently cited instance from the margins—one Faulkner may well have heard—the Choctaw chief David Folsom wrote about his people's feelings to the Presbyterian ministers of the Choctaw nation. " 'We are exceedingly tired,' he wrote. 'We have just heard of the ratification of the Choctaw Treaty. Our doom is sealed. There is no other course for us but to turn our faces to our new homes toward the setting sun.' " Czarina C. Conlan, "David Folsom," *Chronicles of Oklahoma* 4:4 (December 1926): 353, quoted by Arthur H. DeRosier Jr., *The Removal of the Choctaw Indians* (Knoxville: University of Tennessee Press, 1970), 128.

17. William Faulkner, "Mountain Victory," in *Collected Stories*, 759.

I am grateful to Nat Harrold and Ilse Dusoir Lind for their help with this essay.

Faulkner in the Singular

ANDRÉ BLEIKASTEN

Most of the twentieth-century writers whom we have come to value as major figures were somehow ahead of their time. And even now, after their work has at last found an attentive audience and won public recognition and respect, they manage to be still a step ahead of any attempt to trip them up or pin them down, having accumulated enough potential to keep critics busy for generations, if not for centuries. "We are still learning to be Joyce's contemporaries," wrote Richard Ellman at the beginning of his biography. In much the same way, we are still learning to be Faulkner's, still trying to acquire the skills and competencies we need to possess not to misread him. I take it, then, that a conference on "Faulkner at 100" is asking for a progress report on our attempts to become his contemporaries.

The strenuousness of the endeavor is beyond dispute. The secondary literature about Faulkner has grown to enormous proportions. Over the past decades his work has inspired hundreds of books and thousands of articles. On both sides of the Atlantic and even in the Far East, critics have been at pains to dissect his texts and unravel their secrets. The question is what valid insights have been gained in so many years of intensive critical speculation that enable us to understand and appreciate Faulkner's fiction better, more fully and more thoroughly, than it could have been understood and appreciated by those who were contemporary with it in mere chronology, those who, in the late twenties and early thirties, witnessed the emergence of a startlingly new, as yet unidentified and unmapped continent of fiction.

Today, more than thirty years after Faulkner's death, we know of course much more about his life and career, much more about the genesis and development of his work, and we have also learned much more about its various contexts and intertexts. But all this accumulated knowledge is only the precondition of a better-informed understanding of his fiction. The scholar's duty is to gather, order, and make available all the pertinent data; the critic's much more hazardous business—to be confused neither with the scholar's nor with the poetician's—is to determine how Faulkner's texts function and what meanings they produce.

Faulkner, considered a "difficult" author, has solicited the hermeneu-
tic talents of his critics since the fifties. Looking back, one can hardly fail
to realize how faithfully interpretations of his work over the past four
decades have followed critical fashion, how closely their development
reflects the successive trends in American criticism at large. Indeed, most
of them reveal probably as much, if not more, about the stated or un-
stated assumptions and analytical procedures of the critics than about
their presumed object.

As up to the early seventies, American literary studies were by and
large dominated by the formalistic tenets and conservative values of the
New Criticism, a good deal of early Faulkner criticism illustrates what
was then the hegemonic critical discourse. Yet it is worth noting that
none of the first three important book-length studies of Faulkner published in America—neither Olga Vickery's nor Michael Millgate's, and
not even Cleanth Brooks's[1]—can be adequately defined as formalist. And
let me point out that in France critical assessment of Faulkner started as
early as the thirties with the pioneering essays of Malraux and Sartre,
neither of whom had anything to do with New Criticism. The beginnings
of Faulkner criticism, then, should not be oversimplified for the sake of
polemical argument, nor should they be ignored because they rest on
assumptions many of us now find obsolete.

Since then, the critical landscape has been shattered out of recognition. In the late seventies and throughout the eighties, theory, much of it
imported from France, came to dominate criticism in America as it had
never before, and it has deeply altered our thinking about literary texts.
Ideas about language, literature, culture, and history have changed dras-
tically, and have changed at least in part because we have learned how
much they implicate one another. We have been alerted to the wide gap
between world and word, and have come to realize at the same time
how much the codes of language and the tropes of discourse control our
(mis)understanding of ourselves and of the world, and how much historicity predetermines our very conception of literature. There is now a
climate of suspicion, a general questioning of interpretative and evalua-
tive standards, and this questioning has taken many forms, all familiarly
(and at times misleadingly) subsumed under the loose label of "post-
structuralism."

Uncertainty about the functions and purposes of criticism has rendered its practice both more problematic, more open, more pluralistic,
and, it would seem, much more adventurous. As paradigms have shifted,
new avenues of investigation have been opened up and new procedures
put to work. Yet it took time for Faulkner studies to be seriously affected
by the new theoretical mood. Apart from John T. Irwin's provocative

psychoanalytic study,[2] Donald M. Kartiganer's inquiry into Faulkner's modernism,[3] and perhaps my own book on *The Sound and the Fury*,[4] most of what was published on Faulkner in America during the seventies was still meager on theory and offered at best a slight readjustment and refinement of traditional approaches.

The first systematic venture into poststructuralism came only in the early eighties with *The Play of Faulkner's Language*,[5] John T. Matthews's shrewd Derridean reading of four Faulkner novels. In its wake, American Faulkner criticism became increasingly theory oriented, if not in its practice, at least in its terminology. From sloppy underconceptualization it moved, like the rest of American criticism, to compulsive overconceptualization. Most articles and books on Faulkner are now bristling with philosophical, psychoanalytical, and linguistic abstractions; most of them draw ostentatiously upon the French theorists of the sixties and seventies, and indulge almost extravagantly what Pound called "the American habit of quotation." Yet the relative newness of the conceptual tools used in critical practice in no way guarantees the newness of the work done, and, in fact, studies with an impressive array of theoretical references will often turn out on closer inspection to be the most conventional of readings.

Whether there has ever been a strictly "deconstructive" phase in Faulkner criticism is in my opinion very questionable. For all the respect it has deservedly earned, Matthews's first book has had no deep and lasting impact on the younger Faulkner critics, and even Matthews himself has moved on to a much more culture-angled and *marxisant* approach. Today, the paradoxical workings of Faulkner's language and his tortuous textual strategies are clearly no longer major concerns, and of the books published in the early eighties, the one most clearly anticipating the present turn of Faulkner criticism is not Matthews's, but a study published a year later by Eric J. Sundquist, *Faulkner: The House Divided*.[6] Sundquist was the first critic to reassess Faulkner's achievement and to reorder the Faulkner canon according to extraliterary criteria: Faulkner's importance, he argued, is not to be sought in his contribution to the art of the novel but in the seriousness with which he addresses social and historical themes; he only became a major American writer when he came to fully confront within his fictions the difficulty of being white, male, and from Mississippi.

Nearly all recent Faulkner criticism starts from similar premises, and resembles Sundquist's study in its insistence on cultural issues such as race, class, and gender. These issues loom large indeed in novels like *Light in August, Absalom, Absalom!*, or *Go Down, Moses,* and there is none from which they are entirely missing. Relating these novels as accurately and as thoroughly as possible to their sociohistorical or ideological contexts is assuredly a worthwhile and even necessary enterprise, and there is nothing wrong either with reading them in the light of the available theories. This enterprise has been under way for some time now, and has been constantly expanding. The mere list of the titles of the articles and books on Faulkner published over the past few years leaves no doubt as to the primacy of cultural concerns in present Faulkner criticism.

Part of it sheds indeed new light on what is at stake in Faulkner's novels, and contributes to putting the whole Faulkner canon into sometimes startlingly new perspectives. But not all of it is illuminating. No matter how legitimate, concentration on questions of race, class, and gender easily becomes overemphasis, especially if it comes to rule out careful consideration of the specific medium in which and of the specific writer by whom these questions are raised.

One unfortunate consequence of the current dominance of cultural criticism is that Faulkner finds himself once again imprisoned in his Southernness (no other great modern novelist has been as closely and as permanently tied to his region) and that his fictions are increasingly instrumentalized into documents for sociologists and historians of culture to exploit for their own ends. Another perverse by-effect is regression to a naively realistic conception of literature that not so long ago seemed irrevocably outdated. Surprisingly enough, while deconstructionism—at least in its selective American versions—assumed that discourse could only refer to other discourses and so had come to deny language any commerce with reality at all, the culturalists hardly ever question the validity of its referential claims. From radical questionings of language and sophisticated explorations of textuality we have thus reverted to more or less traditional analyses of content, or, to put it more crisply, from poetics to mimetics. Faulkner's fiction is now read again in representational terms; attention focuses once more on characters, and all that seems to matter in a number of recent studies is how much they conform to or deviate from racist or sexist stereotypes. Furthermore, some of the new Faulkner critics treat and evaluate Faulkner's characters as if they were real persons, somehow like the spectator who jumped on the stage during a performance of *Hamlet* to warn the Player King of the approach of the poisoner. Temple Drake in *Sanctuary* is an instructive case in point: after decades of extremely harsh judgment, she is now being reexamined with warm compassion, and feminist critics have been particularly eager to exonerate her from any responsibility for what happens to her and to others at Old Frenchman's place, and, by the same token, to exempt Faulkner from the charge of misogyny. Yet these well-meaning

attempts to transform Temple into an innocent victim of patriarchal violence seem to me badly misconceived because of their failure to acknowledge her fictional status. Temple is a creature out of words with no
existence outside the text; she is nothing more than one of its *effects*.
Whatever the "facts" about her bourgeois family background and her
deplorable education that may be inferred from the novel's diegesis,
whatever may be said in her defense, our responses to her as a character
while we read *Sanctuary* are manipulated throughout by the novelist.
The effect of a portrait depends upon the craft and art of the portraitist,
not upon the features of the model. Faulkner's portrayal of Temple is
pretty harsh, and one must be deaf to his shrill and savage rhetoric to
turn the raving nymphomaniac of the final Grotto scene into the martyr-
saint of male-oppressed womanhood.[7]

Faulkner's novels should first of all be read as novels. True, it is always
possible to read them otherwise, and provided the investigations are conducted with a minimum of methodological rigor, there is nothing intrinsically objectionable about scrutinizing them as cultural artifacts or even
about using them as proof texts for preconceived general views. Whenever we do so, however, whenever we reduce them to mere illustrations
of our ideas about culture and society, we must be aware that our extraliterary interests come to prevail over our involvement with Faulkner and
that we run the risk of losing sight of his achievement as a writer.

Even though theory is indispensable to any kind of criticism, it should
not be allowed to take the upper hand in our examination of specific
texts, and I am tempted to say that to read Faulkner only in the thin, cold
light of theory is not to read him at all. At any rate, with "strong" texts
like his, critical practice, if it is any good, will not content itself with the
mechanical application of theoretical principles but will operate *between*
text and theory, moving back and forth like a shuttle, so as to further
their reciprocal testing and questioning. We can, if we so choose, read
As I Lay Dying through Lacan's lenses, approach *Absalom, Absalom!*
from neo-Marxist premises, process *The Wild Palms* through feminist fil-
ters, but, to be more than a futile academic exercise, reading Faulkner
through Lacan must become something else than reading Lacan into
Faulkner, and it might well, if pursued by an alert and mobile intelligence, reverse itself at some point into reading Lacan with Faulkner.

We should always keep in mind, too, that even the most elaborate
critical and cultural theories are just sets of speculative hypotheses,
which, unlike scientific theories, can be neither verified nor refuted in
any rigorous sense, and therefore should perhaps be regarded as potent
speech acts, complex ways of doing things with words rather than bodies
of reliable knowledge. And yet in current discourses about gender, race,

class, "subject formation" and "social construction," no allowance is ever made for the possibility of dissent. With the newer Faulkner critics, admissions of uncertainty about one's general assumptions or of doubt about one's procedures are seldom to be found. Their textual analyses may be ingenious and even subtle, but their global assertions about cultural issues are all peremptory, their judgments all final, their conclusions all predictible. What they call theory is in fact most of the time an unexamined collection of articles of faith. In other words, theory, supposedly the relentless unmasker of all ideologies, threatens to become in turn one of its deceptive masks. And the suspicion of ideological conformity is the stronger as these critics are disquietingly consensual. Fundamentally, they tend to feel alike, to think alike, and to talk alike; that is, they seldom swerve away from what is approved of within the political culture to which they belong. The respect for "otherness" they claim for minority groups does not extend to other ways of thinking, and while rejecting the old New Critical orthodoxies, they subscribe wholeheartedly to another one.

For the sake of clarity and honesty, literary critics always ought to spell out their theoretical premises. Their first duty, though, is not to theory but to literature. I am aware that today such a statement is by no means self-evident to everybody. For all depends eventually on how literature is defined. "What is literature?" Sartre asked many years ago. Though the word, in its present usage, is fairly recent, the question has been with us since Plato and Aristotle, and the answer of contemporary theorists such as Terry Eagleton is that there is no such thing as literature, that it is at best a "discursive practice" among others, which there is no serious reason to give preferential treatment. Literary criticism, the Eagletons will claim, is only justified inasmuch as it "demystifies" literature and leads on to a critique of society which will promote positive change.

If Eagleton were right, politically engaged cultural criticism would indeed be the only acceptable form of criticism. I think he is demonstrably wrong. That literature is a cultural institution, brought into being by social, legal, and political processes, can hardly be denied, and as such it is inevitably enmeshed in ideology and power relations. I would argue, however, that it is not one institution among others, but, paradoxically, as Derrida has noted, "an institution which tends to overflow the institution."[8] Institutions are normally self-validating and self-perpetuating; literature, at least since Cervantes, has never ceased to put itself into question, the novel has always asserted itself against the novel. At its freshest, freest, and most trenchant, literature cuts across institutionality and any form of sociality, and bypasses the economy of ordinary communication. Insofar as a literary text is determined by its social context and its historical moment, it belongs to instituted/constituted discourse; inso-far as it exceeds them, it becomes, in Merleau-Ponty's phrase, a "consti-tutive language."

Since to be taken seriously these days, you have to buttress all your arguments with the authority of respected names, let me point out that, from Sartre through Merleau-Ponty, Bataille, Blanchot, Derrida, Fou-cault, and Deleuze to Lyotard, none of the innovative French thinkers of this century has held about literature the crude views now circulated by the neo-paleo-Marxists and the half-baked Foucauldians. Not that they grant it a privileged status and revere it as a noble essence in the way the old-school humanists do, but they also refrain from leveling it with ideological discourse in the service of power interests. Literature, to them, or at least the literature (or "antiliterature") they care for and write about, has been since Hölderlin, Flaubert, Mallarmé, and Rimbaud an unpredictable series of dislocations (preceding, accompanying, or follow-ing major ruptures in other fields), and not even Foucault, not even Derrida has departed unequivocally from the French tradition of *mod-ernité*—a notion not quite synonymous with Anglo-American "modern-ism"—for which writing, in the strong sense of *écriture,* has always been thought of as the risky invention of a particular, unheard-of idiom within common parlance, bringing language, *within* language, close to silence. As Blanchot put it, "A literary work, for those who know how to penetrate it, is a rich sojourn of silence, a firm defense and a high wall against this talking immensity which in addressing us, diverts us from overselves."[9] And for Foucault too, "literature . . . implie[s] in every sentence and in every word, the power to modify in sovereign fashion the values and significations of the linguistic code to which in spite of everything it be-long[s]; it suspend[s] the reign of that code in one actual gesture of writ-ing."[10] Silence, suspension. Literature is that which silences the deafening noise of common speech and unsettles common codings and categories. Literature is the site where the relation to reference, mean-ing, and truth is vertiginously suspended. As such, in its refusal to affirm or deny, in its mute dispersal or emptying-out of meaning, it is an un-canny force of provocation and destabilization, a force that resists assimi-lation to what we know and how we think, and hence capable of repelling ideology as well as theory.

Admittedly, these are also unprovable assumptions, but as they happen to be mine, I will try to defend them as best I can. One may of course reject them as idealistic bourgeois delusions, and yet there is at least as much evidence to support them as the assumptions now in currency, and in such matters our reading experience is not to be summarily dismissed. Whoever has read Kafka, Stein, Woolf, Céline, Beckett, or, to take at random more recent examples, Claude Simon, William Gaddis, or Thomas Bernhard, must have felt this strange, turbulent silence, a silence that may arise as well out of the spare, stubborn litanies of *The Unnamable* as of the baroque, torrential prose of *The Flanders Road*. And we can also hear it distinctly in *The Sound and the Fury*, in *As I Lay Dying*, in *Absalom, Absalom!*, and in other Faulkner novels.

These are all books that ran counter to the norms of literature that prevailed at the time they were published, and yet, if they have come to mean more to us than others, it is because they were not just written for the sake of formal experiment, but were born of necessity, out of a sense of urgency, an irrepressible inner compulsion, regardless of the risks incurred. "How can we linger," Bataille wondered, "over books we feel the author was not compelled to write?"[11] Only the books a writer was compelled to write are truly compelling books or, as Kafka eloquently put it in one of his letters, "the kind of books that wound and stab us . . . affect us like a disaster, grieve us deeply, like the death of someone we loved more than ourselves, like being banished into forests far from everyone, like a suicide."[12]

Like Kafka's own, Faulkner's novels possess in their own way the cruel power to "wound and stab us," a pathos that arouses our deepest anxieties, reactivates our earliest griefs, rekindles our oldest rages. And theirs is as well the power to shatter clichés, to break through the sedimented lies of group thinking, and thus to wrench their readers from their certitudes. Faulkner's finest and fiercest fictions have acted and continue to act as rebukes and irritants to established ways of thinking and feeling, and as relentless reminders of the legacies and liabilities of history. As Edouard Glissant, the French Caribbean poet-novelist, emphasizes in his superb recent essay,[13] the whole thrust of Faulkner's vast counterepic has been toward exposure of the Southern myths of grounding, and of their absolute failure to legitimize the foundation of the white, male-dominated South. Yet I would like to add that the scope of Faulkner's demythologizing goes well beyond the denunciation of the patriarchal culture of the South he knew and remembered: in enabling their readers to realize the horrendous costs of the iniquitous order that ruled the slaveholding antebellum South, novels like *Absalom, Absalom!* and *Go Down, Moses* awaken the suspicion that *all* established power is rooted in violence and injustice, that *all* social origins are fatally flawed. From the beginnings of American Faulkner criticism to its latest developments, much energy has been expended to make Faulkner less scandalous, more humane, more hopeful, that is, socially more acceptable. In America, whatever the political affiliation, the intolerance of optimism (or of nostalgia: retrospective optimism) seems inescapable. But in Faulkner there are neither paradises to be lost nor paradises to be regained. As long as he remained true to his deeper tragic insights, he was never a bearer of good news. Nor was he ever, as Cleanth Brooks would have us believe, the bardic voice of his community: he was a traitor to his tribe, to all tribes, as, since the death of the epic, from the anonymous author of *The Life of Lazarillo de Tormes* to Salmon Rushdie, true novelists have always been.

Which is not to say, however, that Faulkner's entire work is miraculously beyond ideology, nor even that his best novels are immune to it. Their capacity to disturb and fracture is an intermittent one, their syntax is not a linear syntax of statement and counterstatement, and it would be wholly mistaken to read them as a systematic frontal critique of Southern society in the realist tradition. Like all the texts we associate with modernism, Faulkner's are deeply heterogeneous. They swarm with opacities and obliquities, with equivocations and contradictions, and one had better admit at once that, with the possible exception of *As I Lay Dying,* even the most admirable of his novels have their moments of cheapness. In *Go Down, Moses,* for instance, not only Ike McCaslin but Faulkner himself (or at any rate his narrator) succumbs from time to time to the vulgarity of ethnic prejudice, as when he refers to the lensless glasses of Fonsiba's black Yankee husband to mock the latter's pretension to literacy and culture. Yet insofar as the effects of Faulkner's fictions elude and exceed the author's intentions, insofar as we must always take account of their suspensive fictionality, they must be examined with extreme caution. In a work like his there is no neat way of filtering out ideological deposits. Nor can its moments of insight be isolated from its moments of blindness. We can never know for sure when exposure *to* ideology turns into exposure *of* ideology. There is no point, therefore, in labeling his fictions as either misogynous or gynophile, racist or antiracist, politically backward or progressive; it is just as preposterous to try to save Faulkner from himself by assigning to his texts a subversive unconscious as to condemn him for offering no alternative social possiblities.

Further commentaries in the inquisitorial spirit of leftish culturalism will no doubt uncover even greater complicity with the patriarchal ideology of race and gender, discover even more offenses against the dignity of women and blacks. Once you have started to look for clues of ideological compromission with a prosecutor's mind, the damning evidence soon becomes inexhaustible. But haven't we known all along about Faulkner's blind spots and limitations? Haven't we known all along that his portrayals of blacks and women seldom show him at his most acute? How could one reasonably expect him to write about women like Virginia Woolf and about African Americans like Toni Morrison? The inventory of his sins can be pursued to his most trifling peccadilloes, but should we go on laboring the obvious? As Joseph Brodsky, a writer in exile whose first-hand experience of and suffering from ideology in action can hardly be contested, noted in his Nobel lecture: "What's wrong with discourses about the obvious is that they corrupt consciousness with their easiness, with the speed with which they provide one with moral comfort, with the sensation of being right."[14]

Smugness is as detestable in literary criticism as in any other field. Judging Faulkner from the imaginary heights of our "advanced" knowledge and superior morality will not take us very far. For what is truly amazing and admirable about Faulkner's fiction is not its embroilment in ideology but the fact that it manages so often to give it the slip. To point up those moments in his work that show him to be in some ways, on certain occasions, as hopelessly prejudiced as the average citizen may be salubrious. No writer is above meanness and foolishness. But it is equally important to acknowledge the brilliance and fertility of Faulkner's formal inventions, the sharpness and depth of his historical sense, his complex awareness of genealogies and inheritances, his keen sensitivity to the violent innocence of the downtrodden, and the capaciousness of imagination that allowed this particular neurotic white Southern male to create characters as much removed from the range of his own experience and background as Benjy and Vardaman, Darl and Addie, Joe Christmas or Rider. I cannot think of any novelist of our century who showed more courage in taking on the challenges thrown up by his particular heritage, more daring in venturing into the labyrinths of time and guilt and into the taboo territories of otherness, more willingness to take risks and to accept failure. Since Melville, there has probably not been a more adventurous, more heroic figure in American literature.

Faulkner is a most *singular* writer, and more than anything else it is his startling singularity, the unique strangeness of his work, that needs to be probed and defined. In saying that Faulkner is a singular writer, I am not at all inviting a romantic celebration of creative individuality. Singularity here is not to be understood as an unalterable predicate of authorial sovereignty; it is that which came to emerge haphazardly from the slow, intricate process of freeing those voices which were inside Faulkner and yet not him, of creating a "cosmos" which, as Philip Weinstein has rigorously demonstrated, was his and yet not his.[15] His novels are singular, not as rare, self-enclosed *objets d'art*, but as acts and interactions, as contingent and dated events, each of them being the (re)enactment and record of a tense encounter, within language, between a writer's evolving self (his "socially constructed subjectivity," if you insist on the fashionable phrase) and a thick, many-layered, and shifting cultural "text." They are singular not because they are timeless, but because they are inscribed in precise moments of irreversible historical time and because they inscribe these moments in their own discourse. And not singular to the point of precluding a whirling plurality of voices and perspectives; not singular to the point of foreclosing generality, because if they did not also belong, no matter how tenuously, to familiar traditions and conventions, if they could not be repeated and did not open themselves to myriads of rereadings, there would be no way of reading them at all. To stress the singularity of Faulkner's texts, then, is in no manner to minimize the import of their various (potentially infinite) contexts but rather to redress the balance by bringing their problematic relationship into proper focus and redirecting attention to what is most valuable and exciting in his work.

If Faulkner's novels live on, it is because their singularity resists the interpretations of their commentators. If they continue to be read (and not only by a small group of experts), it is because they rise triumphantly from their tombs of received opinion to dazzle and baffle us again and again. Whether Faulkner will ever be a popular author is doubtful, but by the end of this century he is certainly more of a living presence than Fitzgerald, Hemingway, Dos Passos, or any other American novelist of his generation. The continuing interest of academics in his work is one sign of its undiminished vitality; it is not the most significant one. The most impressive, most irrefutable evidence of the abiding fascination of Faulkner's fiction is to be found, not in the steady increase of critical studies, but in the many fervent tributes paid to his achievement not only by Southern epigones but by important writers from all over the world. From Gabriel Garcia Marquez to Marios Vargas Llosa, from Carlos Fuentes to Carlos Onetti, there is scarcely a novelist in Latin America today that has not publicly acknowledged his debt. And the same has been true for many years of European writers such as Louis-René des Forêts and Claude Simon in France, Wolfgang Koeppen and Uwe Johnson in Germany, Juan Benet in Spain, Antonio Lobos Antunes in Portugal, to name only the best known. For all these writers Faulkner has been an incomparable master, yet what they say they owe him is much more than a craftsman's debt. "When I read Faulkner, I thought: I must become a writer," said Garcia Marquez in one of his interviews.[16] And Benet: "The greatest influence in my life is Faulkner's. He is my *raison d'être* as a writer."[17] In reading Faulkner, these writers tumbled upon their true vocation. His work, to them, was less a model to emulate than a magnificent lesson of freedom and daring, a cofraternal encouragement to explore creative possibilities to their extreme limits, and with Faulkner the writer they came to feel a kind of spiritual kinship. Let us listen to Marquez again: "Faulkner is the writer who had the most to do with my soul."[18]

For many contemporary novelists Faulkner has come to mean what Flaubert meant to the novelists of his own generation: at once an ideal and tutelary writer figure, the voice of Literature itself. And some, it would seem, have been touched by his books as if by divine grace, and evoke their first encounter with them like the visitation of some luminous angel. Thus Peter Handke celebrates him like his redeemer: "I am saved—I was saved when I read Faulkner at fifteen—and ever since I have been saved again and again."[19] Asked which writer he feels closest to, Pierre Michon, one of today's most talented French novelists, sounds a similar note: "The will to write and the impossibility to write have made me seek for a long time among the great writers the one who would give me the key, the secret, the posture, the incipit from which the text unfolds without effort. Faulkner has given me this key. It is in his shadow and so to speak guided by his hand that I have started to write . . . I was over thirty. I had not written a single line. By mere chance I read *Absalom, Absalom!*, which had just been republished in paperback: there, no sooner had I read the first pages than I found a father and a brother, something like the *father of the text* . . . [Faulkner] is the father of all I have written. Not that I have undergone his *influence,* as the saying goes: I have never been blamed or praised for writing like Faulkner, for having appropriated his sentences or his mannerisms, his themes or his narrative tricks—for the sons dwarfed by their fathers do their best not to resemble him, not to be his epigones. They feed on the father's strength, but in secret, and, while concealing the strength they feed on, they may acquire a force assumed to be their own. Yes, what Faulkner has given me is the permission to enter language with axe strokes."[20]

These personal testimonies of admiration and gratitude have no doubt little to do with literary criticism, but they suggest the possibility of other, less restrictive and prescriptive, readings. Having experienced the dark, daring power of Faulkner's writing with wonder and almost religious awe, these writers have responded to its singularity as one should always respond to it: singularly, and they are probably the most attentive, most intelligent, and most sensitive readers Faulkner has ever had—his only true contemporaries. Their own work has grown out of his, and away from his; they have reread and rewritten Faulkner in their own novels, as James reread and rewrote *Middlemarch* in *The Portrait of a Lady* and Tolstoy *Madame Bovary* in *Anna Karenina.*

True, what Jean Starobinski called "the critical relation"[21] is something different. Literary criticism demands more distance and discipline, and it must therefore follow other paths, but the least we can ask for is that,

in its own ways, with its own language, it attempts to do justice to what
is unique in the texts it sets out to scrutinize. Without some form of
passionate commitment, without the desire to engage Faulkner's novels
in their savage, subtle, and compelling originality, and without the ex-
travagant, slightly insane ambition of an inventive reinscription of one's
reading experience, the enterprise of studying and teaching Faulkner
would soon become boring. Rather than domesticate his work, one
should seek to account for its haunting strangeness, its *Unheimlichkeit*.
To reduce his novels to mere exemplifications of theoretical *a prioris* is
not to enrich their understanding but merely to blunt the strong challenges they offer to the reader.

In future Faulkner studies, I would wish for a lighter touch, a more
flexible and more graceful manner, with a greater readiness for nuance,
a greater willingness for discrimination and qualification. More *esprit de
finesse*, less *esprit de géométrie*. Less priggishness and arrogance would
be welcome too. In reading what has been written about Faulkner in
recent years, one gets all too often the impression that, literature being a
poor relation to theory, there can be no valid interchange between his
novels and their audience without the merciful intercession of the academy, that reading Faulkner as he should be read requires the expert
services of the professional critic. Go-betweens are no doubt needed to
make his work more accessible and relate it with method to other discourses, but before becoming objects of critical investigation, Faulkner's
novels have been part of our reading experience; before subjecting them
to cool scrutiny, most of us have yielded to their strange power of es-
trangement. We must acknowledge this power and respect the troubling
knowledge it conveys. Faulkner, after all, though he was ignorant of deconstruction and though he had little Freud and less Marx, knew more
about the riddles of selfhood and the ruses of language than any of his
critics. The small man, who was also in some ways a little man, was a
gigantic writer and, compared to him, we—teachers, critics, scholars—
are all just scribbling dwarfs.

Not that his work is a monument to be visited with canonical rever-
ence. Faulkner was a literary giant, but not a giant in every line he wrote.
He was neither a letter writer of the order of Flaubert, D. H. Lawrence,
or Kafka, nor a first-rank essayist like Henry James. His speeches are
expendable. And even in fiction, his domain of excellence, the site of his
triumphs, he was, like Balzac and Dostoevski before him, capable of the
best and the worst. As a Frenchman (was it Paul Claudel?) once said,
"With talent you do as you wish; with genius you do what you can."[22]

Genius is another one of those old-fashioned and even faintly ridiculous romantic notions for which contemporary criticism has no longer

any use, but Faulkner was a writer with exceptional gifts and of immense ambitions, and insofar as he managed to fulfill the latter, "genius" may still serve to designate the magnitude of his accomplishment. Art and literature belong to the few spheres of human endeavor where democratic principles do not apply, and like Proust, Kafka, or Joyce, Faulkner deserves to be treated with more than smug and suspicious condescension or pseudoscientific aloofness. We cannot, it is clear, return to the status quo, and I am not at all pleading for a return to the glorification of the Author or to the pious celebration of "verbal icons." I persist in thinking, however, that theorizing Faulkner *à outrance* is not reading him, and that sociologizing and historicizing his novels are precritical steps that take us at best to the threshold of the work yet to be done. For much remains to be done, and from macrocriticism we should perhaps now move on to microanalyses: at this stage of Faulkner criticism, new insights might be gained from sharp and meticulous attention not only to narrative structures but to the grain of the text, to the many ways in which Faulkner's language or rather languages work on the page, to the interplay of their intensities, to their pulses, their rhythms, their timbres, to all that pertains to the fluid zones of the semiotic. And at the other end of the critical spectrum, one might also wish for more philosophically and anthropologically oriented studies, as Faulkner's fiction is also, in its nonconceptual, nonphilosophical way, a work dense with original thought. Three years ago, Julia Kristeva devoted over four hundred pages to Proustian time.[23] How long shall we have to wait for a fresh, learned, and vigorous study of Faulknerian time? Why has no one so far shown serious interest in Faulkner's stunning rendering of sensations and perceptions? And why is there nothing substantial about Faulkner's obsessive brooding on the enigmas of suffering and death?

Many questions, too, lie buried in his books, questions which now we are not even able to conceive and articulate. Each generation has its Faulkner, each new generation will necessarily read and misread him with its own presuppositions and its own concerns. The current interest in the cultural relevance of his fiction is unlikely to last, and there are fair chances that the passage of time will eventually blur their historicity. Even today, at least to a non-American reader, the Civil War seems almost as remote and exotic as the Trojan War in *The Iliad,* and future readers of *Absalom, Absalom!* will probably care no more about Southern history than we do about Scottish history in *Macbeth.* Yet even in a century or two, if there are any readers left, they will respond to the prodigious energy and restless inventiveness of Faulkner's language, and listen to the scandalous wisdom of his tales, and the more astute will recognize his signature at every turn, as unmistakable and as vibrant as a brush-stroke by Van Gogh.

NOTES

1. Olga Vickery, *The Novels of William Faulkner* (Baton Rouge: Louisiana State University Press, 1959); Cleanth Brooks, *William Faulkner: The Yoknapatawpha Country* (New Haven: Yale University Press, 1963); Michael Millgate, *The Achievement of William Faulkner* (New York: Random House, 1966).

2. *Doubling and Incest / Repetition and Revenge* (Baltimore: Johns Hopkins University Press, 1975).

3. *The Fragile Thread: The Meaning of Form in Faulkner's Novels* (Amherst: University of Massachusetts Press, 1979).

4. *The Most Splendid Failure* (Bloomington: Indiana University Press, 1976).

5. *The Play of Faulkner's Language* (Ithaca: Cornell University Press, 1982).

6. *Faulkner: The House Divided* (Baltimore: Johns Hopkins University Press, 1983).

7. For a fuller statement of my reservations about recent feminist discussions of Temple Drake, see "La Réhabilitation de Temple Drake: *Sanctuary* et la critique féministe," *Etudes Anglaises* 48 (October–December 1995): 442–42.

8. " 'This strange Institution Called Literature': An Interview with Derrida," in Jacques Derrida, *Acts of Literature*, ed. Derek Attridge (New York: Routledge, 1992), 36.

9. *Le Livre à venir* (Paris: Gallimard, 1959), 267. My translation.

10. "Madness, the Absence of Work." *Critical Inquiry* 21 (Winter 1995): 296.

11. Foreword to *Le Bleu du ciel* (1957), in *Oeuvres complètes III* (Paris: Gallimard, 1971), 381.

12. *Letters to Friends, Family, and Editors*, trans. Richard and Clara Winston (New York: Schocken Books, 1977), 16.

13. *Faulkner, Mississippi* (Paris: Stock, 1996).

14. "Uncommon Visage," in *On Grief and Reason* (New York: Farrar Straus Giroux, 1995), 54.

15. See *Faulkner's Subject: A Cosmos No One Owns* (Cambridge University Press, 1992).

16. Garcia Marquez to Luis Harris, in *Los Nuestros* (Buenos Aires: Sudamericana, 1966), 396. My translation.

17. Quoted in *Le Monde des livres* (17 April 1992), 30. My translation.

18. "Le Maître Hemingway," *Le Matin des livres* (14 August 1981), 3. My translation.

19. *Phantasien der Wiederholung* (Frankfurt: Suhrkamp, 1983), 95. My translation.

20. *Trois Auteurs* (Lagrasse: Verdier, 1997), 60–82. Originally published in *La Quinzaine littéraire* (1–15 August 1992). My translation.

21. See *La Relation critique* (Paris: Gallimard, 1970).

22. "Avec du talent, on fait ce qu'on veut; avec du génie, on fait ce qu'on peut." My translation.

23. *Le Temps sensible: Proust et l'experience littéraire* (Paris: Gallimard, 1994).

Whose Faulkner Is It Anyway?

SUSAN V. DONALDSON

We've titled our collective response to the conversation held in Oxford commemorating Faulkner's 100th birthday "Whose Faulkner Is It Anyway?" And we've done so precisely because that conversation is as much about ourselves as readers of Faulkner and about the politics and pleasures of reading Faulkner as it is about the work and multiple personae of the master himself. We are all, as Noel Polk suggests, only half-humorously, latter-day Chaucerian pilgrims "telling each other tales that we pretend are about Faulkner when they are mostly about ourselves—who *we* are, where we come from, what we believe, what we seek, and what we *do* with what we discover here," and as Joseph Blotner reminds us in his survey of the Faulkner conference's history, telling tales of Faulkner to each other over the years has been a companionable, sometimes contentious, and ever-expanding endeavor.

Those tales, amazingly enough, continue to generate even more tales—more papers, more essays, more collections, more books—with no foreseeable end in sight, much to the alarm, I think, of bibliographers and library catalogers everywhere. And while we are very much in accord on one basic issue—the pure, visceral pleasure we all derive from reading Faulkner and the profound impact reading him has had on us and continues to have on us—we can indeed be as noisy and as contentious and as insistent on the rightness of our own readings, our own responses, as any chorus of voices haunting Faulkner himself and driving him to the act of writing in an effort at something akin to exorcism. As readers we keep those voices talking because in a sense reading Faulkner as a community and in the ongoing conversations we hold often means to replicate the voices in his texts clamoring for attention, for recognition, as Carolyn Porter suggests, for priority, and for possession. And therein lie both the rich rewards and the pitfalls of telling tales about ourselves as Faulkner's readers—being on the one hand possessed by those texts, by what Philip Weinstein calls the "gorgeous arabesques" of Faulkner's language, and on the other struggling to possess Faulkner's texts, to claim them as our own, to be ourselves their sole owners and proprietors.[1]

Reading Faulkner, after all, is like reading no other American author I can think of—an experience that is intensely private, unsettling, strangely possessive in its nature, and transfiguring.[2] We all envy our students their first reading of *The Sound and the Fury*, James Carothers observed in the teaching Faulkner session—and here he was quoting John Matthews—because as scholars and teachers of Faulkner we can never again experience that first fine rapture of encountering the words of Benjy and Quentin, because we all have our own stories of our first breathless plunges into Faulkner's words. I remember staying up all night reading *The Sound and the Fury* in the shabby parlor of my freshman dorm and then spending half the next day chasing people down the hall to read passages to them. It is no wonder that after a while they fled at the very sight of me.

If that first fine reading of a text like *The Sound and the Fury* is so crucial for so many of us as readers of Faulkner, it is at least partly because reading was so fundamentally important to Faulkner himself. He frequently told aspiring writers to read all they could.[3] The papers by Tom McHaney and Judith Sensibar on Faulkner as reader do a good deal in telling us what reading widely and promiscuously did for the apprentice writer Faulkner, and the direction of inquiry to which their presentations point is one well worth pursuing. As McHaney reminds us, we still don't know enough about Faulkner's intellectual development, about what he read or might have read during those early years of poetic experimentation and voracious reading, and paying closer attention to those blanker periods, like his post office years in the wilderness, will undoubtedly do a good deal to help us reconstruct the intellectual training that he improvised in the absence of formal education. Nor do we know enough, as Judith Sensibar suggests in her paper, about the effect that reading had on Faulkner's psychic development and powers of imagination, about the intensely close relationship between reading and writing—and the gendered associations of those activities as they played out in Faulkner's relationship with another aspiring writer, his future wife, Estelle Oldham Franklin. Reading Estelle's apprentice fiction, Sensibar tells us, reveals the collaborative nature of Faulkner's emerging artistic imagination—his trying on of multiple identities, his susceptibility to merging with other personae, his assumption of other words and other identities.[4]

I find this approach particularly provocative not just because it underscores how crucial reading was for Faulkner's creativity but also because it tells us a great deal about his own implicit model of reading and readers—giving oneself up to the text, relinquishing the firm boundaries of one's own identity, and actively assuming alternative identities and alternative voices. For Faulkner, reading appears to have been a risky and. daring business requiring expeditions into the hinterlands between self and other, and in that respect it is no wonder that today we continue to find reading Faulkner at once deeply unsettling and profoundly personal.

But then again, that might just be why we read Faulkner in the first place, as Richard Moreland suggests in his paper on "Faulkner as Continuing Education." Faulkner forces his readers to question the most basic assumptions about ourselves and our world—even to the extent of making his characters, his texts, and us take embarrassing chances and risks compelling us to acknowledge—as his own novels and stories often do—clumsiness, failures, and limitations. So closely engaged are we as readers with his work that it often seems as though his novels and stories hold up to us an embarrassing mirror of our own failures and inadequacies, as Gail Mortimer suggests in her presentation on Faulkner's use of animals to allegorize the seemingly impassable gap between men and women. Just so does Faulkner appear to underscore our national failures—in particular, that of our longstanding inability to rectify age-old narratives of racial injustice—in the omissions, absences, and erasures of race that Doreen Fowler argues punctuate the narrative of *Absalom, Absalom!* and that Arthur Kinney sees characterizing our critical neglect of the others of Faulkner's others—Native Americans. It just may be, in fact, that Faulkner's ability to unsettle and reproach us is the very quality that we value the most. "At his diagnostic best," Philip Weinstein observes in his paper, "Faulkner shows the madness of the normative—shows, patiently and dizzyingly, how long-sustained cultural structures of recognition and empowerment for some folks are simultaneously—for other folks—structures of nonacknowledgement and abuse."

Ranging widely over national and historical ground, Faulkner nonetheless reminds us that reading him is always a profoundly personal project, intertwined with the way we see and define ourselves and others, and for this reason Kenneth Holditch's paper about his youthful discovery of Faulkner provides useful testimony of the first transformative encounters we've all had with his work. Growing up in Faulkner country, learning of connections between his family and the Falkners, he discovered Faulkner at a time when he was exploring his own aspirations as a writer, finding in his first reading of *Intruder in the Dust* all the things, he says, "I wished passionately and hopelessly that I could have done myself." And when he finally saw Faulkner himself, it was, he says, "tantamount to having one's dreams incarnated."

There is something about reading Faulkner that does indeed produce that singular shock of recognition perhaps because Faulkner is a writer at once utterly private and painfully public and exposed, a writer who, as

John Irwin tells us, unabashedly pillaged his own life, in particular his disappointments in love, to create narratives of unattainable love "that broke the heart and fueled the imagination." He is also a writer whose role-playing, Lothar Hönnighausen suggests, explores a dizzying range of personae and potential selves bobbing and weaving in a sparring match with some of the most bewildering changes of the twentieth century—shifts in cultural definitions of masculinity and femininity, fissures between words and once-stable meanings, master narratives losing credibility and increasingly subject to collapse. Faulkner, Hönnighausen argues, tries on one mask after another—dandy and vagabond, modernist experimentalist and country farmer—and in doing so reveals not just the absence of any one "true Faulkner"—and by implication the absence of the coherent self we associate with earlier, simpler, gentler times—but something very like the dark twin of ourselves, willing to explore the dimmer passages of subjectivity into which we hesitate to venture on our own. This is the Faulkner who reveals himself in the novels, André Bleikasten tells us, that "possess the cruel power to 'wound and stab us,' a power that arouses our deepest anxieties, reactivates our earliest griefs, rekindles our oldest rages." Faulkner's ability to lead us by the hand into those regions where we would just as soon not venture is pronounced and unmistakable, and if anything, we need a fuller explanation of what those masks signify in an era of multiplying signifiers and increasingly problematic personal identity.

There are also a good many things on which I could take issue with Bleikasten's paper—its assessment, for instance, of the contribution, or lack thereof, made by race and gender criticism to Faulkner scholarship. Suffice it to say in the interest of saving time and space for one and all that what we have learned from scholarship over the last fifteen years is that Faulkner is indeed a writer obsessively drawn to issues of gender and sexuality in his writing, for whom the very shape of narrative, marked by the empty centers left by the absent Caddy in *The Sound and the Fury* and the dead Addie Bundren in *As I Lay Dying*, takes on the configuration of desire, as Bleikasten himself has famously argued in *The Most Splendid Failure* and *The Ink of Melancholy*.[5] But what we can agree on—and there is indeed a great deal with which I do agree in his paper—is what he calls the "deeply heterogeneous" nature of Faulkner's work and our own compulsive need to domesticate it, to render it "less scandalous" and more orderly. Faulkner's fellow Mississippian writer Elizabeth Spencer made much the same observation at one of the first Faulkner and Yoknapatawpha conferences when she remarked that readers of Faulkner need to resist that urge to domesticate and to leave his work "pure and difficult—complicated, wild, passionate, dark and dangerous—the real thing."[6]

Michael Millgate, Hans Skei, and Judith Wittenberg all offer useful admonitions on the dangers of pursuing that highly ambiguous project of domestication too fervently. Millgate, for one, recapitulates a "defining moment" in the story of Faulkner's career when Malcolm Cowley supposedly retrieved Faulkner's reputation from oblivion by producing *The Portable Faulkner*. But that project, he notes, for all intents and purposes represented Faulkner as "portable" by essentializing and restricting the range of the writer's work—focusing largely on the short stories, setting the terms for the critical debates to follow, and casting the fiction into a coherent narrative about Yoknapatawpha that eventually evolved into "something you have to get over" for critics to follow. Similarly, Hans Skei reminds us that our all-too-easy references to Faulkner's early career are shaped more by the sense of coherence that we as readers impose upon that period than any intrinsic unity characterizing the years of "Faulkner before Faulkner." Judith Wittenberg in turn suggests that *Absalom, Absalom!* in particular "both celebrates and profoundly questions the feasibility of a career that proceeds by conscious design" and notes that Thomas Sutpen himself serves as a figure for Faulkner both "admonitory and triumphal," one whose design first creates and then exploits all that is "adjunctive" and "incremental."

We would do well to heed their admonitions and to remember the cautionary figure that Sutpen represents, for so impassioned are our individual engagements with Faulkner that we are at times susceptible to trying to drown out each other as we clamor for attention and recognition, as Faulkner's various voices do. We seek, after all, to build our own designs prompted by novels and stories that are very much "participatory texts" as David Minter characterizes them, texts, he adds, that remind us that our need for community and unity emerges as much from the need for order as from the need for interrelatedness. But in our haste to participate, to respond to those compelling texts, to possess them finally, we can, far too easily, I think, replicate the sins of those characters and storytellers who see words and narrative as opportunities to assert an autonomy of self, reluctant to acknowledge interdependence, mutuality, otherness, or even the possibility that stories and storytelling can have very real and very dangerous consequences—and here I am thinking again of storytellers in texts as far ranging as *Absalom, Absalom!*, *The Sound and the Fury*, *Light in August*, and *As I Lay Dying*.

We are still, for instance, very much involved, as Karl Zender, Arthur Kinney, John Matthews, Thadious Davis, Judith Sensibar, and Doreen Fowler assert, in moving countervoices to the foreground from the shad-

ows and margins of Faulkner's narratives—voices of women, white and
black, of black men, and of Native Americans that offer alternatives to the
forceful and sometimes overwhelming cadences of Faulkner's compelling
white male characters. That this is *still* an ongoing task is a measure in
part of the mesmerizing power that Faulkner can exert over us through
some of his most famous creations, such as Quentin Compson, Darl Bundren, Horace Benbow, and Thomas Sutpen. The difficulty of the task
may also be accounted for, as Karl Zender suggestively observes, by the
"tragedy at the heart of Faulkner's fiction" and perhaps even his anger—
"the suspicion," Zender says, "that all male development is a form of
psychic imperialism, a cooptation of some 'other' (generational, sexual,
racial) in the service of the self." Hence a bit of resistance to Faulkner's
texts, Thadious Davis counsels us, is in order—a strong assertion of one's
own self-identity in the act of reading, in her case, an African American
Southern woman, to wrench a seemingly marginal character like Tomey's
Turl onto center stage in *Go Down, Moses*.

Resistance to Faulkner's texts may also take the form, as John Matthews suggests, of reading them as much the products of the American
minstrel tradition as the offspring of international modernism's lofty experiments. Such an approach may indeed reveal that "if there's a black
muse in *The Sound and Fury*, it wears a minstrel mask," that Faulkner,
no less than Mark Twain, no less than the American South, and no less
than American culture, for that matter, is radically dependent on blackness. Such an approach could also reveal that Faulkner may be inadver-
tently echoing what he himself read in earlier texts experimenting with
the minstrel tradition—texts like Twain's *Puddn'head Wilson* and Charles
Chesnutt's *The Marrow of Tradition*—and such a reenactment can have
deeply disturbing implications, as disturbing as our own unwitting echoes of Faulkner's clamoring voices. How far *have* we traveled on issues
of race since the turn of the century, we ask ourselves, when Twain and
Chesnutt published their disturbing and despairing narrative meditations
on the never-ending American obsession with whiteness, blackness, and
the boundaries required for vigilantly maintaining those racial categories? And how far did Faulkner himself travel from the nadir of race
relations in America? Did his fiction in the end travel farther than he
did?

Even as we look past the first one hundred years, then, reading and
being readers of Faulkner promises to continue being an enormously
complicated, emotionally charged, simultaneously public and private enterprise. So insistent do Faulkner's voices continue to be and so irresistible do we constantly find them, that it is highly likely there will still be
someone talking as long as a single Faulkner text remains. Our responsi-

bility, it seems to me, is to keep those voices talking, to resist their more nefarious maneuvers and refusals to listen, to ensure that no voice succeeds in drowning others out, to perpetuate a din that may indeed be noisier and more disorienting than we would like, to realize, finally, that no one reading, no one reader, can or should possess Faulkner.

NOTES

1. Reading theorists and historians of the book suggest that much the same dynamic of desiring possession and being possessed characterizes the general act of reading itself. Barbara Sicherman, for one, has observed: "Reading theorists have argued that reading is not simply a passive form of cultural consumption, that something happens to readers that becomes imperative for them to understand, and that reading stimulates desire rather than simply pacifying it" (Barbara Sicherman, "Sense and Sensibility: A Case Study of Women's Reading in Late-Victorian America," *Reading in America: Literature and Social History*, ed. Cathy N. Davidson [Baltimore: Johns Hopkins University Press, 1989], 216). See also Robert Darnton, "What Is the History of Books?" in *Reading in America*, 27–52.

2. Reading Faulkner evokes the sort of transformative nature of reading envisioned by phenomenological critics like Georges Poulet or the "bliss" of reading that Roland Barthes describes as bestowing upon the reader "a state of loss, the text that discomforts . . . , unsettles the reader's historical, cultural, psychological assumptions." See Poulet's "Criticism and the Experience of Interiority," *Reader-Response Criticism: From Formalism to Post-Structuralism*, ed. Jane P. Tompkins (Baltimore: Johns Hopkins University Press, 1980), 41–49; and Roland Barthes, *The Pleasure of the Text*, trans. Richard Miller (New York: Hill and Wang, 1975).

3. See, for example, his comments in "1947—Classroom Statements at the University of Mississippi," *Lion in the Garden: Interviews with William Faulkner*, ed. James B. Meriwether and Michael Millgate (Lincoln: University of Nebraska Press, 1968), 55.

4. Sensibar explores Faulkner's early masks in *The Origins of Faulkner's Art* (Austin: University of Texas Press, 1984). Faulkner's use of masks and various personae is also explored in Lothar Hönnighausen's *Faulkner: Masks and Metaphors:* (Jackson: University Press of Mississippi, 1997).

5. See in general André Bleikasten, *The Most Splendid Failure: Faulkner's "The Sound and the Fury"* (Bloomington: Indiana University Press, 1976) and *The Ink of Melancholy: Faulkner's Novels from "The Sound and the Fury" to "Light in August"* (Bloomington: Indiana University Press, 1990).

6. Elizabeth Spencer, "Emerging as a Writer in Faulkner's Mississippi," *Faulkner and the Southern Renaissance: Faulkner and Yoknapatawpha, 1981*, ed. Doreen Fowler and Ann J. Abadie (Jackson: University Press of Mississippi, 1982), 137.

Whose Faulkner?

MINROSE C. GWIN

[I've had a bad case of writer's block this week. Maybe it's the enormity of the task, not to speak of a growing sense of Faulknerian doom—the paralyzing knowledge that anything I may say here will be by its very nature hopelessly inadequate, both to the auspiciousness of the occasion and the rich proliferation of the ideas we've heard this week. I've had several suggestions from my esteemed colleagues for my part of this response panel. These range from "What can you say but: 'They came, they gave papers, they left,'" to "maybe you should have written something *before* you came," to "forget the response and offer a prize to the conference participant who took the most showers during the first three days of this week." However, a truly valuable piece of advice came a couple of nights ago from Joseph Blotner, who had gotten this same job several years ago: "Don't try to make it perfect," he said. "Just *do* it." So, here "it," in all its imperfections and limitations, is.]

"Whose Faulkner Is It, Anyway?" is for me a serious and absorbing question, and one I began pondering for the first time here in Oxford a dozen years ago as I sat in the audience listening to the papers being given at my first Faulkner conference. The topic was women, and some of the participants at this conference were also speakers at that one. One morning a very slight middle-aged woman who told me she had ridden a Greyhound bus nonstop from California to attend the conference sat down next to me. The paper we heard that day was about Temple Drake's rape. Its author, Robert Moore, was arguing that *Sanctuary* makes "us" as readers into voyeurs, and hence casts us in the role of passive participants in that act of sexual brutality. "We find ourselves on a roller coaster of ambivalence as we respond to Temple," Moore was saying. "If she demands our sympathy and protective impulses, she is also fair game for our sexual fantasies. . . . We want to turn away from what we see and we want to see more."[1]

After the paper had been read, there was silence in the room. Then the small Greyhound-bus-riding woman stood up, crossed her arms over her chest, and said quietly, "Don't you think it makes a difference who the reader *is*?" This question, which was audacious, even heretical, a dozen years ago—and, I would add, an enormous relief for me to hear someone utter—was in a sense a spatial one: a question of location and position. It was a serious question about the space of the reader—it was gendering and racializing among other things, and it presupposed serious questions about the space of the author and the space of the text, not to speak of the space of Faulkner criticism in general. That was 1985. More than a decade later, I am impressed by the vigor and dexterity of your negotiations and engagements within each of these spaces, an engagement I still do not take for granted.

Anthropologist Henrietta Moore says that space can be read as a text, and certainly, throughout this week, I've had a strong sense of the space of this conference as a text that we all have a responsibility to analyze, negotiate, and mediate. I have found my thoughts turning again and again to the idea of space itself—and by space, I mean what Michel de Certeau calls "a practiced place,"[2] a location in which something is constantly being produced and reproduced, in which space itself is always being produced and reproduced—whether it be the cultural space that has shaped Faulkner's writing and our readings; textual space, the stories Faulkner has told us and we have reproduced, always with a difference, for one another; material/physical space, this very large room in which we practice our retellings; or the psychic spaces that Faulkner occupies within us, those stories we tell ourselves about ourselves in the process of reading his work. We are here, of course, because of the spaces that Faulkner draws us into, the spaces we love.

You as speakers and participants in this conference have drawn us into these spaces; more important, though, you have shown, resoundingly I think, how multiple and at the same time contiguous these spaces are. You have shown how the question of Faulkner's own multiple identities cannot be disconnected from cultural, psychological, interpersonal, or textual practices. For young Kenneth Holditch growing up in Mississippi, Faulkner was a soft-spoken dapper gentleman who looked like genius and who made writing seem both possible and impossible. For Noel Polk, he is "a litany of Faulkners we have created in our evolving images and in our evolving likenesses . . . in which we hear regularly chanted our own cultural and literary histories" and whom we find again and again in the textual spaces of his own creations. Judith Sensibar situates Faulkner within an "erotic and intellectual relationship" of great importance to his art; John Irwin creates a Faulkner and the Faulknerian text as spaces of unfulfilled and highly generative desire; Thomas McHaney gives us a portrait of the artist as an intellectual, an engrossed reader poring over the latest issue of a borrowed periodical a postal customer

should have already received. Like Sensibar, Lothar Hönnighausen sees
Faulkner the artist in a series of masks and maskings.

Mirrorings of Faulkner's career designs and transitions have been
placed within various frames and perspectives: Michael Millgate has
traced Malcolm Cowley's attempts to gather Faulkner's work into a
boundaried (and "portable") textual space Cowley christened the
" 'mythical kingdom,' " of Yoknapatawpha, and Judith Wittenberg finds
the imprint of Faulkner's own conflictual professional aspirations in
Thomas Sutpen's morally ambiguous drive to power. Karl Zender leaves
us wondering whether readers of the postmodern world will continue to
find in the traditional concept of " 'career,' with its emphasis on striving,
on achievement, on triumph, a concept helpful to the reading of Faulkner's fiction," and Hans Skei believes that the whole notion of a coherent
literary career is itself a construction, an effort to pattern spaces of inconsistency into a teleological frame.

How we construct/interpret/enter the textual spaces Faulkner offers
us has emerged as a complicated and volatile question of the conference;
it is as much a question, as I see it, about readership and communities of
readers as it is about Faulkner's novels. André Bleikasten believes that
most criticism of Faulkner focussing on race and gender has resulted in
morally predictable conclusions and "disquietingly consensual" readings
imposed upon Faulkner's texts by those with certain political agendas.
He argues that "Faulkner's novels must first of all be read as novels." As
the week has progressed, however, it has become apparent that about
half of the papers at this conference, and perhaps more, can be placed in
the category of gender and race criticism, and several more than that in
the arena of cultural criticism. (Such criticism, I would add, on the whole
appears as interested in the language as in the cultural matter of Faulkner's writing.) David Minter has argued that gender, race, and class have
always been there in Faulkner's texts "waiting for us before we had the
eyes to see them," while Thadious Davis suggests that, whatever and
however we read and whether we are willing to admit it or not, we are
always reading out of our own subjective and cultural experiences, just
as she, an African American Southern woman, chooses to read Tomey's
Turl at the center rather than the margins of *Go Down, Moses*. John
Matthews explores "how the sense of the world" makes its way into
Faulkner's language, specifically in black dialect, which Matthews links
to the modernistic impulse to challenge standard language, "to transcend
language through language."

Interestingly, I think, one of the most cited names at this conference
has been that of Toni Morrison, an African American writer many see as
the greatest novelist of America's contemporary period, as Faulkner has

become of the modernist period, and a cultural theorist and critic who
has helped us see how the Africanist presence in the white American
literary imagination has been and still is a figuration of white fantasies
and nightmares. Doreen Fowler and Arthur Kinney call on Morrison in
their analyses of, respectively, the erasure of racial merger in Faulkner's
texts and the significant though underanalyzed presence of those "Other
Others," the American Indians, whose presence marks and comments
upon *something else* in Faulkner's stories. Carolyn Porter shows how *Absalom, Absalom!* in particular foregrounds the question of male identity
and recognition within patriarchal order, while Gail Mortimer exposes
the gendered slippages between animals and women. Richard Moreland
cites Morrison's comment about Faulkner's "refusal to look away," and
describes the irony of Faulkner's cultural critique, an irony "pervasive
and profound enough to turn also against itself," allowing space for "an
embarrassing self-exposure" that we as readers must share in. I am offering this litany, not on the pretense of providing adequate summaries of
these complex, nuanced arguments but to suggest that many, perhaps
most, of these readings and others I cited earlier raise issues about cultural approaches to the Faulknerian text and their relation to language.
It is a dilemma Philip Weinstein seeks to negotiate in his assessment that
Faulkner's greatness lies in his knowledge that "culture's most intractable contradictions operate within or beneath language" and in Faulkner's
decision "not to judge but to *cite* that language."

Weinstein's Faulknerian, writerly space is one in which language and
writing are grounded in "self," "experience," and "thought." One might
see critical, readerly space similarly, I would suggest, as "a practiced
place," in which we produce meaning out of a complex process which
not only relies on language, but on a marshalling and, at the same time,
dislocation of self, experience, and thought. Is it not possible, even likely,
that Judith Sensibar's astute description of Faulkner's artistic desire for
access to, and merger with, an other also applies to us as readers?

I will close by describing a Faulknerian space in which I unexpectedly
found myself last year. This past December I, like several others at this
conference, was in Cancun for an American Literature Association conference. Picture this scene: I am riding up a very hot elevator to my room
in the El Presidente hotel. I am clutching my soggy conference paper on
Faulkner and Toni Morrison, which I've been reading at poolside. At the
second floor the elevator stops and a woman in a tennis outfit and sneak-
ers, also a tourist but not with the conference, gets on and pushes the
button for the fifth floor. Between the third and fourth floors she looks
down at my paper and, apparently spying the name "Faulkner" on my
title page, turns to me and confides in a stage whisper: "You know, I have

always thought it was Charles Bon in that burning house, *not* Henry Sutpen."[3] Then the elevator door opens and she is gone.

Whose Faulkner? This conference is not now, nor has it ever been just about reading the novels. It is also about who we are as readers, and more crucially, about who we may become by the reading. As many of the speakers and participants at this conference have shown this week and in weeks past, Faulkner opens these spaces of practice, of becoming. We travel them, mapping their geographies and, as Philip Weinstein says, "submit[ting] to the vehicle,"—but they also travel us, in ways so utterly complex and terrifying and pleasurable that we can never begin to assess them. Reading Faulkner I will never come "home" to the one who began the reading journey; I am laden with others; I am irrevocably changed. And this, I think, is what we come together from long distances and close proximities to celebrate as a community of readers, this intensely personal experience of travel and transformation, this possibility of the *someone else* who returns from the journey.

NOTES

1. Robert R. Moore, "Desire and Despair: Temple Drake's Self-Victimization," in *Faulkner and Women: Faulkner and Yoknapatawpha, 1985*, ed. Doreen Fowler and Ann J. Abadie (Jackson: University Press of Mississippi, 1986), 114–15.

2. Michel de Certeau, *The Practice of Everyday Life* (Berkeley: University of California Press, 1984), 117.

3. Actually this argument is ably presented with supporting details by Nancy Batty in "The Riddle of *Absalom, Absalom!*: Looking at the Wrong Blackbird?" *Mississippi Quarterly* (Summer 1994): 461–88.

A Response in Forbidden Words

WARWICK WADLINGTON

[What follows is a transcription of my response, made from a few notes, to the preceding conference papers. To preserve one participant's spoken reactions at the moment, I have resisted the later temptation to add to or subtract from the substance of what I said on the occasion. I have edited the transcript only to reduce repetitousness and side remarks to the other panelists, to rephrase here and there for greater clarity, and to add a clarifying summational sentence to a paragraph and brief transitions elsewhere.]

In conclusion . . .

Had you going there for a minute, right? That's our favorite part of every paper we ever hear. No matter how much we like the talk, something in us leaps up when those words are spoken: "In conclusion. . . ." So I thought I'd get you on my side right up front before I talked about another kind of conclusion.

Mr. Faulkner, he dead.

That's the news I want to bring to the conference. I don't have to bring the news fully to the other members of the panel, and everything I say from here on doesn't really apply of course to my perfect colleagues here on this panel.

But Mr. Faulkner, he dead.

. . . .

I paused there because I was hoping you would feel yourself breathing. There's only us here. We are not dead. We're alive, as my panel colleagues have said, and so far, with some exceptions, we have been absent from this celebration of Mr. Faulkner, who is, last I heard, dead. If Faulkner is to have an address where he can be located, let's not try "Old Taylor Road, Oxford, Mississippi." Let's not try "Cemetery in Oxford, Mississippi," where we pour good bourbon, I hope, over Faulkner's grave. Let's try, for example, PS 3511 A86. That ought to ring a bell with at least some of us here. That's where Faulkner is. And, for some of us, he's also at PS 3511 A86 Z. . . . He's also at the places around the world that I've seen indicated on nametags at this conference—that's where Faulkner is. There and here, ultimately in us as readers. Mr. Faulkner, he dead. If there *is* going to be a "Faulkner at 150" conference (or at 200, 300, or whatever), it will only be because there will be those who will locate him and keep him alive as their Faulkner.

So far in the conference, we have heard papers which for the most part I would characterize as saying, if I can paraphrase what Phil Weinstein quoted so eloquently, "Faulkner is going to happen to us." But there's a complementary thing Joe Christmas says, which Phil pointedly left out. Christmas doesn't just declare, "Something is going to happen to me." He also says: "I am going to do something."[1] And in the same sense, however much Faulkner "happens" to us, we also ought to be able to say, "I am going to do Faulkner." Faulkner exists only in the collaboration that we award him because he means and speaks for us and to us. But he only speaks if we give him a voice. Faulkner is going to happen to us because we are going to do Faulkner, and in the way we are going to do Faulkner.

I'm holding here a great novel, *Absalom, Absalom!* As I open the book, do you hear anything? No. But now you will, as I read:

> She must have seen him in fact with exactly the same eyes that Henry saw him with. And it would be hard to say to which of them he appeared the more splendid—to the one with hope, even though unconscious, of making the image hers through possession; to the other with the knowledge, even though subconscious to the desire, of the insurmountable barrier which the similarity of gender hopelessly intervened;—this man whom Henry first saw riding perhaps through the grove at the University on one of the two horses which he kept there or perhaps crossing the campus on foot in the slightly Frenchified cloak and hat which he wore, or perhaps (I like to think this) presented formally to the man reclining in a flowered, almost feminised gown, in a sunny window in his chambers—this man handsome elegant and even catlike and too old to be where he was, too old not in years but in experience, with some tangible effluvium of knowledge, surfeit: of actions done and satiations plumbed and pleasures exhausted and even forgotten. So that he must have appeared, not only to Henry but to the entire undergraduate body of that small new provincial college, as a source not of envy because you only envy whom you believe to be, but for accident, in no way superior to yourself: and what you believe, granted a little better luck than you have had heretofore, you will someday possess;—not of envy but of despair: that sharp shocking terrible hopeless despair of the young which sometimes takes the form of insult toward and even physical assault upon the human subject of it or, in extreme cases like Henry's, insult toward and assault upon any and all detractors of the subject. . . .[2]

And the sentence, of course, this being Faulkner, goes on.

That's when Faulkner speaks, when, however inadequately, we give him a voice, aloud or in our own mind, and that passage I plan to return to. Because in it the reaction of those young people is one of *despair* at the power of this androgynous figure who has suddenly appeared in their Mississippi rural purlieu, and they react with despair and at the same time identification with the kind of outrageous danger that he represents to them. I've long thought that passage a partial model for the way Faulkner engages us as readers.

Although this week we have often heard the Faulkner of despair, there's a sense in which, as in this passage, that's still a very young response to Faulkner. If we take into account real readers such as the woman Minrose Gwin talked about who said, "Doesn't it matter who's reading this passage?" then the reading collaborators that I can imagine are not Faulkner, they're not dead, they're not left in the lurch, grieving, by Faulkner's death or his texts, but they're brought to the point that they can go beyond the place where Faulkner brings them, *can* bring them. They can go farther with their own resources, other resources than Faulkner's.

Faulkner does help to make us, as we make him, who we all are, but he's not alone in that. We're made largely in a vast cultural negotiation, and we bring its self-making cultural resources to Faulkner, such that when we get into those dead ends that we've heard so much about here, we have a choice. We can, like Carolyn Porter and others, stab ourselves and wound ourselves with André Bleikasten's knife. And that's a real choice. That's a real danger in reading Faulkner: Faulkner is a dangerous man. But that's not the only choice we have. We are his coauthors and collaborators and we have independent means. And we don't have to read things that way.

I found the speakers converging and diverging in various ways that partly overlap what's been stated here, and I hope to add a little different spin. I think a very important view looks at Faulkner as an educator, providing us an education—the view that in various ways we got from Moreland, McHaney, and really implicitly in many others: Faulkner as a provider of wisdom. And then there's what Phil Weinstein called the nonpedagogical Faulkner, so there is a divergence that I'd like to hear people talk about, if you want to. Another possibility is Faulkner and incest. We've had three different, very provocative views on the question of Faulkner and incest by Karl Zender, John Irwin, and Thadious Davis, and I want to return to them in a little while.

Another issue that I've heard explicitly or implicitly in a lot of the papers has to do with continuity or lack of continuity and coherence in Faulkner's texts and Faulkner's careers or in Faulkner's person. Hönnighausen, Skei, Sensibar, Polk, Irwin, Porter, Minter all touched in one way or another upon that, and others did too.

Yet another is what I alluded to earlier: Faulkner as dead end. Faulkner as someone who reached a point where things were hopeless, and to say "Faulkner is a tragic writer" is taken by the critic to mean "presents us with no hope." "Faulkner as dead end," I think, was travelling around the edges at least of Phil Weinstein's paper; it was there right in the middle of the road in Porter's, and it was there also in Bleikasten's. With Bleikasten and Weinstein we got a celebratory tone about that dead-endness, that lapsing.

On the other side we heard another important Faulkner who was constituted, and who constituted the reader, the critic, as a herald of progressive racial politics. We got that in Jack Matthews. We got that in Zender, and to some degree again in Davis's paper as I understood it.

In the presentations so far, along with too little serious concern with the role of readers, there has been a series of "forbidden words." I feel like George Carlin here—you know George Carlin's old "seven words you can't say on TV" routine? Well, these are not the four-letter kind, but in some ways they're more powerful. One of them I've just been talking about is the *reader's* pleasure and authority, which does not deny the author's, and does not deny the creative pleasure and so on that we've talked about. But we insult ourselves when we don't talk about why we're all here for this occasion.

Whether or not Faulkner teaches us anything, whether or not Faulkner makes or unmakes us, we would not read more than a page if it didn't give us pleasure. And the pleasures readers get are as various as we are, with considerable overlap in some areas, I would say. When Faulkner stops giving pleasure, he's a stuffed animal: nobody will pay attention to anything else in him for long.

And that leads me to the related forbidden word: aesthetics. This was what André Bleikasten was talking about, and it's a word that hovered around the edges of a couple of the other papers. But as André said after his talk: "You notice I didn't use the word; it's a forbidden word. You can't say 'aesthetics' anymore. People will jump down your throat." We apparently don't have aesthetics anymore.

Another phrase captures for me some of that scandalousness that has been referred to in Faulkner, but to my mind not really adequately represented here. The phrase started appearing a lot after awhile in Faulkner's writing: the old meat. Y'all remember that? The old meat. Meat started coming up in Faulkner: for example, "the male furrowed meat," in Rosa Coldfield's fantastically meaty evocation (117). The old meat. You know, critics are puritans and academics and we like to be proper, and so we use words like "the body." And "desire." But Faulkner is dangerous, and he wants to provoke us and remind us of what we are, and I would say again: Mr. Faulkner, he dead. His old meat has presumably by this time, thirty-plus years, rotted away, and so will ours. He reminds us, as in "My mother is a fish," that we are meat, "cooked and et," one way or another. I'll talk about that again, just a little bit more.

There's a related major word having further to do with Faulkner's provocation, his danger, and also his creative power, that moves him from the rather spineless, not very interesting Faulkner of his early writings to that changed figure that in many ways Sensibar, Irwin, and Skei talked about. The important word that didn't come up is *lovelessness*. We heard about how protracted courtship and desire having to do with love transformed Faulkner from a mediocrity to this fantastic writer. I think it's a very important way to understand his development. And it's also a way of talking about his implicit negotiations with us.

So, having said these few loveless, pleasurable, old meat, aesthetic words, let me pick up a further conference theme to rework the forbidden words a little bit, and then I want to hear what you have to say.

At one of the cocktail parties early in the conference I was talking with a couple of people, who I hope will vouch for this, about how in Faulkner, I thought (as in some ways Virginia Woolf), there was not, in the first instance, a strong sense of the human life as story. There was not a sense that the world as one lived it came *inherently* to you as stories, as narratives. It was a pleasure then to hear related ideas emerge in later conference papers. The matter can be seen from a developmental point of view, such as Hans Skei described very nicely for us, as a deficiency in the young Faulkner. He was a lyric writer: he could sketch, he could seize moments, but he was very limited at that point. He didn't have the ability to handle aesthetically narrative material and make it work. What happens to him is the question that, again, Judith Sensibar and others have returned to in various ways. What happened to make this feeble no-story person into a master of narrative? I think one of the things that happens, as in different ways with Virginia Woolf, is that Faulkner learns to make into a strength the sense that there is no necessary story in the world. Human life doesn't have to come packaged in this or that ready-made story—he made that into a theme and writing practice. He shows us stories, what I would call nonnecessary stories, but very convincing and powerful ones, as though being fashioned right before our eyes. In *The Sound and the Fury*, for example; in *As I Lay Dying*, for example; and most obviously in the book that I've quoted from, *Absalom, Absalom!*

Somewhat similarly, David Minter talked about Faulkner in parallel to Wallace Stevens. Both of them, Minter said, give us reminiscences of

narrative; they give us notes toward a supreme fiction. The modern condition, Minter generalized, had wiped out the idea that there was a necessary story to things, at either the micro or the macro level. I'm
paraphrasing part of what I think Minter was saying, and I agree with
that. It rounds out more broadly the kind of individual developmental
progress that we heard about from Skei and Sensibar.

But what happens to Faulkner is not simply love in its varieties as John
Irwin brilliantly presented to us and that Judith Sensibar most brilliantly
captured—a perpetual courtship of sought-after but failed love. What
also happened to Faulkner was that he learned to trust his lovelessness.
To paraphrase the little wordplay that Irwin used, I would say that, between lovelessness and love, Faulkner will take both. Faulkner presents
us these nice little either/ors which the whole text usually warns us away
from, and in fact, he'll throw hate into the bargain. But when I say lovelessness, I don't mean hate. I mean this: one of the things that fascinates
and attracts Harry Wilbourne to the artist figure Charlotte Rittenmeyer
is his sense that there is something in her which doesn't love anybody or
anything. And when he sees that consciously, I think we're meant to
understand that he has a shock of recognition. Their love, which also has
generous dollops of hate in it (and in this they're convincing representations of real people) is partly built upon lovelessness, the lovelessness
that allows Charlotte to create her sculptures. From that lovelessness
comes the cold unflinching gaze that we have so often touched upon in
this conference. It's an unsentimental, loveless eye that doesn't look
away, as Toni Morrison accurately said of Faulkner's work, and Morrison
possesses also in generous measure that same lovelessness, and represents it in characters like Sula Peace. Again I don't mean to say that's the
whole story. The courtship of love is there; there's also more than a modi-
cum of hate, that stirs Faulkner's creative juices and is involved with his
negotiations with us as the implied dangerous author, the Charles Bon.
But there is also that unloving gaze that looks steadily at the encultura-
tion of the old meat in all its cultural, aesthetic, and political meanings
simultaneously. Looks at its reproduction—another word that has come
up a number of times—looks at the ways that lovelessness is involved in
reproduction. And concerning this process I would say with Karl Zender
that for Faulker male identity does have an imperialist quality to it, but
I would add that Faulkner also implies that about identities in general.
For both, or all, the genders and "races." A certain "imperialism," to
whatever degree, is for Faulkner a constituent of being a person.

Reproduction means in Faulkner that, as Quentin says in *Absalom*,
nothing and nobody happen just once. Everything and everybody repeat,
but with a difference every time. We can put together the models of

incest and courtship that we've heard here (and Minrose Gwin has touched upon this)—Sensibar's collaboration model between Faulkner and his in a sense ideal reader; Irwin's courtship model crossed with the political-brotherhood model of Zender; and the Davis model of resistance to the reproduction of the master's image. If we put all these moments together, it seems to me we've got something like a model for Faulkner's courtship of, challenge to, and dangerous risk with the reader, with us. And we take our pleasure—some of us at least—partly by a shock of recognition acknowledging, at some level, that we too are loveless, that we too can earn and learn the courage not to look away from the appalling things that Faulkner shows us.

Here's a final idea that occurred to me in the conference. It again has to do with the impact that Charles Bon has upon the people at that little college, the fictional Ole Miss—the furor that he sets up among those other males, in what is to me clearly a homoerotic, homosocial scene, richly played out throughout *Absalom, Absalom!* in the relationship between Henry and Charles Bon, as well as between Shreve and Quentin. The impact that this sweetmeat Charles Bon has, dropped into this ant-pile of Henry and the rest of those rurals, strikes me as a precursor of what happens with another representative of "animal magnetism," Eula Varner, when she is dropped like a sweetmeat into the ant-pile of all those male suitors who go crazy around her and begin feeling violent, as Gail Mortimer nicely examined. Charles Bon is Eula's predecessor. And both of them focus one revealing possible reaction Faulkner invites to him as an implied powerful, sensuous figure—a representative of the ineluctable power of breathing, eating, sleeping, mating or not, reproducing or not, and dying (dying for sure), all of which is the trajectory of the old meat.

For some readers of Faulkner, there is "a happy marriage of speaking and hearing." For others, it is perhaps better to say there is a protracted happy *courtship* of speaking and hearing, with a wariness that this fellow who wants to seduce us may have a corncob in his pocket. And that we'd better keep an eye on ourselves as well.

Don Kartiganer told me that I would have the last word as a speaker at this conference, and in answer to that I've scribbled down a quotation that also brings me back to my joking and yet serious beginning. It's a quotation from Rosa Coldfield you all know, as she contemplates "the rubbishy aftermath to clear away from off the very threshold of despair." She says, "That was all. Or rather, not all, since there is no all, no finish." (121).

NOTES

1. William Faulkner, *Light in August*, The Corrected Text (New York: Vintage International, 1990), 104.

2. William Faulkner, *Absalom, Absalom!*, The Corrected Text (New York: Vintage International, 1990), 75–76. All subsequent references are to this edition.

Me and Old Uncle Billy and the
American Mythosphere

ALBERT MURRAY

There was nothing at all avuncular about the impression he made on me when I began reading William Faulkner during the first term of my freshman year at Tuskegee in the fall of 1935. At that time he, along with Ernest Hemingway, John Dos Passos, F. Scott Fitzgerald, Sherwood Anderson, Gertrude Stein, and James Joyce, and also such poets as T. S. Eliot, Ezra Pound, Archibald McLeish, Carl Sandburg, Robert Frost, Edwin Arlington Robinson, and such playwrights as Eugene O'Neill, Maxwell Anderson, Robert E. Sherwood, and Clifford Odets of Broadway, and William Butler Yeats and John Middington Synge of the Abbey Theatre, was very much a part of what the current literary news and commentaries in newspapers and magazines in the periodicals room of the Hollis Burke Frissell Library were about.

At the time my main literary interest was drama, and the book that led me to anthologies and surveys of world literature was *The Theater: Three Thousand Years of Acting and Stagecraft* by Sheldon Cheney, who was also the author of *A Primer of Modern Art*, from which by that next spring I had become familiar with such aesthetic terms as Impressionism, Postimpressionism, Cubism, Futurism, Expressionism, Dadaism, Surrealism and so on, including Vorticism and Constructivism.

By which time because of such weekly magazines as the *Saturday Review of Literature*, the *New York Times Book Review*, the *New York Herald Tribune Book World*, the *New Republic*, and the *Nation*, none of which had been available to me in high school, I was already spending more of my extracurricular reading time on contemporary fiction, poetry, and critical theory than on drama and stagecraft, although I was also keeping current on what was happening on the Broadway stage and on the screen and radio.

Come to think of it, although I was not really aware of it at the time, the shift of my primary reading interests from drama to prose fiction probably had already begun between mid-September and mid-November. In any case, along with Ernest Hemingway, who was writing about Florida and Cuba in sequences from *To Have and Have Not* and correspondence dispatch observations about the craft of fiction as such in current issues of *Esquire* magazine, there was also one William Faulkner whom I still remember as if it all happened yesterday. Because I will always remember the faded red print on the blue and beige binding of the Jonathan Cape-Harrison Smith edition of *These Thirteen* that was right there on the tilted display tray at your elbow on the checkout counter in the main reading room on the second floor of the Hollis Burke Frissell Library.

So it all began with "Dry September," "Red Leaves," "That Evening Sun," "A Rose for Emily," "A Justice," and "Hair." Then came the blue embossed sun-bleached meadowland beige bound Harrison Smith-Robert Haas edition of *Light in August,* bringing Joe Christmas and Lena Grove and Byron Bunch and Joe Brown and Lucas Burch and Reverend Gale Hightower, Old Man MacEachern, Old Doc Hines, Miss Addie Burden, and the sheriff, plus Percy Grimm to be sure.

Then came *Absalom, Absalom!* hot off the press in 1936. *Soldiers' Pay, Sartoris, Mosquitoes, The Sound and the Fury, As I Lay Dying,* and *Sanctuary* were not available at Tuskegee at that time. Gerald Hamilton, my favorite classmate of all time, had already read *Sanctuary* back in Detroit, his home town, where he had also seen a movie version entitled *The Case* (or *Story*) *of Temple Drake.* I don't remember him saying anything about any of the others, so I assume that he had not yet read any of them either, because I can't imagine him not saying anything about the stylistic innovations that Faulkner employed in the Benjy and Quentin sections of *The Sound and the Fury,* and I still think about how much fun it would have been to have him there with his input on the decoding of those first two hundred twenty-two pages. What with him already checked out as he alone among the undergraduates I knew was on such contemporary writers as James Joyce and Marcel Proust and such stylistic innovations in narration as the stream of consciousness, the fourth dimension, free association, imagism, symbolism, and so on.

Which, of course, is why both *Light in August* and *Absalom, Absalom!* were so much easier going for him than for me. But I was no less captivated even so. And I still think of both, which I reread immediately, as belonging as much to me as to anybody. Incidentally, the fact that the current reviews of *Absalom, Absalom!* were hardly laudatory had no negative effect on our enthusiasm whatsoever. Both novels were like tunes you keep humming to yourself because you like them for yourself, regardless of what anybody else thinks.

Hamilton was back up north when *The Unvanquished* arrived in 1938.

So I made what I made of the Civil War and Reconstruction escapades of Bayard Sartoris and Ringo on my own. But there was something about the curiosity that the two of them shared and running mate games they played that reminded me time and again of how things were when he was there. Young Bayard Sartoris was no Huck Finn to be sure. Although in some ways he and Ringo were personally closer than Huck and Jim, who, after all, was an adult, not Huck's age peer. And I had serious doubts about the naiveté of Ringo's devotion to the Confederacy. But Faulkner's rendering of Ringo's competitive curiosity and self-confident ingenuity are not condescending, and his account of Ringo's efforts to conceive the concrete image of a functioning railroad train, something he not only has never heard of before Bayard comes back from a trip and tells him about one but has nothing to compare it with, is as profoundly insightful as it is hilarious.

And yet, as far as I know, Faulkner never got around to coming to terms with an emancipated and reconstructed Ringo. There was the formidable Lucas Beauchamp of *Go Down, Moses* and *Intruder in the Dust* to be sure and several others not unlike him who exemplify the traditional orientation to the dignified bearing and noble aspirations of their "high class" white relatives in the Edmonds, MacCaslin, and Sartoris families. But what about the ex-slaves, mulatto or not, who became leaders, teachers, professionals, and businessmen? The Reconstruction was not a farce, nor was it mostly a disaster perpetrated by corrupt carpetbaggers. In spite of the widespread hostility and all of the horrendous acts of terrorism by the likes of Nathan Bedford Forrest and others, the transition from people freed from slavery to responsible U.S. citizenship and unimpeachable patriotism is unexcelled by any other stories of the making of any other Americans.

The last Faulkner novel I read before graduating from Tuskegee in 1939 was *The Wild Palms*, in which the nightmarish Old Man River flood story came across very effectively in spite of the way it was seemingly arbitrarily interwoven with the totally different narrative sequences of the Harry Wilbourne-Charlotte Rittenmeyer fiasco, the implications of which became richer later on when I eventually got around to reading Faulkner's New Orleans based equivalent to the influential 1920s *Wasteland*-oriented efforts of the poet T. S. Eliot, the novelist F. Scott Fitzgerald, and others in such books as *Soldiers' Pay*, *Mosquitoes*, *Pylon*, and *New Orleans Sketches*. Then very belatedly there was also *Sartoris (Flags in the Dust)* for all its benchmark status in the Yoknapatawpha chronicles.

William Faulkner's stylization of the idiomatic particulars of the Deep South is very much a part of what impressed me about his fiction from the very outset. Moreover, even then it was not simply a matter of regional or provincial atmosphere or local color, not as such. Even then there was something about it that had the effect of transforming all too familiar everyday down home environmental and demographic details into the stuff of poetry, the stuff that the so-called avant-garde poetry of T. S. Eliot, Ezra Pound, e.e. cummings, Marianne Moore, and Robinson Jeffers among others was made of.

For me, the "mot juste" prose of Ernest Hemingway's *In Our Time* and *The Sun Also Rises* was also the stuff of such poetic endeavor. But whereas the poetry of Hemingway's prose struck me as being all-American in a Walt Whitmanesque sense (also with overtones of syndicated wire service vernacular to be sure) Faulkner's Southerners' linguistic Southernness, not unlike the unmistakably Irish idiom of James Joyce's *Dubliners*, was no less potentially international in its avant-garde chicness and already no less immediate in the universality of its implications. (For me, at any rate, what André Malraux made of *Sanctuary* recalls what Beaudelaire and the French made of Poe!) Stylization could make small-town down-home stuff, even Mississippi small-town down-home stuff as universal as anything from anywhere else.

Also when I think of the near symphonic orchestral convolution of some of Faulkner's prose as compared with the streamlined precision of Ernest Hemingway's *Kansas City Star* disciplined 4/4-like incantation, it is as if Faulkner were a not quite not Thomas Sutpen Mississippi planter and occasional river boat to New Orleans dandy and sometime gentleman rider-huntsman who inhabits a haunted antebellum mansion on what is left of a vast plantation inherited from ancestors whose accruals were derived directly from owning and exploiting human slaves. Some of them very close relatives indeed. A prop-laden stage set for costume drama with ever so historical resonances.

Whereas for me, it was as if Hemingway's style was that of some species of all-American sportsman in leotards on a clean well-lighted starkly symbolic, multi-level stage set for ritual sketches. And of course much goes to show that it is the ritual sketch that the costume drama however elaborate must add up to. Which well may be as good a reason as any why "The Bear" in *Go Down, Moses* may be regarded as a crucial if not definitive Faulkner achievement.

No, there was nothing about the impression that William Faulkner made on me during those early years that was yet avuncular. But even so, he had become Old Faulkner almost as fast as Little Louis Armstrong had become Old Louis and the handsome young Duke Ellington had become Old Duke. That was because at a very early age, he had his own way of doing what he did that commanded serious attention and respect not only of his peers but also of his elders as well. Indeed what it meant was that he was already on his way to becoming an elder himself. Because there was something about the way that he did what he did that left you more bemused and/or astonished and impressed withal than aghast and outraged. In any case, I submit that he had already become Old Faulkner early on because it was already so obvious that he was headed for the status of the legendary and who knows, perhaps eventually the status of a classic.

As an undergraduate I associated the idiomatic particulars of Faulkner's role as a regional elder in the arts with what I regarded as a post-Confederate Southern small-town seed-store, feed-store courthouse square sensibility. Not that I had any firsthand experience of such places. I had grown up hearing fireside tales, tall and otherwise, about such potentially explosive Southern small towns as Atmore, Bay Minette, Flomaton, and so on in Alabama. But Magazine Point, where I spent the first nineteen years of my life, was a small suburb of the international seaport city of Mobile, to the downtown municipal and business center of which we were directly connected by a trolley car ride of only a matter of perhaps thirty minutes or less and a short walk of less than an hour. So the small courthouse square Macon County seat of Tuskegee was actually my very first ongoing contact with a small courthouse square town with a Confederate statue like Faulkner's town of Jefferson. So Jefferson was just as real as Tuskegee town and the town of Tuskegee was just as much a part of a story book world as Faulkner's Jefferson.

In all events when as a graduate whose literary context by that time included Thomas Mann, André Malraux, James Joyce, Marcel Proust, Arthur Koestler, Ignacio Silone, and Franz Kafka among others, including such poets as Auden, Spender, and C. Day Lewis, I came back around to reading Faulkner when *The Hamlet* and then *Go Down, Moses* were published, my image of the idiomatic dimension of him as a Deep South elder became that of a book-oriented corn whiskey drinking cracker barrel lie swapper and hot stove yarn spinner, whose cosmopolitan literary awareness was as natural to him as was his comprehensive courthouse square awareness of local, regional, national, and global affairs. None of which seemed to have very much if anything to do with drawing room chic but was clearly of a piece with the nuts and bolts stuff of local politics and ever so confidential inside gossip. And thus perhaps not little to do with motives underlying narrative action.

It was when he became more and more involved with the Snopes people and the Varners that I realized that along with everything else that had made him Old Faulkner there was also something that made him Old Uncle Billy as far as I was personally concerned. My having grown up in the Deep South as I had, he was my own personal very special big house equivalent to and literary extension of my traditional brownskin fireside, barber shop, and storefront loafers rest bench Uncles Bud, Doc, Ned, Pete, and Remus, with pipe whether sometimes alternating with cigar or not.

Because just as it was as if Old Uncles Bud, Doc, Ned, Pete, and Remus existed to make you aware of attitudes, acts, and implications that you were not yet old enough to come by on your own for all your ever alert and even ingenious curiosity, so were Old Uncle Billy's books there to pull you aside and provide you with inside insights not readily available to you as an everyday matter of course because you were neither white nor a personal servant.

So the quest for universality in aesthetic statement being what it is, and despite his avowed but ambivalent desire for anonymity, Old Faulkner became and still is my very own idiomatic Old Uncle Billy. Not for all intents and purposes to be sure, but for quite a few even so. In all events, anywhere his concerns and curiosity took him I could go also and so can you. For such is indeed the nature and function of literary artistic endeavor in the human scheme of things.

Thus what William Faulkner's avuncular status with me comes down to is precisely the role of the literary artist in the contemporary American mythosphere, a term I am appropriating from my friend Alexander Eliot. In other words there is the physical atmosphere of planet Earth which is said to extend some six hundred miles out into space in all directions and consists of the troposphere in which we live, and beyond which is the stratosphere beyond which are the mesosphere, the ionosphere, and exosphere.

The mythosphere is that nonphysical but no less actual and indispensable dimension of the troposphere in which and in terms of which human consciousness exists and as we all know, the primary concern of all artistic endeavor is the quality of human consciousness, whether our conception of things is truly functional, as functional as a *point* or *moral* of the classic fables and fairy tales. But that is quite a story in itself. Let me just say that I assume that the role of the serious literary artist is to provide mythic prefigurations that are adequate to the complexities and possibilities of the circumstances in which we live. In other words, to the storyteller actuality is a combination of facts, figures, and legend. The goal of the serious storyteller is to fabricate a truly functional legend, one that meets the so-called scientific tests of validity, reliability, and comprehensiveness. Is its applicability predictable? Are the storyteller's anecdotes truly representative? Does his "once-upon-a-time" instances and episodes imply time and again? I have found that in Old Uncle Billy's case they mostly do.

*Photographs of the Tuskegee Albert Murray knew when
he first began to read Faulkner. Courtesy of Albert Murray.*

WILLIAM FAULKNER

    noun, place, and verb
memory he said believes he said
and himself did who was himself
memory and did himself believe
and then remember to recollect,
whose name was william faulkner
whose place was mississippi
and whose verb was tell.

memory he wrote believes before knowing
remembers. believes longer than recollects
longer than knowing even wonders
knows remembers believes, he himself said
believing himself and mississippi august skylight
mississippi thickets in september twilight,
believing the dry hysteria: *something
is going to happen I am going to do something
something is going to happen to me*

and memory no less in mississippi than elsewhere
believes knows tells t•.is:
the mississippiness of ancient oracles
of albatross sins ancestral; recollects remembers this:
presummersmell of wisteria
oldentime ladies in rooms unsanctuary
amid mississippi gothic behind cottonwhite
totems doric corinthian scotch irish
*(O clytemnestra my black one
              O my firstborn son and brother)*

and this also believes: cypress and gum trees
beach, cane and briar and three-note birdsong ·
reflections in branch water; mississippi distant horns
and gas engines smells fading beyond now and fury
and this recollects and knows the significance of
*black human blood red on butcher knives
white female blood on phallic corn cobs.*

memory believing yoknapatawpha indian doom
did not mistake the wilderness for sanctuary
either but wished it so as huntsman
but wishing does not know
forgets and gallops confederate cavalry in gale tone hightower sermons
wish-fulfilling knighthood (without negroes)

wish-forgiving arrogance and the outrage of human bondage
wish-denying antebellum nightmares
while celebrating those who could survive them
but wishing is believing too
because the bones remember
(*O canaan look away from dixie*
away from bedford forest O railroads
underground freedom bound)

and memory knowing this
knows more (believes infers
more complications than even those
miss rosa coldfield's perhaps once glittering
eyes gave quentin compson, who said:
and wants it told)!

memory believes knows recollects in him (*whose nouns*
were courage and honor and pride and
he says pity and love and even justice
and liberty) believes knows and wonders at:
wishing become man-horse-demon
with twenty negroes (shackled) begetting
with one french architect (shanghaied) sutpens
hundred (*without gentleness begot,* miss rosa
coldfield says); wonders remembers
aghast but knows: mississippi dynasties
of somewhat
oedipal innocence with black
queen-mothers and half brothers
knows jefferson the man and town
and public confederation of decorum; and also knows
remembers eighty miles to memphis
and miss reba's sanctum sanctorum of law and order
and sportsmanship
                    believes remembers
recollects, records in commissary ledgers
pharoah-tale-accounts compounded in confounding
convolutions of all-too-human-impacted
good intentions which at any rate
reveal (or partly unconceal) himself:
william faulkner, hamlet-hounded master
of mulatto metaphors among macbeths
in county courthouse castles out demographed
by ever in-creeping miscegenated thickets

nigger? the sheriff said in hot pursuit
of the inherently elusive mississippi christmas,

nigger? he said. maybe nigger, maybe not
they told him then
whose memory like theirs believed in shadows
as well as men

Following his talk and the reading of his poem, Mr. Murray related a few anecdotes and responded to some questions from the audience.

During World War II, I was plans and operation officer at the Tuskegee Army Air Field. Recalled from the Reserves for Korean War service, I stayed on, and I retired as a major in 1962. That's when I turned to writing full time. I had been a college teacher before that, but while I was at Tuskegee during the war I was rereading Faulkner, and one day the commanding officer came in. He was a Mississippian; his name was Noel F. Parrish and he was a very conscientious guy, along with the other instructors, most of whom were white Southerners who had volunteered to make up the instructional staff for what began as the 99th Pursuit Squadron. Some of these guys had been over with the Flying Tigers with Chenault. Some were very hot pilots, but they trained these cadets very very well and were largely responsible for the outstanding record our fliers had in Europe. Colonel Parrish was a very curious guy and he was very much interested in all dimensions of American history. The big book at that time was Gunnar Myrdal's *American Dilemma*, which Colonel Parrish would talk about in Officers' meetings and at other times. He came by my office and I had these synthetic gunnery trainers, the instrument trainers, and all kinds of stuff; but I also had these books, and he saw *Go Down, Moses* and *The Hamlet* on my desk, and other books of Faulkner. So he wanted to tell me stories about Faulkner. He said, when Faulkner found out that he, a Mississippian, was in charge of this black unit of airmen—oh, he would give anything to go up there *and help him train these guys.* "What I couldn't do with me a squadron of these guys. Jeez, we would tear up Europe!" He never got up there, but it sent him back into all his fantasies that went all the way back to the Canadian Air Force.

Every time Faulkner would see Parrish, he would tell him, "I gotta get up to Tuskegee, see how those boys are doing up there. That should be my squadron, that should be my group, I should have one of those." So that was another connection: I was reading him and he was dreaming about being in the air force.

Another tale I was thinking about was what Ralph Ellison wrote me the day he won the National Book Award for *Invisible Man*. He sent me a copy of the speech he gave and he also sent me an account of how events went that day. They went to Saxe Commins's office at Random House, and Faulkner was there. Commins said, "Ralph, put your things here and come meet Bill Faulkner." So Ralph went in and met Faulkner. They shook hands, and Ralph said, "Well, Mr. Faulkner, you got a lot of children scattered around. Some of 'em you've never seen, and might never see, and some of them you might claim and you might not, but they're out there all the same." And Faulkner said, "Yaaas. It's surprising how the stuff gets around." But then Ralph went on to say, "Man, you hear this talk about his beat-up clothes and stuff like that. Don't believe it. Man, he is as sharp as we are!" He said, "he had a sport coat that wouldn't quit. He had his tie all right, and he had a collar that rolled down, and I mean down."

Later on, Faulkner mentioned him in Faulkner at Nagano. They were asking him about black writers. He said, "Well, most of them are more interested in being black than in being writers. But there's one, Ellison—he's very much interested in being a writer. He doesn't have to worry about being black—he was already that—he wanted to see how much literature he could get out of it.

Question: How much contemporary literature did you read at Tuskegee Institute?

I think I was among the first teachers at Tuskegee to put in contemporary literature as such. In fact a number of the teachers who had taught me became interested in twentieth-century literature because of me. My favorite English teacher had to go back and do *The Wasteland* with me. He used his better French to translate the several poems of Eliot's that were written in French. We translated them together because he knew French better.

They were teaching traditional courses in the novel. In fact, I was just fictionalizing that yesterday. They were teaching courses in the English novel—Richardson, Sterne, Fielding. So my roommate and I were reading all this stuff, plus the contemporary stuff. *Ulysses* was locked up in the librarian's office. You had to get special permission to read it. But on the shelves—it was a very good library. You think of Tuskegee as being like a Big Ten school, agricultural and technical. The other schools—people thought I should have gone to Morehouse or Talladega, which were strictly liberal arts schools, but their libraries were no better than the Tuskegee library. It depended on who was staffing the library.

They kept up with the contemporary stuff. So I was reading all these anthologies of world literature and the current literary magazines, and reading the Louis Untermeyer anthologies of modern American and British poetry. It led me to comprehensive reading, because I was a literary person, and that's what I wanted to do. But the material was there. They just had missed—I don't know why they didn't get those other books on time, but it took me that many years to get to *Sanctuary*, for example, and *Mosquitoes*—it took a long time to get to that. Another book I missed, I don't know why, was *Pylon*, which came out when I was a sophomore. But the next book I got after *Light in August* was *Absalom, Absalom!* I was hooked forever with that.

Question: Can you say anything about how Faulkner may have misled us?

He may have misled us a few times in public utterances, but that was not his actual literary work. Nothing pops to my mind, except what I mentioned in passing, and that is that he did not deal with Ringo after Ringo was free. That's a big gap in Faulkner, because that's me, so far as I'm concerned. Because Ringo is as smart as Bayard, so how do you get Hampton and Howard and Tuskegee and Morehouse and all these leaders and these doctors and lawyers and all that? They come from Ringo. Faulkner didn't deal with that. That's all right for Lucas, who has the great dignity. But there were other guys who were leaders and achievers right there in Mississippi. In that sense there was that gap. But the basic humanity, and in terms of the intrinsically human, Faulkner couldn't, he just wouldn't cheat, he wouldn't distort deliberately. Because those are very profound, existential things which you can't avoid, he had to confront them.

But after all, Faulkner was human and he had his weaknesses, and as a human being: I mean he was right on the verge of being a very pathetic person. But many great writers are. They're at their best when they're doing what they do best. So it's worth all that. I was out at Rowan Oak. All I was thinking was, boy this must have cost so many trips to Hollywood, just to put in some grass and some trees, and things like that. He wasn't filling the house up with luxuries. But he liked the place.

By the way, I think Hollywood had a beneficial effect on his writing. It helped him to be one of the most convoluted of all writers. And I feel that it's not worth trying out if it's not worth convoluting. I like that part of his literary identity.

CODA

William Faulkner Centennial Celebration

The University of Mississippi
Fulton Chapel

September 25, 1997
2:00 p.m.

PROGRAM

Prelude
Quartet for Piano and Strings in G minor, K. 478
Wolfgang Amadeus Mozart
    Allegro
    Andante
    Rondeau

The Oxford Piano Quartet
Diane Wang, piano; Robert Riggs, violin; Dan Haley, viola;
    Tien-sheng Li, cello

Welcome
Robert C. Khayat
Chancellor
The University of Mississippi

Greetings
The Honorable Patricia Chadwick Lamar
Mayor
City of Oxford

Remarks
The Right Reverend Duncan Montgomery Gray Jr.
Bishop Emeritus, Episcopal Diocese of Mississippi
Former Chancellor, University of the South

Testimonials
Donald M. Kartiganer
Howry Professor of Faulkner Studies
Director, Faulkner and Yoknapatawpha Conference
The University of Mississippi

Richard Howorth
Proprietor, Square Books
Oxford, Mississippi

Larry Brown
Author
Oxford, Mississippi

Introduction to Readings
Evans Harrington
Professor Emeritus of English
Founding Director, Faulkner and Yoknapatawpha Conference
The University of Mississippi

Artist's Considered Perspectives
Dramatic Readings Adapted by Evans Harrington
   from the Works of William Faulkner

From "Introduction to *The Sound and the Fury*"
George Kehoe

From "Letter to Joan Williams"
L. W. Thomas

From "Interview with Jean Stein"
George Kehoe

From "Colloquies at Nagamo Seminar"
L. W. Thomas

From "Nobel Prize Acceptance Speech"
L. W. Thomas

From *A Green Bough*
George Kehoe

Postlude
"We Shall Behold Him" Dottie Rambo
"Center of My Joy" Gloria and William Gaither, Richard Smallwood

Delbert Collins, baritone and piano; Deaundrea Thomas, soprano

Welcome

ROBERT C. KHAYAT

It is a great pleasure to welcome you today. Please join me in thanking the Oxford Piano Quartet for their beautiful music.

Please welcome our platform party. . . .

It is humbling to celebrate William Faulkner's one hundredth birthday. He is so much a part of this University and this community. However, today gives us an opportunity to be even more reflective of his impact on us, our literature, and the world.

In his Nobel Prize Award Speech in 1950, Mr. Faulkner stated that the prize was not being given to him but to his work. Today, we pay homage to him—the man, the writer, the father, the brother, the uncle, a friend, the postal worker, the compassionate observer of humanity—and we honor his "life's work" about the "agony and sweat of the human spirit" that was the inspiration for his thought and writing.

In 1964, my mother and father gave me a volume of Martin Dain's wonderful work *Faulkner's County: Yoknapatawpha*. At the time, thirty-three years ago, I enjoyed the photographs—familiar scenes of Mr. Faulkner, the Square, the town, and the county—this place many of us call home. So, this gift became a part of me.

As we celebrate one of the most remarkable writers of the twentieth century—we recognize that this reclusive, quiet man, through his gift, has become a part of each of us. And by us, I mean not only those of us who live in this county, but the world community as well.

His spirit, his sensitivity, his honesty regarding the limits of man and his pain—all of these characteristics endure within us. His fictional characters—Isaac McCaslin, Benjy, Dilsey, Temple, Boon, and others—are people we know as if they lived in our town, on our street, or perhaps in our homes. He enabled us to smell tobacco on his grandfather's leather vest, to understand the feeling of the wilderness, to recognize the cultural boundaries that exist and that individuals must face.

He is so much a part of us and how we think—so embedded in our cultural and literary heritage that only when we sharpen our focus on a day like today, do we realize that he is speaking through us.

His contributions are immense and are grounded in "the intensity and sincerity with which he has depicted the complexities of human experience measured by the progression of history"—one hundred years of history now.

Time is uncontrollably pushing us toward the twenty-first century, but the same human issues continue to surface, and we, who love and admire Faulkner and who continue to celebrate his life, are assured that his work will undeniably have permanence, just as his wilderness, his Yoknapatawpha, and his spiritual truths have.

Thank you for sharing this historic event with us at the University.

A Eulogy for Faulkner

THE RIGHT REVEREND DUNCAN M. GRAY JR., D.D.

It is both a pleasure and a privilege to be a part of this one hundredth birthday celebration of a man whose writings have meant so much to me over the years and whom I was privileged to know during the last five years of his life. As many of you know, I served as Rector of St. Peter's Episcopal Church here in Oxford from the fall of 1957 until the fall of 1965, and this was the parish church with which the Faulkner family was affiliated. I officiated at the funeral of Mr. Faulkner's mother, Maud Butler Falkner, and at the funeral of Mr. Faulkner himself; and I think that's the reason I was asked to say a few words this afternoon. Indeed, it was suggested to me that I might read certain portions of Scripture that were read at Mr. Faulkner's funeral *and* that I might recall some of the things that I had to say at his funeral. The first of these things I can do, and I will in a moment; but the second is much more difficult, since I made no comments at Mr. Faulkner's funeral—there was no sermon or eulogy. I just read the Burial Office from the Episcopal Church's Book of Common Prayer.

That was the prevailing practice in the Episcopal Church in those days: no sermon, or eulogy, at a funeral. In those days we made much of the fact that death is the great equalizer. Fame and fortune and other human distinctions mean little at this point; and the funeral service was to be essentially the same for everyone, whoever or whatever he or she might be. The practice has changed somewhat in recent years, but thirty-five years ago we were acting very much in the Episcopal Church's tradition with no sermon, no eulogy, at Mr. Faulkner's funeral.

The service was held in the parlor at Rowan Oak with only the family and a few close friends present. I read the Burial Office there, and then we moved to St. Peter's Cemetery for the interment and the graveside service—again from the Book of Common Prayer. But here again, no sermon, no eulogy.

All of which calls to mind something that Mr. Faulkner wrote in an article for *Holiday* magazine in 1954. We have all heard about Mr. Bill's "preaching" Mammy Callie's funeral in Rowan Oak back in January 1940. Mammy Callie had been born into slavery before the Civil War. She was freed at age sixteen, and she had been the Faulkner family's house servant for many, many years. Mr. Bill felt especially close to her. We have a record of some of the words that he spoke at Mammy Callie's funeral, and they were words of love and affection, respect and appreciation, for one who had been so much a part of the Falkner family. In recalling all of this in that 1954 magazine article, Faulkner wrote the following, referring to himself in the third person:

> And the middleaging (man) did indeed lay back and preach the sermon, the oration, hoping that when his turn came there would be someone in the world to owe him the sermon which all owed to her, who had been, as he had been from infancy, within the scope and range of that fidelity and that devotion, and that rectitude.

. . . hoping that *when his turn came* there would be *someone in* the world to owe *him* the *sermon* which all owed to her.

Certainly, on that weekend of July 6 and 7, 1962, the world was filled with testimonials of praise and respect for William Cuthbert Faulkner—eulogies, if you will, proclaimed through every medium available; but there was no sermon, no eulogy, in the parlor of Rowan Oak that day; only the Burial Office from the Book of Common Prayer. But that, of course, was precisely what he had requested; that his funeral be brief and simple, family only, no flowers, no fuss—"Just like Mother's," as he put it. Of course, I had done his mother's funeral, and his—the service itself—*was* just like hers in almost every respect.

The priest and family do have some options as to what Psalms are to be used, what other passages of Scripture may be read, and what additional prayers might be said. For William Faulkner's funeral, considering his preoccupation with human suffering and what its meaning might be, along with what I see as his ultimate optimism with reference to the future of the human race, I read, among other things, these verses from the 46th Psalm:

> God is our hope and strength, a very present help in trouble.
> Therefore will we not fear, though the earth be moved, and though the hills be carried into the midst of the sea;
> Though the waters thereof rage and swell, and though the mountains shake at the tempest of the same.
> There is a river, the streams whereof make glad the city of God; the holy place of the tabernacle of the Most Highest.
> God is in the midst of her, therefore shall she not be removed; God shall help her, and that right early.

Be still then, and know that I am God: I will be exalted among the nations, and I will be exalted in the earth.

The Lord of hosts is with us; the God of Jacob is our refuge.

And I read these words from Paul's Epistle to the Romans:

As many as are led by the Spirit of God, they are the sons of God. For ye have not received the spirit of bondage again to fear; but ye have received the Spirit of adoption, whereby we cry, Abba, Father. The Spirit himself beareth witness with our spirit that we are the children of God; and if children, then heirs; heirs of God and joint-heirs with Christ; if so be that we suffer with him, that we may be also glorified together. For I reckon that the sufferings of this present time are not worthy to be compared with the glory which shall be revealed in us. For the earnest expectation of the creature waiteth for the manifestation of the sons of God. . . . What shall we then say to these things? If God be for us, who can be against us? . . . Who shall separate us from the love of Christ? Shall tribulation, or distress, or persecution, or famine, or nakedness, or peril, or sword? Nay, in all these things we are more than conquerors through him that loved us. For I am persuaded that neither death, nor life, nor angels, nor principalities, nor powers, nor things present, nor things to come, nor height, nor depth, nor any other creature, shall be able to separate us from the love of God, which is in Christ Jesus our Lord.

Then, in addition to the prescribed prayers and just before the final blessing, I used that well-known prayer for evening that seems to speak so well to the end of life as well:

O Lord, support us all the day long until the shadows lengthen and the evening comes, and the busy world is hushed, and the fever of life is over, and our work is done. Then in thy mercy grant us a safe lodging, and a holy rest, and peace at the last. Amen.

This is a bit of what was read and said at Mr. Faulkner's funeral. But now, at this late date, exactly one hundred years after his birth, and some thirty-five years after his death, I want to add a brief "sermon that I owe to him," as he put it in that *Holiday* magazine article; a testimonial, if you will, that might surprise him, but which I feel is so true and which is important to me.

I give thanks today for all that William Faulkner has meant to me, primarily as a writer; but also as a friend during those last five years of his life. But I want to thank him especially for being for me something of what he was for Walker Percy, who, you will remember, called Faulkner "a *theologian* in spite of himself." I think there is a lot of truth in that description, and I discovered it for myself as long ago as my days in theological seminary when I chose to write a paper for one of my classes on *The Sound and the Fury* and *As I Lay Dying*. I was fascinated then, as I am now, with his use of Holy Week as the framework for *The Sound and the Fury* and with Dilsey's Easter faith providing what seems to be the only note of triumph in the whole Compson saga. I know there is much disagreement about the meaning of all this, just as there is about the innumerable other Biblical references in Faulkner's writings up to and including *A Fable*, which is built entirely around Holy Week and Easter. But I still see the man as Walker Percy did: as "a theologian in spite of himself."

Apart from a few broad themes such as the triumph of the Snopeses over a fading aristocracy, I don't think Mr. Faulkner spent much time in figuring out what "message" he wanted to get across in his writings—and certainly he was not concerned with some specifically "religious" message. As he said himself so many times, he was primarily a storyteller, not a man of ideas. And yet, writing from the depths of his being inevitably he communicates a lot about himself in his writings; who he is and where he's coming from; his basic ideas about human life on this planet. And his writings do exhibit some common theological themes.

For example, whatever he may have called it, he certainly had a strong belief in what the Church has always called Original Sin! He saw that we human beings have in common a basic self-centeredness that tends to dominate our outlook on life and that is at the root of so much of the evil and injustice with which the world is filled. . . . He understood sin and guilt as profoundly corporate, as well as individual, in nature; and he knew how profoundly individual behaviour could be influenced by corporate sin and guilt. . . . Certainly doom and damnation are favorite Faulkner themes, but he also has lots to say about human dignity; a dignity that is manifested by some men and women in their rebellion against that doom that is set before them; by proving through compassion and pity, patience and endurance, love and action, that they are, indeed, superior to circumstance.

And then there are those instances in which Faulkner goes somewhat further than this. Remember the closing scene from *Requiem for a Nun* that speaks once again of doom and damnation, but which also takes a tentative look through Nancy Mannigoe at what must be our only ultimate hope. Temple, the mother of the infant child whom Nancy has killed, but who also shares in the guilt, says to Nancy: "Is there a heaven, Nancy?" And Nancy answers, "I don't know. I believes."

                    Temple
Believe what?

                    Nancy
I don't know. But I believes.

Then a few moments later, Temple asks:

Nancy. . . . What about me? Even if there is one (a heaven) and somebody waiting in it to forgive me, there's still tomorrow and tomorrow. And suppose tomorrow and tomorrow, and then nobody there, nobody waiting to forgive me——

And Nancy replies:

Believe.

Temple
   Believe what, Nancy? Tell me.

                                    Nancy
Believe.

Just believe. ". . . a faith that shall prevail, that the world cannot conquer, nor Yoknapatawpha County defeat. . . ." (Gabriel Vahanian)—that's what Nancy represents; and I think this may very well represent Mr. Faulkner as well: a nonspecific, rather generalized conviction that what he called the "eternal verities" would ultimately prevail.

The William Faulkner I knew considered himself a Christian—at least in the broadest sense of that word. He would not have passed any test of theological orthodoxy, nor would he have wanted to; nor did he have close ties with organized religion. However, he did consider himself a member of St. Peter's Church, albeit a rather inactive one, and he thought of the Rector of St. Peter's as his Pastor—or "Padre," as he put it. He thought of himself as a somewhat unorthodox, or even maverick, Christian; but he said grace at meals—at least in my presence—and he believed in a God who cared about the world that He had made and about the people in it. . . . The crucifixion of Jesus held a fascination for him because of his own preoccupation with the meaning of human suffering. . . . He believed in some sort of life after death, and he expressed the same to me on more than one occasion. And I believe this belief became stronger as his own days grew shorter. . . . Apart from these few basics, I think he would have pled agnostic; about the ultimate nature of God and the nature of God's relationship with His creatures; about the details of a systematic theology. . . . I think he wrestled with such things in much of his writing, but I'm sure he never saw it as "doing theology!" Still, I wonder sometimes about what has been called his "obsession" with Christian symbols and themes; about his intimate knowledge of the Bible and his so very frequent references to it; and about his apparent fondness for Bishop Jeremy Taylor's two little books *Holy Living* and *Holy Dying*—devotional tracts usually read only by devout Christians.

In any event, I think I can best close with a quote from someone who shares my perception of William Faulkner as "a theologian in spite of himself." Dr. Robert Johnson, in an address at one of the early Faulkner conferences some twenty years ago here at Ole Miss, had this to say, and I would like to say it with him:

> Faulkner is for me a witness to the Christian story of sin and redemption. His power seems anchored in that of the Black Christian community. His vision, like theirs, is cruciform in character, a vision that knows more about exile than exodus, more about crucifixion than resurrection, but a great deal about the capacities of the human heart for survival. It is a prescient, unsophisticated faith. (As with the powerful singing coming from the black church at the end of *Soldiers' Pay*): "It was nothing, it was everything. . . .

That, Mr. Bill, is the "sermon I owe you," even if it is thirty-five years late! Thank you for being a "theologian in spite of yourself"; and congratulations on number one hundred!

"He Was Writing"

Donald M. Kartiganer

Sherwood Anderson once said to Faulkner: "You've too much talent. You can do it too easy, in too many different ways. If you're not careful, you'll never write anything." As we look back now on Faulkner's life and career, it is abundantly clear that indeed he had talent, enormous talent, and that he could realize it in many different ways. He might have done it "easy"—as Anderson shrewdly warned him—but instead he became one of the most daring, most innovative writers of his time, in virtually every novel trying something new, something he had not done before, often something no one else had done either. He once wrote, "I'm trying to say it all in one sentence, between one Cap and one period. I'm still trying to put it all, if possible, on one pinhead. I don't know how to do it. All I know to do is to keep on trying in a new way."

Writing was his life; in a strange sense it seems to have been all of his life. There are several fine biographies of Faulkner, and yet in all of them there is always that impenetrable corner of his identity to which biographers invariably come: some secret self in front of which he placed the various roles he played, the masks he put on: the long history of poses and posturing: the wounded World War I pilot, the bohemian artist, the dandy, the town bum, the tough-guy bootlegger, the farmer, the gentleman rider. Apart from those roles, his habit was often silence, an apparent remoteness that even his longtime Oxford acquaintances could not penetrate. Phil Mullen put it succinctly: "Bill Faulkner and I were not what you could call intimate friends. I doubt if he had any."

A Hollywood friend described Faulkner's well-known capacity for silence. He would occasionally take Faulkner on long drives: "I always talked," he later recalled, "because [Faulkner] never said a thing; he never said one word. I found the silence a little difficult to stand, so to fill the silence, I would talk about hunting or trucking trips I had made out of Fresno in my youth. Once, during one of my transitions or pauses, Bill said, 'Bud,' and I said, 'Yeah, what is it, Bill?' He said, 'Bud, you're an animal, but I'm just a vegetable.' "

What did he mean? A vegetable because he had nothing to say? Or because he required the most attentive cultivation? Or because, although forced to exist among animals, he was of another species entirely?

An incredibly keen observer of the world, he chose either to stand apart from it or to relate to it only through the screen of his masquerades. What was it that the masks, the remoteness protected? Was there a self he dared not reveal, or one he did not know and wished in his roles to discover? Was he afraid that the world would not accept him as he was, or did he know, beneath it all, that he was simply, and supremely, an artist?

When I first visited Oxford, at the 1987 Faulkner conference, I heard a story, several versions of which I have heard since—not, as it turns out, describing the same incident, but referring to an incident which happened more than once. A woman at the conference, who had grown up in Oxford but since moved away, remembered how as a four- or five-year old in the 1950s she once encountered the famous writer. She was playing on the sidewalk outside her home, when she noticed a man walking toward her—tweed jacket, khaki trousers, pipe—headed for the Square. As he came abreast, she said "Good morning." The man kept on walking without saying a word. The little girl burst into tears and dashed into the house. Upon questioning by her mother, she explained what had happened. The description of the man (and possibly his behavior) left no doubt in the mother's mind as to his identity. Immediately she was on the phone to Maud Falkner, William's mother. "Miss Maud, this is ——; you have *got* to do something about that son of yours! He just walked past my little girl in the street without so much as a hello, and she's standing here crying her heart out!"

"That son of yours," was, of course, over fifty years old at the time, and already the recipient of the most prestigious literary honor in the world. And apparently Maud Falkner—who had three sons at the time, two of them living in Oxford—did not have to ask *which* son had committed the social infraction. "I will talk to Billy," she said, but she urged the mother to tell her daughter that he meant no harm. "He just didn't see her," Maud insisted, "he was writing."

He was writing. This is what he did, this is what he was. It was not that the life around him meant nothing to him or that it could not touch him, sometimes with delight, sometimes with despair. But whatever occurred, his devotion to his work was staggering in its intensity and, ultimately, in the greatness of what he wrote. During his most productive years, the fourteen-year period from 1929 to 1942, Faulkner published ten novels and wrote seventy short stories. Six or seven of the novels, a score of the stories, are among the indisputably major works of American literature.

In the midst of it all, he was by no means immune to hardship: to the economic impact of the Great Depression or to devastating personal tragedy. Because of the financial difficulties that dogged him for most of his career, he was forced to do eight different tours of duty, of varying length, as a screenwriter in Hollywood. In 1931, his first child died shortly after her premature birth; in 1935 his youngest brother Dean was killed in a plane crash. His terrible sorrow over daughter and brother are well-known; yet the fact is, nothing could stop him. The year that his daughter died, he published sixteen stories and began *Light in August*, which he completed in six months. Following the death of his brother, he moved into his mother's house, where his widowed sister-in-law was also staying. He was there for several weeks, during which time, working nights on the dining room table, he completed the final chapters of his greatest novel, *Absalom, Absalom!*

Perhaps as much as the books themselves, Faulkner's commitment to them, his dedication, astonishes us and moves us. Asked once about his writing schedule, he simply said: "I write when the spirit moves me, and the spirit moves me every day." As for the real life he wondrously articulated in fiction, it became the necessary arena within which he acted, but outside of which he chose to live. He seemed to stride the world a foot above it, observing, absorbing all of it, even as he passed it by, pursuing what he once called the "dream of perfection."

As his mother said: he was writing.

For Literature, for Faulkner

RICHARD HOWORTH

In the process of preparing the commemorative booklet I hope you received when you came in, and in thinking about what on earth I might say here today, I've done a bit of research, a good deal of ruminating, on William Faulkner, his books, his life here in our town, the life of our town, the life of the bookstore, and how—regarding William Faulkner—those things and perspective about those things, have grown, changed, affected each other, and so on.

It's complicated, and fortunately for you there isn't time here for me to fully expound on all that.

So many questions, especially recently, I'm asked on these matters. Most, particularly the press, for their own good reasons, want short answers. There are no good short answers—not that I have, anyway. Scholars have written books, often centered on a single theme. In fact, more than fifteen hundred books have been written about Faulkner's work, more than on any other American writer.

There is one question many people ask me for which there is a short answer: How does he sell? Between April and September this year (I know this period because a magazine recently asked for my top paperback fiction sellers in this period), *Absalom, Absalom!* was number four, and *The Sound and the Fury* was number eight.

But for the more complex matters, regarding his life, his history, his work, there are no easy answers. Before Square Books had become a year old, I was already dealing with this, trying to sharpen my own judgment with the much greater wisdom of others. In the spring of 1980 I wrote Joseph Blotner, Elizabeth Kerr, Cleanth Brooks, John Pilkington, and Robert Penn Warren and asked each what Faulkner work and what works about Faulkner they'd recommend to the novice Faulkner reader.

Elizabeth Kerr sent me her entire syllabus. Dr. Pilkington recommended *Sartoris* and, for criticism, Cleanth Brooks's three indispensable books. Joe Blotner felt the most accessible novel is *Light in August*, although "some people have been grabbed by *As I Lay Dying* and others by *The Sound and the Fury*, hard as it is." (The problem many novice

Faulkner readers have is the tendency to jump in with his most famous books, which are also his most difficult.) For criticism Blotner also recommended Brooks, and Calvin Brown's *A Glossary of Faulkner's South* (a great book, now out of print. So much Faulkner material flows in and out of print).

Cleanth Brooks, after remarking that "there has been an enormous amount of rubbish written about Faulkner's life and especially his work," recommended Blotner and Malcolm Cowley's *Portable Faulkner*, the book which, when it came out in 1946, reinvigorated Faulkner's career.

Robert Penn Warren's response came on a typed, plain postcard which I had tacked on the wall of the bookstore for many years. He, too, recommended Brooks and Cowley.

Faulkner himself frequently pointed beginning readers to *The Unvanquished*, and I like to suggest, along with these, *The Reivers* and the short stories, the latter in part because I think Faulkner sometimes is not recognized enough for his mastery of short fiction.

One of the earliest and best pieces on Faulkner, my personal favorite, is the essay Warren wrote that appeared in the *New Republic* in 1946. Among other things, Warren truly understood Faulkner on the subjects of race and the South.

But of all the things I've considered and read by and about Faulkner, what serves as my touchstone (not just for Faulkner, but as a way of measuring all literature or any writer) is Robert Penn Warren's essay "On Reading Fiction."

In that piece he makes a very convincing point that the reason we read fiction is because it is the best way for us to have the experience of life we can't have for ourselves, because drama or "story" in life simply isn't there all the time. Let's face it: life is mostly pretty boring. Or it just is not available to us, nor practical for us, to experience at will, and personally, great danger or passion, triumph or deep failure, the way that we can vicariously through characters in fiction.

There is no learning of life like the personal experience of life. It is fiction successfully rendered, then, that informs us, better than anything, about our own lives. Faulkner did this—created in fiction history and characters and stories that enrich our lives—more vividly and completely—better than, okay?—any writer has, most agree, since Shakespeare.

If I can take a brief detour here as a way to salute today living writers along with the dead (I think it's something Faulkner would like me to do, though I must add I am reluctant to invoke "what Faulkner would want" because we've heard a bit much of that lately. I'm reminded of my youngest child, who the other day came home from school with a bracelet.

"What is that?" her mother and I asked. "A bracelet. Everybody in my class has one." We noticed the letters "W.W.J.D.?" on it. "Where did you get it?" "Wal-Mart," she answered. "What does 'W.W.J.D.?' mean?" "It means," she said, "What Would Jesus Do?" So I've been thinking I'll have made some bracelets—to sell in the bookstore—W.W.F.D.?"— "What Would Faulkner Do?" Not really, of course. I won't do that, and nobody else in this town had better try it, either.)

At any rate, I want to mention one of the other things I found digging through old papers and letters to find the notes from Mr. Warren and the others. It's an essay by Cleanth Brooks called "An Affair of Honor: Larry Brown's *Joe*." I think it appeared only in a newsletter publication from Larry Brown's publisher, Algonquin.

It opens by saying "Larry Brown's hometown is the same as William Faulkner's, Oxford, Mississippi. But his novel, *Joe*, is not imitation Faulkner. Brown has his own style and is quite comfortable in it. Nevertheless, the Beat Four district of Yoknapatawpha County peeps through in it." We don't have time for the whole thing—it's a wonderful piece—but he later says, concerning the title character, Joe Ransom, that "to shape and present this special kind of character convincingly is a formidable test of any author's powers." And that "a story has been told to us, a story that is significant."

That Faulkner chose to use for his material, as Larry Brown has, this world around us, right outside the doors of Fulton Chapel here, giving us the Bundrens and the Compsons, the McCaslins, the Sartorises, Joe Christmas, Lucas Beauchamp, and all the others, is something for which I feel remarkably lucky. Sometimes some of us here feel that the beam of scholarship and publicity on Faulkner shines a little too bright for the rest of us, this week especially. That's a light that shines on our own lives. But there's probably no better way to understand it than through the fiction of William Faulkner.

A Tribute to William Faulkner

LARRY BROWN

A long time ago when I was a boy, I was an avid reader of "boy and dog" stories like *Goodbye My Lady* by James Street, *Old Yeller* by Fred Gipson, *Where the Red Fern Grows* by Wilson Rawls, and *Stormy*, by Jim Kjelgaard. I had dogs of my own and when I wasn't in school I prowled the river bottoms and wooded ridges around Tula, the vast hardwood forests known by their names almost like people: the Big W, London Hill, Round Station, Old Dallas, the Crocker Woods. There were little sand roads that curved through these holdings of timber, and the woods were alive with deer and squirrels, bobcats and raccoons, foxes and hawks and owls, and birds of every variety, even the pileated woodpecker, known to the old folks as the Indian hen. I hunted at first with a single barrel twelve gauge Victor Special given to me by my great-uncle, Dave Hallman. It was already an old gun when it was passed down to me, but it would still shoot. For a while, it would. The breech lock was so worn down that somebody had built it back up with a torch and a brazing rod, but sometimes it would fly open after the shot. I remedied that by tying the barrel to the receiver with a strip of leather, but one day the whole thing simply flew apart in my hands. Where it leans now reassembled in my gun cabinet, it is missing the trigger guard, and the badly scarred stock bears a deep yellow vein of glue that some former owner must have used to fix a long crack, and all the metal parts wear the same brown and dull sheen common to antiques, not rust, just old age. But it was my first gun, and for a long time it was the only one I had, and having it rest in the gun cabinet among the newer and shinier models is kind of like putting a favorite horse out to pasture, feeding him well, and letting him live out his days in peace. But the old shotgun holds another, more special meaning to me. I was using that gun when I first started reading William Faulkner.

I was born in Oxford but was taken to Memphis at the age of three, and for the next ten years I was educated in the Memphis city schools, learned to skate on steel wheels on Memphis sidewalks, and spent years watching the great trains rumble down the length of the Southern Avenue tracks. Another thing I did was visit my relatives in Lafayette County, my grandmother and aunts and uncles and cousins, who farmed, had milk cows and chickens and dogs. They fished and they hunted. My cousins played baseball on a red dirt field at a place called Yocona. I remember Oxford as a magical place with dime stores on the square and dusty pickup trucks loaded with watermelons and tomatoes and purple hull peas, men on the sidewalks wearing overalls. Back then you saw a lot of snap brim hats, and people sat on the benches under the oaks around the courthouse talking and spitting tobacco juice. I remember the Golden Rule, Metts Hardware, Winter's Cafe. I loved to go to the square when I was a boy in hopes that I would see my grandfather, Max Brown, who sold shoes for Grace Crockett, or to walk into a store that sold candy and buy a nickel's worth in a small white bag.

But those trips were rare. They only lasted for a couple of days most of the time, and then we'd go back to Memphis and school. I knew I belonged in Mississippi and I longed to be in Mississippi, specifically, at Tula, where most all my closest connections lived, but it wasn't until 1964 that we came back home for good.

I was not a rebellious boy but I felt like there were many important boy things I had missed: I had never owned a dog. I had never fired a gun. I didn't know how to swim. I had never been able to run wild in Mississippi, and I knew by then that this was my birthright, irrevocably, undeniably mine. So when the chance came, that's what I did. I studied only enough to get from one grade to the next. I spent most of my time totally unencumbered, running around with the other eight or ten boys my age who lived around Tula, camping out, smoking grapevines or swinging on them, catching fish, riding bicycles for miles over dirt roads, sitting around the store listening to old men tell stories, growing up at long last in the country. And then I began to hunt. There were many nights I should have been studying that were spent roaming black woods with high rubber boots and six volt flashlights and following bellowing dogs, blueticks, black and tans, redbones. We'd go hunting with fifteen dogs, an entire pickup load of them, speckled and spotted, gigantic hounds named from the Bible: Nimrod, Naman, Lisa, rigid tails curved over their backs, growling, snarling, fights breaking out sometimes, even going down the road. And I loved every minute of it. When I was that young I could sit frozen for hours under a tree on the white frost that covered the leaves and wait for a deer to step down a trail or for a squirrel to drop a hickory nut at the wrong time. I loved hunting, the life, the woods, the cold, the blood, the smells and the sounds. There was not much land posted in Lafayette County at that time. A boy could go just about anywhere he wanted to with his dog and his gun. And I availed myself of it fully, at every chance I got. One day I climbed the highest cypress in the Yocona River bottom, and I spent nearly one whole day lost in the Holly Springs National Forest. And I read books about the outdoors and hunting by Ernest Hemingway, Frank Buck, Jack London, and finally, William Faulkner.

A joiner-planer is a machine that runs a cutting edge at high speed. It's used to cut a piece of wood into a certain shape. We had one in our shop at Lafayette County High School, and one day about thirty years ago, a friend of mine accidentally stuck two of his fingers into it and lost the fingernails and the flesh attached to them. Gary had to go to the hospital and stay for a while, and I suppose one of the teachers got up the idea for all of us to chip in and buy him some books to read while he was recuperating. One of those books was *Big Woods*, and after Gary had healed up and come back to school, the books were passed around to his classmates and friends. And that was where I discovered "The Bear."

It's sometimes hard to remember an actual reading experience when that much time has passed, but I knew when I was sixteen years old that I had never seen anything like it. There was so much in there that touched me: the brooding wilderness and what it looked like, the quest for one dog that could bay and hold the great bear until the men could arrive with the guns, the steady encroaching of civilization into the wild place that the boy Ike McCaslin knew like the back of his hand, and the irrevocable changing of the landscape by what man calls progress, which to me then and still is now the saddest part of that story. And just imagine, I thought: a man made up that story. I probably can't honestly say that I appreciated the story on the level I now appreciate it. Back then I had never written any stories or books of my own. I simply loved reading, loved a good story, loved to go to another world through pages and leave this one behind. To me the true test of a piece of writing is a story that does not die in the mind, that is never forgotten, and the characters in the story are like people you have met in your life, who will be friends until like the preacher says death do you part. That story lives on in my mind and Ike McCaslin still walks those woods, and the bear still roams, and the dogs still follow him. I said earlier that he made it up, but that was not totally accurate. He had to know what a pack of hounds sounds like when they're all funneling down a ridge with a leaping buck ahead of them, and their cries and howls are echoing up and down the length of the woods, and he had to know about the buck's warm breath coming cloudlike into the cold air, and how incredibly fast he comes, and how hard it is to hit him on the run. He had to know about the fellowship of men in the woods, cooking and eating and drinking and playing cards in deer camp, and how quickly dark comes at the edge of a black slough in a river bottom when the dogs' voices are fading, going out of hearing. It was about a simpler time of horses and mules and wagons, a time before bulldozers and four-wheelers invaded into the deepest reaches of the forest and stilled the cries of those Indian hens. It was written like a legend or a myth and to me it is a legend and a myth, able to stir in a forty-six-year-old man the same feelings it invoked in a sixteen-year-old boy, timeless and not lessened or diminished by a span as long or as short as thirty years.

Since that time I've read the story again and again, and it never fails to hold a certain wonder for me, and in a large part because "The Bear" compelled me to start reading his other books, his other works, the stories and the novels that are known throughout the world. In later years they became more than just great books to read; they became tools for learning how to create my own characters and settings. They taught me what to write about and how to say things, how to portray the landscape as a vast background for the action that plays out among characters. They taught me that the little touches are important in fiction, the slash of a cold rain on the face or the warble of a bird sitting on a springtime branch. They taught me determination and perseverance, to keep on writing in the face of constant failure.

His work is the solid proof of what one man can do as a writer if he is deeply committed to his craft and is willing to spend those thousands of days and nights alone with the work. He continues to hold up a standard for young writers everywhere, a greatness to aspire to, because every young writer has to have hope, has to have somebody to look up to.

When I think about him walking around the streets of this town, I think of him with pipe in hand, maybe a little cloud of smoke following him, wearing a scuffed tweed jacket and deep in thought, not brooding or unfriendly, but probably thinking about what he had just written or what he was about to write. I never fail to be touched by the peace and the solitude of Rowan Oak whenever I'm down there, and the quietness that just pervades that place. It's almost as if you're scared to raise your voice, as if there might be some chance he's sitting in there at that old Underwood, the pipe in the tray beside it, the clacking of the keys going, a story in progress.

The most inspiring thing for me is to look at that house and to know about him sitting in that room back there, all alone, unmindful of the world about him when the work was at hand, and to think about all the books and stories that came out of there. It's almost as if I can feel him still there, if in nothing more than the way the wind blows through those tall cedars on a pretty fall afternoon, in the quiet crunch of your shoes going up the drive through the pea gravel and under those big trees.

What was more than a good hunting story held the quiet longings of a boy's heart, and the passing of an era, as his has passed now too. He must have worried and struggled like all other men worry and struggle, to put bread on the table and buy clothes and insurance, but none of that can be seen from reading his books. It is the work that remains, and the names of the people who live in the books are immortalized: Flem Snopes, Sam Fathers, Emily Grierson, Major de Spain, Joe Christmas, Temple Drake, Addie Bundren, Boon Hogganbeck, Ike McCaslin.

I can only wish now that somehow I could have seen him just one time walking around the square, for somebody to nudge me, point to him, and say: "There goes William Faulkner."

A young writer starts out knowing nothing and trying to write about it, and it's only after enough time and work that he or she finds out that the condition of the human being is endlessly varied and an inexhaustible source of material for fiction, and that the truths of the human heart are the only things worth writing about, exactly as Mr. Faulkner has said.

He and a handful of other writers have been the people I've looked up to in trying in my own way to write about he human condition, and his example is still ongoing and invaluable to me. I'm still in awe of the sentences he was able to make, the stories he was able to tell, the people he was able to create. Those people walk around in my mind long after the book has been closed, and his contribution to the world's literature has already been made solid and lasting by that great leveler of all things, time.

I'm particularly proud to be known as a Mississippi writer, and I'm probably happier than anything about having the great good luck to be born in the town that Mr. Faulkner called home. As sad as it is to think about him not being here to see the things that have been done today, it's wonderful to know that what he did with his life will always live on in the bookshelves of the world.

I thank him deeply for what he has done, and on this day, like everybody else in town today, I wish him a Happy Birthday.

"Like a Big Soft Fading Wheel": The Triumph of Faulkner's Art

ROBERT W. HAMBLIN

Upon the occasion of his receiving the Nobel Prize for Literature in Stockholm in 1950, William Faulkner responded with a speech which is now generally acknowledged to be the best (certainly it is the most famous) ever given by a Nobel recipient. In the memorable phrasing of that speech Faulkner celebrated both finished works of art and the artists who craft them, calling attention to artistic achievement that is made even more impressive and ennobling because it is produced through "anguish and travail," "in the agony and sweat of the human spirit." Few in Faulkner's 1950 audience could know how much of his own personal history was embodied in such words as "anguish" and "agony." Today, of course, because we have read biographies of Faulkner by Joseph Blotner and others, we are better able to understand and appreciate not only the greatness of Faulkner's art but also his greatness as an individual artist, one whose literary genius and unswerving dedication to his art conjoined to enable him to transform personal misfortune and disappointment and tragedy and grief—to use his words, "anguish" and "agony"—into novels and stories that continue to give every evidence, even in a world much different from the one Faulkner lived in, that they will "endure and prevail."

Even though Faulkner once claimed it was "[his] ambition to be, as a private individual, abolished and voided from history, leaving it markless, no refuse save the printed books," I believe it is incumbent upon us, as we gather here in Faulkner's birthplace to commemorate the one hundredth anniversary of his birth, to recall and celebrate both the work and the man, not only the monumental work that survives to delight and instruct its readers but also the dedicated artist who struggled and sacrificed and suffered to create that work. In the hope of accomplishing this dual purpose, I shall frame my remarks with a discussion of the text and context of a short story Faulkner wrote in 1942 entitled "Shall Not Perish." While no one, I think, would contend that this is one of Faulkner's greatest stories, and while Faulkner himself labeled the story as "Topical, not too good," "Shall Not Perish" serves my intention well because it includes some of Faulkner's most serious reflections on the nature of art and the artist.

In "Shall Not Perish," Faulkner movingly describes the reaction of a small boy from rural Mississippi upon observing for the first time the paintings that hang in a town museum much like the Mary Buie Museum in Oxford. There the youngster views paintings like the one executed by William Dunlap as part of this Centennial celebration—as Faulkner describes them,

> pictures from all over the United States, painted by people who loved what they had seen or where they had been born or lived enough to want to paint pictures of it so that other people could see it too; pictures of men and women and children, and the houses and streets and cities and the woods and fields and streams where they worked or lived or pleasured, so that all the people who wanted to, people like us from Frenchman's Bend or from littler places even than Frenchman's Bend in our county or beyond our state too, could come without charge into the cool and the quiet and look without let at the pictures of men and women and children who were the same people that we were even if their houses and barns were different and their fields worked different, with different things growing in them.

Later, after leaving the museum and boarding a bus for the return trip home, the boy cannot forget the paintings he has viewed, and through them he feels an intimate kinship with the places and people he has seen depicted in the art. Faulkner writes:

> And so, even though the bus ran fast again, when the road finally straightened out into the long Valley stretch, there was only the last sunset spoking out across the sky, stretching all the way across America from the Pacific ocean, touching all the places that the men and women in the museum whose names we didn't even know had loved enough to paint pictures of them, like a big soft fading wheel.

Faulkner emphasizes the importance of this wheel metaphor by returning to it at the end of the story, as the boy recalls again the way the museum paintings have created in him a recognition of the identity between his small provincial world and the larger world beyond.

> It was like the wheel, like the sunset itself, hubbed at that little place that don't even show on a map, that not two hundred people out of all the earth know is named Frenchman's Bend or has any name at all, and spoking out in all the directions and touching them all, never a one too big for it to touch, never a one too little to be remembered:—the places that men and women

have lived in and loved whether they had anything to paint pictures of them with or not, all the little places quiet enough to be lived in and loved and the names of them before they were quiet enough and the names of the deeds that made them quiet enough and the names of the men and the women who did the deeds, who lasted and endured. . . .

The passages I have just quoted are among Faulkner's most powerful tributes to artists and the art they create. Here Faulkner pays homage to the capacity of art to both record and transcend the life it captures and, as a result, to inspire its participants to a greater awareness and understanding of the human condition. In "Shall Not Perish" the artists celebrated are painters, but that detail hardly disguises the fact that Faulkner's comments embrace his own specialty of literary art as well. In fact, as I hope to demonstrate, there are some deeply personal elements encoded in Faulkner's text.

First of all, we should note the context in which the Grier boy's visit to the museum occurs. "Shall Not Perish" takes place during the first few months of World War II; and the boy's older brother Pete, the reader learns, has been the first casualty of that war from Yoknapatawpha County. Now word has just been received that a second soldier, the son of Major de Spain of Jefferson, has also been killed. Mrs. Grier, accompanied by her remaining son, who is only nine years old, goes to Jefferson to offer sympathy and comfort to Major de Spain in his bitterness and despair. Following the visit to de Spain, Mrs. Grier takes her young son to the town museum, where he views the paintings that, like his mother's commiseration with Major de Spain, celebrate human empathy and solidarity. Not insignificantly, Faulkner's text identifies the museum as "a house like a church," an altogether appropriate description since in the museum the young boy experiences something very like a religious epiphany, a rush of sudden insight in which he comes to understand his kinship with human beings from other places and times. Thus, we note, Faulkner encapsulates a tribute to art, and the humanizing effect of that art, within a text that treats the personal and communal tragedies of war, death, and grief.

This merging of art and death is hardly coincidental. In numerous interviews and public statements, Faulkner expressed his belief that all artistic endeavors are ways of "saying No to death," of "scratch[ing] 'Kilroy was here' on the last wall of the universe," or, as he expressed it in *Absalom, Absalom!*, of leaving "an undying mark on the blank face of the oblivion to which we are all doomed." But art is not only the artist's personal protest against time and death; it is also, as Faulkner noted in his Nobel Prize Acceptance Speech, "one of the props, the pillars to help

[man] endure and prevail." It accomplishes that goal, as do the paintings in "Shall Not Perish," "by lifting [man's] heart, by reminding him of the courage and honor and hope and pride and compassion and pity and sacrifice which have been the glory of his past."

Morever, it is important to note that Faulkner wrote "Shall Not Perish" not only during a time of national catastrophe but also during a period of extreme artistic, financial, and personal distress. His letters of this period to his agent Harold Ober and others reflect the desperation of his situation. For example, when he sought Ober's assistance in placing the story "Knight's Gambit" with a magazine, he enclosed a letter which stated: "As always, I am broke. If and when this sells, will you get the check to me as soon as you can." A short while later, in agreeing to rewrite another story, "Snow," according to Ober's request, Faulkner wrote: "Thank you for advance two weeks ago. If you have anything else of mine which any editor ever intimated he might buy if it were simplified, send that back too. As usual, I am not quite a boat's length ahead of the sheriff."

An index of how terribly low Faulkner's spirits had sunk is the letter he wrote to Whit Burnett, the noted editor, who had asked Faulkner to recommend one of his stories for an anthology Burnett was compiling. Faulkner wrote:

> Choose anything of mine you want to and that is convenient. I have become so damned frantic trying to make a living and keep my grocer etc. from putting me in bankruptcy for the last year that nothing I or any body else ever wrote seems worth anything to me anymore. Sorry I couldn't have helped you and best wishes for the anthology. I thought I had written you before to this effect, but I have been so worried lately with trying to write pot-boilers and haunting the back door of the post-office for checks that dont come to keep a creditor with a bill from catching me on the street, that I dont remember anything anymore.

Faulkner's inability to earn a living from his writing at this stage of his career led him to seek a commission in the naval reserve, which he anticipated would secure him a desk job with the Bureau of Aeronautics in Washington, D.C., at a salary of $3,200 a year. While the patriotic and militaristic side of Faulkner's nature was attracted to the possibility of serving his country during wartime, the projected salary was far less than that needed to satisfy his debtors. For this reason Faulkner had also initiated a search for a screenwriting job in Hollywood. In late June 1942 Faulkner described his rapidly deteriorating financial situation in a letter to Bennett Cerf, one of his publishers at Random House.

> I have 60c in my pocket, and that is literally all. I finished a story and sent it in yesterday, but with no real hope it will sell. My local creditors bother me,

but so far none has taken an action because I began last year to give them notes for debts. But the notes will come due soon and should I be sued, my whole house here will collapse: farm, property, everything.

Within a month of writing this letter Faulkner had found temporary relief from his dire financial circumstances by signing a lengthy movie contract with Warner Bros. He began work for the studio on July 27, 1942, at a salary of $300 a week, considerably less than the salaries writers of Faulkner's stature usually commanded in Hollywood, but somewhat more than the "anything above $100" weekly figure Faulkner had indicated to Harold Ober that he would be willing to take in order to obtain a regular salary. Faulkner spent much of the next three years in Hollywood, working on more than a dozen film projects; and while he resented the time movie work took away from his fiction, he was nevertheless grateful that the money he made ($500 a week by 1945) enabled him to pay off most of his debts. But the fact that he made this money from what he called "whoring" in Hollywood rather than through the sales of his novels and stories led him to question even more his stature and future as a serious writer. For example, in early 1944 he wrote Malcolm Cowley: "My mail consists of two sorts: from people who dont write, asking me for something, usually money, which being a serious writer trying to be an artist, I naturally dont have; and from people who do write telling me I cant." A little later in the same letter Faulkner lamented that he seemed destined "to leave no better mark on this our pointless chronicle than I seem to be about to leave."

Looking back on Faulkner's doleful situation in the early '40s from our perspective over a half-century later, with our knowledge of his eventual triumph over both critical neglect and financial difficulty, his Nobel Prize award, his ever-expanding international fame and reputation, his now-familiar picture adorning a commemorative stamp, and this month his centennial birthday being celebrated by events like this all around the world, we are struck with amazement and incredulity that this writer, the one who is unquestionably the greatest American novelist of the twentieth century, the one who has been called "the American Shakespeare," should, at age forty-five, with his greatest work already accomplished, have found himself largely unread, unappreciated, unmarketable, and unrewarded.

Our amazement and incredulity become even greater when we consider the nature of the artistic achievement Faulkner had already accomplished by age forty-five. In little more than a single decade, beginning with *The Sound and the Fury* in 1929 and continuing through *Go Down, Moses* in 1942, Faulkner produced, initially at the rate of one per year, a succession of truly outstanding novels, nearly every one of which has been advanced by one critic or another as his masterpiece. In keeping with our desire to pay tribute to Faulkner during this centennial celebration, let's briefly recount the history of those marvelous years of creativity.

In 1929, following a somewhat unimposing apprenticeship that included a volume of rather mediocre poems and three promising but largely undistinguished novels, Faulkner burst upon the literary scene like a giant meteor, producing *The Sound and the Fury*, the novel that would always remain Faulkner's personal favorite because, he said, it represented his "most magnificent failure." *The Sound and the Fury* recounts the tragic story of the collapse of the once-aristocratic Compson family, a poignant story made even more remarkable by the experimental strategy of narrating the action from four different perspectives, the first three of which are brilliant interior monologues of the type utilized by James Joyce and T. S. Eliot. The next year, 1930, Faulkner stretched this narrative device to its ultimate in *As I Lay Dying*, employing fifteen different characters to narrate the mock-epic journey of the rural Bundren family to transport the corpse of Addie, the wife and mother, to her burial place in Jefferson. In 1931 Faulkner published *Sanctuary*, which traces the moral corruption of an Ole Miss coed who is abducted and controlled by an amoral Memphis gangster. *Sanctuary* is one of the great horror stories in American literature and, interestingly, a novel that French critics have always championed as one of Faulkner's finest.

Light In August followed in 1932, with its brilliant counterpointing of the tragic lynching of Joe Christmas and the happy resolution of Lena Grove's search for a father for her newborn child. *Light in August* is not only a powerful indictment of racial hatred and religious fanaticism but also a testament, through Lena's successful quest, of mankind's ability, as Faulkner later expressed it, to "endure" and "prevail." In 1936 appeared *Absalom, Absalom!*, which many critics, including the present speaker, now rank as Faulkner's greatest novel. In this novel of miscegenation and the Civil War, readers meet Thomas Sutpen, unquestionably one of the supreme tragic heroes in all of literature. To speak of Sutpen is to speak of a character who belongs in the rare company of the biblical David, Hamlet, Lear, Adam of *Paradise Lost*, Faust, Ahab, Roskolnikov, or Kurtz—those individuals who seem to possess almost unlimited potential but tragically self-destruct because of significant weaknesses of character. It is one of the great ironies of American literary history that *Absalom, Absalom!*, which was ridiculed in the *New Yorker* by the influential Clifton Fadiman and generally ignored by the reading public, was published the same year as a far lesser novel of the Civil War, Margaret Mitchell's

Gone with the Wind, which went on to become an international bestseller and a world-famous movie.

In 1940 Faulkner published *The Hamlet*, the comic masterpiece which emulates the tradition of Mark Twain and the Southwestern humorists to trace the rise to power of the shrewd and rapacious Flem Snopes, surely one of the most despicable characters in modern literature. As Sinclair Lewis had done with "Babbit" and Joseph Heller would later do with "Catch-22," Faulkner with "Snopes" succeeded in adding a new term to the common vocabulary of the English language. In 1942 Faulkner closed out his greatest period of creativity with *Go Down, Moses*, dedicated to his beloved Negro mammy, Caroline Barr, and presenting his most passionate plea for racial justice and equality. The climax of this narrative is the section entitled "The Bear," which has been frequently printed as a separate story and is now universally acclaimed as one of the finest short narratives in the English language.

In addition to the seven masterpieces listed above, the period 1929–1942 also saw the publication of four additional novels; two impressive collections of short stories, including such world-renowned ones as "Red Leaves," "A Rose for Emily," "That Evening Sun," "Dry September," and "Wash"; and a second volume of poems. All in all, this period of Faulkner's career, which Melvin Backman has called "The Major Years" and John Pilkington has called "The Heart of Yoknapatawpha," represents a magical run of creativity that, in the aggregate, is unmatched in the annals of American, and perhaps world, literature. Merely to list the names of a few of the major characters that Faulkner invented during this period is to call attention to the monumentality of his achievement: Compson, Sutpen, Sartoris, McCaslin, Beauchamp, Snopes, Hightower, Varner, Dilsey, Temple Drake, Popeye, Ratliff, Stevens, Sam Fathers, Old Ben. Among novelists only Charles Dickens supplies us with as lengthy a list of memorable characters.

Now, having reviewed the remarkable artistic successes during his miracle years, as well as the critical neglect and financial distress that Faulkner was experiencing, I'd like to return to "Shall Not Perish" to consider what it reveals about Faulkner's ideas concerning his own artistic creation.

First of all, it seems quite evident that Faulkner, whether consciously or unconsciously, is paralleling the descriptions of the paintings that the young Grier boy views in the Jefferson museum to his own fiction. The wheel metaphor alluded to earlier is one that Faulkner often applied to his artistic creation, most notably in *Requiem for a Nun, The Mansion*, and the maps he drew of Yoknapatawpha County—the "hub" being the

courthouse and Jefferson square, the "spokes" being the roads and rivers
leading outward, as he put it, "from Jefferson to the world." Moreover,
all of the paintings are characterized by their particularity, by their relation to specific places, that is, the homes of the individual artists, "the
houses and streets and cities and the woods and fields and streams where
they worked or lived or pleasured." The same observation, of course,
may be made of Faulkner's Yoknapatawpha novels and stories. Indeed,
like Thomas Hardy's Wessex or James Joyce's Dublin or Nathaniel Hawthorne's New England, Faulkner's Yoknapatawpha County is inextricably
rooted in the actual landscape and history of its creator's native region.

Faulkner himself recognized the degree to which his best work was
identified with his "own little postage stamp of native soil," and he dated
the beginning of his genuine success from the time he realized that this
native region "was worth writing about and that [he] would never live
long enough to exhaust it." In this conclusion he was partly following the
advice of Sherwood Anderson, who told him in New Orleans in 1925,
"You're a country boy; all you know is that little patch up there in Mississippi where you started from." Faulkner probably also learned a great
deal from his older contemporary, Willa Cather, whose *My Antonia* and
other novels set on the Nebraska frontier provided models for the use of
native materials. And, of course, looming like a mountain peak over
Faulkner and all the writers of his generation was the example of Mark
Twain's *Adventures of Huckleberry Finn*, which elevated local color realism from sub-genre into genuine literature. "In my opinion," Faulkner
once observed, "Mark Twain was the first truly American writer, and all
of us since are his heirs."

Whether from Anderson, Cather, Twain, and/or others, Faulkner
learned well the lesson that wider, even universal, concerns may be expressed in the language, geography, and customs of a particular locale.
Open any Yoknapatawpha novel or story at random and you'll quickly
discover descriptions of places, persons, and events that are easily recognizable as unique to Faulkner's native region. Consider, for example, the
famous description of the mule powering the sorghum mill in *Sartoris*:

> Round and round the mule went, setting its narrow, deerlike feet delicately
> down in the hissing cane-pith, its neck bobbing limber as a section of a rubber
> hose in the collar, with its trace-galled flanks and flopping, lifeless ears and its
> half-closed eyes drowsing venomously behind pale lids, apparently asleep with
> the monotony of its own motion. Some Homer of the cotton fields should sing
> the saga of the mule and of his place in the South. . . . Father and mother he
> does not resemble, sons and daughters he will never have; vindictive and pa-
> tient (it is a known fact that he will labor ten years willingly and patiently for
> you, for the privilege of kicking you once). . . .

Or consider the following description of a landscape in *The Mansion:*

> The road had ceased some time back to be even gravel and at any moment now it would cease to be passable to anything on wheels; already, in the fixed glare . . . of the headlights, it resembled just one more eroded ravine twisting up the broken rise crested with shabby and shaggy pine and worthless black-jack. The sun had crossed the equator, in Libra now; and in the cessation of motion and the quiet of the idling engine, there was a sense of autumn after the slow drizzle of Sunday and the bright spurious cool which had lasted through Monday almost; the jagged rampart of pines and scrub oak was a thin dike against the winter and rain and cold, under which the worn-out fields overgrown with sumac and sassafras and persimmon had already turned scar-let, the persimmons heavy with fruit waiting only for frost and the baying of potlicker possum hounds.

Or, to cite just one more example, consider the authentic Southern idiom employed by characters such as Anse Bundren in *As I Lay Dying:*

> Durn that road. . . . A-laying there, right up to my door, where every bad luck that comes and goes is bound to find it. I told Addie it wasn't any luck living on a road when it come by here, and she said, for the world like a woman, "Get up and move, then." But I told her it wasn't no luck in it, because the Lord put roads for travelling: why He laid them down flat on the earth. When He aims for something to be always a-moving, He makes it long ways, like a road or a horse or a wagon, but when He aims for something to stay put, He makes it up-and-down ways, like a tree or a man.

How thoroughly Faulkner's work is linked to the people, places, sights, and sounds of his native region is demonstrated each year, of course, by the legions of visitors from around the world who tour Oxford, New Albany, Ripley, and other settings utilized in Faulkner's books.

In considering the close ties of Faulkner's fiction to the region of his birth and residence, we cannot ignore, even on this day of celebration and triumph, the negative characterizations that Faulkner sometimes presents of the South. As a realist, of course, Faulkner well understood that an honest and accurate depiction of life—anywhere, anytime, not merely in the twentieth-century South—must include the ugly and the ignoble as well as the beautiful and the admirable. But many of Faulk-ner's contemporaries were not inclined to view his work from such a detached philosophical perspective, and they responded to his incidents of violence, murder, racism, incest, sodomy, and fanaticism with the same question that Shreve asks Quentin at the end of *Absalom, Absalom!*: "Why do you hate the South?" Today, I think, readers, even loyal South-erners, are more prepared, more willing to view Faulkner's work in the context he intended, that is, as a critical reassessment of Southern mores and traditions, the bad as well as the good. In this regard it is helpful to recall that such fellow Southerners as Hodding Carter and Robert Penn Warren defended Faulkner from charges of perversity and cruelty and, indeed, quite to the contrary, saw in his novels and stories the striving of a moral conscience under siege by the forces of darkness. In this regard, too, we should recall Faulkner's own words at the end of his loving tribute to Mississippi, published in *Holiday* magazine in 1954: "Loving all of it even while he had to hate some of it because he knows now that you dont love because: you love despite; not for the virtues, but despite the faults." As this statement makes clear, Faulkner did not belong to the "love it or leave it" school of thought; rather he practiced what Adlai Stevenson once called "the hard kind of patriotism," that is, a love of homeland that is so honest and intense that it compels one to identify, expose, and hopefully eradicate the evils that threaten its continuance. Admittedly, it is a tough kind of love that Faulkner directs toward his native land, but it is nonetheless a love that is genuine and sincere.

While Faulkner is in many ways the most Southern of our Southern writers, it is also paradoxically true that had he been *merely* a Southern writer his work would be relegated to the level of minor regionalists like, say, James Branch Cabell, Donald Davidson, and Erskine Caldwell, and we would not be here celebrating his life and work. But Faulkner's regional elements, like those of Twain and Hawthorne, whom he equals in ability and stature, are always employed in the interest of larger concerns. The fact that the Faulkner Centennial is being celebrated in places as diverse as Moscow, Tokyo, Beijing, Venice, and Paris, as well as various sites in the United States, both south and north, attests to the universality of Faulkner's appeal.

Faulkner himself well understood and acknowledged that it was not the regional aspects but the universality of his art upon which his achievement must ultimately be judged. As he wrote to Malcolm Cowley in 1944, "I'm inclined to think that my material, the South, is not very important to me. I just happen to know it, and dont have time in one life to learn another one and write at the same time." He was still voicing this opinion when he visited the Philippines a decade later: "I write about American Mississippi simply because that is what I know best. The Filipino would write about his country because it is what he knows best. The Chinese about his country because that's what he knows best." But for any writer to be truly great, Faulkner believed, he must subordinate the local, regional, or even national particularities to the greater service of universal truth. As Faulkner told the cadets at West Point just weeks before his death,

> The writer is simply trying to use the best method he possibly can find to tell you a true and moving and familiar old, old story of the human heart in conflict with itself for the old, old human verities and truths, which are love, hope, fear, compassion, greed, lust . . . eternal verities which haven't changed too much since man first found how to record them.

Faulkner's insistence that there are only a relatively few basic story lines that are repeated over and over down through the centuries places him with other writers of his time—notably Joyce, Eliot, Cather, Hemingway, O'Neill, MacLeish, Steinbeck, and Warren—who interwove their poems and narratives of contemporary life with ancient stories that have survived from primitive folklore, Greek or Roman mythology, or the Bible. Eliot gave this distinctly modern way of writing a name, calling it "the mythical method," and Faulkner became one of the method's greatest practitioners.

For instance, in the monumental compendium of primitive man's religious customs, James George Frazer's *The Golden Bough*, one of the most influential books upon modern literature, Faulkner read the account of the killing of the sacred bear—an account he drew upon years later in writing "The Bear." In *Light In August* Faulkner incorporated the ancient Greek notion of an earth goddess into his characterization of Lena Grove. And, of course, on numerous occasions Faulkner retold biblical material, using, for example, the story of King David and his rebellious son in *Absalom, Absalom!*, the story of the Exodus in *Go Down, Moses*, and the Eden and Christ stories in *The Sound and the Fury* and various other works. In all of these instances Faulkner seems clearly intent on reminding his readers that human nature has not changed a great deal down through the centuries, that humanity's deepest needs and desires, what he called "the old verities and truths of the heart," are the same in the modern world as they have been from the beginning. And, as Faulkner well knew, it is only a literature that treats these universal concerns that deserves to "endure and prevail." In the paintings in "Shall Not Perish" the people live in different kinds of houses, and build different types of barns, and grow different crops; but they are still "the same people" because they all share a common humanity that, even as it confronts the ravages of war, injustice, suffering, grief, and death, nevertheless longs and quests for identity, peace, love, and community. And, in Faulkner's view, it is only an art that expresses these universal conflicts and values that can ever possess the power to truly move its viewers and readers. Faulkner's choosing to emphasize that point through the responses of a nine-year-old boy, I would submit, merely demonstrates just how fundamental, indeed how elementary, he considers the point to be.

There is one other aspect of Faulkner's work that persuades readers that it deserves the claim of universality. I have reference here to his blending of pathos and comedy. All of our truly greatest writers— Shakespeare of course being the best example—possess both a tragic and comic sense, enabling them to be true to the contradictions and polarities of existence. As Shakespeare's genius ranged from the despair and pessimism of *King Lear* to the madcap comedy of *A Midsummer Night's Dream* to the utopian vision of *A Tempest*, so too did Faulkner's muse express itself in a wide variety of tones and moods—tragic, comic, grotesque, fantastic, satiric, elegiac. And such moods, like the character types and plots in Faulkner's work, are universal, not limited by geography or era.

I conclude my remarks with a few comments suggested by Faulkner's title, "Shall Not Perish." Faulkner lifted this phrase, of course, from Lincoln's Gettysburg Address, and readers should not forget that the lines offering such great hope and promise for our nation—"the proposition that government of the people, by the people, and for the people shall not perish from the earth"—were first delivered at a military cemetery marking the battlefield of an earlier conflict when the American nation had faced perhaps an even greater peril than World War II. Like Lincoln's speech, Faulkner's story treats the death of soldiers but also presents those individual tragedies in the context of a corporate history that could, hopefully and possibly, have a happy ending. The mythic pattern here is the ancient and oft-repeated one of *felix culpa*, "the fortunate fall," which dramatizes how positive results of a greater good can sometimes evolve from negative situations. It is a pattern that Faulkner employed again and again in his books, not only because he recognized it as a central myth of human desire and history but also because he lived out that recurring story in his own personal life and career. As noted earlier, Faulkner was often plagued by serious doubts about his ultimate place in literary history; yet at the same time he continued to find the inner strength and courage to maintain his faith in himself as an artist and to produce stories like "Shall Not Perish" that hold out at least the hope of an ultimate triumph over apparent defeat and failure. And on December 10, 1950, in Stockholm, he received into his hands from King Gustaf Adolf of Sweden the tangible proof that his faith in himself and his work had not been mistaken.

And this week, here and at similar events being held around the world, we and readers like us are reminded that we have received from Faulkner's hands a double legacy—an impressive number of literary masterpieces that rank among the best the world has ever produced, and the inspirational example of a dedicated writer who demonstrated that a life devoted to imagination and creativity is well worth the "anguish and tra-vail," all the "agony and sweat." And both of these legacies, we can be quite sure, "shall not perish," because, to rephrase the ending of that story, "North and South and East and West . . . the name of [who he was and what he did] became just one single word, louder than any thunder, it was [Faulkner], and it covered all the . . . earth."

Faulkner Centennial Celebrations

The centennial of William Faulkner's birth on September 25, 1987, in New Albany, Mississippi, was celebrated throughout the world. A sampling of events follows.

OXFORD, MISSISSIPPI—JANUARY 9, 1997
Square Books sponsored the first observance of the year with a program of readings on the occasion of the publication of *William Faulkner and the Tangible Past: The Architecture of Yoknapatawpha* by Thomas S. Hines. The author, a noted architectural historian, talked about Faulkner's buildings during a program that also included readings of relevant passages from the fiction of Yoknapatawpha.

ASHLAND, VIRGINIA—MARCH 3–6
Randolph-Macon College's "The Achievement of William Faulkner: A Centennial Conference" included John Maxwell's performance of *"Oh, Mr. Faulkner, Do You Write?"*; a showing of the films *The Reivers* and *Tomorrow*; and a discussion by panelists Joseph Blotner, Thadious M. Davis, and Lothar Hönnighausen. Thomas Inge, Blackwell Professor of Humanities, was in charge of the event.

NEWARK, DELAWARE—MARCH 17–JUNE 20
The University of Delaware, drawing entirely from its library collections, sponsored the exhibition *William Faulkner: A Centenary Celebration*.

NOTTINGHAM, ENGLAND—JULY 12, 1997
The University of Nottingham hosted a one-day conference on "Faulkner and Modernism" to commemorate the author's one-hundredth birthday. Richard King, American and Canadian Studies, was in charge of the event.

OXFORD, MISSISSIPPI—JULY 1–SEPTEMBER 30
Photographs of Faulkner and his home environment by Jack Cofield and Martin Dain were exhibited at the University of Mississippi. The Cofield exhibition was at Barnard Observatory, and the Dain exhibition

was at the University Museums. The Center for the Study of Southern Culture organized the exhibitions.

OXFORD, MISSISSIPPI—JULY 27–AUGUST 1

The 1997 Faulkner and Yoknapatawpha Conference celebrated the author's centennial by bringing together more than twenty Faulkner scholars to discuss his work. Addresses by scholars who spoke on the conference theme "Faulkner at 100: Retrospect and Prospect" are included in this volume.

OXFORD, MISSISSIPPI—JULY 27–DECEMBER 27

Special Collections at the University of Mississippi Libraries sponsored *A Faulkner 100: The Centennial Exhibition*. Thomas M. Verich, university archivist, organized the exhibition and wrote the catalog, published in five hundred numbered copies. Leila Clark Wynn, a generous donor of Faulkner and other items to Special Collections over the years, was sponsor of the catalog.

CAPE GIRARDEAU, MISSOURI—SEPTEMBER 2–30

"A Faulkner Centennial Celebration" at Southeast Missouri State University offered lectures, including "Faulkner and the Visual Arts" by Max Cordonnier, an exhibit of the Brodsky Collection, and an art contest and exhibit based on Faulkner's life and work. Robert W. Hamblin, Center for Faulkner Studies, was in charge of the celebration.

COLUMBIA, SOUTH CAROLINA—SEPTEMBER 4–5

The Institute of Southern Studies at the University of South Carolina sponsored a program of centennial lectures by American scholars Thadious Davis, Tom McHaney, and Noel Polk; Richard Gray, of England; Peter Nicolaisen, of Germany; and Hans Skei, of Norway.

OXFORD, MISSISSIPPI—SEPTEMBER 25

The City of Oxford dedicated a statue of William Faulkner by Mississippi sculptor William Beckwith during a program that included comments by public officials and authors Shelby Foote and Willie Morris. The morning event was followed in the afternoon by a University-sponsored program of tributes to Faulkner and readings from his work. The tributes are included in this volume.

NEW ALBANY, MISSISSIPPI —SEPTEMBER 25–27

A community birthday celebration on Thursday evening, September 25, was followed by Faulkner Education Day in the New Albany and

Union County schools on Friday, September 26. That evening, John Maxwell presented *"Oh, Mr. Faulkner, Do You Write?"* Events on Saturday, September 27, included an address by Faulkner scholar Robert W. Hamblin, area historic tours, music, workshops for teachers and students, announcement of winners of a creative writing context, a mule auction, and mule races. The day ended with an evening performance of *As I Lay Dying*, performed by Nashville singers and songwriters.

RENNES AND PARIS, FRANCE—SEPTEMBER 22–25

Fondation William Faulkner at Rennes 2 University sponsored a four-day program with literary seminars and workshops, readings, concerts, award presentations, and exhibitions. On Thursday, September 25, the program moved to Paris for an official ceremony, a visit to the Luxembourg Gardens, and the installation of a commemorative plaque.

NEW ORLEANS, LOUISIANA—SEPTEMBER 28

Faulkner House Books and the Pirate's Alley Faulkner Society hosted a birthday party.

TBILISI, REPUBLIC OF GEORGIA—SEPTEMBER 28

Scholars from institutions throughout the Republic of Georgia gathered at Tbilisi State University for a conference in celebration of the centennial of Faulkner's birth.

STATEN ISLAND, NEW YORK—OCTOBER 1–31

The College of Staten Island sponsored an exhibition from the collection of Dr. Karl J. Leone, a Staten Island dentist and lifelong Faulkner admirer. Edmund Volpe, former president of the college and author of *A Reader's Guide to William Faulkner*, spoke at the opening of the exhibition.

DALLAS, TEXAS—OCTOBER 3

The William Faulkner Society offered a special session on "A Century of Faulkner and His Critics" during the annual meeting of the South Central Modern Language Association.

BEIJING, CHINA—NOVEMBER 1–4

Peking University sponsored the International Conference on William Faulkner in Celebration of His Centennial. Cosponsors were the East-West Center of Hong Kong Baptist University and the Hong Kong-America Center of the Chinese University of Hong Kong.

ANN ARBOR, MICHIGAN—NOVEMBER 7–8

The University of Michigan sponsored a conference featuring lectures by Faulkner scholar Robert W. Hamblin; William Boozer, editor of the *Faulkner Newsletter*; and Engelsina Pareslegina, librarian at the Gorky Institute of World Literature in Moscow. The Special Collections Library also sponsored an exhibition of materials from the Irwin T. and Shirley Holtzman Faulkner Collection.

VENICE, ITALY—NOVEMBER 13–15

The University of Ca'Foscari sponsored a Faulkner Centenary International Conference, with the focus on problems of translation and problems of language and style.

CONWAY, SOUTH CAROLINA—NOVEMBER 21–22

Coastal Carolina University sponsored "William Faulkner and Southern History," a centennial conference organized by Charles Joyner and including presentations by Edwin M. Yoder Jr., Joel Williamson, and James B. Meriwether, among others.

MOSCOW, RUSSIA—DECEMBER 1–5

Scholars from Russia and the United States gathered at the Gorky Institute of World Literature in Moscow for a three-day program commemorating William Faulkner.

TOKYO, JAPAN—DECEMBER 7

The University of Tokyo sponsored a seminar titled "The South Beyond Boundaries: William Faulkner and the Marginal" with lectures by scholar Kenzaburo Ohashi, literary critic Kojin Karatani, and novelist Hideki Ikezawa. The program marked the publication of the final two volumes of the twenty-seven volume *Complete Works of William Faulkner*.

Contributors

André Bleikasten, professor of American Literature at the University of Strasbourg, has published numerous works on Faulkner in French and in English. Among the latter are *Faulkner's "As I Lay Dying," The Most Splendid Failure: Faulkner's "The Sound and the Fury,"* and *The Ink of Melancholy: Faulkner's Novels from "The Sound and the Fury" to "Light in August."*

Joseph Blotner's six books on William Faulkner and his work include *Faulkner: A Biography* (two volumes, 1974) and *Faulkner: A Biography* (one volume, 1984). With Noel Polk he is coeditor of The Library of America's four volumes of Faulkner's novels. In 1977 he was William Faulkner Lecturer at the University of Mississippi. Professor of English Emeritus of the University of Michigan, he is a member of the Fellowship of Southern Writers.

Larry Brown is the author of two story collections—*Facing the Music* and *Big Bad Love*—and the novels *Dirty Work, Joe,* and *Father and Son. On Fire* is a nonfiction account of his years as a firefighter in Oxford, Mississippi.

Thadious M. Davis is the Gertrude Conaway Vanderbilt Professor of English at Vanderbilt University. Editor of four books and the author of over forty critical essays, she has written *Nella Larsen, Novelist of the Harlem Renaissance: A Woman's Life Unveiled* as well as several works on Faulkner, including *Faulkner's "Negro": Art and the Southern Context.*

Susan V. Donaldson, professor of English at the College of William and Mary, is the author of *Competing Voices: The American Novel, 1865–1914* (1998) and co-editor, with Anne Goodwyn Jones, of *Haunted Bodies: Gender and Southern Texts* (1997). She is also associate editor of *The Faulkner Journal* and editor of *The Faulkner Journal*'s 1993/1994 special double issue *Faulkner and Sexuality* (published in 1995) and the Fall 1999/Spring 2000 special issue *Faulkner and Masculinity*. The author of thirty articles on Faulkner, Eudora Welty, Walker Percy, Ellen Douglas, Sheila Bosworth, and Robert Penn Warren and on southern literature, culture, and art, she is currently completing a book titled "Reluctant Visionaries and Southern Others: The Politics of Storytelling in the Modern South" and has just started writing a book on Faulkner, modernism, and masculinity.

Doreen Fowler, professor of English at the University of Kansas, is the author of *Faulkner: The Return of the Repressed* and *Faulkner's Changing Vision: From Outrage to Affirmation*. She is also coeditor of twelve volumes of proceedings of the annual Faulkner and Yoknapatawpha Conference.

Duncan M. Gray Jr. is bishop emeritus of the Episcopal Diocese of Mississippi and a former chancellor of the University of the South. He served as rector of St. Peter's Episcopal Church, the Faulkner family parish, from the fall of 1957 until the fall of 1965

Minrose C. Gwin, professor of English at the University of New Mexico, is the author of *Black and White Women of the Old South: The Peculiar Sisterhood in American Literature* and *The Feminine and Faulkner: Reading (Beyond) Sexual Difference*. She is the editor of three additional books and is currently at work on "Space Travel: Gender, Reading, and the Motion of the Imagination."

Robert W. Hamblin is professor of English and director of the Center for Faulkner Studies at Southeast Missouri State University. In addition to publishing essays on Faulkner in various books and journals, he is coeditor of *Faulkner: A Comprehensive Guide to the Brodsky Collection* and is coeditor of *A William Faulkner Encyclopedia*.

W. Kenneth Holditch, professor emeritus of English of the University of New Orleans, is the author of numerous essays on various Southern writers and editor of *In Old New Orleans* and *The Tennessee Williams Journal*. He is currently coediting the Two Tennessee Williams volumes for the Library of America and is writing the text for a photographic study of Tennessee Williams and the South.

Lothar Hönnighausen is professor of English in the Nordamerikaprogram at the University of Bonn. He is the author of *William Faulkner: The Art of Stylization* and *Masks and Metaphors*, published by the University Press of Mississippi.

Richard Howorth is proprietor of Square Books in Oxford, Mississippi. He is an organizer of the Oxford Conference for the Book and is president of the American Booksellers Association for 1998–2000.

John T. Irwin, professor of English at Johns Hopkins University, is the author of *Doubling and Incest/Repetition and Revenge, American Hieroglyphics: The Symbol of the Egyptian Hieroglyphics in the American Renaissance*, and *The Mystery to a Solution*. He is also the author, under the name John Bricuth, of two volumes of poems, *The Heisenberg Variations* and *Just Let Me Say This About That*.

Donald M. Kartiganer is the William Howry Professor of Faulkner Studies at the University of Mississippi and director of the Faulkner Conference. He is the author of *The Fragile Thread: The Meaning of Form* *in Faulkner's Novels* and coeditor, with Malcolm Griffith, of *Theories of American Literature* and, with Ann J. Abadie, of six volumes of proceedings of the Faulkner and Yoknapatawpha Conference.

Robert C. Khayat has been chancellor of the University of Mississippi since 1995.

Arthur F. Kinney is Thomas W. Copeland Professor of Literary History at the University of Massachusetts, Amherst and adjunct professor of English at New York University. He is the author of *Faulkner's Narrative Poetics: Style as Vision* and *Go Down, Moses: The Miscegenation of Time*, coeditor of *Approaches to Teaching "The Sound the and Fury*," and editor of a five-volume series on Faulkner's families, four of which have been published.

John T. Matthews, professor of English at Boston University, is the author of *The Play of Faulkner's Language* and *"The Sound and the Fury": Faulkner and the Lost Cause*. He is currently writing a book titled "Raising the South: Literary Modernism and the Imagination of History," for which he received a fellowship from the National Endowment for the Humanities.

Thomas L. McHaney, Kenneth M. England Professor of Southern Literature at Georgia State University, has published on Faulkner for more than thirty years. His edition of a long lost manuscript of Faulkner's second novel, *Mosquitoes*, a facsimile and transcription, recently appeared.

Michael Millgate, University Professor of English Emeritus of the University of Toronto, is the author or editor of over twenty-five books, including *The Achievement of William Faulkner*, twelve volumes in the *William Faulkner Manuscripts* series, and his most recent study, *Faulkner's Place*.

David Minter is Bruce and Elizabeth Dunlevie Professor of English at Rice University. He is coeditor of *The Harper American Literature* and *The Columbia Literary History of the United States* and author of *A Cultural History of the American Novel: Henry James to William Faulkner*, *William Faulkner: His Life and Work*, and *The Interpreted Design as a Structural Principle in American Prose*.

Richard C. Moreland, associate professor of English at Louisiana State University, is the author of *Faulkner and Modernism: Rereading and Rewriting* and *Learning from Difference: Teaching Twain, Ellison, and Eliot*.

Gail L. Mortimer is professor of English at the University of Texas, El Paso. She is the author of *Faulkner's Rhetoric of Loss: A Study in Perception and Meaning* and *Daughter of the Swan: Love and Knowledge in Eudora Welty's Fiction*.

Albert Murray is the author of numerous works of fiction and cultural criticism, including *The Omni-Americans: New Perspectives on Black Experience and American Culture, South to a Very Old Place, The Hero and the Blues, Train Whistle Guitar, Stomping the Blues, The Spyglass Tree, The Seven-League Boots: A Novel* and *The Blue Devils of Nada.* He recently received the Ivan Sandrof Award for "a notable contribution to American arts and letters."

Noel Polk, professor of English at the University of Southern Mississippi, is the author of *Faulkner's "Requiem for a Nun": A Critical Study, Eudora Welty: A Bibliography, Children of the Dark House: Text and Context in Faulkner,* and *Outside the Southern Myth.*

Carolyn Porter is professor of English at the University of California at Berkeley. She is the author of *Seeing and Being: The Plight of the Participant Observer in Emerson, James, Adams, and Faulkner,* as well as numerous essays on Melville, Twain, James, Faulkner, Ann Beatty, and American cultural history. She is currently at work on a book, "Grim Sires and Spectral Mothers: Gender and Family in Faulkner."

Judith L. Sensibar is professor of English at Arizona State University. Her books include *The Origins of Faulkner's Art, Faulkner's Poetry: A Bibliographical Guide to Texts and Criticism* and *William Faulkner's Vision in Spring* (ed. and intro.). Her essays on Faulkner and other Modernists have appeared in journals such as *American Literature, Journal of American Studies, Prospects* and in various collections including the Faulkner and Yoknapatawpha Conference Proceedings series and the Cambridge American Novel series (*New Essays on Go Down, Moses,* ed. Linda Wagner-Martin). Her current book project is called "Faulkner and Love: A Family Narrative."

Hans H. Skei is professor and chairman of the Department of Scandinavian Studies and Comparative Literature at the University of Oslo. In addition to numerous books in Norwegian, he is the author of *William Faulkner: The Short Story Career, William Faulkner: The Novelist as Short Story Writer,* and *Reading Faulkner's Best Short Stories.* He has translated the Snopes trilogy (Norwegian) and is editor of *William Faulkner's Short Fiction: An International Symposium.*

Warwick Wadlington is Joan Negley Kelleher Centennial Professor of English at the University of Texas, Austin. He is the author of *The Confidence Game in American Literature, Reading Faulknerian Tragedy,* and *"As I Lay Dying": Stories out of Stories,* as well as a wide range of essays on American fiction and culture.

Philip Weinstein is Alexander Griswold Cummins Professor of English at Swarthmore College. He is the author of *Henry James and the Requirements of the Imagination, The Semantics of Desire: Changing Models of Identity from Dickens to Joyce, Faulkner's Subject: A Cosmos*

No One Owns, and *What Else But Love? The Ordeal of Race in Faulkner and Morrison*, and editor of *The Cambridge Companion to William Faulkner*.

Judith Bryant Wittenberg is professor of English Emerita at Simmons College and Associate Director of the Commission on Institutions of Higher Education, New England Association of Schools and Colleges.

Karl F. Zender, professor and chair (1993–98) of the Department of English at the University of California at Davis, is the author of *The Crossing of the Ways: William Faulkner, the South, and the Modern World*. He has written the Faulkner section of six editions of *American Literary Scholarship: An Annual* and coauthored the Faulkner section for *Sixteen Modern American Authors: A Survey of Research and Criticism* Volume 2.

Index